C0-AZS-687

Texts, Ideas, and the Classics

Texts, Ideas, and the Classics

Scholarship, Theory, and Classical Literature

Edited by
S. J. HARRISON

OXFORD
UNIVERSITY PRESS

Great Clarendon Street, Oxford OX2 6DP

Oxford University Press is a department of the University of Oxford.
It furthers the University's objective of excellence in research, scholarship,
and education by publishing worldwide in

Oxford New York

Athens Auckland Bangkok Bogotá Buenos Aires Cape Town
Chennai Dar es Salaam Delhi Florence Hong Kong Istanbul Karachi
Kolkata Kuala Lumpur Madrid Melbourne Mexico City Mumbai Nairobi
Paris São Paulo Shanghai Singapore Taipei Tokyo Toronto Warsaw

with associated companies in Berlin Ibadan

Oxford is a registered trade mark of Oxford University Press
in the UK and in certain other countries

Published in the United States
by Oxford University Press Inc., New York

First published 2001

British Library Cataloguing in Publication Data
Data available

Library of Congress Cataloging in Publication Data
Data applied for
ISBN 0-19-924746-3

1 3 5 7 9 10 8 6 4 2

Typeset by Regent Typesetting, London
Printed in Great Britain
on acid-free paper by
Biddles Ltd., Guildford & King's Lynn

In memoriam
Don Fowler
† 15.10.1999

Preface

This volume is the result of a conference held at Corpus Christi College, Oxford, in April 1997 under the title 'Working Together: Scholarship and Theory in Classical Literature', and under the auspices of the Corpus Christi Centre for the Study of Greek and Roman Antiquity. The conference could not have taken place without generous grants from the Charles Oldham Trustees of Corpus Christi College, Oxford, and from the Humanities Research Board of the British Academy; further much-appreciated financial help came from the Craven Committee of the University of Oxford, the Jowett Copyright Trustees of Balliol College, Oxford, and the Society for the Promotion of Hellenic Studies. To all these bodies are due most grateful thanks.

Thanks are also owed to many friends and colleagues for practical help. To my co-organizer, John Birchall, who provided the first impetus to hold the conference and was the source of much-appreciated ideas and support during the planning process; to the panel directors, Ewen Bowie, Susanna Morton Braund, Don Fowler, Michael Reeve, and Michael Silk, who played a vital role in choosing speakers, chairing panels, and contributing panel introductions to this volume; to Simon Swain, who very kindly wrote the panel introduction on 'Historicism'; to Pat Easterling, who with characteristic generosity chaired a panel at an extremely busy time; and to Peter Wiseman, who provided prompt and valuable support in the search for funding. I would also like to thank all other speakers and attenders, who made the conference a memorable academic event, and Colin Holmes, the Domestic Bursar of Corpus, and his staff, who with typical kindness and efficiency ensured its smooth operation.

In the editing stage, I am grateful once again to Hilary O'Shea and the staff of Oxford University Press for their help and support; to Niall Rudd, who kindly read and commented on my introduction; to Robin Osborne and Tony Brett at Corpus, who kindly helped with computing issues; and to Rachel Pearson for generous last-minute help in the preparation of texts. Though it was not the main project for my tenure of the award, the first stages of editing this book were facilitated by a Leverhulme/British Academy Senior Research Fellowship for 1997–8, which gave precious time for research and writing activity, and for which I am extremely grateful.

While this volume was being assembled, Don Fowler died at the tragically early age of 46, a grievous loss to the world-wide community of classics and to Oxford classics in particular. As already recorded above, he gave characteristically generous help and encouragement to this project, and it is only fitting that this book, concerned with a topic so close to his interests, should be dedicated to him.

SJH
July 2000
Corpus Christi College, Oxford

Contents

List of Contributors

ALESSANDRO BARCHIESI is Professor of Latin at the University of Siena in Arezzo. His writings include *La traccia del modello: effetti omerici nella narrazione virgiliana* (Pisa, 1984), a commentary on Ovid *Heroides* 1–3 (Florence, 1992) and *The Poet and the Prince: Ovid and Augustan Discourse* (Berkeley, 1997).

SUSANNA MORTON BRAUND is Professor of Classics, Yale University. Her books include *Beyond Anger: A Study of Juvenal's Third Book of Satires* (Cambridge, 1988) and a commentary on Juvenal *Satires* I (Cambridge, 1996).

JERZY DANIELEWICZ is Professor of Greek at the Adam Mickiewicz University, Poznań, Poland; he is the author of a study of the morphology of the Greek hymn (Poznań, 1976), of *The Metres of Greek Lyric Poetry* (Bochum, 1996), of an edition with commentary of selected Greek lyric poets (Warsaw/Poznań, 1999), and other books and articles on Greek literature.

IRENE DE JONG is Academy Professor of Ancient Greek Literature at the University of Amsterdam. Her books include *Narrators and Focalisers: The Presentation of the Story in the Iliad* (Amsterdam, 1987), and *Narrative in Drama: The Art of the Euripidean Messenger Speech* (Leiden, 1991).

INGRID DE SMET is Senior Lecturer in French Studies at the University of Warwick and Fellow of the European Humanities Research Centre, Oxford. She is the author of *Menippean Satire in the Republic of Letters 1580–1655* (Geneva, 1996), and co-editor with Philip Ford of *Eros et Priapus: érotisme et obscénité dans la littérature néo-latine* (Geneva, 1997).

LILLIAN DOHERTY is Associate Professor of Classics at the University of Maryland at College Park, and author of *Siren Songs: Gender, Audience and Narrators in the Odyssey* (Ann Arbor, 1995).

DON FOWLER was until his death in 1999 Fellow and Tutor in Classics at Jesus College, Oxford. His most important articles are collected in his *Roman Constructions: Reading in Postmodern Latin* (Oxford, 2000).

STEPHEN HARRISON is Fellow and Tutor in Classics at Corpus Christi College, Oxford, and Reader in Classical Languages and Literature in the University of Oxford. He is the author of a commentary on Vergil *Aeneid* 10 (Oxford, 1991) and of *Apuleius: A Latin Sophist* (Oxford, 2000).

JOHN HENDERSON is Reader in Classics at the University of Cambridge and Fellow of King's College. His books include *Fighting For Rome* (Cambridge, 1998) and *Writing Down Rome* (Oxford, 1999).

JOHN MOLES is Professor of Latin at the University of Newcastle. He is author of a commentary on Plutarch's *Life of Cicero* (1988) and of many articles on Roman literature and culture.

MICHAEL REEVE is Kennedy Professor of Latin in the University of Cambridge and Fellow of Pembroke College. His publications include Teubner texts of *Daphnis and Chloe* (1982; 3rd edn. 1994) and *Cicero: Pro Quinctio* (1992) as well as many articles on the interpretation and transmission of Latin literature.

PETER LEBRECHT SCHMIDT is Professor Emeritus of Latinistik at the University of Konstanz. His writings include books on Cicero's *De Legibus* (Rome, 1969) and on Claudian (Konstanz, 1976).

MICHAEL SILK is Professor of Greek Language and Literature at King's College London. His books include *Interaction in Poetic Imagery* (Cambridge, 1974), *Homer: The Iliad* (Cambridge, 1987), *Aristophanes and the Definition of Comedy* (Oxford, 2000), and (with J. P. Stern) *Nietzsche on Tragedy* (Cambridge, 1981).

CHRISTOPHER STRAY is Honorary Research Fellow in the Department of Classics at the University of Wales, Swansea, and author of *Classics Transformed: Schools, Universities and Society in England, 1830–1960* (Oxford, 1998), and editor of *Classics in Nineteenth and Twentieth Century Cambridge* (Cambridge, 1999).

SIMON SWAIN is Professor of Classics at the University of Warwick and author of *Hellenism and Empire: Language, Classicism and Power in the Greek World, AD 50–250* (Oxford, 1996).

MARCUS WILSON is Senior Lecturer in Classics at the University of Auckland and author of many articles on Latin literature.

I

General Introduction: Working Together

Stephen Harrison

This book derives from a conference, held in Oxford in 1997 under the title 'Working Together', which aimed to promote a simple idea: that, in the contemporary context of the study and interpretation of classical literature at universities, conventional classical scholarship and modern theoretical ideas need to work with each other in the common task of the interpretation of texts. The Oxford conference arose directly from another conference held in London in 1995 on the theme of 'The Language of Latin Poetry' (now published as Adams and Mayer, 1999), at which a distinguished colleague raised the issue of the absence of more theoretically minded scholars at that gathering, and suggested that greater dialogue and co-operation represented the way forward. In my view such dialogue and co-operation is not merely desirable; it is essential to ensure the survival and relevance of the study of classical literature in the twenty-first century.

Such talk of a common interest might seem banal and truistic; but the issue remains far from uncontroversial. 'Theory wars' became a major feature in the literature departments of US universities in the 1980s, and literary classicists in the UK, as ever with transatlantic time-lag, have in recent years been urged to 'cast out theory' in a presidential address to the Classical Association,[1] and told from a different perspective that the opposition between traditional classical scholarship and modern theory is a 'war', that 'there ain't no neutral ground', and that 'there is no point in being falsely eirenic'.[2] Though these statements were, of course, made in both cases with some degree of rhetoric and irony, they represent a conflict which is genuine enough and which has major

[1] For a convenient account of the US debates on theory from a classical point of view cf. Galinsky (1992), 21–7. West (1995) has the title 'Cast Out Theory: Horace *Odes* 1.4 and 4.7'.

[2] Citations from Fowler (1993).

consequences within universities. While in no sense wishing to discourage forceful debate,[3] this book enters a plea to the two 'sides' for mutual tolerance and understanding, in the cause of mutual interest and enrichment, and to argue for their common ground and interdependence. Each can and should learn from the other if the subject is not to become undesirably polarized and weakened. Part I of this introduction is something of a personal manifesto on this general issue from my own limited perspective, that of a traditionally trained and formalistically inclined classical scholar and literary interpreter who has some interest in the application of contemporary theory to the reading of texts. Part II is concerned with the contents of this volume in particular.

I

The arrival of various types of theory need not represent an alien modern incursion into a hallowed and seamless tradition of the study of classical literature. That tradition itself has owed much of its considerable strength and durability to its capacity to develop and change, and many aspects of the study of Greek and Roman texts have always (and inevitably) moved with the times. An illustration of this is a piece written by Niall Rudd in 1972,[4] in which he pointed out the paucity of literary treatments of classical texts in the Anglophone academic world before 1950, and the sea-change that had taken place since then under the influence of the New Criticism, resulting in a rich flow of books and articles concerned with literary criticism, and in welcome interchange with literary scholars and critics in other disciplines. The same could be said of the situation in the 1990s: at least in some parts of the study of classical literature, the influence of the New Criticism has now been supplemented and overtaken by a whole variety of more recent critical ideas, just as the New Criticism itself displaced much of the sentimentalizing pseudo-biography which passed for literary criticism in the first half of this century.

[3] I would here agree with many of the academic benefits of intellectual controversy laid out by Graff (1997). For a bracingly forceful anti-theoretical approach set in the context of the US university system, provocatively hyper-conservative but also with some home truths for modern academics on the dangers of entropy and the importance of undergraduate teaching and a broader appeal, cf. Hanson and Heath (1998).

[4] Rudd (1972).

On the other hand, the continuities which link the contemporary study of classical texts with a long history of scholarship need not be rejected in the wake of the recent advent of a range of theoretical approaches. As in the case of the arrival of the New Criticism, as Rudd himself argued, the arrival of new ideas need in no way displace the more conventional disciplines of classical scholarship—the editing of texts, the study of manuscripts, the thorough knowledge of ancient languages, or the writing of commentaries, to give but a few obvious examples. Indeed, the last at least has obvious potential to be enriched and expanded by wider theoretical horizons, as modern commentaries allocate more space to broader literary analysis and ideas, and become more flexible in format. Here the aspect of interdependence arises. Theory cannot manage without scholarship, which provides the very basis for its operations: new literary interpretations and approaches rely, for example, on the use of texts, established by the labours of editors, and on an expert semantic knowledge of those texts, either wielded by the interpreters themselves or mediated through commentaries and translations. Furthermore, as we shall see, some of the most effective theoretical readings incorporate traditional scholarly methods. But can scholarship manage without theory, at least in a general sense? Many classical scholars would claim that they merely pursue their activities in an untheoretical and pragmatic way, and that what they do is simply not influenced by larger ideas: they appeal to such notions as 'scholarly method', 'balanced judgement', and 'common sense'. But are these values as neutral and uncontroversial as they seem? My answer to the question 'can literary scholarship be divorced from theoretical preconceptions?' would be a resounding 'no', on two levels.

First, in principle and at a very general level, any activity with a text involving interpretation, even (on occasion) choosing between readings transmitted by manuscripts, requires more than a mechanical process, and can never be fully objective or scientific. Even editors of texts bring their own personal agenda to their work in so many ways: not just their idea of what an *apparatus criticus* should look like, but their own 'feeling' for a particular author's text and its possibilities, not to mention their own ideological approach to the interpretation of literature in general. Any claim to neutrality and pure scholarship in literary studies involving acts of interpretation, in my view, ignores a crucial and central consideration: the practical impossibility of objectivity in the judgements of human intellectual activity. Individual views on almost everything are affected by a vast congeries of individual circumstances—temperament, education, environment, political or social preference (to take just a few)—and we cannot claim that we come to any situation freed from this kind of ideological influence. Of course, there are many important aspects of working with classical texts where quasi-scientific values can be said to apply (for example, some aspects of work on manuscript traditions, metre, or the facts of poetic diction), but this is simply not so for most kinds of larger literary interpretation. There we may claim to judge in an unprejudiced and open-minded way, but we are always already predisposed in certain directions. Theory itself, with its emphasis on clarifying and enunciating the interpreter's principles of operation, has had an important role in stressing and demonstrating this state of affairs.[5]

It might seem strange to extend this fundamental subjectivism to the problem of deciding, for example, something as apparently technical and trivial as whether to print *prima* or *summa* in an edition of Vergil *Aeneid* 10.100. There the poet describes Jupiter's supremacy over creation; Mynors' Oxford text there prints *tum pater omnipotens, rerum cui prima* potestas, 'then the all-powerful father, who has the prime power over creation', rather than summa potestas, 'who has the greatest power over creation'. The testimony of the most important manuscripts is equally divided on this point.[6] The editor is consequently thrown back on his or her feeling about whether to prefer *prima* for a typically Vergilian alliteration with the following word *potestas*, or to prefer *summa* since the combination *summa potestas* is found in a similar final position in the hexameter in Lucan, Statius, and Silius, all of whom can imitate Vergilian diction closely.[7] The consequent conflict of the principles of euphony and the application of later parallels is not easily resolved except by editorial personal preference, a prefer-

[5] On this whole topic see now Fowler (2000), esp. 3–4.

[6] Mynors (1972); I might now disagree with my favouring of *prima* in Harrison (1991). Of the three late antique capital MSS here available, equal in authority, R has *prima*, P has *summa*, and M has *prima* in the first hand, *summa* in the second; the later Carolingian MSS are equally split.

[7] For similar final alliteration, supporting *prima*, cf. e.g. *Aeneid* 10.113, *flumina fratris*. Lucan *BC* 8.494 has *quis rerum summa potestas*, supporting a Vergilian *rerum cui summa potestas*; *summa potestas* is also found in final position in the hexameter at Statius *Silvae* 1.2.37 and Silius *Punica* 2.270.

ence which may be affected, for example, by an early teacher's enthusiasm for alliteration in Vergil, or by a feeling inherited from the 'authoritative' tradition of traditional commentary that argument from parallels is somehow the true path to scholarly virtue. Even in the apparently 'objective' realm of textual criticism, the approach of practitioners can sometimes be subject to a range of influences which they may often be unable to articulate, but which nevertheless fundamentally affects the ways in which they work and the technical decisions they make.

Thus the first step in critical self-examination for literary scholars is to admit that what they do in dealing with the interpretation of literary texts is in some degree subjective, that they all necessarily bring their individual agendas to bear in the act of interpretation.[8] This does not mean that all interpreters are 'really' applying elements of contemporary theory without knowing it. But it does mean that they are all much more 'theoretical' (in terms of having an approach governed by particular and underlying interpretive beliefs and principles) than they intuitively think, and that arguments which reject explicitly theoretical approaches to literary interpretation as too dogmatic and ideological are themselves likely to be equally ideologically informed. The assertions of 'natural' views and 'common sense' against 'unnatural' theories creates a false dichotomy, though this is certainly not to exclude the notion that some ideas and interpretations can be more generally persuasive and convincing than others. The 'natural' views must in fact be based on unspoken critical assumptions, probably in fact connected with older literary theories. J. M. Keynes' well-known dictum on economics is fully applicable, *mutatis mutandis*, to literary work in classics: 'Practical men, who believe themselves to be quite exempt from any intellectual influences, are usually the slaves of some defunct economist.'[9]

The second level at which scholarship cannot manage without theory is in the specific context of universities. Most academic practitioners in classical literature pursue their professional activities within a framework of both teaching and research, with the instruction of students occupying a major part of their time. Even if university teachers of classical literature disagree with much or all of the theoretical work which has been emerging, as many do

[8] See again Fowler (2000), esp. 3–4.

[9] Keynes (1973), 383.

and are entitled to do, they have at least some responsibility to their students to make them aware of the wide variety of approaches to literary texts which are now available, and not simply to provide them with the fare which they themselves individually favour. This is particularly important in the education of graduate students: these are the academics of the future, and it is crucial that they receive as wide a training as possible within the field of classical literary studies, a training which, in my view, should range from textual criticism to literary theory. The ideal graduate student of the twenty-first century in classical literature should be able both to analyse and discuss the relative merits of variant manuscript readings, and to give a coherent account of the basic features of narratology and reader-response theory, and their possible effects on literary interpretation.

There is another, increasingly important issue within universities which points to the necessary co-operation of theory and scholarship within the study of classical literature. The rise of comparative literature and cultural studies, and the consequent growth of literary and cultural work which spans more than one period and culture, has led to rewarding interpretations of classical texts by non-classicists, often employing some degree of theory. Literary classicists naturally wish to communicate and discuss common interests with their literary colleagues in other fields, and to utilize their interpretations in their own teaching and research. On the other hand, literary classics needs to maintain a strong and unified field, with a major interdisciplinary tradition of scholarship of its own, as well as functioning as a subject able to interact with other related academic areas. This is especially relevant in a generation which has seen a considerable upsurge in the number of those studying classical literature in translation, where on the one hand wider literary concerns and interrelationships are naturally to the fore, and on the other, expert translators and annotators fulfil an increasingly important role in the broader communication of classical texts.

An approach which allows a place to both traditional scholarship and theory can negotiate this mild dilemma: this avoids both an undesirable dilution of classics into 'just another' form of literature, and a disastrous retreat into the bunker of an ever-narrowing specialism. Literary classics needs a broad but firm agenda of its own—the exploration of significant ancient literatures with a range of approaches, incorporating both a rich and individual scholarly tradition and modern tools common to other literary fields. I am not arguing here that every literary classicist should become an active theorist, but rather for an awareness that in a larger sense there is no non-theoretical literary interpretation; that there is much interesting theoretically informed interpretation about, especially in interdisciplinary work; and that consequently literary interpreters need to take some account of explicitly theoretical discourse.

But the sceptical will need convincing here of the effectiveness of theoretical approaches in the interpretation of classical literature; the brief examples which follow are largely drawn from my own field of Roman literature, though similar instances could be adduced for Greek texts.[10] Three general points are worth making.

The first is that the new perspectives offered by literary theory can lead to new insights which can revolutionize (no less) the interpretation of a text. One example which comes to mind is the application of narrative theory (with a mild deconstructive flavour) to Apuleius' *Metamorphoses* by Jack Winkler. This has, by common consent of Apuleian specialists, begun a whole new era in the study of that work: Winkler's sceptical and ambivalent approach has ensured (among many other things) that the crucial last book of the *Metamorphoses* can never again be used as a 'straight' source for Apuleian biography or the history of religion.[11]

The second is that the application of theory, with its technical terminology, can effectively and efficiently codify and focus the investigation of phenomena which non-theoretical scholars had more vaguely indicated as important: again, narratology has in my view been strikingly successful here, as (for example) in the work of Don Fowler and others on poetic closure.[12] Here, however, it should be noted that clarity is crucial: technical terms, when introduced, should be adequately glossed and referenced, and there

[10] e.g. Vernant's application of the *pharmakos* to Sophocles' *Oedipus Tyrannus* and Vidal-Naquet's relation of Sophocles' *Philoctetes* to *ephebeia*, both to be found in English in Vernant and Vidal-Naquet (1988), or the use of narratology in the analysis of Homer by de Jong (1987), or the employment of gender theory in Halperin, Winkler, and Zeitlin (1990).

[11] Winkler (1985); for an assessment see e.g. the review of Dowden (1987), and for my own views Harrison (2000), 238–52.

[12] Fowler (1989), like Fowler (1997) a commendably clear and scholarly exposition of a theoretical idea and its impact on the close reading of texts, both now reprinted in Fowler (2000); see also Roberts, Dunn, and Fowler (1997).

should be no assumption that all readers can slip naturally into the world of theoretical idiolect, which unless elucidated can become the exclusive and opaque discourse of the self-chosen few.

The third point is that theoretical considerations have a salutary role in the interpreter's own realization of his or her own ideological agenda, something already touched on above. An analysis which openly reveals its own theoretical basis involves the explicit adoption of a set of principles of interpretation, while a 'non-theoretical' or 'non-ideological' analysis in fact involves an implicit adoption of the same. It is surely better for an interpreter to declare his or her underlying viewpoint rather than to leave it to be constructed from what he or she writes or says in an apparently neutral manner; there are many ways of effectively indicating a critical standpoint or affinity through indirect means (the approving citation of explicit theoretical positions, for example), but some orientation for the reader or audience is extremely helpful in a world of competing ideologies. Modern interpreters are increasingly following this route, with an explicit theoretical or methodological section at the beginning of a piece, a trend which is to be encouraged for its transparency.[13]

In the recent study of Latin poetry, one of the most significant strands of criticism has been that associated with Gian Biagio Conte and other Latinists connected with Pisa.[14] Its effective combination of traditional classical scholarship and modern theory has made it especially influential, despite some initial jargonizing. In particular, Conte's reassessment of the function of allusion, revealingly analysed as a poetic figure equivalent to metaphor in the rich texture of Augustan and other poetry, has been especially valuable, combining detailed analysis of linguistic and thematic echoes with stimulating broader interpretative ideas about the nature of genre; the intertextual transformation of Homer has been pursued along these lines in a fine study by Alessandro Barchiesi,[15]

[13] This clearly relates to the issue of the personal voice in classical scholarship, raised by Hallett and Van Nortwick (1997); for a good discussion of the issues see Nisbet (1997).

[14] For further remarks on the Pisan school cf. e.g. Segal (1986), Fowler (1995), and Fowler (1997). Conte (1986) condenses in English two volumes of his previous work; within a generally formalist approach, his concern with 'codes' shows clear structuralist affinities (cf. e.g. Conte (1986), 31), while his concern with the competence of the reader intersects with reader-response ideas (cf. e.g. Conte (1986), 30).

[15] Barchiesi (1984).

author also of an important book on Ovid and Augustus which similarly combines the traditional and the modern.[16]

One example in Conte's own work is here worth considering. A matter of great debate amongst literary classicists is the interpretation of Vergil's tenth *Eclogue*, in which the love-poet Gallus appears in a bucolic landscape, makes a speech in which he tries to become a bucolic character and escape from love, but is able only to rehearse the topics of love-poetry, and withdraws again.[17] Through an analysis of what he calls the 'bucolic code' and the 'elegiac code', that is, through collecting and considering traditional scholarly material on the language and themes of these two genres and how they interact within the poem, and through an application of more theoretical ideas about the interplay of genres, Conte arrives at a rich interpretation of the poem which makes sense of its complexities. The poem is, he thinks, about exploring the boundaries of literary genres and the life-choices they represent: 'the confrontation between two adjacent genres makes their relationship come to life, rescuing both from the conventionally static nature of literary institutions. By being made vivid and vital in this way, the conflict between forms is able to mediate . . . a conflict present in life.'[18] While I would not go as far as Conte in arguing that a debate about life-choices is necessarily implicated in the debate between literary genres, the crucial insight is that the poem is about a clash of types of poetry: Gallus' mysterious presence in the poem, and his strange speech stuffed with the topics of love-elegy, represent that type of writing and its confrontation with pastoral, a confrontation from which Gallus, the unshakeable love-elegist, eventually withdraws: the two genres cannot merge, however hard they try. This essential insight seems to me to move the interpretation of the poem on to a whole new plane through the application of both theoretical ideas about genre and traditional scholarly material.[19]

Also significant here, as others have noted, is the series of

[16] Barchiesi (1997a), a revised translation of Barchiesi (1994).

[17] Conte (1986), 100–1 gives some background; see also Clausen (1994), 288–92, which shows the problems on which Conte provides such a sharp focus, though Coleman (1979), 295–6 shares some of Conte's points in a good discussion.

[18] Conte (1986), 128 (the complete interpretation of *Ecl.* 10 occupies pp. 100–29).

[19] Note too that this generic debate is staged at a point where the *Eclogue* collection itself is explicitly concluding (10.1 *extremum . . . laborem*), a natural point for generic self-consciousness following Callimachus fr. 112. 9.

studies on Roman Literature and its Contexts edited by Denis Feeney and Stephen Hinds. The eight volumes so far published have represented a range of topics and approaches: deconstruction and elegy from Duncan Kennedy; deconstruction, translation, and reception theory from Charles Martindale; post-Freudian theory from Philip Hardie; the textual reception and representation of the city of Rome from Catharine Edwards; literature and religion from Denis Feeney; Intertextual allusion from Stephen Hinds; slavery in literature from William Fitzgerald; and women in Roman epic from Alison Keith.[20] Though I at least would not agree with all of the ideas proposed by all of the authors, these volumes fulfil well the programme set out by the editors for the series, that it should promote interdisciplinary discussion between Latinists, other classicists, and other scholars in the humanities. That programme also makes an essential point in noting that such interdisciplinary activity is by no means alien to the traditional discipline of classics: 'the pursuit of contacts with cognate fields such as social history, anthropology, history of thought, linguistics and literary theory is in the best traditions of classical scholarship.'[21] For me, the qualities of the series are best brought out by Philip Hardie's *The Epic Successors of Virgil*, where careful close readings of a traditional kind are allied with Bloomian ideas of the 'anxiety of influence' to cast a new and convincing light on the relationship between post-Vergilian epic and the *Aeneid*.

The eclectic but consistently theoretical approach of this series, and its aim of stimulating debate rather than laying down doctrine, seems to me to provide some good prospects for classical literary studies. One of the chief difficulties raised in the field of literary theory, especially in the context of deconstruction, is how the matter of interpretation can be usefully debated: X has one theory or reading, Y has another, while Z suggests that all interpretations are equally possible. What is the criterion for decision? Can there ever be such a criterion? Is there anything beyond a purely subjective and individual reading of a text? Can one reading be 'better' than another? And if not, what is the point of the discipline of literary interpretation, other than mere self-display by individual interpreters selling their competing products? While I share the

[20] Kennedy (1993), Martindale (1993), Hardie (1993), Edwards (1997), Feeney (1998), Hinds (1998), Fitzgerald (2000), Keith (2000).

[21] Set out at the beginning of each volume—e.g. Kennedy (1993), p. iv.

doubts of many theorists about the simply asserted 'natural' or 'common-sense' interpretation, and do not believe that a modern interpreter can indubitably reconstruct the intentions of an ancient author, I do not myself believe that literary interpreters should despair of reaching adequate (if provisional) conclusions about whether one interpretation can be preferred to another.

Here I would appeal (perhaps naively) to reader-response theory and the notion of 'interpretive communities'.[22] Classical literary interpretation is, in my view, aimed at such a community (primarily, literary academic classicists, their students, and others with cognate interests), and it is their views which must count most, given that they (collectively) have a special training and competence in the technical knowledge required (knowledge of texts and languages, training in the analysis of literature, relevant data about history and culture, and so on); as in scientific fields, peer judgement is crucial. If objective interpretation of texts is (as I would hold) impossible since interpretation is simply never an objective activity, there remains the possibility of a significant and well-informed group of individuals agreeing on an interpretation, of intra-subjective acquiescence in particular readings. One view of what we are doing in literary interpretation is that we are constructing a hypothesis, plausible to us, for the consideration of our fellow-interpreters, for debate and negotiation (hence the importance of discussion, seminars, conferences, and publications); our goal is to persuade our audience or readership that our views are worth their consideration or acceptance. Hence the provisionality of interpretation: what is agreed or tolerated as an interpretation by one group or generation may not be acceptable to another.[23]

This raises a clear issue concerning the identity of the appropriate interpretive community: do we count only the judgement of the ideologically like-minded peer group as significant? In the more technical reaches of classics the interpretive community will perhaps be small and select; but in the field of the general interpretation of texts I would argue for a wide and pragmatic perspective, for the broadest possible communication and negotiation within

[22] The idea is that of Fish (1980); for its application to classics see Fowler (2000), esp. pp. vii–ix. I recognize the real problems inherent in defining the limits of such an interpretive community for literary classicists. As well as the question of narrowing the community by appealing only to select groups within classics, raised above, there is the question of broad appeal to (e.g.) specialists in comparative literature or the larger literary public.

[23] See again Fowler (2000), pp. vii–ix.

the practice of literary classics. This means taking some account of theory. As the history of literary studies in classics pointedly shows, we are all necessarily children of our time and environment, and so are our interpretations. As our time and environment become increasingly informed by theory (whether we like it or not), we need to take theory increasingly into account, at least in reading the interpretations of others, unless we want to communicate with only part of our interpretive community, and damagingly polarize further our often-threatened discipline. By the same token, literary theory, as it emerges from the margins into the centre of the field of literary classics, must make itself even more accessible and transparent to those without a theoretical background.

II

The 'literary classics meets theory' book is already a genre in its own right. Some have aimed at presenting a debate between parties of opposing views;[24] others have been concerned with the contribution of a particular type of theory to classics;[25] yet others have attempted to show to the unconvinced the use of different types of theory in the interpretation of different kinds of literary material.[26] This book falls largely (but not entirely) into the last category: its purpose is protreptic, to speak to both the sceptical and the non-sceptical, and to suggest to both the importance of its topic. The areas of interest chosen for the 1997 Oxford conference, reflected in this book, were in no way intended as exhaustive, and many significant topics are wholly omitted for simple lack of space. Those selected were chosen by a panel of distinguished practitioners as traditional areas of classical literary studies where the importance of the co-operation of theory and scholarship could be shown in different ways by scholars who ranged widely in their views. The final headings under which papers are grouped in this volume are 'literary language', 'narrative', 'genre', 'historicism', and 'reception and history of scholarship': individual section introductions within the book will discuss the particular papers, but

[24] e.g. Galinsky (1992).

[25] e.g. Benjamin (1988) on post-structuralism, Rabinowitz and Richlin (1993) and McManus (1997) on feminism, or Fowler (2000) on postmodernism.

[26] e.g. Hexter and Selden (1992), implicitly theoretical and with a strong interdisciplinary thrust; more explicitly theoretical, de Jong and Sullivan (1994).

here I want to set each of the topics chosen in a briefly outlined general framework.

First, literary language. The consideration of language in the work of Saussure and early structuralism put linguistic interpretation at the centre of theoretical discussion early on. The issue of literary style, a traditional topic of classical scholarship, thus meets theory at a number of points—whether in terms of the application of linguistic theory to the literary analysis of classical texts (as in Jerzy Danielewicz's paper in this volume), or in terms of aesthetics and pre-1960s literary theory, whose contribution is too often forgotten (as Michael Silk's contribution effectively reminds us). As in other areas, theory can be used to create useful categories, and for sharp and focused analysis of particular elements. It can also reflect the concerns of analysts of poetic style in a striking way: even Derrida's radical notion of *différance*, the idea (roughly speaking) that the meaning of a piece of language is never fully closed and must always be deferred,[27] has some affinities with those parts of Greek and Roman poetic style where traditional analysis has felt that richness, compression, or ambiguity leaves meaning open to some degree. In my own field of Latin, suitable examples from Vergil might be the identity of the shedder of the tears at *Aeneid* 4. 449: *lacrimae volvuntur inanes*, 'the tears roll down in vain' (Aeneas' or Anna's?); or the ultimate sense of *quisque suos patimur manis*, 'we all endure our own ghosts' (?) at *Aeneid* 6.743—issues which have been extensively and inconclusively discussed through long centuries of classical scholarship.[28]

Secondly, narrative. The application of narratology to classical texts has been a success story,[29] and the three papers included here build on previous work which has achieved much of value in interpretation (two indeed build on significant previous work by the authors themselves). There are perhaps several reasons for this. First, the terms of narratological analysis are themselves not entirely foreign to classicists, since many of them derive from evidently Greek roots and even from the categories of Greek literary criticism: Genette's use of *diegesis* and its cognates, for example,

[27] For Derrida's own characteristically difficult exposition cf. Derrida (1984), and for a useful and clearer account cf. Jefferson and Robey (1986), 114–15.

[28] For discussions of the two passages see Austin (1955), 135, Austin (1977), 227–9.

[29] See e.g. the essays by Don Fowler picked out in n. 12 above.

owes something to the ancient use of that term.[30] Secondly, the pioneers of narratology themselves received extensive classical educations and sometimes treat classical texts (an example would be Todorov's piece on the *Odyssey*[31]); their approaches are thus likely to be useful to classicists. Thirdly, and perhaps most importantly, classical texts themselves display the kind of narrative complexities which narratology can help to unravel and categorize: this is partly due to the universal importance of narrative categories such as order, duration, frequency, mood, and voice (to cite those employed by Genette), but is also partly owed to the rich narrative texture of texts like the *Odyssey*, with its four-book inserted tale, its flashbacks, and its manipulation of the double strands of events on and off Ithaca and involving or not involving Odysseus; or of Plato's *Symposium*, in which, in a multiple-layer embedded narrative, Apollodorus repeats to an unnamed friend his own previous conversation with Glaucon about the famous party, a conversation which consisted largely of reporting the narrative of Aristodemus concerning that occasion; or of Apuleius' *Metamorphoses*, where the last book seems to require a reassessment of the whole preceding narrative, and where the inserted tales seem to reflect and anticipate the events of the main story.[32] Narratological analysis requires a close and careful reading with the tools of traditional scholarship, but provides a new and often highly stimulating way of looking at familiar texts (for example, Don Fowler's work on focalization in the *Aeneid*); it also has natural affinities with other areas of theory, as, for example, with feminism in the work of Lillian Doherty, which makes it a good entry-point into theory as a whole.[33]

Thirdly, historicism. In the context of the conference, this included the role of history in interpreting texts and the necessary historical situatedness both of ancient texts and of the writing about them, as well as the more obvious New Historicism and its impact on classics.[34] In a general way, one might say that classicists have in fact been doing New Historicism for some time. This is

[30] See Genette (1980) and useful terms such as intradiegetic, extradiegetic, metadiegetic, etc. For the use of *diegesis* in ancient literary-critical contexts see e.g. Plato *Republic* 2.392c ff., discussed by Genette (1980), 164–75, Aristotle *Poetics* 3.1448a ff.

[31] In Todorov (1977).

[32] See esp. Winkler (1985) and Tatum (1969).

[33] Fowler (1990); Doherty (1995)—see also her piece in this volume. As noted above (n. 8), De Jong (1987) provides an accessible narratological account of a major text.

[34] On New Historicism see the useful reader of Veeser (1989).

partly because the nature of classics, centred on other cultures and their motive forces, favours the anthropological drive central to New Historicism, and partly because of the sparse nature of evidence for classical cultures (often literary texts) and the need of classicists to generalize from it. Something closely akin to the New Historical dense reading of texts which seeks to open up the realities of cultural forces and social power has been practised in, for example, readings of Augustan poetry since the 1960s, though it has become more sophisticated in recent years.[35] Similarly, recent work on Attic tragedy has stressed much more its interrelation with the historical culture of the Athenian *polis* in negotiating (a central New Historicist term) major social and political concerns;[36] while the work on ancient sexuality by Foucault, who would oppose the label 'historicist' but whose concern with the manipulation of power through institutions and other forms of discourse has plain links with New Historicism, has been creatively applied to Greco-Roman culture and texts.[37] As interpreters of cultures and texts from a dimension in many ways alien to our own (and much more alien than was thought a century ago), we need to be particularly aware of crucial difference and distance, the way in which our own cultural and historical location colours and affects our view of Greco-Roman antiquity. To take a controversial example, the arguments of Martin Bernal that much of Greek culture is derived from Africa through Egypt may not convince all readers in a scholarly sense,[38] but the controversy serves some useful general purpose in reminding classicists of the 'otherness' of the Greeks.

Fourthly, genre. This has been a major concern of modern literary theorists, especially the interface between genre and ideology or social culture, and the issue of whether traditional genres break down in modern literary practice.[39] In Greco-Roman literary texts,

[35] Barchiesi (1997) again provides an excellent example.

[36] For work on Attic tragedy cf. e.g. Winkler and Zeitlin (1990).

[37] For applications and discussions of Foucault in classical contexts cf. Halperin, Winkler, and Zeitlin (1990) and Goldhill (1995); for Foucault himself see esp. Foucault (1986), (1987), and (1988) and the useful guide by Merquior (1985).

[38] Bernal (1987); see the response in Lefkowitz and Rogers (1996).

[39] On genre and ideology see especially Todorov (1990), 19; on the modern 'dissolution of the genres' see e.g. Genette (1982) 67. On genre-theory in general, for a typically complex but influential contribution cf. Derrida (1992), 221–31; for a stimulating discussion see Todorov (1990), for a more pragmatic and user-friendly guide Fowler (1982). A useful reader in genre theory is Genette and Todorov (1986).

above all in poetry, generic codes and conventions can be seen as specific, firm, and vigorous, with a history and identity stretching back to generic predecessors through detailed and carefully manipulated allusion of previous texts and literary traditions (I think here again of the work of Gian Biagio Conte).[40] The investigation of genre thus constitutes a field in which stimulating modern work on the theory of genre can be combined with rigorous traditional scholarship to produce new results. One particular area of interest for literary classicists is the question of the interplay of genres: ever since Wilhelm Kroll in the 1920s formulated the notion of the *Kreuzung der Gattungen*, the crossing of the genres, a formulation acutely analysed by Alessandro Barchiesi in this volume, the way in which poets (especially) creatively combine and confront different genres has been seen as one of the chief features of the extraordinary efflorescence of poetry in the early Augustan period.[41] Generally innovative here, and not without influence, has been the work of Francis Cairns, whose analysis of poetic texts in terms of speech-genres from prescriptive rhetorical handbooks has added a new dimension, though it has also made more difficult the task of defining 'genre' in the context of classical literature.[42] Mention should also be made here of the effective application, in recent study of the problem of the genre of the ancient novel, of the Russian Formalist Mikhail Bakhtin's stimulating discussions of the novel genre, discussions which themselves dealt with the ancient novel at length.[43]

Finally, reception and history of scholarship. Though it might be argued that this is an aspect of literary interpretation only in the sense of forming part of its history, reception-theory argues conversely, with some force, that our own interpretations derive much from those of others, often over a long period.[44] This can be particularly true of the models of scholarship which literary classicists encounter in their training, encounters which, when effectively conducted, continue to be fruitful and creative rather than mere antiquarian exercises. Literary classicists of the highest

[40] Conte (1986) and esp. (1994).

[41] Kroll (1924), 202–24. For some good examples see Conte (1986), 100–29, or Hinds (1992).

[42] Cairns (1972).

[43] For Bakhtin's own views cf. Bakhtin (1981), and for their application to the ancient novel see Slater (1989), Branham (1995).

[44] For a stimulating exposition in the context of Roman literature see Martindale (1993).

quality have often been ready to look back to the long history of their own discipline and to their critical predecessors: the work of Pfeiffer and Wilamowitz in particular comes to mind.[45] History of scholarship might strike some as the ultimate conservative practice, preserving the past and holding it up for imitation, and as intellectually naive, with its tendency towards catalogue-form and a biographical approach to scholarship.[46] More recently, however, more detailed research and closer contextualization has combined with a consciousness of underlying ideologies to produce a new kind of history of scholarship, with clear affinities to New Historicism.[47] Not only are past interpreters brought more effectively to life, with a wealth of detail about their texts and practices, but the resources of sociology and a consciousness of the importance of the academic and political frameworks of the time are applied to analyse their intellectual activities, which can then be interpreted in a greatly enriched way. Again, this type of approach provides a salutary reminder to all interpreters of our own historical and cultural situatedness: we too are potential specimens for future contextualized analysis.

In sum, I hope that this volume will encourage sceptically inclined literary classicists to believe that the application of literary (and other) theory can provide new and enriching resources for their traditional scholarship, and remind the more theoretically inclined that they need and rely on traditional scholarship and must continue to train the academics of the future in its fundamental disciplines and practices. To cite the excellent 'Guidelines for Contributors' to the *Transactions of the American Philological Association*: 'theoretical insights, to be plausible, must be grounded on sound philology, while illuminating philological investigation requires an informed awareness of underlying theoretical postulates.[48] Above all, I hope that this book stresses that a rich mixture of traditional learning and modern ideas, tested and contested

[45] Pfeiffer (1968), Wilamowitz (1982).

[46] This is rather the feel of the monumental three volumes of Sandys (1903–8); see Brink (1985), 6.

[47] For a more focused and historically contextualized approach to the history of scholarship see e.g. Brink (1985) and Jocelyn (1988), (1996), though neither would claim to be a 'theorist', and Grafton's work on Scaliger (1983, 1993). For a more explicitly sociological perspective see Stray (1998) and his piece in this volume, the group of articles on the history of scholarship in *TAPA* 127 (1997), and the recent treatment of J. E. B. Mayor by Henderson (1998d).

[48] Skinner (1997).

through discussion and negotiation, can only nourish the community of academic classicists in their contact with each other and with colleagues in related fields, and further their working together in the common task of the interpretation of classical texts.

Literary Language

2

Introduction

Stephen Harrison

As already noted in my General Introduction to this volume, the issue of literary language has been a central topic in both literary theory and classical scholarship in the twentieth century. Auerbach's *Literary Language and its Public*, translated in 1965, states that 'a literary language is distinguished from the general language of daily life by its selectivity, homogeneity and conservatism',[1] and classical scholars have often followed this traditional emphasis on linguistic register and lexicon as the key features of literary and (especially) poetic language.[2] However, a larger perspective can also be applied, by which the developing concerns of twentieth-century classical scholars can be seen as consonant with developments in linguistic and literary theory more generally. The turn in Saussure and structuralist thought towards language as system, the deep preoccupation with language in linguistic philosophy generally, the close analysis of literary language which is a common concern of both Formalism and New Criticism, and the radical destabilization of language and its capacity to signify in post-structuralist theory, have all to some extent been reflected in the work of literary classicists, even when there is no apparent formal connection.

For instance, the central concern with Homeric language as system in the work of Milman Parry and his successors might plausibly be seen as having some structuralist affinities (indeed, it is not impossible that Parry had some acquaintance with Saussure's *Cours de linguistique général*, published posthumously in Paris in 1915, during his studies in Paris in 1923–8),[3] while linguistic

[1] Auerbach (1965), 249.

[2] e.g. the ongoing controversy about 'poetic' and 'unpoetic' language in Latin poetry—cf. Axelson (1945), Williams (1968), 743–50, Watson (1985).

[3] For Parry's connections with French scholars in these years see Parry (1971), pp. xxii–iv.

philosophy, Formalism, and New Criticism have had an important impact on literary interpretation in classical scholarship from the 1950s.[4] Post-structuralist approaches to literary language in Greek and Latin have produced some stimulating work on Roman poetry and Greek tragedy;[5] but the already-noted tendency of classical linguistic scholarship towards close categorization of the varieties of literary language has naturally found it difficult to coexist with modes of theory in which infinite possibilities of signification can be opened up. As a result, the formal analysis of literary language is a field in which traditional scholars and modern theorists sometimes find communication difficult, though (for example) the more traditional discipline of linguistics has sometimes been used to good effect in the analysis of literary texts.[6]

The rise of New Criticism in English studies in the 1950s transferred to classics in the 1960s, and I have already noted the major impact of this change in the General Introduction to this volume.[7] The concern of New Criticism with the 'verbal icon' and the consequent close analysis of (especially) poetic texts as autonomous aesthetic artefacts,[8] naturally promoted an approach concerned with bringing out the richness and variety of classical literary language, a ripe object for the New Critical concerns of irony and ambiguity. As I noted, such searches for indeterminacy even raise an analogy with Derrida's radical notion of *différance*, the idea (roughly speaking) that the meaning of a piece of language is never fully closed and must always be deferred.[9] Furthermore, the concern of New Criticism with the (accessible) text rather than the (less accessible) author and historical context showed an interest-

[4] The rise of the New Criticism in classical literature in the Anglophone world is particularly associated with the journal *Arion*, founded in 1962, with the series of volumes *Critical Essays on Roman Literature* published by Routledge and Kegan Paul under the initial editorship of J. P. Sullivan (Sullivan 1962 and 1963), and with the Cambridge volumes edited by Tony Woodman and David West (especially Woodman and West 1974). Silk (1974), an important study of poetic imagery, provides perhaps the most subtle and well-informed application of formalistic literary theory to the study of the language of classical poetry.

[5] e.g. Goldhill (1983) and some of the pieces in Henderson (1998).

[6] Here I think of the role of traditional linguistics in the analysis of the literary style of prose authors—e.g. Callebat (1968) on Apuleius, or Petersmann (1977) on Petronius; for a recent example by a distinguished linguistic theoretician cf. Pinkster (1998).

[7] Cf. p. 2–3 above.

[8] The phrase 'verbal icon' is taken from the title of a key New Critical work, Wimsatt and Beardsley (1954); for another cf. Brooks (1947).

[9] Cf. p. 13 above.

ing affinity with the 'death of the author' associated with contemporary structuralist/post-structuralist thinking.[10] New close analyses of familiar texts brought renewed vitality to the literary interpretation of the classics: this phenomenon is particularly associated in the UK with the journal *Arion*,[11] with the series of volumes *Critical Essays on Roman Literature* published by Routledge and Kegan Paul under the initial editorship of J. P. Sullivan,[12] and with the Cambridge volumes edited by Tony Woodman and David West.[13] Work of this kind encouraged classicists to move beyond their primary concerns with linguistic register to larger issues of syntax, imagery, themes, and literary structure, and could also incorporate Formalist concerns in pursuing the special features of literary and poetic language.[14]

This mild coalescence of literary and theoretical concerns in the analysis of literary language has continued towards the end of the twentieth century. One branch of the study of literary language in which theory and scholarship have successfully worked together is in the study of literary allusion and/or the more postmodern 'intertextuality'.[15] As already noted in the General Introduction, scholars of Latin poetry have perhaps been the prime movers here, especially Gian Biago Conte and those influenced by his work in Italy, the USA, and the UK.[16] These approaches, generally speaking, combine a traditional concern with textual detail, literary history, and (even) authorial intention with structuralist-influenced ideas of poetry and its genres as a literary system, a formalistic approach to literary texture, and a reader-response approach to interpretation.[17] The key insight here is that, within the system of ancient poetry, allusion functions as a type of rhetorical figure,

[10] Cf. esp. Barthes (1977).

[11] For a representative anthology see Rudd (1972).

[12] e.g. Sullivan (1962) and (1963).

[13] Esp. Woodman and West (1974).

[14] Here one thinks of the links between the debate on Latin poetic diction noted in n. 2 above and the central formalist concept of literary language heightened through 'defamiliarization' (for a convenient account of the latter with some original sources cf. Lodge (1988), 15–30). Silk (1974), an important study of poetic imagery, provides perhaps the most subtle and well-informed application of formalistic literary theory to the study of the language of classical poetry.

[15] For a good discussion of the two terms see Fowler (1997). One reason why intertextuality did not feature in the Oxford conference which is the origin of this book is that it was the subject of another Oxford conference in 1996 whose proceedings are now published in *MD* 39 (1997).

[16] See most recently Hinds (1998); on Conte's work in general, see General Introduction, pp. 8–9.

[17] See esp. Conte (1986).

bringing with it the baggage of other texts and their contexts, to be recognized by the alert and learned reader. Such allusions often advertise their allusive status in a self-conscious and metapoetical way—an element which clearly appeals to postmodern notions of the self-conscious text.

A well-known example from Conte's work will make the point. In Ovid's *Fasti*, Ariadne, abandoned by Bacchus, makes her complaint (3. 471–4):

> en iterum, fluctus, similis audite querellas!
> en iterum lacrimas accipe, harena, meas!
> dicebam, memini, 'periure et perfide Theseu!'
> ille abiit, eadem crimina Bacchus habet.

As Conte shows, the iterative force of *en iterum* and *similis* and the self-conscious memory of *memini* point inescapably to Ovid's poetic model, Ariadne's previous lament, at Catullus 64. 133–201, after being similarly abandoned by Theseus, an episode firmly indicated by *periure et perfide Theseu*: she is reliving her literary past in this intertextual allusion. 'Ovid's Ariadne has "lived" her experience as a poetic self, in Catullus' poem, and she remembers the tears she wept there—the tears and lamentations of Catullus' Ariadne.'[18] The simple building-blocks of poetic language in Ovid's text are here fundamentally enriched by the reactivation of another famous Ariadne-text,[19] and the application of the theory of poetic memory ensures that the relationship between the two is not one of static ornament but of dynamic reshaping. The echo is thus given an important role in interpretation, pushing the alert reader towards recalling the Catullan context and identifying the self-conscious literary gymnastics of Ovid's text.

Allusion is, of course, only one field in which the nature of literary language can be illuminated by theoretical concerns, though I have concentrated on it here since it is a particularly fashionable (and important) topic, which happens not to be one of the central topics of this book. It has been a particular, though of course not exclusive, concern of Latinists; by contrast, both the papers in this section deal with the theoretical links of Greek literary style,

[18] Conte (1986), 61.

[19] 471 *similis audite querellas!* ~ 64.195 *meas audite querellas*, 473 *periure et perfide Theseu* ~ 64.133 *perfide . . . Theseu*, 474 *ille abiit* ~ 64.167 *ille autem prope iam mediis versatur in undis*.

though in very different ways. Through an analysis of passages of Pindar and Plato, Michael Silk mounts a plea for the restoration of the concept of the value of literature to the debate about literary theory, and against the fetishizing of postmodernism and consequent discarding of valuable earlier ideas: the richness of literary language, he argues, is fundamentally linked with notions of the values underlying literature which postmodern theory has been inclined to discount. The reminder that there was literary theory before 1968 is salutary, especially from a scholar who has himself applied such theory to classical texts in an important and pioneering book.[20] Jerzy Danielewicz, on the other hand, seeks to incorporate the concept of 'metalanguage' from linguistic philosophy into a practical and functional analysis of how Greek lyric poems use metatextual signposts to point to their own status as uttered and performed texts and to promote coherence and continuity, thus uniting theoretical concerns with the traditional questions of the unity and performative aspects of ancient lyric poetry. Here we see literary analysis using a central philosophical idea to support a particular interpretative approach.

[20] Silk (1974).

3

Pindar Meets Plato: Theory, Language, Value, and the Classics

Michael Silk

The recently published third edition of the *Oxford Classical Dictionary* contains a long article on 'Literary Theory and Classical Studies' (pp. 873–5) by Don and Peta Fowler, which on more than one count might be seen as a representative discussion. What it represents I wish to elucidate, partly by way of agreement, but also, and substantially, by way of critique.[1]

Fowler and Fowler begin:

> One of the most striking features of twentieth-century intellectual life has been the attention paid to literary theory, especially from the time of the 1960s. This intellectual ferment has produced a confusing variety of approaches . . .

. . . for which (however) the Fowlers offer, not a 'path through the minefield', but rather 'a way in', because 'twentieth-century theorizing has a great deal to offer classical studies'. The general character of this 'great deal' is indicated by the remark that 'many of the most significant twentieth-century theories of language and literature stress a slippery indeterminacy in discourse that is at odds with the pretence to scientific objectivity', and, in the paragraphs

[1] Hornblower and Spawforth (1996) 871–5. At various points the critique extends or is complementary to the argument of Silk (1995): see notes below. I take the opportunity to express my gratitude to various members of the original audience at the 'Working Together' conference, to OUP's anonymous reader, and then to Tania Gergel, Charles Martindale, and Alessandro Schiesaro for some valuable comments, and especially to Don Fowler for graciously accepting the propriety of my using the Fowlers' article as a point of departure in the first place. The untimely death of Don Fowler, between the time of the conference and the publication of this volume, is a sad loss to all who care about the Classics and the future of the Classics; I hope and believe that Don would have encouraged me to put my arguments on record, irrespective of his opportunity or lack of opportunity to respond.

that follow, this opposition between 'science' and 'theory' is placed by a passing reference to the argument between Nietzsche and Wilamowitz[2] and by a list of assumptions ascribed to 200 years of traditional classical 'philology' and said to characterize it still:

> the assumed scientific objectivity of the critic, the focus on the surface psychology of the author, the belief that all the [textual] 'clues' will point to a single coherent picture, the aspiration to that overall master interpretation, and especially the belief that the hermeneutic tools used to interpret texts are timeless.

These assumptions are said to have been challenged by 'various different theoretical positions' and are pronounced 'unhelpful'.

Let me note, by way of clarifying matters at this early stage, that I readily agree with the Fowlers that these positions are indeed characteristic of and significant for the 'traditional' classical study of literature; and that these positions have indeed been significantly challenged by 'various different' kinds of theorist in the last hundred years; and also that (in crude multiple-choice terms) this cluster of 'assumptions' is indeed unacceptable—as a whole. One must at once lodge a protest, however, against the bland way that the items in question are lumped together. Literary critics are indeed not, and cannot be, 'scientifically objective', if only because they are, or should be, concerned with what D. H. Lawrence famously called 'values that science ignores'.[3] Focus on the *surface* psychology of 'the author' and the belief that hermeneutic tools of interpretation are 'timeless' are indeed, to say the least, 'unhelpful': for myself, I would choose stronger language. But the belief (or the correlative aspiration) about single coherent pictures is, in itself, no less, or more, laudable than its converse, though it is at least pragmatically more plausible: in life, in literature, as no doubt in much-derided science, it makes more sense to *expect* a single 'answer' unless and until we are forced to conclude otherwise. Already one is aware that the Fowlers have their own questionable, and unstated, assumptions—this one, that simplicity is suspect, negligible, or else even impossible. The 'Flavian epicists', we learn later in this article are no longer to be viewed as 'servile imitators of Virgil', but as 'machines for producing striking intertextual

[2] For the argument see Silk and Stern (1981), 90–131, esp. 95–107, 129–30.
[3] Lawrence (1936), 539.

complexities': this is, if not a false, at least an opaque disjunction—and I for one would rather be called an imitator than a machine—but the implicit value judgement in 'complexities' is clear enough.[4]

In the main part of their article the Fowlers proceed to juxtapose and characterize twentieth-century alternatives and challenges to traditional classicistic scientism—from the Formalist emphasis on literature as autonomous system to Saussurian linguistics and its concept of meanings as relationships; from New Criticism, with its particular interest in irony and ambiguity, to the structuralist focus on text as part of a wider (not necessarily literary) system; and then the contrasting offshoots of structuralism, narratology and intertextuality, where the Fowlers rightly distinguish between the traditional interest in specific *allusion* and the postmodern insistence (associated, above all, with Kristeva) that 'all texts are'—equally—'shot through with the presence of other texts'.

After structuralism comes post-structuralism, first in the shape of the Derridean philosophy of language: text has in a given sense nothing outside it; the world is constructed as and through language, where language consists of an infinite regress of frustrated signification (not quite the Fowlers' formulation, this).[5] We move on to deconstruction and the argument that text, however seemingly stable in its systematic or hierarchical relationships (assumed to be oppositional relationships), in fact conceals an endless, therefore inconclusive, 'play of meaning' which the deconstructive process of critical decentring reveals—so that all discourses and all texts are credited with a suppressed centre and a suppressed counter-play of meaning, which then (as if by a sort of inversion of the Hegelian principle of synthesis) calls for a further process of recentring and . . . (again, not quite how the Fowlers present the case). Derridean and deconstructive thinking is then broadly—and uncontroversially—associated with postmodernism, its 'incredulity towards metanarratives' (Lyotard), its dismissal of (or disbelief in) 'objective features' of text, and its credo that 'there is no single right way to do anything'.

At which point one pauses to protest again. No single right way to do anything? Really? No single right way to turn a key? No single right way to spell 'Derrida'? The objections—not the

[4] Cf. n. 34 below.

[5] Cf. Silk (1995), 120–4, 127–8.

Fowlers' objections: they offer and seem to expect none—are not facetious. The moment one grants that, yes, there are of course some resting-places in the 'real world' (also the world in which, perhaps, university teachers meet students or get paid) where there *is* a single right way, then the question turns into a vastly more intransigent, but also more productive, set of questions: where does this 'real world' begin and end, and why? When is there a single right way and when not? When (perhaps) is there a multiplicity of right ways? And in a case when there are no single right ways, are there still always *wrong* ways? What questions at this juncture could be more important? Do they not even deserve a mention? And if not, then there is a further two-part question waiting in that 'real world': what are we—we classicists and other *littérateurs*, who are mostly university teachers—meeting students *for*, and what are we getting paid *for*?

From postmodernism, the Fowlers move on to neo-Marxism (eccentrically, perhaps, citing not only New Historicism in this connection, but also Bakhtin), psychoanalytic criticism, and feminism. In their closing statement they point out that theirs has not been 'a comprehensive survey', either of the literary theories of 'the second half of the twentieth century' or of the classical studies 'inspired' by them. They conclude by stressing the 'importance of modern literary theory for classics':

> both as an important and salutary invitation to examine the presuppositions and preconceptions of our individual practices, and as a wealth of techniques and approaches which will enable classical scholars to play their full part in the cultural dialogue that is a central justification for the study of antiquity.

As the Fowlers would be the first to agree, there can be no such thing as a neutral account of literary theory and theories, and theirs is conspicuous for what it says and doesn't say, for what it foregrounds and doesn't foreground. In the main, what the Fowlers do foreground is specifiable literary-theoretical (and associated) movements—rather than individual theorists or individual works of theory—and especially fashionable movements. Their treatment of these movements is largely uncritical: one could hardly claim that the movements are assessed against each other or against any literature or literary or other considerations from outside. Nevertheless, a broad postmodern sympathy is apparent. And overall, the clear impression is given that the history of literary theory, though not actually *beginning* around 1950/60, falls into two parts: pre-1950/60s versus post-1950/60s.

In many ways, what the Fowlers have provided is an admirable survey of the last forty years of literary theory—or at least of the last forty years of fashionable theory—and some of their particular emphases and formulations are striking and felicitous. At the same time, various of their premisses, their assumptions, and their silences are (I suggest) deeply questionable, and a discussion in the realm of literary language (on which they, and their favourite theorists, are relatively muted) is as good a way as any of raising the questions that need to be raised. Then again, perhaps, it is the best way, because literature (however one understands the term) is created of and from language and is accessible only through its language, and in this sense language is fundamental to literature as nothing else can be.[6]

My concrete examples of literary language in action are a pair of passages from Pindar (*Pythian* 8. 76–100) and Plato (*Republic* 10. 617d–e): two related passages, I suggest, and in any case two of the most remarkable passages in Greek literature.[7] Pindar first:

τὰ δ' οὐκ ἐπ' ἀνδράσι κεῖται· δαίμων δὲ παρίσχει,
ἄλλοτ' ἄλλον ὕπερθε βάλλων, ἄλλον δ' ὑπὸ χειρῶν.
μέτρῳ κατάβαιν'· ἐν Μεγάροις δ' ἔχεις γέρας,
μυχῷ τ' ἐν Μαραθῶνος, Ἥρας τ' ἀγῶν' ἐπιχώριον
νίκαις τρισσαῖς, ὦ Ἀριστόμενες, δάμασσας ἔργῳ·
τέτρασι δ' ἔμπετες ὑψόθεν
σωμάτεσσι κακὰ φρονέων,
τοῖς οὔτε νόστος ὁμῶς
ἔπαλπνος ἐν Πυθιάδι κρίθη,
οὐδὲ μολόντων πὰρ ματέρ' ἀμφὶ γέλως γλυκὺς
ὦρσεν χάριν· κατὰ λαύρας δ' ἐχθρῶν ἀπάοροι
πτώσσοντι, συμφορᾷ δεδαγμένοι.

[6] This is equally true irrespective of whether our understanding of 'literature' tends towards crypto-essentialism or towards (e.g.) post-Macherey constructivism.

[7] Text for Pindar essentially as Turyn (1952); the translation quoted is based on Race (1997); for the Plato, both text and translation are, for convenience, Shorey's (1930). I know of no discussion of the relationship between the two passages. Discussions that relate Plato to Pindar are usually concerned with Pindaric anticipation of 'Platons Ideendenken': thus Fränkel (1962), 556. I have myself touched on the Pindar passage in Silk (1980), 103–4.

ὁ δὲ καλόν τι νέον λαχών
ἁβρότατος ἔπι μεγάλας
ἐξ ἐλπίδος πέταται
ὑποπτέροις ἀνορέαις, ἔχων
κρέσσονα πλούτου μέριμναν. ἐν δ' ὀλίγῳ βροτῶν
τὸ τερπνὸν αὔξεται· οὕτω δὲ καὶ πίτνει χαμαί,
ἀποτρόπῳ γνώμᾳ σεσεισμένον.

ἐπάμεροι· τί δέ τις; τί δ' οὔ τις; σκιᾶς ὄναρ
ἄνθρωπος. ἀλλ' ὅταν αἴγλα διόσδοτος ἔλθῃ,
λαμπρὸν φέγγος ἔπεστιν ἀνδρῶν καὶ μείλιχος αἰών.
Αἴγινα φίλα μᾶτερ, ἐλευθέρῳ στόλῳ
πόλιν τάνδε κόμιζε Δὶ καὶ κρέοντι σὺν Αἰακῷ
Πηλεῖ τε κἀγαθῷ Τελαμῶνι σύν τ' Ἀχιλλεῖ.

But those things do not rest with men; a god grants them,
exalting now one man, but throwing another beneath the hands.
Enter the contest in due measure. At Megara you hold the prize
and in the plain of Marathon; and with three victories you
mastered Hera's local contest, O Aristomenes, by your effort.
And upon four bodies you fell from above
with hostile intent,
for whom no homecoming as happy as yours
was decided at the Pythian festival,
nor upon returning to their mothers did sweet laughter
arouse joy all around; but staying clear of their enemies
they shrink down alleyways, bitten by failure.

But he who has been allotted a new success
is inspired by hope at his great splendour
and takes flight
on the wings of manly deeds, having
aspirations superior to wealth. In a short time the delight
of mortals burgeons, but so too does it fall to the ground
when shaken by a hostile purpose.

Creatures of a day! What is someone? What is no one? A dream
of a shadow,
man. But whenever Zeus-given brightness comes,
a shining light rests upon men, and a gentle life.
Dear mother Aigina, on its voyage of freedom
safeguard this city, together with Zeus and king Aiakos,
Peleus and noble Telamon, and with Achilles.

This is the end of the famous ode that commemorates a victory by the boy Aristomenes of Aegina in the wrestling competition at the Pythian games of 446. After due celebration of the heroes of the island and the exploits of the victor's family, Pindar makes a characteristic claim: these things are not up to mankind (*τὰ δ' οὐκ ἐπ' ἀνδράσι κεῖται*, 76), but to a *δαίμων* (*δαίμων δὲ παρίσχει*, 76), a *δαίμων* which puts one man on top (like a wrestler) and another underneath, *ὑπὸ χειρῶν* (like a wrestler). Aristomenes' victories, culminating in his new Pythian triumph, are now ticked off (78–82), and there follows a vignette of the boys who lost: down the back alleys they slink home, with no *γέλως γλυκύς* from mother when they get there (83–7). These losers are *συμφορᾷ δεδαγμένοι* (87), whereas the winner, *καλόν τι νέον λαχών* (88), takes flight, borne up by his achievement (90–1). But then again, there is a general law, *ἐν δ' ὀλίγῳ | βροτῶν τὸ τερπνὸν αὔξεται* (92–3); and here we move into an interactive image of human felicity (93–4), that grows (like the image growing out of the neutral form, *αὔξεται*) and wilts, *ἀποτρόπῳ γνώμᾳ σεσεισμένον* (94).[8]

And now the idiom suddenly changes: the apostrophe, *ἐπάμεροι* (95), marks an address to humankind (however we hear it), not just Aegina in 446 BC, but equally us—*any* 'us'—on the eve of the third millennium AD, along with all points between and beyond. The apostrophe is followed by a short, abrupt, general question of almost embarrassing simplicity, both a rhetorical and a very real question: *τί δέ τις;*—almost, what *is* this 'any us'? And then that simple general question is followed, and countered, by a second simple general question, which is both its seeming negation and also its confirmation, *τί δ' οὔ τις;*—what is no one? what isn't anyone?—as if possibilities were (what?) endless? non-existent? yes? no?

And now another sudden change: *σκιᾶς ὄναρ | ἄνθρωπος* (95–6). We switch from the simple if elusive interrogations to a quite unforeseen stylistic idiom. Our answer comes in the form of a three-noun sentence, without articles, particles, or anything but these three nouns. And though this *is* the answer, *yet* (*ἀλλά*, 96) there is also, one can also hope for, an *αἴγλα διόσδοτος* and thus a truly *λαμπρὸν φέγγος*: a *bright* light, a light of *fame*.[9] At which point Pindar moves to his closing prayer (98–100). *Αἴγινα φίλα μᾶτερ*: so/and/but, Aegina, *mother* Aegina, look to the city that bears and

[8] The interactive mechanism is pivotal: Silk (1974), 90, 93.

[9] i.e. there is a further stage of interactivity in the image: Silk (1974), 119.

shares your name, you, with the great heroes of the land, from Aeacus to Achilles (*κρέοντι σὺν Αἰακῷ . . . σύν τ' Ἀχιλλεῖ*, 99–100), and with Zeus too (*πόλιν τάνδε κόμιζε Δὶ καὶ . . . σὺν . . .*, 99).[10]

The 'still point' of all this remarkable 'turning' is the three-noun sentence. Here Pindar reaches for a new idiom, correlative to his new articulation of the classic-archaic pessimism which underwrites his epinician poetry. The sentence constitutes a perfect example of what the Russian Formalists called defamiliarization.[11] Everyday discourse *automatizes* its messages. Pindar's sentence, by its strangeness, not only puts the spotlight on itself, but forces its listeners or readers to listen afresh to its 'message'. This is achieved through the compressed idiom, through the contrast of this patch of semantic density with what precedes and follows it, through, above all, the un-Greek cast of the three-noun sentence itself.[12]

Compare and contrast the final climactic section of Plato's great dialogue, containing the Myth of Er and in particular the following passage (617d–e):

σφᾶς οὖν, ἐπειδὴ ἀφικέσθαι, εὐθὺς δεῖν ἰέναι πρὸς τὴν Λάχεσιν. προφήτην οὖν τινὰ σφᾶς πρῶτον μὲν ἐν τάξει διαστῆσαι, ἔπειτα λαβόντα ἐκ τῶν Λαχέσεως γονάτων κλήρους τε καὶ βίων παραδείγματα, ἀναβάντα ἐπί τι βῆμα ὑψηλὸν εἰπεῖν. Ἀνάγκης θυγατρὸς κόρης Λαχέσεως λόγος. ψυχαὶ ἐφήμεροι, ἀρχὴ ἄλλης περιόδου θνητοῦ γένους θανατηφόρου. οὐχ ὑμᾶς δαίμων λήξεται, ἀλλ' ὑμεῖς δαίμονα αἱρήσεσθε. πρῶτος δ' ὁ λαχὼν πρῶτος αἱρείσθω βίον, ᾧ συνέσται ἐξ ἀνάγκης. ἀρετὴ δὲ ἀδέσποτον, ἣν τιμῶν καὶ ἀτιμάζων πλέον καὶ ἔλαττον αὐτῆς ἕκαστος ἕξει. αἰτία ἑλομένου· θεὸς ἀναίτιος. ταῦτα εἰπόντα ῥῖψαι ἐπὶ πάντας τοὺς κλήρους, τὸν δὲ παρ' αὐτὸν πεσόντα ἕκαστον ἀναιρεῖσθαι, πλὴν οὗ· ἓ δὲ οὐκ ἐᾶν· τῷ δὲ ἀνελομένῳ δῆλον εἶναι, ὁπόστος εἰλήχει.

Now when they arrived they were straight-way bidden to go before Lachesis, and then a certain prophet first marshalled them in orderly intervals, and thereupon took from the lap of Lachesis lots and patterns of lives and went up to a lofty platform and spoke, 'This is the word of Lachesis, the maiden daughter of Necessity. Souls that live for a day, now is the beginning of another cycle of mortal generation where birth is the

[10] On the ellipse of *σύν* cf. Gildersleeve ad loc. The effect of the ellipse (not discussed by Gildersleeve) is to foreground Zeus himself—momentarily inexplicable, finally in his place.

[11] On defamiliarization, see briefly Silk (1995), 119–20.

[12] On partial parallels see n. 15 below.

beacon of death. No divinity shall cast lots for you, but you shall choose your own deity. Let him to whom falls the first lot first select a life to which he shall cleave of necessity. But virtue has no master over her, and each shall have more or less of her as he honours her or does her despite. The blame is his who chooses: God is blameless.' So saying, the prophet flung the lots out among them all and each took up the lot that fell by his side, except himself; him they did not permit. And whoever took up a lot saw plainly what number he had drawn.

The great mythical culmination of the great dialogue offers us a glimpse of what happens after death, between death and rebirth. To assist his exposition, Plato enlists the *προφήτης* of *Λάχεσις*, who has the *ψυχαί* of the dead sorted out into a kind of military order (*ἐν τάξει*), takes from the *γόνατα* of Lachesis 'lots and patterns of lives', then speaks. His words, addressed to the *ψυχαί*, are given verbatim. He begins with a five-noun sentence: *Ἀνάγκης θυγατρὸς κόρης Λαχέσεως λόγος*. And in case one had not quite made any particular connection with earlier literature, Plato at once adds the allusive trigger, *ψυχαὶ ἐφήμεροι* (Pindar wrote *ἐπάμεροι*), by which the two very different statements about life and the hereafter are linked. In the words and sections that follow, Plato offers further corroborative verbal links,[13] culminating in the very last sentence of the *Republic*, in which he invites his readers to accept that the soul is immortal, that we should pursue *δικαιοσύνη*, and that, if we do, we shall eventually have our reward, *ὥσπερ οἱ νικηφόροι*, 'like the winners in the games' (621d).

In the meantime, and in the passage quoted, we have not only a majestic Platonic statement about these issues, but a cluster of Platonic counter-statements to Pindar. For Pindar, in his poetic world of victors and heroes, and victors *evoking* heroes, death is

[13] At 616b there is a *φῶς λαμπρότερον* (cf. Pindar's *λαμπρὸν φέγγος*, 97), at 621b a *σεισμόν*, and in between at 617c we hear *ὑμνεῖν . . . Ἄτροπον . . . τὰ μέλλοντα* (cf. Pindar's *ἀτρόπῳ γνώμᾳ σεσεισμένον*, 94). Once an allusion is established, of course, such very subsidiary evocations are more readily picked up. The allusion overall, one might add, indicates that the passage in *P* 8 was as memorable for a sensitive fourth-century reader as it is for many of us. In later antiquity too it was much regarded, to judge from its many citations (see Turyn's app. crit., ad loc.). For earlier antiquity it is worth considering whether the proverb attested already in Aristophanes (*Vesp*. 191 and fr. 199 K–A) and Sophocles (fr. 331 R) as *ὄνου σκιά* originates as some sort of comic allusion (the Soph. is from a satyr-play) to Pindar's *σκιᾶς ὄναρ*. If so, the fame of Pindar's passage must have been virtually instantaneous. The possibility is not mentioned in the otherwise comprehensive note on the proverb by MacDowell on *Vesp*. 191.

death, but perhaps, in a moment of supreme achievement, the *αἴγλα διόσδοτος* redeems it.[14] For Plato death is only an interstice. For Pindar good or bad fortune is all-but random and a god brings it to effect: *δαίμων δὲ παρίσχει*. For Plato—

εἶναι δὲ καὶ δοκίμων ἀνδρῶν βίους, τοὺς μὲν ἐπὶ εἴδεσι καὶ κατὰ κάλλη καὶ τὴν ἄλλην ἰσχύν τε καὶ ἀγωνίαν, τοὺς δ' ἐπὶ γένεσι καὶ προγόνων ἀρεταῖς, καὶ ἀδοκίμων κατὰ ταὐτά, ὡσαύτως δὲ καὶ γυναικῶν· ψυχῆς δὲ τάξιν οὐκ ἐνεῖναι διὰ τὸ ἀναγκαίως ἔχειν ἄλλον ἑλομένην βίον ἀλλοίαν γίγνεσθαι· τὰ δ' ἄλλα ἀλλήλοις τε καὶ πλούτοις καὶ πενίαις, τὰ δὲ νόσοις, τὰ δὲ ὑγιείαις μεμῖχθαι, τὰ δὲ καὶ μεσοῦν τούτων

and there were lives of men of repute for their forms and beauty and bodily strength otherwise and prowess and the high birth and the virtues of their ancestors, and others of ill repute in the same things, and similarly of women. But there was no determination of the quality of soul, because the choice of a different life inevitably determined a different character. But all other things were commingled with one another and with wealth and poverty and sickness and health and the intermediate conditions—

for Plato good or bad fortune has its divine sanction, but in its particularity is a matter of human choice. The *προφήτης*, in another moment of compressed Greek (this one more Gorgianic than the first), is explicit: *αἰτία ἑλομένου· θεὸς ἀναίτιος* (617e). Unmistakably, too, the dispensations now seen to be effected by human choice include that most Pindaric of preconditions for achievement, *προγόνων ἀρεταί* (618b), the 'ancestral glories' which in Pindar are restored, if only for a moment, *by* a moment of illuminated glory in the games. It follows, among much else, that *ὁ λαχών* in Plato (617e) is very different from *ὁ . . . λαχών* in Pindar (*Pythian* 8. 88): in Plato the whole role of *Λάχεσις* is in effect problematized and recast.

The relation of Plato's five-noun sentence to Pindar's three-noun sentence is intriguing. It has the same compressed idiom, the same semantic density in active contrast to the words preceding, and the same un-Greek cast. It differs, of course, in so far as the burden of allusion changes its perceived weight. It also differs in that, instead of a momentary effect, Plato's words introduce a

[14] This facet of Pindaric ideology is nowhere more sensitively or sympathetically expounded than by Finley (1955), 23–56, summed up on 40–1. The neglect of Finley's book (notwithstanding the randomness of some of his 'symbolic' interpretations) is regrettable.

whole sequence, of which they constitute, admittedly, the stylistic peak, but a sequence in which the strange idiom is part-converted into a new mode. Thus the five-noun sentence is followed by another sentence of striking density, with light and little words excluded, albeit now adjectives are allowed in as well as nouns: *ψυχαὶ ἐφήμεροι, ἀρχὴ ἄλλης*—the lightest item in the sentence, but still a significant one—*περιόδου θνητοῦ γένους θανατηφόρου*, which is followed by a distinctly Gorgianic parallelistic sequence that begins *οὐχ ὑμᾶς δαίμων λήξεται, ἀλλ' ὑμεῖς δαίμονα αἱρήσεσθε*, and ends with the dense parallelism already quoted: *αἰτία ἑλομένου· θεὸς ἀναίτιος*. One way or another, the *προφήτης* of *Λάχεσις*, dealer in final truths, can claim a special mode of utterance: hear the word of the Lord.[15]

My account of the two passages has looked to squeeze significance out of their relationship. I would propose that we squeeze further. The Pindar passage has two mothers, the human one in 85 (*οὐδὲ μολόντων πὰρ ματέρ'*) and mother Aegina (*Αἴγινα φίλα μᾶτερ*) in 98: the one who nurtures the heroic victor, or would-be victor, and the other who raised the 'real' heroes. Pindar's epinician poetry is a poetry of relationships: between man and his ancestors, ancestors and gods, man and gods, and between the poet and all of these points of reference. It is a poetry of meaning and value in life as experienced and as re-enacted by his epinician constatations. Whatever may be said of Plato's philosophy as a whole, this poetic myth of his, certainly, has no such tale to tell. With an almost devastating directness, it informs us that life has a concealed philosophical meaning: as experienced, without that meaning, life is (in the strictest sense) inconsequential. This is a poetry of rejection and new proposals, of choice and new beginnings. In literary-historical terms, we have here a confirmation of Nietzsche's way of seeing Plato, as an appropriator of the traditions of existing Greek poetry, as a reconstitutor and renewer, a successor but also a subverter. As Plato's Socrates succeeds and outmodes the tragic hero, so Plato's poetic *sophia* (which is a new philosophy) succeeds and

[15] In itself the noun-clustering idiom is quite different from the Gorgianic (however striking the latter), and very different too in effect from the occasional noun-heavy sentence that occurs 'spontaneously' in Greek (on the model of e.g. *ὦ βασιλεῦ, Τέλλον Ἀθηναῖον*, Hdt. 1. 30). An interesting discussion of the 'ritualistic' affinities of Gorgianic idiom is provided by Thomson (1953) (I owe the reference to Michael Reeve), but this collection of material contains nothing that bears decisively on the present discussion or the Plato–Pindar passages.

buries Pindar's (which is no philosophy, as Plato would understand it): or such is Plato's aspiration.[16]

But we can squeeze again, beyond the literary-historical, by turning back once more to ponder Plato's stylistic mode, so strange, so striking—and so assertive. As in Pindar, the all-noun idiom admits of no doubt, no syntactic nuance, no modality. But in Pindar those nouns were enveloped within doubts, questions, cancellations, alternatives, confrontations: *τί δέ τις; τί δ' οὔ τις;* In Plato there is no doubt and no alternative, only truth beyond implication, beyond statement indeed, and only assertion succeeded by greater assertion: *αἰτία ἑλομένου· θεὸς ἀναίτιος.* It is no coincidence that such assertion can only be delivered outside the civilities of Socrates' conversational mode, at the final stage in the great dialogue, where in fact all pretence at *actual* dialogue has been abandoned.[17] And yet this is—is it not?—a philosophy of choice: *αἰτία ἑλομένου.* It is as if Plato's philosophical cards are democratic, while his literary-linguistic cards are, in the final analysis, dictatorial. *Ἀνάγκης θυγατρὸς κόρης Λαχέσεως λόγος*: it simply *is*, and yet there *is* no 'is', even: there is no claim to be denied, no choice at all.[18]

In Plato the new mode thus points to a concealed inner contradiction. In Pindar, by contrast, it reveals a new, perhaps surprising, coherence: his new idiom, like Plato's, asserts a would-be truth beyond dispute, but it is only momentary; and the momentary assertive cluster stands at the epicentre of all the attendant doubts, questions, yes/no images, buts, and negations. Pindar's poetry is, of course, deeply aristocratic, yet at this point, and on this level, the aristocrat is shown to be a free thinker and this free thinking is made part of the aristocratic ideology: there are no

[16] Nietzsche (1872), ch. 14: recent discussions, like that by Nightingale (1995), tend to lose the sharpness of the point. Nietzsche himself has nothing to say by way of relating Plato and Pindar, but finely re-articulates the tradition of Greek religious pessimism of which Pindar is a unique representative: Silk and Stern (1995), 160–2.

[17] 'To bring something to an end is a clear sign of power': Barchiesi (1997a), 207.

[18] One might also note the small, but significant, part played by the seductive lambdas (*Λαχέσεως λόγος*) in Plato's overall linguistic manoeuvre. They seem to whisper: 'you want to challenge this? forget it!' For ancient testimony to the 'seductive' power of λ, see Stanford (1967), 52. I make no comment here on the coercive, or non-coercive, character of Plato's philosophy 'as such', but I would add that any interpretation that seeks to bypass the linguistic particulars through which philosophy (or anything else) is presented is reductive in the worst possible sense.

cracks here, no intriguing contradictions.[19] Faced with ultimate issues of value, Plato closes down, Pindar opens out.

In supra-historical terms, Plato's confrontation with Pindar tells us as much about Pindar as about Plato. Pindar has a different look, once Plato has confronted him. As Eliot said, the past is altered by the present,[20] and such alterations are seen to take place irrespective of, and over the heads of, 'the authors'—but then, as Foucault demonstrates in his brilliant essay 'What Is an Author?' (or rather, in the brilliant part of his very uneven essay 'What Is an Author?'), the concept of *author* is in any case strictly a *post eventum* construct, whereby we make sense of the writing or writings under the sign of the name.[21]

What kind of theory is needed to reach these conclusions? It is apparent, I imagine, that the theoretical affiliations of the discussion have been composite. This was hardly a 'scientific' analysis, and one can only agree with the Fowlers that literary study is not a science—which is not, however, to say that interpretation or indeed evaluation are arbitrary, or need be; and, if nothing else, one would do well to steer clear of the philosophical tangles of the objective/subjective dichotomy here.[22] In part, the categories used have been 'traditional' (pre-nineteenth-century) or at least com-

[19] One could also argue that the passage reflects in concentrated form the consistent impression of ideological uncertainty embodied elsewhere by such problematic series as *N* 11. 43–4 *τὸ δ' ἐκ Διὸς ἀνθρώποις σαφὲς οὐχ ἕπεται | τέκμαρ*, *I* 5. 52 *Ζεὺς τά τε καὶ τὰ νέμει*, *I* 5. 28–9 *μελέταν δὲ σοφισταῖς* [sc. poets] *Διὸς ἕκατι πρόσβαλον σεβιζόμενοι* [sc. heroes or their modern counterparts].

[20] Eliot (1920), 50.

[21] Foucault (1979): the brilliant part includes most of the analysis of the 'author-function' (pp. 148–53), the extraordinary conclusion, 'the author is the principle of thrift in the proliferation of meaning' (p. 159), and the insight that the notion of a *work* is arguably tied to that of an author (pp. 143–4). Contrast the frivolity of the final page (p. 160, 'as our society changes') and the appalling irresponsibility of the way Foucault succeeds in ducking the question whether *works*, as given, may have something to offer their readers which their reconstituted fragments do not. One also notes, *passim*, the very uncertain grasp that Foucault has on intellectual, cultural, and literary history: e.g. he is unaware that the concept of authorial property is already implicit in antiquity (from Theognis 19–23 onwards) or that, in antiquity, Homer provides a test case for his proposition that 'work' is inconceivable without 'author': compare and contrast Silk (1987), 13.

[22] If there was ever a distinction that deserves to be called 'unhelpful', this must be it; in this connection I commend Leavis's much undervalued concept of the 'third realm'—see e.g. Leavis (1962), 27–8—implicit in which is the essential understanding of the *provisional* nature of judgements about the interpretation of literature.

patible with 'traditional' categories; under this heading one might, for instance, include the principle that language *enacts*, a principle that can be traced back from, for instance, Genette to Aristotle.[23]

But the whole thrust of the discussion is, no doubt, in one or other sense distinctively 'modern'. A student of the history of theory might, for instance, diagnose a New Critical/Formalist treatment of poetic texture, allied to the organicist premisses of a Coleridge, who (along with other critics and theorists of the last 200 years, beginning with Coleridge's own mentors, Schelling and A. W. Schlegel) pointed the way to the translation of Aristotle's concept of organic structure onto the level of style, but with the additional insight that the various levels of a work of literature are *themselves* liable to interrelation: this was never better grasped than in the criticism of F. R. Leavis.[24] The appeal to the defamiliarizing effect of Greek—or *un*-Greek—idiom was an appeal to a Russian Formalist principle, which is one of the handful of truly significant advances made by twentieth-century theory (regrettably overlooked by the Fowlers); unfamiliar idiom can, poetic idiom often does, startle its audience into a new response; ancient poetry (and oratory) exudes response to the principle; ancient theory is wholly ignorant of it.[25] And if the literary-historical discussion of Plato's allusion to Pindar was in itself unremarkably nineteenth/twentieth century, the a-historical comparison that followed owed a good deal to Eliot and something, also, to the deconstructional exposure of suppressed possibilities. In deconstruction theory, however, there are supposed to be no stopping-places, and an unrestrictedly free play of meanings, with each deconstruction inviting a further deconstruction—all of which one need not suppose, partly because no good reason for supposing it has been advanced, partly because the practical products of such unrestrictedly free plays (at Yale or elsewhere) are wont to seem futile, self-indulgent, and (yet) self-defeating: the disproof of the deconstructive pudding is in the endlessly reductive regurgitating. Let us discriminate.

The discussion of Plato and Pindar came to rest on issues of

[23] Cf. Silk (1995), 112–25. On the correlation of 'traditional' and 'pre-nineteenth-century', see. n. 34 below.

[24] On Coleridge, Schelling, Schlegel, see e.g. Wellek (1955), 151–87. For Leavis and interrelated levels, see e.g. his discussions of Milton: Leavis (1952), 9–43.

[25] See e.g. Aristotle on 'strange words' (τὰ ξενικά, *Po.* 22); 'Marcellinus', *Vit. Thuc.* 35, on Thucydidean 'obscurity'; 'Longinus', *Subl.* 3 on Gorgias.

value. It is, sadly, one of the most prominent weaknesses of much literary theory of the past forty or fifty years that it has failed to engage with either the value *of* literature (of *this* literature against *that* literature) or the values promoted by, explored within, defamiliarized, or enacted by, works of literature—or indeed the close relationship between the two. Feminists and neo-Marxists have, in various cases, been honourable exceptions; postmodernists have been the worst offenders, tending to evade engagement either by silence or by bland recourse to the mantra of 'deferral'.[26] Yet all literary traditions, and so-called 'classical' literature more obviously than most, are built on values and a concern for values; and some literature does have more to offer us (*any* 'us') than other literature—which is not to say that study of the latter, and especially comparison with the former, is not a valuable activity. But why bother with literary traditions and literature at all, if values are of no consequence? The truth, of course, is that in 'real life' issues of value are equally and inevitably of consequence to every individual (including a postmodern individual) and every collectivity (including, were such a thing imaginable, a postmodern collectivity), and literature (as innumerable texts from different cultures have made clear) is one of the characteristic testing and defining grounds for such issues. And the rather well-known fact that communal, let alone global, agreement on the specific designation and hierarchization of values is, at the end of this millennium, at least as far away as ever only adds urgency to the need to confront such things.[27]

> What for—what ultimately for? what do men live by? . . . In coming to terms with great literature we discover what at bottom we really believe.

That credo (which is Leavis)[28] is both blunter and more individualist than some might wish; it is, nevertheless, the right way round. One can learn *from* literature and not just *about* literature; and it is, and always must be, one of the chief tasks of literary study to

[26] My argument here complements that in Silk (1995); for larger critiques of this and related aspects of postmodernism, see the bibliography cited there at p. 132, nn. 51–2, and add e.g. Eagleton (1996) and Devaney (1997).

[27] In this connection the defeatism about agreement on values expressed by, notably, Hirsch—esp. Hirsch (1976), 110–24, without reference, even, to postmodernism—seems quite misplaced.

[28] Leavis (1962), 23.

suggest how and why. It *is* the right way round, and no amount of wriggling on the 'slippery indeterminacy' of discourse (which is a theoretical *issue*, not a given) can make it otherwise: the indeterminacy factor may make the task more delicate; perhaps it makes it more urgent; certainly it does nothing to invalidate it. It is not that reading literature just 'makes people better';[29] and of course people can read literature without 'coming to terms with it'; and, among others, George Steiner's long agonizings about the coexistence of literary culture and horrific modern atrocity demand attention. Here, certainly, 'more delicate *and* more urgent' seems the appropriate, provisional, designation of the consequential task. If it helps, one might stress at this point that it is in the nature of language, and of literature, and of speaking of value in literature or about literature, to be provisional. What do definitive answers look like? Like Plato, of course.

What does this argument tell us about 'theory', and in particular the versions of 'theory' demarcated by the Fowlers? In the first place (simple truth) it reminds us that indeed all response to literature has theoretical status and theoretical implications. There are no theory-neutral readings, and the Fowlers are right to make that clear. Then again (another simple truth), it suggests that we do need to have and cultivate a critical, discriminating attitude towards theory—towards any theory and, not least, towards fashionable ones. On inspection, it is clearly the case that recent theoretical articulations vary greatly in quality; and on mature reflection, it will not perhaps seem to be the case that the theory of the last forty or so years has definitively superseded earlier theory. If, for instance, one wishes to understand why it *is* 'unhelpful' (the Fowlers' word) to 'focus on the surface psychology of the author' and why it *may* be misguided to assume that textual 'clues' point to a 'single coherent picture', one would do much better to put postmodernities to one side and look to the oeuvres of Bakhtin (who is on the Fowlers' list) and Eliot (who is not), both of whom help to explain why we should be concerned with literature, as well as with these and other questions about literature, in the first place. Values again. Within postmodernism itself, one should also discriminate. Among de Man's best-known essays, for instance, we

[29] So first the Aristophanic Euripides (*Ran.* 1009–10): *βέλτίους τε ποιοῦμεν | τοὺς ἀνθρώπους ἐν ταῖς πόλεσιν.*

find the lucid piece 'Semiology and Rhetoric',[30] which, after treating the last line of Yeats' 'Among School Children' to an impartial and surprising reading, converts the findings into paradigmatic status in a way that is both elegant and deeply thought-provoking. Here, if anywhere, the deconstructive mind is on plausible display, even if its insights and its mannerisms are often, in Oscar Wilde-ish fashion, bundled up together:

> Literature as well as criticism—the difference between them being delusive—is condemned (or privileged) to be forever the most rigorous and, consequently, the most unreliable language in terms of which man names and modifies himself.[31]

'Rigorous *and consequently* unreliable' is intriguing; 'condemned *or privileged*' is worth more than it sounds; 'the difference . . . being delusive', couched in the same language of paradox, is essentially a ritual genuflection to one of the emptier postmodern beliefs. Yes, and once again, critical prose cannot be 'scientific', or not for long; and yes, some critical prose *may* be 'literary' by its eloquence (Johnson), its associations (Eliot), its Jakobsonian-poetic qualities (Nietzsche); but no, that does not make the difference 'delusive'—and the distinction denied is in any case affirmed by the first four words of the sentence, without which affirmation the denial is incomprehensible. Yet such irritants apart, the discussion impresses. Compare and contrast de Man's equally well-known 'Genesis and Genealogy in Nietzsche's *The Birth of Tragedy*'—which is opaque, intellectually shoddy, and in part shockingly ill-informed.[32]

Why should such almost elementary discriminations be necessary? Not just because the Fowlers avoid making them, but because it is part and parcel of their postmodernism that they do. It is symptomatic, perhaps, that their story should be so largely a general account of theoretical movements (at the expense of any particular books or essays by particular theorists), for which the absence of critical comment seems less untoward. Yet it is not, after all, that critical comment *is* totally absent from the Fowlers' discussions—as we recall from their enthusiasm for the 'striking

[30] Cited from Harari (1979), 121–40: de Man (1973).

[31] De Man in Harari (1979), 140.

[32] De Man (1972). The criticisms of this article made in Silk and Stern (1981), 427, n. 72, are restrained.

intertextual complexities' of the 'Flavian epicists' and their disparagement of the notion that those poets are 'servile imitators of Virgil'.[33] Not only have we here the conventional twentieth-century valuation, arguably overvaluation, of complexity; we also have an unacknowledged respect (perhaps surprising: certainly not unwelcome) for the well-known Romantic concept of originality.[34] The crucial absence, however, is that the critical relationships are nowhere discussed: on all levels, from operative criteria to the goals of living, values are not taken seriously enough to be made explicit, let alone argued, but are merely assumed. Needless to say (or is it?), valuing is also implicit in the mere choice of *which* text to study, *which* text to avoid. Why is a text worth reading? If we study the work of the 'Flavian epicists', we are implicitly raising the question, albeit not necessarily answering it, 'what value do we attach to their poetry?'—especially in such a case, where only relative value ('silver', against Virgilian 'gold') has been attached in the past. And classicists, in particular, can hardly fail to acknowledge that the literature in their custody has almost all been pre-sifted on the basis of perceived value (be it 'gold' or 'silver'), albeit a long time ago and by generations whose judgements we do not necessarily share. The responsible interpreter or critic does not wish such implications away, but draws them out and perhaps challenges them—or not—and here, as elsewhere, looks to theory for support.

The equality, in fact the superiority, of pre-postmodern theory is nowhere more evident than in the area of literary language, especially the language of poetry. Rather little of the theory itemized by the Fowlers caters to poetry anyway (as they might, but fail to, point out). And in any case, the understanding of literary language displayed by the Formalists, by New Critics, by independent critics like Leavis, is both more comprehensive, more sophisticated, and more convincing than (for instance) the strange cluster of dogmas associated with Derrida's ill-judged concept of deferral/

[33] Above, pp. 27–8.

[34] Access to which, along with a defining author-centred expressivism, determines that the true dividing-point in the history of theory comes not *c.* 1950, but *c.* 1800. See e.g. the classic discussion of Abrams (1953), and note that the obsession with *authors*, albeit now a problematizing one, is as characteristic of much twentieth-century theory—Eliot as much as Foucault—as it was of Wordsworth. On the fetishization of *complexity*, cf. the admirable sharp thrust by Schiesaro (1998), 147–8; one can see a parallel in the modern preoccupation with *showing* as against *saying*: Silk (1995), 117–18 with n. 41, 127 with n. 66.

difference (itself little more than a speculative inference from the more problematic side of Saussurian linguistics), whereby all language is taken to be flawed, failed, and unfulfilled, signifying nothing.[35]

Some language *may* indeed signify nothing; but then look at Pindar, Plato, and many others, who put language to work and make it signify more, not less, than we had thought it could. Postmodern theory is often strikingly totalitarian: *all* language signifies nothing: *all* language is involved in an (if you please) infinite play of meaning; there is no single right way to do *anything*; *all* literature is equally intertextual, deconstructible, self-referential.[36] Like Plato, postmodernism purports to glorify choice (*infinite* plays of meaning?), but in practice tends to deny it. Conversely, the beauty of Foucault's discussions of 'the author' is that he shows that the concept of 'author' is a construct, where the force of his demonstration depends on the implicit assumption that not everything *is* a construct—because if everything *was*, there would be no point in knowing or demonstrating that some *one* thing *is*.[37]

The particular lesson I would wish to draw from my own discussion is that we cannot profitably discuss 'theory', let alone use 'it', until we know *which* theories and *why*. And we find that out by testing and exploring theories in as wide a perspective as possible and, in any case, in conjunction with the literature that the theories purport to subsume. Surprising and unfashionable though it may be to say so, classicists are, or should be, in a special, even privileged, position here,[38] because we have distinctive access both to

[35] See Silk (1995), and (1996), 462–4. As representative instances of 'the understanding of literary language' shown by Formalists, New Critics, and Leavis, respectively, one might point to (say): Shklovsky (1965: orig. 1917) and the style-related aspects of Bakhtin (1981); the earlier chapters of Empson (1947: orig. 1930); Leavis (1968), p. 231–48 (orig. 1945). It is piquant, in this connection, to note de Man's comment, in Harari (1979), 122: 'from a technical point of view, very little has happened in American criticism since the innovative works of the New Criticism.'

[36] This last, and least rewarding, of all the postmodern dogmas is—to their credit—quietly suppressed by the Fowlers: on the dogma itself see Silk (1995), 122–3.

[37] It might be objected, perhaps, that my insistence on relating literature to values is equally 'totalitarian'. I think not, and would be delighted to have the relationship discussed, qualified as necessary, and above all, tested: *are* there cases where literature and significant questions about literature somehow point in some value-free direction? Totalitarianism and open discussion are incompatible.

[38] Cf. Silk (1995), 114–15.

the most defining literature in the Western tradition and to the full continuum of theory, from Aristotle to Derrida and beyond: the defining literature and the theoretical continuum that, all in all, make the centrality of values so unmistakably plain—just as Plato and Pindar, in their revealingly different ways, make it so plain.[39]

One can only welcome the Fowlers' closing call to use theory to help scrutinize our individual practices[40] and to help us, as a profession, 'play our full part' in a wider 'cultural dialogue'. However, we will not do this by meekly accepting 'modern literary theory' as some kind of unchallengeable given, or—if we do—the scrutiny and the dialogue are worth very little. Modern theory has (as the Fowlers insist) something to offer us—but we also have something to offer it. Our urgent task is to take an active interest in the development of theory and its reclamation for the common good. The current theoretical debate needs to be problematized and reoriented. The totalitarian preoccupations of many current theorists, and their disinclination to value and to deal with values, bear the marks of classic displacement activity, designed to avoid facing up to real problems by creating illusory ones. I am all for progress: please, when can we start?

[39] On Pindar cf. incidentally Fränkel (1962), 556: 'Pindars Dichtung ist . . . auf den Wert [ausgerichtet]; und zwar so ausschliesslich, dass alles ignoriert wird was keine positive oder negative Beziehung zu Werten hat.'

[40] By implication the Fowlers are telling us that 'questioning our presuppositions' will postmodernize us. I would expect that, properly done, such questioning would tend to do the opposite.

4
Metatext and its Functions in Greek Lyric Poetry

Jerzy Danielewicz

This discussion is mainly intended to draw attention to a metatextually oriented approach by showing its advantages and practical applicability to the interpretation of literature. It is hoped that this point of view will interest the students of Greek lyric poetry; I am deeply convinced that already an awareness of the existence of the metatextual level in texts can stimulate the reader to go deeper into their linguistic structure. Since the notion of metatext is not yet popular among classicists, I attach some preliminary remarks on its usage in literary studies, exploiting the results of earlier reflection on the nature of language.

In contemporary linguistics there exists a firmly established notion of 'metalanguage'. Although the term itself is relatively new, the underlying conception was developed as early as the Middle Ages by schoolmen (for example, Wilhelm Shyreswoode, d. 1249), who introduced the notion of *suppositio materialis* as opposed to *suppositio formalis*. Whereas a word in the 'formal supposition' denotes any object, a word in the 'material supposition' is in itself the object of statement.[1] Contemporary logic, too, differentiates between the level of 'object language' and that of 'metalanguage', the latter describing the language itself.[2] As Carnap formulates it, 'in order to speak about any object language . . . we need a metalanguage'.[3] It is Jakobson's merit to observe that such operations, labelled 'metalinguistic' by the logicians, prove to be an integral part of our customary linguistic activities.[4] Whenever the participants of a conversation want to make sure whether they understand each other, they ask the other person

[1] See Weinrich (1976), 90–112.

[2] The terms were invented by the Polish logician Alfred Tarski—Tarski (1933).

[3] Carnap (1960), 4.

[4] Jakobson (1971), 248.

such questions as 'What do you mean by that?' or 'Am I making myself clear?' Appreciating this very aspect of communication, Jakobson[5] expanded the traditional scheme of Bühler (*Ausdruck, Darstellung, Appell*) by adding the metalinguistic function—supplementing the 'poetic' and 'phatic' types.[6]

The function under discussion here appears, as Weinrich rightly remarks,[7] only in concrete utterances ('parole' according to Saussure's terminology).[8] A text cannot be composed exclusively of metalanguage; it contains at the most only some metalinguistic elements. Sometimes it may be difficult to mark the limits of metalinguistic utterances within a literary text, since in contrast to artificial languages, for example, the language of mathematical logic (where the two levels are formally separated), every natural language provides for the possibility of speaking about what is expressed in that language, thus becoming its own metalanguage.[9]

In a restricted sense the status of metatext cannot be attributed to a word, phrase, sentence, and so on unless it is used in the 'material supposition', as, for example, the word 'lyre' in the sentence '*Lyre* is a noun of Greek origin'.[10] Jakobson, however, would deem the whole of this explanation metalinguistic.[11] Weinrich goes still further, being inclined to regard any utterances about literary texts (interpretations, reviews, even discussions) as 'in hohem Maße reflexiv-metasprachlich'.[12] To qualify 'meta' utterances longer than one sentence, some scholars use a more convenient term 'metatext'.[13] The broadest meaning is given to the notion of metatext by Popovic,[14] who includes in the category even such forms as parody, translation, or plagiarism since they all originate from another text, called by him 'prototext', on which they are, as it were, superimposed. Genette speaks in such a case of 'hypertextuality',[15] meaning the relation linking the text of second degree (that is, the derived text) with the earlier text, called 'hypotext'. 'Hypertext', usually derived from works of fiction, retains their fictional character. The notion of metatext is reserved by Genette for interpretative considerations, such as those parts of Aristotle's *Poetics* which

[5] Jakobson (1971), 248.
[6] Bühler (1934).
[7] Weinrich (1976), 102.
[8] Saussure (1916).
[9] Weinreich (1970), 75.
[10] Okopien-Slawinska (1985), 44.
[11] Jakobson (1960), 356.
[12] Weinrich (1976), 111.
[13] Advocated in Poland by Wierzbicka (1971) and Mayenowa (1974).
[14] Popovic (1978); cf. Bakula (1994), 31–2.
[15] Genette (1982).

comment upon *Oedipus Tyrannus*. Hypertext retains, however, to a certain extent, the quality of metatext: pastiche or parody are for Genette 'criticism in action'.

This discussion will concentrate on the narrower definition of metatext as an intratextual phenomenon, paying less attention to its status as an intertextual phenomenon. Accordingly, I shall confine my investigation each time to the sphere of 'meta' references within the same text, especially those announced explicitly by means of conventionally established formulae. To demonstrate the typical aspects of metatext in Greek poetry, let us begin with the brief 26th Homeric Hymn, to Dionysus:

Κισσοκόμην Διόνυσον ἐρίβρομον ἄρχομ' ἀείδειν
Ζηνὸς καὶ Σεμέλης ἐρικυδέος ἀγλαὸν υἱόν,
ὃν τρέφον ἠΰκομοι νύμφαι παρὰ πατρὸς ἄνακτος
δεξάμεναι κόλποισι καὶ ἐνδυκέως ἀτίταλλον
Νύσης ἐν γυάλοις· ὁ δ' ἀέξετο πατρὸς ἕκητι
ἄντρῳ ἐν εὐώδει μεταρίθμιος ἀθανάτοισιν.
αὐτὰρ ἐπεὶ δὴ τόνδε θεαὶ πολύυμνον ἔθρεψαν,
δὴ τότε φοιτίζεσκε καθ' ὑλήεντας ἐναύλους
κισσῷ καὶ δάφνῃ πεπυκασμένος· αἱ δ' ἅμ' ἕποντο
νύμφαι, ὁ δ' ἐξηγεῖτο· βρόμος δ' ἔχεν ἄσπετον ὕλην.
Καὶ σὺ μὲν οὕτω χαῖρε πολυστάφυλ' ὦ Διόνυσε·
δὸς δ' ἡμᾶς χαίροντας ἐς ὥρας αὖτις ἱκέσθαι,
ἐκ δ' αὖθ' ὡράων εἰς τοὺς πολλοὺς ἐνιαυτούς.

I begin to sing of ivy-crowned Dionysus, the loud-crying god, splendid son of Zeus and glorious Semele. The rich-haired Nymphs received him in their bosoms from the lord his father and fostered and nurtured him carefully in the dells of Nysa, where by the will of his father he grew up in a sweet-smelling cave, being reckoned among the immortals. But when the goddesses had brought him up, a god oft hymned, then began he to wander continually through the woody coombes, thickly wreathed with ivy and laurel. And the Nymphs followed in his train with him for their leader; and the boundless forest was filled with their outcry.

And so hail to you, Dionysus, god of abundant clusters! Grant that we may come again rejoicing to this season, and from that season onwards for many a year.

(trans. H. G. Evelyn-White)

In this hymn there are two clearly metatextual places: its beginning and its end. The phrase *Διόνυσον . . . ἄρχομ' ἀείδειν* presents, among other things, the addressee of the poem, which is, at the same time, an indirect indication of its content and character (a hymn to a god). The fact that in the opening sentence the first person is used is very significant. Bearing in mind the circumstances of the performance of poetry in Greece, we should avoid referring it exclusively to the poet as creator of text. Ancient practice apart, one can come to a similar conclusion by merely considering the unique status of the personal form. As Benveniste has observed,[16] an utterance containing *I* belongs to the pragmatic type of language, which includes, with the signs, those who make use of them. In every act of speech the speaker posits himself as 'subject'. In other words, in every instance of discourse the pronoun *I* is appropriated by a concrete person, not necessarily the poet himself, but, for example, a performer, or even a group of performers. In my further considerations I will, naturally, take the possibilities for granted; nevertheless, one cannot forget that it was the poet who wrote the text.

As far as the 'subjective' *I* is concerned, I am interested first of all in cases where it is accompanied by an announcement (for example, by a *verbum canendi/dicendi* followed by a direct object), since this is one of the simplest forms of metatextual statement, aiming, among other things, to signal the poem's general topic, which itself can constitute the starting-point for a following narration. This kind of utterance has also interested Calame as an instance of the *I*'s focal position in conveying the thematic information in the text itself.[17] His concept of the 'énonciation énoncée', or the way in which the 'énonciation' of a text is represented in that text ('énoncée'), verges conceptually upon the notion of metatext, although he never in fact introduces that actual term. What makes his method less pertinent to the purpose of this discussion is the fact that it mainly concentrates on the mutual relationship between *I* and *you* (the invoked Muse being included in this category), as well as their actantial roles, in order to enucleate the subtleties of installing in the text the elements indicative of its 'énonciation'. For my investigation, the kind and functional complexity of information conveyed by metatextual announcements, not limited to personal interrelations, is more essential; answering the question of who is formally made to introduce the following narration does not resolve the whole issue.

After these expository remarks we may proceed to the interpre-

16 Benveniste (1971). 17 Calame (1986).

tation of the end of the poem under discussion. The salutation *Καὶ σὺ μὲν οὕτω χαῖρε* proves an instrumental function of the hymn intended to give the god pleasure and win his favour. The poet/performer declares he is about to finish his utterance and emphasizes his role in creating the text: *οὕτω*, 'in this way', implies the meaning 'having received the hymn in the form I have given to it'.

The metatextual frame of the hymn with its deictic expressions[18] refers also to the situation of performance.[19] Particularly interesting is the formula *ἄρχομ' ἀείδειν*, giving information which is, as a matter of fact, redundant from the point of view of the audience but quite normal as a conventional pronouncement. One can assume that uttering the phrase 'I begin to sing' by the performer is something more than just saying the words. The issuing of such an utterance is the performing of an action. The phrase *οὕτω χαῖρε* corresponds to *ἄρχομ' ἀείδειν* in this respect too. To use the terminology of Austin,[20] the imperative reveals its performative nature when supplemented by an explicit performative, for example, 'I pray you . . .', and the utterer of such formulae performs both a locutionary and an illocutionary act.

Finally, one should add that the initial formula fulfils an important function of linking two different levels of text. *Ἀείδειν* used as a transitive verb requires a direct object. The shift from the 'meta' level to the object language is made by means of the relative clause *ὃν τρέφον κτλ.*, which itself stands only halfway to the narration proper (in the third person): *ὁ δ' ἀέξετο κτλ.* I used the phrase 'finally' to emphasize that the last function is by no means the only one.

The Homeric hymn gives but a sample of possible perspectives from which metatext can be viewed. Its role in lyric poems seems to be much more differentiated, although the state of preservation of many a fragment makes it difficult to generalize. The complete poems, however, allow us to draw firmer conclusions, and in the case of fragments it is often possible to analyse their beginnings, that is, that part in which metatext manifests itself most clearly.

Here are some examples of explicitly metatextual utterances. Fragment 698 *PMG* ascribed to Terpander contains the dedication:

[18] Cf. Danielewicz (1990), 8.

[19] For this issue see Danielewicz (1976), 7–9.

[20] Austin (1980).

Ζεῦ σοὶ πέμπω ταύταν ὕμνων ἀρχάν

Zeus, to you I send this beginning of my hymns.
(trans. D. A. Campbell)

alluding to the traditional name of the first part of the *nomos*: ἀρχά (although the poem itself does not come into this category of compositions[21]). The poet/performer with the demonstrative *ταύταν* points to his own text being just performed. We are informed who is the addressee of the poem (*Ζεῦ*), how it can be classified in respect of genre (*ὕμνων*), and which part of the performance it belongs to (*ἀρχάν*). In the formula of Alcman's fr. 29 Davies:

ἐγὼν δ' ἀείσομαι
ἐκ Διὸς ἀρχομένα

and I shall sing beginning from Zeus
(trans. D. A. Campbell)

the metatextual information pertains to the sequence of topics to be spoken about. It is worth noticing that here metatext takes into account the sex of the performers (note the feminine form of the participle), which testifies that the lyric poets composed their songs with future performance in view.

Using the first person of a *verbum canendi/dicendi* in the future tense was a natural way to announce the topic—compare Archilochus 168 W.:

Ἐρασμονίδη Χαρίλαε
χρῆμα τοι γελοῖον
ἐρέω, πολὺ φίλταθ' ἑταίρων,
τέρψεαι δ' ἀκούων

Fitzdarling, delight of the people,
I've got a funny story
to tell you, my dearest companion,
and I guarantee you'll like it.
(trans. M. L. West)

Addressing a hearer with a funny nickname to tell him an amusing story (*χρῆμα . . . γελοῖον*), sounds like an independent, extra-textual utterance about the poem which will be immediately recited.

[21] For this issue see Gostoli (1990), 132–6.

Pindar's encomium for Thrasybulus (fr. 124 Maehler) begins with a dedication which is by its nature a metatext:

> *Ὦ Θρασύβουλ', ἐρατᾶν ὄχημ' ἀοιδᾶν*
> *τοῦτο ⟨τοι⟩ πέμπω μεταδόρπιον, ἐν ξυνῷ κεν εἴη*
> *συμπόταισίν τε γλυκερὸν καὶ Διωνύσοιο καρπῷ*
> *καὶ κυλίκεσσιν Ἀθαναίαισι κέντρον·*

O Thrasyboulos, I send this gear of racing and lovely
songs to you for the end of your revels. So may you share it
with them who drink beside you, sweet instigator to them, to the yield
of Dionysos' abundance and the flagons of Athens . . .

(trans. R. Lattimore)

The poet mentions the addressee by name and points out the suitability of the song for the symposium. In the initial lines of Solon's *Salamis* (fr. 1 W.):

> *αὐτὸς κῆρυξ ἦλθον ἀφ' ἱμερτῆς Σαλαμῖνος*
> *κόσμον ἐπέων ᾠδὴν ἀντ' ἀγορῆς θέμενος.*

I bring my own dispatch from lovely Salamis,
adopting ordered verse instead of speech.

(trans. M. L. West)

the form of utterance is defined: it will not be a public speech (*ἀγορή*), but a piece of fine poetry.

In the examples quoted above metatext was mostly connected with the poet's statements in the first person. The repertoire of possibilities is, of course, much larger and includes, among other things, rhetorical questions, as in Pindar's prosodion to Artemis (fr. 89a Maehler):

> *Τί κάλλιον ἀρχομένοισ(ιν?) ἢ καταπαυομένοισιν*
> *ἢ βαθύζωνόν τε Λατώ*
> *καὶ θοᾶν ἵππων ἐλάτειραν ἀεῖσαι;*

Is there any nobler theme for our commencing or for our closing strains, than to sing the deep-zoned Leto, and the goddess that driveth the swift steeds?

(trans. J. E. Sandys)[22]

[22] Cf. Pind. *Ol.* 2.1ff.: *ἀναξιφόρμιγγες ὕμνοι, | τίνα θεόν, τίν' ἥρωα, τίνα δ' ἄνδρα κελαδήσομεν | ἤτοι Πίσα μὲν Διός· Ὀλυμπιάδα | δ' ἔστασεν Ἡρακλέης | ἀκρόθινα πολέμου | Θήρωνα δὲ τετραορίας ἕνεκα νικαφόρου | γεγωνητέον . . .*

A similar way of introducing the topic may be found in Mimnermus 1 W.:

> *τίς δὲ βίος, τί δὲ τερπνὸν ἄτερ χρυσῆς Ἀφροδίτης;*
>
> What's life, what's joy, without love's heavenly gold?
> (trans. M. L. West)

The meaning of this question is best paraphrased with a declaration such as: 'I believe life without love has no value at all'; the point is then supported with arguments. In questions like this metatext is not verbalized; the missing information is simply implied by the position of the rhetorical figure.

The topic can be announced also through negation, when one rejects potential themes until, at the end of the enumeration, the accepted one is chosen (the so-called 'priamel'), as in Tyrtaeus 12 W.:

> *οὔτ' ἂν μνησαίμην οὔτ' ἐν λόγωι ἄνδρα τιθείην*
> *οὔτε ποδῶν ἀρετῆς οὔτε παλαιμοσύνης,*
> *οὐδ' εἰ Κυκλώπων μὲν ἔχοι μέγεθός τε βίην τε*
>
> *ει μὴ τετλαίη μὲν ὁρῶν φόνον αἱματόεντα,*
> *καὶ δηίων ὀρέγοιτ' ἐγγύθεν ἱστάμενος.*
>
> I would not rate a man worth mention or account
> either for speed of foot or wrestling skill,
> not even if he had a Cyclops' size and strength
> unless he can endure the sight of blood and death,
> and stand close to the enemy, and fight.
> (trans. M. L. West)

Among the traditional methods of giving information about the content of the poems, the apostrophe to the Muse is particularly popular. Let us recall its less typical variation in Alcman 14 Davies:

> *Μῶσ' ἄγε, Μῶσα λίγηα πολυμμελὲς*
> *αἰὲν ἀοιδὲ μέλος*
> *νεοχμὸν ἄρχε παρσένοις ἀείδην.*
>
> Hey Muse, euphonious Muse, full of melodies,
> ever the singer,
> make start of a new song for the girls to sing!
> (trans. M. L. West)

The attributes of the Muse (sonority, melodiousness) are expected to become the features of the song being presented.[23]

From our point of view, the initial invocation of the Muse, or another deity, is a formality device which is used to commence the poem and indicate its content and character. Further metatextual qualities can be seen also in the more sophisticated invocations of Pindar's and Bacchylides' odes.[24]

Metatext refers sometimes to the planned accompaniment, as in Bacchylides 20B S.-M.:

> *Ὦ βάρβιτε, μηκέτι πάσσαλον φυλάσ[σων*
> *ἑπτάτονον λ[ι]γυρὰν κάππαυε γᾶρυν·*
> *δεῦρ' ἐς ἐμὰς χέρας· ὁρμαίνω τι πέμπ[ειν*
> *χρύσεον Μουσᾶν Ἀλεξάνδρωι πτερόν*
> ——
> *καὶ συμποσ[ίαι]σιν ἄγαλμ' [ἐν] εἰκάδεσσιν,*

My new lyre, cling to your peg no longer, silencing your clear voice with its seven notes. Come to my hands! I am eager to send Alexander a golden wing of the Muses, an adornment for banquets at the month's end,

(trans. D. A. Campbell)

As a result of Pindar's inclination to stress his own originality, metatextual information about new aspects of the musical side of the composition can appear in the initial parts of his epinicians in addition to the routine elements—compare *O.*3.1, 1 ff. S.–M.:

> *Τυνδαρίδαις τε φιλοξείνοις ἁδειν*
> *καλλιπλοκάμῳ θ' Ἑλένᾳ*
> *κλεινὰν Ἀκράγαντα γεφαίρων εὔχομαι,*
> *Θήρωνος Ὀλυμπιονίκαν*
> *ὕμνον ὀρθώσαις, ἀκαμαντοπόδων*
> *ἵππων ἄωτον. Μοῖσα δ' οὕτω ποι παρέ-*
> *στα μοι νεοσίγαλον εὑρόντι τρόπον*
> *Δωρίῳ φωνὰν ἐναρμόξαι πεδίλῳ*
> *ἀγλαόκωμον·*

I pray that I may please Tyndareus' gracious sons | and lovely-haired Helen | as I sing of glorious Akragas, | raising the Olympian victory hymn | in honor of Theron and his thunder-hoofed horses. | For so the

[23] Cf. Stesich. 210 PMGF Davies: *Μοῖσα σὺ μὲν πολέμους ἀπωσαμένα πεδ' ἐμοῦ | κλείοισα θεῶν τε γαμοὺς ἀνδρῶν τε δαίτας | καὶ θαλίας μακάρων.*

[24] Cf. the beginnings of Bacchyl. 1; 3; 9; 12; 19; Pind. *O.* 3;10;14, *P.* 4; 9, *N.* 3; 9; 10.

Muse stood at my side | when I discovered this new mode of song, | the shine still in its fabric: | voice and Dorian sandal fitted together for the dance | of splendor.

(trans. F. J. Nisetich)

Pindar does not restrain himself from praising his own creativity in such contexts (*I* 4. 1 ff. S.–M.):

Ἔστι μοι θεῶν ἕκατι μυρία παντᾷ κέλευθος,
ὦ Μέλισσ', εὐμαχανίαν γὰρ ἔφανας Ἰσθμίοις
ὑμετέρας ἀρετὰς ὕμνῳ διώκειν·[25]

By the will of the gods | I have a thousand roads in every direction | To follow your deeds of greatness in my song— | for you, Melissos, have given me the power by winning at Isthmos . . .

(trans. F. J. Nisetich)

In our discussion the role of demonstratives deserves special attention.[26] Their metatextual function appears whenever the poet uses them to refer to the text as a whole or, more frequently, to its parts. To discuss the latter usage let us return to Tyrtaeus 12 W., beginning with line 13 of that elegy:

ἥδ' ἀρετή, τόδ' ἄεθλον ἐν ἀνθρώποισιν ἄριστο·

This is the highest worth, the finest human prize
(trans. M. L. West)

which summarizes the considerations about 'man worth mention or account'. The demonstratives of the sentence are used anaphorically: 'this' is here an equivalent of 'what I have said above'. The metatextual perspective reappears in lines 15 ff.:

ξυνὸν δ' ἐσθλὸν τοῦτο πόληΐ τε παντί τε δήμωι,
ὅστις ἀνὴρ διαβὰς ἐν προμάχοισι μένηι κτλ.

It benefits the whole community and state
when with a firm stance in the foremost rank
a man bides steadfast . . .
(trans. M. L. West)

where the demonstrative *τοῦτο* is cataphoric (an explanation

[25] Similarly Bacchyl. 5. 31–3: *τὼς νῦν καὶ ⟨ἐ⟩μοι μυρία πάνται κέλευθος | ὑμετέραν ἀρετάν | ὑμνεῖν . . .*

[26] On their deictic function in general see esp. Danielewicz (1990).

follows), and in lines 20 and 43ff., where the same pronoun is again anaphoric. One should mention in this connection also the demonstrative and articular *ὁ, ὅ, ὅς* followed by a particle[27] with their exclusively anaphoric reference, for example *ὁ δ'*, meaning 'he', 'the person I have just mentioned', *τό* denoting 'what has been said above', and so on. Let us consider an example from Pindar, *N.* 4. 9–11 S.–M.:

> *τό μοι θέμεν Κρονίδᾳ τε Διὶ καὶ Νεμέᾳ*
> *Τιμασάρχου τε πάλᾳ*
> *ὕμνου προκώμιον εἴη·*

So would I raise to Zeus Kronidas, | to Nemea and the wrestling skill of Timasarchos, | the prelude of my hymn:

(transl. by F. J. Nisetich)

Having expounded in the first lines of the ode his views on the importance of eulogies, the poet refers to them summarily by means of the anaphoric *τό* in the antistrophe.

Reference forward (cataphoric) and reference backward (anaphoric) is a common function of expressions signalling the beginning or end of quotations in direct speech, such as *εἶπεν . . . τοιοῦτον τι ἔπος·* or *ὣς φάτο*, the sense of which can be paraphrased as 'he uttered the following words' and 'he uttered the words I have cited above', respectively. In cases like that one sees the poet in action, that is, as creator of the text.

A demonstrative placed in the opening lines of a poem can refer to the whole text, as in Pindar's encomium for Thrasybulus (fr. 124 Maehler, quoted above):

> *Ὦ Θρασύβουλ', ἐρατᾶν ὄχημ' ἀοιδᾶν*
> *τοῦτο ⟨τοι⟩ πέμπω μεταδόρπιον.*

In Pindar's fr. 52b, 1–4 Maehler the demonstrative *τόνδε* goes together with the name of the genre, identifying the poem as a paean:

> *Ναΐδ]ος Θρονίας Ἄβδηρε χαλκοθώραξ*
> *Ποσ]ειδᾶνός τε παῖ,*
> *σέθ]εν Ἰάονι τόνδε λαῷ*
> *παι]ᾶνα [δι]ώξω*

[27] For a long list of such uses see Slater (1969), 364–70.

Abderus, with breast-plate of bronze, thou son of the Naiad Thronia and of Poseidon! beginning with thee shall I pursue this paean for the Ionian folk.

(trans. J. E. Sandys)

Also the indefinite pronoun *τις*, when placed at the beginning of the poem, implies forward reference, meaning 'a/an' in the sense 'the one that will follow'. The usage, common in the popular language of fable,[28] is testified to by Archilochus in fr. 185 W.:

> *ἐρέω τιν' ὕμιν αἶνον, ὦ Κηρυκίδη,*
> *ἀχνυμένηι σκυτάληι,*

> I want to tell you folk a tale, your Honour,
> —oh, it's a mournful dispatch!
> (trans. M. L. West)

Deictic expressions are sometimes used to support one's words with an authority, which is a typically metatextual operation—see Pindar, *P.* 4.277 f. S.–M.:

> *τῶν δ' Ὁμήρου καὶ τόδε συνθέμενος*
> *ῥῆμα πόρσυν'· ἄγγελον ἐσλὸν ἔφα τι-*
> *μὰν μεγίσταν πράγματι παντὶ φέρειν·*

Versed as you are in the lore of Homer, | ponder this saying of his as well: | 'A good messenger | furthers any enterprise'

(trans. F. J. Nisetich)

and Bacchylides 5. 191 ff. S.–M.:

> *Βοιωτὸς ἀνὴρ τᾶδε φών[ησεν, γλυκειᾶν*
> *Ἡσίοδος πρόπολος*
> *Μουσᾶν, ὃν ⟨ἂν⟩ ἀθάνατοι τι[μῶσι, τούτωι*
> *καὶ βροτῶν φήμαν ἔπ[εσθαι.*

A man of Boeotia, Hesiod, minister of the (sweet) Muses, spoke thus: 'He whom the immortals honour is attended also by the good report of men'.

(trans. D. A. Campbell)

Simonides (564. 4 *PMG*) saying:

> *οὕτω γὰρ Ὅμηρος ἠδὲ Στασίχορος ἄεισε λαοῖς*

> so have Homer and Stesichorus sung the tale to all.
> (trans. M. L. West)

[28] Cf. e.g. Aesop. 32. I–II, 35. II–III, 42. III, 47. I, 52. III Hausrath.

states: 'The version of events I have presented agrees with that of Homer and Stesichorus, and is therefore reliable.'

The lyric poets elaborated a number of methods of conveying metatextual observations. They often do not speak directly of the composition of text, but prefer making use of metaphors. This is how Pindar justifies his decision concerning the choice of myth in the first Isthmian Ode (lines 14 ff.):

ἀλλ' ἐγὼ Ἡροδότῳ τεύ-
χων τὸ μὲν ἅρματι τεθρίππῳ γέρας,
ἀνία τ' ἀλλοτρίαις οὐ χερσὶ νωμάσαντ' ἐθέλω
ἢ Καστορείῳ ἢ Ἰολάοι' ἐναρμόξαι νιν ὕμνῳ.
κεῖνοι γὰρ ἡρώων διφρηλάται Λακεδαίμονι καὶ
Θήβαις ἐτέκνωθεν κράτιστοι·

But I, composing in Herodotos' honor | a prize for victory in the four-horse chariot, | because he guided the reins himself, | with his own hands, | desire to join him | to a Kastor-song or a hymn of Iolaos. | For among heroes in Lakedaimon and in Thebes, | they were born to be the mightiest charioteers.

(trans. F. J. Nisetich)

In the same ode the poet comments on the restraints caused by the format of the song (1. 60ff.):

πάντα δ' ἐξειπεῖν, ὅσ' ἀγώνιος Ἑρμᾶς
Ἡροδότῳ ἔπορεν
ἵπποις, ἀφαιρεῖται βραχὺ μέτρον ἔχων
ὕμνος.

but the song, | with its brief measure, forbids | listing all the triumphs | Hermes god of contests has given | to Herodotos and his horses.

(trans. F. J. Nisetich)

Pindar also pleads a law of convention (*τεθμός*) which restricts him in composing his text (*N.* 4.33 f. S.–M.):

τὰ μακ'ρὰ δ' ἐξενέπειν ἐρύκει με τεθμός
ὧραι τ' ἐπειγόμεναι·

But the laws of the song and passing time | forbid dwelling on a theme at length.

(trans. F. J. Nisetich)

In the Archaic age Alcman could pass on to another subject without justifying his decision; the poetic 'I' marked the point of transition (1. 37–40 Davies):

ἔστι τις σιῶν τίσις·
ὁ δ' ὄλβιος, ὅστις εὔφρων
ἡμέραν [δι]απ'λέκει
ἄκ'λαυτος· ἐγὼν δ' ἀείδω
Ἀγιδῶς τὸ φῶς·

There's such a thing
as God's requital. Fortunate is he
who in good heart plaits up his day sans tears.
Now my song's of the radiance
of Agido

(trans. M. L. West)

Bacchylides and Pindar in such cases make use of a repertoire of *loci communes*, introducing, for instance, the motif of the chariot of song:

λευκώλενε Καλλιόπα,
στᾶσον εὐποίητον ἅρμα
αὐτοῦ.

(B. 5. 176 f. S.–M.)

White-armed Calliope, halt your well-made chariot here

(trans. D. A. Campbell)

ὦ Φίντις, ἀλλὰ ζεῦξον ἤ-
δη μοι σθένος ἡμιόνων,
ᾇ τάχος, ὄφρα κελεύθῳ τ' ἐν καθαρᾷ
βάσομεν ὄκχον, ἵκωμαί τε πρὸς ἀνδρῶν
καὶ γένος·

(Pi. *O* 6.22 ff. S.–M.)

But come, Phintis! bridle those mighty mules of yours | as fast as you can, so I may mount the chariot, drive | on the clear road and reach, | at last, the source of this clan.

(trans. F. J. Nisetich)

To make a metatextual remark, 'It is time to finish. One cannot proceed with the story to infinity.' Pindar (*N.* 49, 69ff. S.–M.) uses a nautical metaphor:

> *Γαδείρων τὸ πρὸς ζόφον οὐ περατόν· ἀπότρεπε*
> *αὖτις Εὐρώπαν ποτί χέρσον ἔντεα ναός·*
> *ἄπορα γὰρ λόγον Αἰακοῦ*
> *παίδων τὸν ἅπαντά μοι διελθεῖν.*

The darkness beyond Gadeira cannot be crossed: | sail back again to Europe, back to land! There is no way | I could run through the whole | saga of Aiakos' sons.

(trans. F. J. Nisetich)

Metatext in the final parts of the preserved lyric poems is more often implicit than explicit. Mimnermus ends his elegy (1) with a kind of conclusion: *οὕτως ἀργαλέον γῆρας ἔθηκε θεός*. Pindar, at *O.* 10. 100, just uses the past tense of a *verbum dicendi*: *αἴνησα*, 'I have praised', viz. *laudandum*; in *O.* 1 115 f. the poet signals the end with a prayer for Hieron's and his own continued success:[29]

> *εἴη σέ τε τοῦτον ὑψοῦ χρόνον πατεῖν,*
> *ἐμέ τε τοσσάδε νικαφόροις*
> *ὁμιλεῖν πρόφαντον σοφίᾳ καθ' Ἕλ-*
> *λανας ἐόντα παντᾷ.*

For the time we have, may you continue to walk on high, | and may I for as long consort with victors, | conspicuous for my skill among Greeks everywhere.

(trans. F. J. Nisetich)

But with this example we have already reached the sphere of indirect metatextual information ('closural' themes), presented in all its variety by Rutherford.[30]

It is time to comment on the utility of investigations taking into account the existence and role of metatext as opposed to other, more traditional interpretative methods. The profit we can derive from this new approach lies, among other things, in perceiving the text in its complexity—as a whole consisting of two complementary levels. Traditionally the text is analysed on one plane only,

[29] For the frequency of prayers for the future at the end of poems cf. Gerber (1982), 175.

[30] Rutherford (1997).

which results in including metatextual elements within the world presented in the poem; compare Bowra's remarks on the relation between Alcman and the Muse in fr. 27 Davies:

> *Μῶσ' ἄγε Καλλιόπα θύγατερ Διὸς*
> *ἄρχ' ἐρατῶν ϝεπέων, ἐπὶ δ' ἵμερον*
> *ὕμνωι καὶ χαρίεντα τίθη χορόν.*
>
> Hey Muse, daughter of Zeus, Calliope,
> make me a start of delightful poetry:
> give my song charm, and beautiful dancing.
> (trans. M. L. West)

'So he summons Calliope by name and explains to her the kind of song he wishes to compose.'[31] The metatextual perspective, retaining the internal plane, allows us to see in the same utterance something more than an appeal to the Muse: a declaration of the poet, *poietes* in the primary sense of the word, who uses a conventional motif to inform the recipients about his own intention. The audience, and not the Muse, are given the signal 'I promise you a sweet song'; after all, the information was communicated during the performance. The poet's words run side by side with the active hearers' perception of the text, a process observed by Bakhtin,[32] reinforcing their hypotheses relative to its delimitation, structure, line of reasoning, and so on. It is at this juncture that an important function of metatext, namely, making textual coherence more visible, is fulfilled. Although the global coherence of the whole composition is, as a rule, successfully grasped by the recipients who reconstruct the semantic links between its segments, a kind of support on the part of the poet facilitates this task. The role of metatext becomes greater when thematic continuity is broken. Thus, a metatextually oriented approach adds to our understanding of the unity of the lyric poems. Generally speaking, it undoubtedly enriches text analysis. This does not mean, however, that it can claim to replace any other interpretation. What I should like to state clearly in conclusion, is that such an approach is a very useful, but only a supplementary method of investigating poems as polyphonic texts.

[31] Bowra (1967), 29.
[32] Bakhtin (1986), 359.

Narrative

5

Introduction

Don Fowler†

The analysis of narrative has a history almost as long as narrative itself, and it is not difficult to find passages in ancient commentators like Servius which 'anticipate' (to use a word which self-reflexively emphasizes the omnipresence of plot) later observations. The modern discipline of 'narratology' however is a twentieth-century phenomenon. One branch of the subject begins with the *Morphology of the Folk Tale* of V. Propp[1], and has as its most famous practitioner C. Lévi-Strauss.[2] Propp and Lévi-Strauss, however, though they have had great influence through the Paris School on structuralist readings of Greek literature,[3] were concerned primarily with the analysis of story-patterns themselves, rather than the relation between a particular story and its tellings, an approach which found its most abstract and algebraic representation in the work on narrative positions of A.-J. Greimas.[4] On a more concrete and stimulating level, R. Barthes produced a number of important studies during the period of high structuralism, not least the essay 'Introduction to the Structural Analysis of Narratives' first published in 1966, and the major analysis of Balzac's *Sarrasine in S/Z*.[5] But although such a 'narratologia dell'histoire' is included within most discussions of the study of narrative, the 'narratologia del récit' has proved more productive in literary studies.[6]

[1] Propp (1928/1958). [2] Lévi-Strauss (1958/1963), Leach (1970).

[3] Cf. e.g. F. Zeitlin's introduction to Vernant (1991), 6.

[4] Greimas (1966/1983). [5] Barthes (1988), 95–135, Barthes (1974).

[6] The terms are those of Fusillo (1985), 14. I keep the mixture of Italian and French, because one of the main problems of narratological work is that the same or similar terms are used differently by different theorists, and translations into other languages can cause further problems. The basic level of analysis, for instance, is for most people the 'story', *histoire*, but Bal prefers the original Russian formalist term *fabula*, reserving 'story' for the next level up (*sjuzhet*, *discours*, discourse) because she wants to distinguish between a focalized version of a set of events and a particular textual representation of that version. On the problem of terminology see e.g. Toolan (1988), 9–11.

The term 'narratology' comes into English from the French 'narratologie', coined by T. Todorov in his *Grammaire du Décameron* (Todorov 1967). The most obvious 'parents' of the new discipline, however, were G. Genette and M. Bal. In 1972 Genette published in Paris a study of Proust's *A la recherche du temps perdu* as part of a collection called *Figures III* (Genette 1972). The distinction between 'what happens' in a story and 'the way it is told' goes back to the Russian formalist critic V. Shlovsky,[7] but Genette provided not only a clear set of headings under which the manipulations of story-telling might be analysed—the classic quintet of order, duration, frequency, mood, and voice—but also a demonstration of the power of these tools in his reading of Proust. The study was published in English in 1980 as *Narrative Discourse: An Essay in Method*, and remains the most important foundational text of the new discipline (Genette 1980). M. Bal published her introduction to narratology in French in 1977, and with the revised English translation of 1985 it provided the first real 'manual' of narratology (Bal 1985).[8]

Both Genette and Bal have continued to publish both on narratology and more widely, and have certainly not felt themselves to be bounded by the techniques to which they gave birth. The 1970s and 1980s in particular saw a large number both of theoretical studies of narratology and of practical applications: the current MLA bibliography lists 138 items under the subject keyword 'narratology' (and 7,322 titles contain the word 'narrative'). The discipline quickly acquired such indispensable signs of status as not one but two *New Accents* introductions and an extremely helpful *Dictionary of Narratology* by Gerald Prince.[9] The moves in the 1980s and 1990s away from anything that sniffed of formalism towards 'cultural studies' and the New Historicism undoubtedly brought about a fall in the discipline's market share, but as with other theoretical positions of recent times that was only because the essential elements of narratological analysis had been absorbed into the reading practice of almost all scholars. Whatever else is

[7] Cf. Shlovsky (1965).

[8] Although Genette and Bal perhaps represent the 'main line', there is a mass of works by other theorists which any adequate history of narratology would have to take into account: cf. e.g. Martin (1986), Mihailescu and Hamarneh (1996), and Peeters (1998).

[9] Rimmon-Kenan (1983), Cohan and Shires (1988), Prince (1987); see also Prince (1982).

done to stories, order, duration, frequency, mood, and voice frequently remain basic categories from which analysis begins. There has been much discussion in recent literature of the relationship between narrative analysis and gender and sexuality, and one particularly interesting development has been the integration of narratological approaches with psychoanalytic theories of the reading process, as in Peter Brooks' outstanding *Reading for the Plot* (Brooks 1984).[10]

Classicists were not slow to take up the new methods of analysis, with, for instance, the Italian critic Massimo Fusillo producing an interesting study of Apollonius Rhodius' *Argonautica* which was particularly indebted to Genette (Fusillo 1985).[11] The most influential work for classical studies, however, has been that of Irene de Jong, a pupil of M. Bal. It was her fine *Narrators and Focalizers: The Presentation of the Story in the Iliad* of 1987 which first drew the attention of the majority of classical scholars to the possibilities offered by Genette's notion of 'focalization', and which stimulated a number of studies in this area.[12] Perhaps the most celebrated study which avows itself narratological, however, is J. Winkler's book on Apuleius' *Metamorphoses*, *Auctor & Actor*.[13] This owes more to Barthes than to Genette, but is a striking demonstration of how narratological analysis can have far-reaching conclusions at the level of content. Brooks' *Reading for the Plot* was a major influence on one of the most stimulating recent books on the classical epic tradition and its reception, David Quint's *Epic and Empire*,[14] and has also been prominent in other studies. But as with literary studies more generally, narratology is now everywhere, even where its underlying assumptions are most explicitly interrogated.

Narratology, then, has to offer both broad perspectives and detailed interrogations, and the pieces in this volume show some

[10] See also Brooks (1994); for further work on narratology, gender, and sexuality see esp. Lanser (1986) and (1996).

[11] Fusillo has gone on to produce some of the best work in classical narratology, most notably on the ancient novel (Fusillo 1989/1991) and in his article 'narrative, narration' in the third edition of the Oxford Classical Dictionary. Narratology has received a great deal of attention within Italian classical studies: see e.g. *Semiotica* (1986) and *Ars Narrandi* (1996).

[12] De Jong (1987); see also her study of Euripidean messenger narratives (1991) and her contribution to de Jong and Sullivan (1994), with a good bibliography on narrative and classical studies. On Homeric narrative see also Richardson (1990).

[13] Winkler (1985). See Stephen Harrison's General Introduction, p. 7 above.

[14] Quint (1993).

of that range. Stephen Harrison's opening piece is concerned with narrative anticipation, both intra- and extradiegetic: in its wide-ranging analysis of the relationship between visual and verbal art, it picks up a theme which has been of particular importance within classical studies,[15] but which has also received more general discussion. Irene de Jong's piece, also concerned with narrative anticipation, is marked as always in her work by a great sensitivity to the nuances of texts, and a refusal to treat narratological analysis as a merely mechanical process; her treatment of the way in which prolepsis or anticipation functions within the text of Herodotus' *History* again shows how larger issues of interpretation may be affected by small details of narrative stylization. Lillian Doherty's concluding essay situates the concerns of narrative analysis within the gendered oppositions that structure the reading of a text like the *Odyssey*, and well shows what may be at stake in the stories we tell about texts as well as in the texts themselves.[16]

Three pieces, then, working with the narratological tradition which is now, in true postmodernist fashion, just one more set of tools and approaches available to the critic. All three show how the methods of narratology have still to offer a great deal to critics as ways into texts. Narratology is a good area with which to begin this collection, as it is an approach which has been taken up and adapted even by classicists relatively hostile to theory: terms like 'prolepsis', 'intradiegetic', and 'focalization' are now as familiar to classical scholars as such non-jargon terms as 'syllepsis', 'propemptikon', or 'prosopopoia'. The enthusiasm with which these terms have been taken up suggests indeed that it is not jargon which is the usual problem with the reception of theory. Viewed as a bundle of techniques, narratology fits as easily into such traditional concerns as the construction of authorial intention (why did Vergil narrate this event before this event?) or of historical 'reality' (is this detail focalized from Thucydides' point of view or that of one of his characters?) as it does into postmodernism. Here surely is an area where we can all 'work together', as the warm reception accorded by both theorists and hard-bitten ancient historians to Simon Hornblower's brilliant narratological introduction to the volume of essays *Greek Historiography* demonstrates.[17]

[15] Cf. Barchiesi (1997a), with bibliography, Fowler (2000), 64–108.

[16] See also her book, Doherty (1995).

[17] Hornblower (1994).

But there are still some raw nerves. If historians and literary scholars have accepted that narratology has a role to play in the analysis of ancient texts—and not just literary ones—they have been less eager to accept (*experto crede*) that their own productions also merit analysis in the same way, that their own discourse is not a privileged scientific meta-discourse but more story-telling. It is too easy if we reduce narratology just to a bundle of tools with which we analyse other people's texts: the study of narrative should problematize our views of our own discourse and its status, should make us more aware of how we construct our stories in both writing and reading. It is perhaps significant that some of the most stimulating work on narratology has come not from literary critics but from theologians like Don Cupitt, whose *What Is a Story?* emphasizes just what is at stake in questions of how we plot what we say and do.[18] As I have remarked elsewhere, twentieth-century literary theory has to offer classical studies both a set of methods and an interrogation of foundations: if it is through the former that it is easiest for people of different viewpoints to come and work together, the potential of the latter for making them argue when they do should not be neglected. One of the nice things about the conference on which this volume is based is that we did not agree all the time: the very possibility of working together depends on recognizing just that.

[18] Cupitt (1991).

6

Picturing the Future: The Proleptic Ekphrasis from Homer to Vergil*

Stephen Harrison

The work of modern literary theory on narrative has since the 1980s come to be applied with some fruitfulness to the texts of classical antiquity.[1] One aspect which has drawn particular attention is that of ekphrasis or description, and its role within narrative: do passages of formal description, often long and apparently digressive, play an organic or functional role in the narratives in which they appear, or are they mere decorations, examples of 'narrative pause'?[2] Don Fowler, in an important treatment of the theoretical aspects, has indicated that the organic view is clearly correct for at least some classical instances;[3] the purpose of this paper is to support this notion through practical analysis and an attempt at categorization. I shall attempt to identify a particular type of organic ekphrasis briefly alluded to by Fowler and familiar

* Earlier versions of this paper have been delivered at the Newcastle Narrative Seminar, Harvard University, Yale University, and the Universities of Washington, Cape Town, Mannheim, Heidelberg, and St Andrews, as well as at the Oxford conference from which this book derives. I am most grateful to all these audiences for much helpful comment, to the late Don Fowler for generous bibliographical help, and to Rachel Pearson for her kind aid in production.

[1] For such applications see esp. the work of de Jong (1987) and Doherty (1995) in Greek, Winkler (1985), and Fowler (1990, 1991) in Latin (now collected in Fowler 2000). For some classic texts of narratology cf. Todorov (1977), which includes a piece on the *Odyssey*, and Genette (1980); for useful introductions Bal (1985) and Rimmon-Kenan (1983), and for a reader which gives some idea of the current range of approaches within narratology, Onega and García Landa (1996). For work on ekphrasis in classical literature see the standard collection of material by Friedlander (1912), the more recent treatments by Ravenna (1974), Perutelli (1978), 32–43, Bartsch (1989), Fowler (1991), and Laird (1993), and a number of important papers in Goldhill and Osborne (1994) and Elsner (1996).

[2] For the theoretical problem cf. Genette (1982), 127–44 on the 'frontiers of narrative', esp. 133–43 on narration and description.

[3] Fowler (1991).

in general terms to readers of classical texts, that in which the matter or scenes described in the ekphrasis of an artefact anticipate by some kind of parallel the events of the plot: the basket in Moschus' *Europa* and the coverlet of Catullus 64 are the standard examples.[4]

In terms of narrative theory, an ekphrasis anticipating the plot is clearly a prolepsis, a device by which a future portion of the *story* is recounted out of temporal sequence in the *narrative*; I will follow the practice of some narratologists in using the term 'story' to describe the events, plot, or content of a piece of narrative, and 'narrative' to describe the text itself which constitutes the story's vehicle.[5] The use of ekphrasis in this proleptic role also raises the question of point of view or narrative focalization, another technique recently applied to classical texts with interesting results.[6] If a description within a narrative signifies future events, it is likely to do so from a particular point of view, focalized by a particular character. The characters of the narrative, unless they themselves have gifts of foresight or of prophetic interpretation, will naturally be unable to recognize the significance of the proleptic ekphrasis in predicting the future course of the narrative, and the resulting gap of knowledge between the non-omniscient character and the omniscient character (for instance, a divinity), omniscient narrator, or omniscient (second-time) reader, is frequently a source of dramatic irony and pathos. Finally, there sometimes arises the issue of whether a prolepsis is intradiegetic, anticipating events in the story of the narrative where it occurs, or extradiegetic, anticipating events outside the literary work but familiar to its readers.[7] By their nature, most proleptic ekphrases in classical narrative texts are intradiegetic, but as we shall see, there will be examples of the extradiegetic kind, and indeed cases where it is difficult to decide. This issue in turn (like that of irony) raises the question of the role of the reader: where knowledge of events outside the story

[4] Cf. e.g. Nisbet (1995), 208–9.

[5] This should be set within the threefold distinction commonly made by narratologists between the 'story' (a series of related events), the 'text' (written or spoken discourse which represents them), and the 'narrative' (the act of communication as voiced by a particular narrator or narrators in the text); not all theorists agree on the terminology, but most are clear about the three fundamental divisions. Cf. Genette (1980), 25–9, Bal (1985), 5–6, Rimmon-Kenan (1983), 3–4, de Jong (1987), p. xv.

[6] Cf. esp. de Jong (1987) and Fowler (1990).

[7] For these terms see Genette (1980), 227–31.

is required, we are clearly dealing with the horizons of expectation or the 'repertoire' of the intended reader of the work, without which such prolepsis will not function.[8]

The range of texts treated in this paper comprises those which are self-conscious literary fictions; this excludes the texts of Greco-Roman historiography, more for reasons of space than because they are in my view fundamentally different in this narratological aspect.[9] The origins and development of the technique of proleptic ekphrasis will be treated chronologically and in both Greek and Latin texts; examples will necessarily be selective, but an attempt will be made to deal with the most important. In many cases (though not in all) the particular points of scholarly interpretation made are those of others; the point of this piece is to draw attention to the technique of proleptic ekphrasis and its interpretative power, and to show that it can provide new readings of familiar passages from a narratological point of view. It is notable that all the examples I have chosen are descriptions of artefacts: this not only reflects the balance of the evidence,[10] but also brings out the resemblance between the artificial, constructed nature both of the artefact itelf and of the literary work in which the description of the artefact occurs. Though none of the ekphrases cited is a strict *mise en abyme*, in terms of replicating in miniature the whole plot of the text in which it is situated, this term is often used more loosely to describe a subsection of a narrative which mirrors some part of a larger narrative in which it is set,[11] and in this broader sense the intradiegetic examples of the phenomenon of proleptic ekphrasis can also be seen as a species of *mise en abyme*.

ARCHAIC AND CLASSICAL GREEK TEXTS

The beginnings of the proleptic ekphrasis may be seen in the *Iliad* and *Odyssey*, texts which respond well in other respects to narrato-

[8] These terms are derived from reader-response theory: 'horizons of expectation' comes from Jauss (1982), 'repertoire' and 'implied reader' from Iser (1974). The last term conveniently codifies what kind of reader any particular work paradigmatically demands, the first two what that reader might need to know for successful interpretation. For a useful introduction to the different strands of reader-response theory cf. Tompkins (1980).

[9] See e.g. Irene de Jong's paper in this collection.

[10] Artefacts constitute the vast majority of proleptic ekphrases, though descriptions of landscapes may have a similar effect: cf. e.g. Nisbet (1995), 209.

[11] On *mise en abyme* see most helpfully Dällenbach (1989).

logical analysis.[12] Here some of the ekphrases, often considered as mere decoration, can be seen as having a more complex narrative function. The two most substantial examples in the *Iliad*, both unsurprisingly describing weapons or armour, are in fact presented as part of the continuing narrative rather than as descriptive digressions, thus stressing that ekphrasis need not be equivalent to a pause in the progress of the narrative even in the most obvious sense. The armour of Agamemnon is described as he puts it on (*Iliad* 11.15–46), the shield of Achilles in the course of its manufacture by Hephaestus (18.478–608).

The decorative scheme of the shield of Agamemnon, which as in the case of Achilles stands out from the rest of the armour as the main device-bearing piece, contains the figures of the Gorgon and of Dread and Terror (11.36–7):

> *τῇ δ' ἐπὶ μὲν Γοργὼ βλοσυρῶπις ἐστεφάνωτο*
> *δεινὸν δερκομένη, περὶ δὲ Δεῖμός τε Φόβος τε.*

And upon it was embossed a fierce-eyed Gorgon, staring horribly, and about her Dread and Terror.

An ancient commentator in the T-scholia rightly notes here that these are devices intended to frighten the enemy, and that the shield recalls the aegis of Zeus, Agamemnon's divine counterpart, from whom he receives his authority and power (2.101–8, 477–8);[13] the aegis also has the Gorgon's head on it, for much the same intimidatory reason (5.738–42). This interesting piece of characterization might be supplemented by some form of narrative foreshadowing. These depictions of Dread and Terror might anticipate the terror which Agamemnon is actually about to inspire in the Trojans: his great aristeia will dominate the first part of this book until his wounding at 248ff., an aristeia of which the arming-scene is a significant and prophetic beginning. Thus a proleptic narrative function is at least arguable here; but one might equally claim that Dread and Terror represent Agamemnon's general character and intentions as a warrior, rather than an actual anticipation of his deeds in this particular case. As often, there is an ambiguity between general characterization and specific anticipation of future events.

[12] Cf. de Jong (1987) on the *Iliad* and Doherty (1995) on the *Odyssey* (see also Doherty's further piece in this collection).

[13] T-scholia on *Iliad* 11. 37.

No specifically proleptic elements seem to appear in the Shield of Achilles episode, the longest and most complex Homeric ekphrasis, about which so much has been written.[14] Its multiple scenes of cosmic setting, cities at war and peace, disputes at law, the killing of men and cattle, agricultural activities, and dancing have been persuasively related to the themes of the *Iliad* and even to the particular events of its plot.[15] However, none of this mass of material seems specifically to anticipate the events of the *Iliad* after Book 18 or of the subsequent stages of the Troy saga, a strong contrast with the firmly proleptic function of the shield of Aeneas in the *Aeneid* (see below); this is despite the fact that it is manufactured by Hephaestus, and therefore has the possibility of presenting a divine character's knowledge of the future (as with the shield of Aeneas). No obvious parallels are provided for the death of Hector, the burial of Patroclus, the reconciliation between Achilles and Priam, the death of Achilles himself, or the taking of Troy, and the clear opportunities for this kind of foreshadowing which exist in the subject-matter of the shield seem not to be taken: the dispute at law on the shield is not resolved (that is, there is no theme of reconciliation to match *Iliad* 24), its besieged city is not captured, and it does not display the death or burial of a notable individual.

The *Odyssey* also provides two interesting examples of artefact-ekphrasis, one of which seems to have some proleptic character. This occurs at *Odyssey* 19.226–31, where Odysseus in his lying tale to Penelope describes a brooch worn by himself, probably an artefact invented for the sake of the tale:

> αὐτάρ οἱ περόνη χρυσοῖο τέτυκτο
> αὐλοῖσιν διδύμοισι· πάροιθε δὲ δαίδαλον ἦεν·
> ἐν προτέροισι πόδεσσι κύων ἔχε ποικίλον ἐλλόν
> ἀσπαίροντα λάων· τὸ δὲ θαυμάζεσκον ἅπαντες,
> ὡς οἱ χρύσεοι ἐόντες ὁ μὲν λάε νεβρὸν ἀπάγχων,
> αὐτάρ ὁ ἐκφυγέειν μεμαὼς ἄσπαιρε πόδεσσι.

And on his cloak there was a brooch of gold with double sheaths [sc. for the pins]. On the face the brooch was richly wrought; there was a hound with a dappled fawn in the grip of its front paws, keeping tight hold of it as it gasped. Everybody marvelled at it, at the two beasts, and the way that, though they were made of gold, one had the fawn in his grip and was

[14] Most of the large literature is cited in Stanley (1993) and Becker (1995), the most extensive recent treatments.

[15] Cf. Taplin (1980), Edwards (1991).

throttling it, while the other, desperate to escape, was jerking its feet, convulsed.

Richard Rutherford has suggested in his recent commentary on this passage that 'we might see an analogy between Odysseus (as hunter and warrior) and the dog, and between the suitors and the fawn'; this hint can be amplified.[16] First, as Rutherford notes, Odysseus' future revenge on the suitors is characterized elsewhere in the poem through the image of a strong predator dispatching weak prey (*Odyssey* 4.335–40 = 17.126–31). Likewise, when it does actually occur in the narrative, the slaughter of the suitors is compared to vultures killing smaller birds (22.302–9), and Odysseus is compared to a lion who has killed an ox (22.401–6). The similar image here suggests a similar anticipation of the predatory slaying of the suitors. Secondly, at the point where the brooch is described Odysseus is addressing Penelope, and although he does not reveal his identity at this point, he does swear to her in the same conversation that Odysseus will return (19.300–9). Thus the prospect of Odysseus' open return and revenge, to be finally revealed in Book 22, figures prominently in this scene, and an anticipation or hint of these events in the ekphrasis narrated by Odysseus himself to Penelope, and naturally focalized through him and his interests, would be appropriate; if the brooch is as fictional as the rest of Odysseus' tale, it may well have been invented for the purpose. Again, as for Agamemnon, this suggests that any proleptic significance here represents Odysseus' general intentions at this point, that is, it may be more a matter of characterization rather than true anticipation of the narrative, though as before the two are hard to disentangle.

Another significant ekphrasis in the *Odyssey* is that of the baldric of Heracles as seen by Odysseus in the Underworld (11.609–12):

> *σμερδαλέος δέ οἱ ἀμφὶ περὶ στήθεσσιν ἀορτὴρ*
> *χρύσεος ἦν τελαμών, ἵνα θέσκελα ἔργα τέτυκτο,*
> *ἄρκτοι τ' ἀγρότεροι τε σύες χαροποί τε λέοντες,*
> *ὑσμῖναί τε μάχαι τε φόνοι τ' ἀνδροκτασίαι τε.*

And a dreadful sword-belt was about his breast, a golden baldric, on which marvellous deeds were wrought, bears and wild boars and shaggy lions, battles and fights and killings and slayings of men.

[16] Rutherford (1992), 169–70.

Here the grisly design clearly represents Heracles' career of slaying beasts and men. But any echo of the deeds of Heracles must be retrospective (analeptic) rather than proleptic here; there is no room for narrative anticipation within the *Odyssey* or outside it, since Heracles is already dead and in the Underworld. An apparently similar use of ekphrasis is found in the most substantial non-Homeric instance, again connected with Heracles, the description of the hero's shield in the pseudo-Hesiodic *Aspis*.[17] The hero arms for his fight with Cycnus, and his shield is described at great length (*Aspis* 139–320), in an ekphrasis longer than that of the shield of Achilles in the *Iliad* and disproportionate to the length of the poem itself (only 480 lines, with the story of Heracles and Cycnus beginning only at line 57). The details of the description are worth some consideration in the present context.

Several depictions on the shield of the *Aspis* draw something from three artefacts already considered. The list of fierce abstract deities with which the description begins (144–60: Fear, Strife, Advance, Retreat, Clamour, Killing, Slaying of Men) clearly echoes the appearance of Dread and Terror on the shield of Agamemnon (*Iliad* 11.37; indeed, the same pair appears again at *Aspis* 195); the herds of boars and lions (168–77) recall those on the baldric of Heracles (*Odyssey* 11.611); while the depictions of a city of men, a battle, agricultural activities, and the circling river of Oceanus (238–317) recall a large proportion of the shield of Achilles. Other scenes, which are not drawn from Homer, have more relevance to the immediate context, where Heracles is about to face Cycnus in battle. Of general relevance are the depiction of Lapiths and Centaurs (178–90), a great battle parallel to that which Heracles is about to enter, and the depiction of Perseus after slaying the Gorgon Medusa (216–37), suggesting perhaps that Heracles will emulate his great-grandfather in defeating a monstrous opponent.[18] More particularly apposite are the adjoining depictions of Ares and Athene in battle-gear and of Apollo and the Muses (191–206); these surely mark the role of the three divinities in the narrative of the poem. The allusion to Apollo may be retrospective, for we have already been told that Apollo has incited Heracles against Cycnus (69 ff.), but the juxtaposition of Ares and Athene, both prepared to fight, may well be anticipatory,

[17] See Becker (1992) for a useful modern account.

[18] For Heracles' relationship to Perseus cf. e.g. Apollodorus *Bibl.* 2. 4. 3–8.

looking forward to their opposing roles in the battle itself (325 ff., 441 ff.), though both have already appeared in the poem as supporters of their favourites (58 ff., 126 ff.). Thus there is arguably some proleptic material here, though the Perseus-image might merely be an ancestral badge, and the allusions to the three gods could pick up their previous appearances in the poem rather than their subsequent roles.

The main ekphrases of fifth-century Attic tragedy continue in this epic tradition, especially the two descriptions of the shield-designs of the Seven against Thebes (Aeschylus *Septem* 369–652, Euripides *Phoenissae* 1104–40). The Aeschylean scene[19] provides an interesting case of prolepsis, for in several cases the conquering intentions expressed by the boastful shield-designs of the Seven, reported by a messenger with some explanatory glossing, are instantly reinterpreted as specific anticipations of their defeat by the listening Eteocles, naturally concerned to discount the bravado of his opponents. Tydeus' shield (387–90) has a moon in the heaven, clearly a boastful statement of his martial supremacy,[20] but viewed by Eteocles as portending Tydeus' death because of its dark background of the night sky (400–6). Capaneus' unambiguous shield-device (432–4) is a man carrying a torch, with the words 'I will burn the city', interpreted by Eteocles as a prophecy of Capaneus' death by thunderbolt (444–6). Hippomedon's design (492–6) has the monster Typhon, clearly a token of monstrous strength and destruction,[21] but matched by Eteocles with the Zeus-device of the Theban Hyperbius, who will conquer Hippomedon just as Zeus overcame Typhon (510–14).

In these three cases Eteocles clearly provides a polemical and alternative reading of the shields which turns out to be correct in terms of the subsequent story: all three will die as Eteocles suggests, Capaneus even in the manner suggested. Here at least we should see some specific narrative prolepsis in the use and interpretation of ekphrasis, and indeed some play with ambiguity and focalization: the devices have one (misleading) interpretation seen from the point of view of the bearers, glossed by the messenger, another (true) interpretation seen from the point of view of the watching Eteocles. Eteocles is of course forced by the dramatic

[19] On the Aeschylean shields see most usefully Zeitlin (1982) (complex but illuminating), Hutchinson (1985), Vidal-Naquet (1988), and Conacher (1996), 49–52.

[20] So Hutchinson (1985), 109.

[21] So Hutchinson (1985), 123.

situation, poised for battle, to reinterpret the shield-devices as he does to encourage his own side, but he may be granted some kind of prophetic insight here, perhaps because of the imminence of his own end; heroes near death often show foresight.[22] There is considerable dramatic irony here, since Eteocles can foresee the deaths of others but not his own.

Similar boastful devices can be found in the briefer descriptions of the shields of the Seven by Euripides (*Phoenissae* 1104–40),[23] but these simply refer to the intentions of the Seven to sack Thebes, to local or family associations, retrospective rather than prospective, or to the character of the bearer, in the manner of the baldric of Heracles in the *Odyssey*; no truly proleptic explanations are given, and nothing seems to anticipate future plot-events (there is not even an allusion to Capaneus' fiery end). More rewarding is the description of the shield of Achilles offered by the chorus of Euripides' *Electra* (452–75):[24]

Ἰλιόθεν δ' ἔκλυόν τινος ἐν λιμέσιν
Ναυπλίοις βεβῶτος
τᾶς σᾶς, ὦ Θέτιδος παῖ,
κλεινᾶς ἀσπίδος ἐν κύκλωι
τοιάδε σήματα δείματα
Φρύγια τετύχθαι·
περιδρόμωι μὲν ἴτυος ἕδραι
Περσέα λαιμοτόμαν ὑπὲρ ἁλὸς
ποτανοῖσι πεδίλοις κορυφὰν Γοργόνος ἴσχειν,
Διὸς ἀγγέλωι σὺν Ἑρμᾶι,
τῶι Μαίας ἀγροτῆρι κούρωι.

ἐν δὲ μέσωι κατέλαμπε σάκει φαέθων
κύκλος ἁλίοιο
ἵπποις ἃμ πτεροέσσαις
ἄστρων τ' αἰθέριοι χοροί.
Πλειάδες Ὑάδες, Ἕκτορος
ὄμμασι τροπαῖοι·
ἐπὶ δὲ χρυσοτύπωι κράνει
Σφίγγες ὄνυξιν ἀοίδιμον ἄγραν
φέρουσαι· περιπλεύρωι δὲ κύτει πύρπνοος ἔσπευ-
δε δρόμωι λέαινα χαλαῖς
Πειρηναῖον ὁρῶσα πῶλον.

22 Cf. conveniently Harrison (1991), 249.
23 For commentary see Craik (1990).
24 Cf. Walsh (1977), King (1980), and Cropp (1988).

From a man of Troy sojourning
at Nauplia harbour I heard,
O son of Thetis,
that on the circle of your famous shield
were wrought these emblems,
terrors for the Phrygians:
on the rim's encircling field
was Perseus over the sea with flying sandals,
holding, throat severed, the Gorgon's head,
   in company with Zeus's herald Hermes,
the rustic child of Maia.

On the buckler's centre radiant shone down
the circle of the sun
on wingéd horses,
and constellations dancing in the heaven,
Pleiads and Hyads, to turn back
the eyes of Hector;
and on the helm of beaten gold
were Sphinxes bearing in talons their song-trapped
prey; and on the hollow corslet, breathing fire,
   sped at a run the lioness on clawed feet
as she beheld Peirene's colt.

Here there are a number of parallels with the overall plot of the *Electra*. First, there seems to be some general parallel between the past arrival of Achilles at Troy, the point of departure and subject of this choric ode, and the future arrival of Orestes at Argos, which has of course taken place already in the play, though concealed from the chorus. The vengeful return of Orestes is in the air at this point for the chorus, since Electra has sent a message pleading for it in the previous episode (332–8). The resemblances between the Achilles of this ode and the Orestes of the *Electra* are significant. Each is a young man set to perform a crucial task of killing at the beginning of his career, each as a result of adultery by a daughter of Tyndareus (Helen and Clytemnestra). Each task of killing requires a special journey: Achilles goes to Troy to kill Trojans, Orestes returns to Argos to kill Aegisthus and Clytemnestra. This establishes a context where the whole ode can look forward to Orestes' killing of his mother at the climax of the play.

Secondly, specific details in the description of Achilles' shield also seem to have an anticipatory function. Perseus is depicted after his slaying of the Gorgon (458–64), a device drawn of course from the shield of the *Aspis* (*Aspis* 216–37), but highly significant in its new context: many have noted that Orestes' killing of Clytemnestra in this play as described by himself at ll. 1221–2 has certain resemblances to Perseus' slaying of Medusa in the veiling of the slayer's head, and Orestes' revenge on Aegisthus is specifically compared to Perseus' deed later in the play.[25] The comparison of the avenging Orestes to the Gorgon-slaying Perseus is also found in Aeschylus' *Choephoroe*.[26] Both slayers are similarly approved by the gods: Perseus in the ekphrasis is accompanied by a protecting Hermes, while later in the play Orestes claims to carry out his killing under divine auspices (890–2). Moreover, the death of the Chimaera at the hands of Bellerophon, another scene on the shield (470–5), has similar anticipatory qualities: the description of the Chimaera as a lioness (474) looks forward to 1163–4, where Clytemnestra is described as acting like a mountain-lioness when she killed Agamemnon,[27] and Bellerophon, killer of the Chimaera, accordingly seems (like the monster-slaying Perseus) to parallel the avenging Orestes.

In the narrative context of the play, all this anticipation naturally represents hope rather than knowledge from the chorus' point of view: at this point in the action they do not even know that Orestes has returned, let alone that he will accomplish his revenge successfully, and they are not gifted with any form of foresight. Any proleptic force in the ekphrasis is thus from the writer's point of view, and not from the speaker's; the chorus' words will turn out to be truer than they now know, and the images of Gorgon and lioness will return with pointed dramatic irony for the attentive reader.

In general, the technique of proleptic ekphrasis seems to develop in specific ways between Homer and Euripides. In the looser frameworks of Homer and the *Aspis* it is not clear that any of the ekphrases allude to future plot-events rather than to events of the past or to what the character associated with the artefact intends, proclaims, or is likely to do at that narrative point; even Odysseus' description of his brooch, apparently quite specific about coming events, may represent his intention at the time

[25] *Electra* 855–7.
[26] Aeschylus *Choephoroe* 831–7.
[27] 474 λέαινα, 'lioness', is picked up by λέαινα at 1163.

rather than providing detailed anticipation of future actions, and many of these prophetic images occur in descriptions of shields, a natural place for hopeful boasts about martial prowess. In the more tightly structured plots of Attic tragedy, on the other hand, we begin to see proleptic ekphrases more closely related to plot-events than to the intentions or nature of a character. This enables the development of a gap between the intentions or knowledge of the character associated with the ekphrasis and the meaning of the description for the future course of the narrative. This in turn allows the introduction of a range of sophisticated literary effects. For example, a character can voice a proleptic ekphrasis in hope or prophecy, without the possibility of foreknowledge; much dramatic irony and pathos can result. Or a true proleptic interpretation of an ekphrasis can be set against a misleading one, as with Eteocles in the *Septem*, raising the question of ambiguous significance and focalization (who designs? who sees? who interprets?). Or a proleptic ekphrasis can form part of a larger complex of thematic parallels and images, which help to define its nature and function, as with the shield of Achilles in the *Electra*, where the link between Achilles and Orestes needs to be established for the narrative anticipation to work. These are all characteristics which we will see more openly displayed in later examples of the proleptic ekphrasis, but which first come to prominence in fifth-century texts.

HELLENISTIC POETRY

It is only natural that Hellenistic poetry, with its fondness for narrative complexity and sophistication, should show some prime examples of proleptic ekphrasis. Here the two most prominent Hellenistic instances will be treated, briefly since much has been said on both by others: the cloak of Jason in Apollonius (Ap. Rh. *Argonautica* 1.730–67), and the basket of Europa in Moschus (*Europa* 43–62). Jason's cloak earns a grand ekphrasis in the epic style, at the point where he disembarks with his crew on Lemnos;[28] the point has been well made that with it he is armed for the forthcoming erotic encounter with Hypsipyle and the later affair with Medea, just as Achilles in the *Iliad* is armed for real battles with

[28] On Jason's cloak see most usefully Lawall (1966), 154–9, Shapiro (1980), and Hunter (1993), 52–9.

his shield, neatly pointing the contrast between Homeric and Apollonian heroism.[29] Jason is a hero of the bedroom, not of the battlefield. All the scenes on the cloak are significant, some generally characterizing Jason and the expedition, appropriate since the Argonaut story is near its beginning, and some specifically anticipating future events of the plot. Apart from the first scene of the labouring Cyclopes forging a thunderbolt for Zeus (730–4), which stresses that the cloak too is of divine manufacture, made by Pallas Athene (cf. 721), and the last two scenes of Apollo, another of the voyage's divine sponsors (759–62), and of Phrixus and the ram, which identifies the object of Jason's expedition, the Golden Fleece (763–7), the intervening four scenes all refer to future themes of the narrative, and are worth considering in detail as instances of proleptic ekphrasis.

Aphrodite's depiction holding the shield of Ares (742–6) anticipates events in Book 3—the power of love, represented by Aphrodite, prefiguring the role of Medea, will succeed where military heroism alone, represented by Ares' shield and prefiguring the role of Jason, cannot. This message is underlined by the juxtaposition on the cloak of a scene of fruitless and destructive war of the old heroic kind, with the bloody stalemate between the Teleboans and the sons of Electryon (747–51). The same triumph of subtlety over crude violence is made in the preceding panel of Amphion and Zethus building the walls of Thebes (735–40): Amphion's music accomplishes much more than the brute force of his brother. Slightly different is the scene of Pelops and Hippodameia (752–8), which stresses the seamier side of Jason's heroism, justly prominent in modern discussions;[30] this clear mythological analogy anticipates that Jason too will have problems with a cunning potential father-in-law who will try to bring about his death, and that he too will solve these by treacherous violence in the context of a tight and dangerous pursuit, by the killing of Absyrtus in 4.450–81. These are multiple and specific proleptic ekphrases, setting out near the beginning of the work several of its major themes and events; like the shields of Achilles and Heracles, the cloak is a divine artefact, and perhaps represents the omniscient divine per-

[29] Cf. Hunter (1993), 55–6, who also notes that the description of Jason's cloak recalls and reworks in detail the more warlike artefacts of Achilles' shield in the *Iliad* and Heracles' shield in the *Aspis* (see above).

[30] Cf. e.g. Beye (1969).

spective, summarizing the plot in advance. The primary focalization within the narrative is that of the women of Lemnos, who all gaze at Jason in his resplendent clothes (1.774–86), and who cannot understand anything of the cloak's significance; there is perhaps some irony in their failure to realize that Jason is a destructive force as well as an attractive male.

This element of multiple anticipation, a Hellenistic extension of the technique of the shield of Achilles in Euripides' *Electra*, is matched in the famous ekphrasis of the basket in Moschus' *Europa* (43–62):[31]

> ἐν τῷ δαίδαλα πολλὰ τετεύχατο μαρμαίροντα·
> ἐν μὲν ἔην χρυσοῖο τετυγμένη Ἰναχὶς Ἰώ
> εἰσέτι πόρτις ἐοῦσα, φυὴν δ' οὐκ εἶχε γυναίην.
> φοιταλέη δὲ πόδεσσιν ἐφ' ἁλμυρὰ βαῖνε κέλευθα
> νηχομένῃ ἰκέλη, κυάνου δ' ἐτέτυκτο θάλασσα·
> δοιοὶ δ' ἕστασαν ὑψοῦ ἐπ' ὀφρύσιν αἰγιαλοῖο
> φῶτες ἀολλήδην θηεῦντο δὲ ποντοπόρον βοῦν.
> ἐν δ' ἦν Ζεὺς Κρονίδης ἐπαφώμενος ἠρέμα χερσί
> πόρτιος Ἰναχίης τήν θ' ἑπταπόρῳ παρὰ Νείλῳ
> ἐκ βοὸς εὐκεράοιο πάλιν μετάμειβε γυναῖκα.
> ἀργύρεος μὲν ἔην Νείλου ῥόος, ἡ δ' ἄρα πόρτις
> χαλκείη, χρυσοῦ δὲ τετυγμένος αὐτὸς ἔην Ζεύς.
> ἀμφὶ δὲ δινήεντος ὑπὸ στεφάνην ταλάροιο
> Ἑρμείης ἤσκηντο, πέλας δέ οἱ ἐκτετάνυστο
> Ἄργος ἀκοιμήτοισι κεκασμένος ὀφθαλμοῖσι.
> τοῖο δὲ φοινήεντος ἀφ' αἵματος ἐξανέτελλεν
> ὄρνις ἀγαλλόμενος πτερύγων πολυανθέι χροιῇ,
> τὰς ὅ γ' ἀναπλώσας ὡσεί τέ τις ὠκύαλος νηῦς
> χρυσείου ταλάροιο περίσκεπε χείλεα ταρσοῖς.
> τοῖος ἔην τάλαρος περικαλλέος Εὐρωπείης.

On this there were many shining well-wrought elements; there was Io daughter of Inachus, wrought in gold, still in the form of a heifer, and without woman's shape. Wandering, she stepped with her feet upon the salt paths of the sea as if swimming, and the sea was made of dark blue metal. Two men stood close together high on the brows of the seashore, and gazed on the cow crossing the sea. And on it was Zeus the son of Kronos, touching gently with his hands the heifer daughter of Inachos, whom beside the seven-mouthed Nile he changed back to a woman from a well-horned cow. The stream of the Nile was in silver, and the heifer in bronze, but Zeus himself was wrought in gold. And around the circular

[31] On its proleptic aspect cf. Zanker (1987), 92–3, Campbell (1991), 52–3.

basket, under the rim, was an image of Hermes, and near him there lay stretched out Argos, equipped with his sleepless eyes. And from his crimson blood there arose a bird which gloried in the many-flowered hue of its wings; unfolding these like a ship swift over the sea, he covered the lip of the golden basket with his plumes. Such was the basket of the fair Europa.

This basket, like Jason's cloak, is of divine manufacture, made by Hephaestus (38) and exceptionally constructed of metal, and again represents the omniscient divine perspective. It depicts Io, Europa's ancestor, whose story provides many parallels for what is about to happen to her descendant (we may compare the story of Perseus, ancestor of Heracles, on his descendant's shield in the *Aspis*). Both Io and Europa are virgins raped by the same god, Zeus, and in both stories love is the motive for a bovine transformation of beloved (Io) or lover (Zeus); Io crosses the sea from Europe to Asia, Europa from Asia (Phoenicia) to Europe; both stories end with a return to human form; and both are implicitly aetiological.[32] None of these resemblances would have occurred to Europa at the narrative time in the poem, since at that point she is peacefully gathering flowers in a meadow, and nothing significant has happened; this produces dramatic irony and pathos, for Europa is in effect given a coded warning which she cannot decipher and which only the reader and omniscient divine maker can unscramble. Thus the proleptic ekphrasis here functions as a device for raising sympathy with a character as well as informing the reader of multiple future developments in the plot.

ROMAN POETRY: CATULLUS AND VERGIL

The first identifiable proleptic ekphrasis in Roman poetry is the famous description of the coverlet in Catullus 64 (50–266).[33] An account of the tale of Theseus, Ariadne, and Bacchus is depicted on the coverlet for the wedding-couch on which Peleus and Thetis, in the main plot of the poem, are about to inaugurate their marriage, and this tale functions as an embedded narrative. This narrative is notoriously long within the volume of the poem, filling 217 of its 408 lines, and given its strategic central location in both

[32] These points are well made by Campbell (1991), 54.

[33] From the huge bibliography cf. Klingner (1956), Perutelli (1979), 33–41, Bramble (1970).

poem and marriage-ceremony must have some significance which is more than decorative. It is difficult to avoid drawing some parallel between the frame story of the wedding of Peleus and Thetis and the inset story of Theseus, Ariadne, and Bacchus; modern commentators are agreed that there is a parallel, but generally see it as one of momentary contrast between the happy marriage of Peleus and Thetis and the unhappy liaison between Theseus and Ariadne, thus celebrating and praising their union.[34] This is unsatisfactory, and there are several considerations urging the opposite point of view, that the coverlet represents an unhappy, not a happy future for the couple being married.[35]

First, the insert story is not a tale of one couple, Theseus/Ariadne, but of two, Theseus/Ariadne and Bacchus/Ariadne. Thus the inset story provides two tales of male/female union which may be offered as parallels for the main story: one of two mortals whose love is broken by treachery and desertion, and one of a mortal and a god whose love is apparently strong and passionate, and crowned by wedlock. This second story of Bacchus and Ariadne is clearly more closely similar to that of Peleus and Thetis, and a suitable complimentary design for their bridal coverlet. But the inset itself concentrates for over 90 per cent of its space on the unhappy Theseus/Ariadne story (50–250), and not on the happy Bacchus/Ariadne story, introduced at the end of the ekphrasis almost as an afterthought (251–66); this suggests that the union of Peleus and Thetis will not be an ideal one, and seems to look forward proleptically to darker events after the end of the poem rather than contemplating the current moment of connubial felicity.

This is the first recognizable instance of what was alluded to at the outset as extradiegetic prolepsis, an anticipation of future events *outside* the current literary narrative, *beyond* the end of the story told by the writer as a whole but implicitly familiar to its readers, and deserves further consideration. Such extradiegetic prolepses naturally depend on the reader knowing what happened after the current narrative ends. In the case of Catullus 64 the second-time reader has been made to think forward to the later relations of Peleus and Thetis by the later prophetic and unpleasant summary of the career of their unborn son Achilles, and there

[34] Cf. e.g. Klingner (1956), 69–70, Perutelli (1979), 40, Syndikus (1990), 134–9.

[35] It will be obvious that I favour the 'darker' view of the poem, most powerfully put by Bramble (1970).

is a prominent account of the future state of the Peleus/Thetis marriage in Apollonius, an author to whom the author and reader of the poem might naturally turn.[36] In Apollonius (*Argonautica* 4.866–79) it is clear that Peleus and Thetis live apart, and that Thetis left Peleus for good when the latter misunderstood her attempts to make the baby Achilles immortal. This desertion and separation matches the tale of Theseus and Ariadne as depicted in the ekphrasis, and suggests that their story is told as a parallel for the imminent future relations of Peleus and Thetis.

Indeed, even the union of Bacchus and Ariadne, which seems to commence as the ekphrasis closes, need not itself have been a happy one. Most common is the version where Bacchus married Ariadne on Naxos and set her wedding-crown in the heavens as the constellation Corona,[37] but a much darker story appears as far back as Homer. In the catalogue of heroines encountered by Odysseus in the Underworld, mention is made of Ariadne (*Od.* 11.321–5), who, after helping Theseus in his escape from Crete, was killed by Artemis 'on the evidence of Dionysus'. This might allude to Ariadne being unfaithful to Dionysus and being punished by the goddess of chastity, but whatever it means,[38] it suggests that relations between Bacchus and Ariadne were, in at least one version, far from ideal.

This proleptic function is increased by the thought that this extraordinary coverlet, like the presents given at the wedding, is likely to be of divine manufacture, and may express an authoritative prophetic view of the future. Its spectators, on the other hand, through whose point of view we seem to see it in the poem, are mortals and know nothing of the future, a powerful irony—they are celebrating a marriage whose marriage-bed, unknown to them, predicts its failure. The proleptic function of the ekphrasis in Catullus 64 is thus at a higher level of sophistication than those previously examined. First, the ekphrasis provides two models for the future which appear to be mutually exclusive, but which can be made to point the same way through the application of know-

[36] See the excellent article by Clare (1996).

[37] For the happy union of Bacchus and Ariadne on Naxos see (apart from Strauss and Hofmansthal's *Ariadne auf Naxos*) Apollonius *Arg.* 4. 431–4; for the Corona cf. Nisbet and Hubbard (1978) on Horace *Odes* 2. 19. 13, Mynors (1990) on Vergil *G.*1.222.

[38] Modern Homeric commentators suggest this is the only remnant of an early story later displaced by a happier one—cf. Heubeck and Hoekstra (1989), 97.

ledge external to the text: the poem relies on a reader who is not only alert, but also equipped with the relevant mythological and literary knowledge, an appropriate 'repertoire' in the terms of reader-response theory. Secondly, the length, relevance, and narrative complexity of the ekphrasis itself questions and even breaks down the boundaries between narrative and description, an important general issue raised at the beginning of this paper; can an apparent digression which itself tells a tale evidently parallel to the main story, and itself has digressions and flashbacks, itself count as a digression? This is writing of high artistry which is determined to make the reader work hard for his or her interpretation.

The *Aeneid* of Vergil, which learnt so much from Catullus and from the Hellenistic tradition in general, contains three proleptic ekphrases of great skill: the pictures in Dido's temple (1.450–93), the shield of Aeneas (8.626–731), and the baldric of Pallas (10.495–505); all have been much discussed.[39]

The pictures in Dido's temple depict scenes from the Trojan war, and Aeneas' famous reaction to seeing them (462, *sunt lacrimae rerum, et mentem mortalia tangunt*) is one of relief that he has apparently reached a place where his past history and sufferings are known and may bring sympathy (cf. 1.450–2), as indeed is about to occur with Dido. As critics have stressed, there is some splendid irony here: the temple is of course being built by Dido to Juno, Aeneas' arch-enemy, no doubt in celebration of that goddess's aid to the victorious Greeks at Troy—it is surely not intended as the monument to Trojan courage perceived by Aeneas, and stresses the natural hostility of Dido and her people towards the Trojans (cf. 1.297–304).[40] Furthermore, as Keith Stanley has argued, each of the scenes depicted chooses an incident from the story of the fall of Troy as told in the *Iliad* and the Epic Cycle which will be in some sense repeated within the *Aeneid*.[41] This stresses the crucial point that Aeneas' war in Italy is a repetition and inversion of the war at Troy, a second *Iliad* which takes up in detail the themes and episodes of its Homeric original.[42]

[39] Putnam (1998) offers a large-scale treatment of all three. Though Fowler (1991) and Laird (1996) have applied some narratological considerations to the passages from Book 1 and Book 8, they have not stressed the proleptic aspect.

[40] Cf. e.g. Johnson (1976), 103. For bibliography cf. Fowler (1991), 31, n.40.

[41] Cf. Stanley (1965), an unjustly neglected article.

[42] On this theme cf. e.g. Anderson (1957), Gransden (1984), Barchiesi (1984).

The appearance of Achilles (468) anticipates the Achilles-role to be played by Aeneas himself in Books 10–12, and the exceptional depiction of Aeneas himself in his Iliadic role suggests that he will have to fight again in the same manner in Italy (488). The night-expedition involving Rhesus and Diomedes (469–73) looks forward to the night-expedition of 9.176–502; the Trojan women entreating the inexorable Athene (479–82) look ahead to the similarly unsuccessful approach to the same deity by the Italian women in 11.477–85; and the appearance of the Amazon Penthesilea (490–3) is an obvious parallel for the later appearance of the virgin warrior Camilla in 7.803–17 and 11.498–867, as several elements make clear (it also doubles as an anticipation of the imminent appearance of Dido, herself a forceful huntress). Likewise, the death of Troilus, the young warrior ill-matched with a great hero (474–8), prefigures the deaths of Pallas, Lausus, and even Turnus in similar circumstances in Books 10–12,[43] while the picture of Priam lamenting over the body of Hector, abused but eventually returned by Achilles (483–7), anticipates the grief of Evander over the body of Pallas, stripped by Turnus, in 11.139–81, and that of Mezentius over the body of Lausus in 10.821–56, and perhaps even the presumed grief of Daunus over the body of Turnus anticipated in the last scene of the *Aeneid* (12.932–6).

Aeneas, of course, through whom the ekphrasis is primarily focalized, has no idea that these scenes refer to his future as well as his past; his reading of them can be partial at best. The full knowledge required to appreciate the prolepsis here is naturally that of the second-time reader of the poem, though the first-time reader is aided by the prophecy of Jupiter, unknown to Aeneas, which has predicted the war in Italy a few hundred lines before (1.257–96). This dramatic irony, together with his own misinterpretation of the temple-decorations as pro-Trojan, arouses pathos and sympathy for Aeneas: the prospect of a tough war and of a replay of the *Iliad* in Italy contrasts movingly with Aeneas' present hopes for rest and a sympathetic reception in Carthage. Again, as in several of the cases already discussed, the distinction between narrative and description is largely broken down; we see the paintings through the eyes of Aeneas as he wanders around the temple, a narrative event, not as a separate digression.

This distinction between narrative and description appears to

[43] On this theme see esp. Barchiesi (1984), 55–73.

be maintained, however, in the account of the shield of Aeneas (*Aeneid* 8.626–731), with its collection of scenes from the future victories of Rome. Here I will be brief, since once again the critical literature is vast.[44] In *Aeneid* 8 the status of the shield as separate artefact is stressed by the text, which specifically distracts us from the main story: the narrative effectively stands still as the reader is shown the shield—Aeneas is at rest in the cool grove of Caere as it arrives (8.607), and rises to return to his task with the shield on his shoulder as the description concludes (729–31). The focalization operating is made clear both at the beginning and the end of the shield's description: it is being viewed through the eyes of Aeneas (617–18, 729–30). This, however, is necessarily not the only point of view being applied: Aeneas himself cannot know the identity of the scenes he is seeing from future Roman history, just as he needs Anchises to tell him the identities of the figures in the show of heroes in the Underworld in Book 6, and this is explicitly pointed out by the narrating poet at the end of the book—he knows nothing of the subject-matter, but likes the pictures (730, *rerumque ignarus imagine gaudet*). Again, as in *Aeneid* 1, Aeneas is not able to read the artefact with full information, and in both cases this surely stresses his isolation and human virtue in soldiering on without a reliable guide to the future. There is a second focalizer with a more informed view, the divine maker of the shield, Vulcan, who as a god has knowledge of the future in manufacturing the shield (the poet tells us this explicitly at 626–8, *illic res Italas Romanorumque triumphos haud vatum ignarus ventrurique inscius aevi facerat ignipotens*). This 'omniscient' viewpoint is also, of course, that of the third focalizer, the Roman reader, for whom all these predicted events are already confirmed by their occurrence in past history.

The future depicted on the shield would seem to be entirely outside the events of the *Aeneid*; the account of Roman history which it gives begins with the foundation of Rome, many generations in the future from the time of the poem. In the terms of this paper, the shield of Aeneas seems to be an instance of a wholly extradiegetic proleptic ekphrasis: its anticipatory function appears to lie entirely outside the events of the poem. However, the shield does arguably have an internal anticipatory function in the plot of the *Aeneid*. It is to be used by Aeneas in the forthcoming war in which he will lay the foundations for the Roman people, and thus, with

[44] For a recent discussion with some bibliography cf. Harrison (1997).

its depictions of the foundation of Rome and future Roman victories, acts as a symbol and guarantee of Aeneas' own victory within the poem; the triumphs of Rome, and in particular the ultimate triumph of Augustus at Actium, parallel the victory of Aeneas against his own adversaries in the poem, in a conflict which, like that of Actium, can be viewed as both a foreign and a civil war.[45]

I end with a final Vergilian example.[46] As the young Pallas is killed by Turnus and his sword-belt brutally stripped off and put on by the victor in defiance of the usual practice of dedicating such spoils to a deity, we are given a description of the design on the belt (*Aeneid* 10.495–505):

> et laevo pressit pede talia fatus
> exanimem rapiens immania pondera baltei
> impressumque nefas: una sub nocte iugali
> caesa manus iuvenum foede thalamique cruenti,
> quae Clonus Eurytides multo caelaverat auro:
> quo nunc Turnus ovat spolio gaudetque petitus.
> nescia mens hominum fati sortisque futurae
> et servare modum rebus sublata secundis!
> Turno tempus erit magno cum optaverit emptum
> intactum Pallanta, et cum spolia ista diemque
> oderit.

And so saying he pressed the corpse with his left foot, stripping off the monstrous weight of Pallas' baldric and the abomination stamped upon it: the foul slaughter of a band of young men under the cover of one wedding-night, and bloodstained marriage-chambers, which Clonus the son of Eurytus had embossed with much gold. In this booty Turnus now triumphed, and rejoiced at his acquisition. How ignorant of destiny and of their future lot are the minds of men, and how unable to observe due measure when uplifted by good fortune! There will be a time for Turnus when he will wish he had bought Pallas' safety at a great price, and when he will hate these spoils and the day he got them.

Commentators have rightly taken this as a subtle reference to the Danaids' mythological slaying of their cousin-husbands on their wedding night, a theme popular in Augustan poetry owing to the portico attached to Augustus' temple of Palatine Apollo in which

[45] For this point cf. Harrison (1988).

[46] I have recently treated this passage much more fully from a slightly different perspective in Harrison (1998); for a classic treatment see Conte (1986), 185–96.

there was a famous representation of the Danaids. This description occurs at one of the crucial narrative points of the *Aeneid*, at the moment when Turnus in effect seals his own death at the hands of Aeneas, and so possesses a certain amount of weight, stressed by the narrating poet in the lines which immediately follow (501–5). There is an interesting question of focalization here. The belt cannot be seen from the dead Pallas' point of view, but it also seems unlikely that the victorious Turnus, swiftly grabbing his trophy in the heat of battle, is imagined as taking the time to examine the design upon it. Thus neither of these are available to read or misread the design, and since the design is explicitly the product of mortal craftsmanship, we cannot, as with the shield of Aeneas, ascribe any proleptic force in it to divine foreknowledge. It is the epic narrator who looks, and who directs the reader's gaze towards this portentous artefact, thus manipulating his own narrative and emotional reactions to it.

Here there is great potential for moving dramatic irony, since the dreadful design on the belt clearly refers to disaster in some sense, but cannot be accurately read by any of the characters at the crucial narrative point. If the disaster portended on the belt is that of Pallas, then Pallas has ignored the message of his own belt and gone to his death unaware of a message which might have prevented it; if the disaster is that of Turnus, then at least that is to come, but Turnus spares no time to consider the belt's device before rashly strapping it on. But to what precisely does the dreadful design on the belt refer? Here there is some proleptic force. The legend of the Danaids and their slaughtered bridegrooms seems to have anticipatory reference to the end of Turnus, whose Argive descent is much stressed in the *Aeneid*, and who is also doomed to die before celebrating his marraige, like the young men on the belt; though it is also clear, as Conte has effectively argued, that Pallas too is like the young men on the belt in being cut down before marriage. Thus we are offered a dual perspective of flashback (analepsis) and prolepsis—flashback to the recent death of Pallas, prolepsis of the future death of Turnus—a characteristically subtle Vergilian manipulation of this narrative technique.

CONCLUSION

There are many interesting examples of proleptic ekphrasis in post-Vergilian epic, but that would be the topic for another paper.[47] I hope that I have given some account of the technique's development from Homer to Vergil, and in particular, that I have stressed that many features of ekphrasis which we think of as subtle and Hellenistic occur as early as classical and archaic Greek literature, though of course there is some linear progress in terms of increasing sophistication and subtlety. Specific developments to note are the emerging categories of intradiegetic and extradiegetic prolepsis, and the way in which the latter increases considerably in importance, reflecting a learned readership with an increasingly broad repertoire of literary and mythological knowledge; the varieties of focalization in reading these artefacts (who sees—characters, author, reader—and—which of these readings is effective and authoritative?); and the consequent effects of dramatic irony and pathos. These elements show that classical narratives can rival modern texts in their richness and complexity, and that modern narrative theory can help us to bring new and valuable perspectives to the critical appreciation of familiar ancient texts.

[47] For example, an instance in Statius (the arms of Capaneus at *Thebaid* 4. 165–77) is treated by Harrison (1992); for analysis of an extensive ekphrasis in Silius (*Punica* 6. 653–97, his version of the pictures in the temple (cf. *Aeneid* 1), clearly non-proleptic and referring to past history only) see Fowler (1996), reprinted in Fowler (2000). Valerius Flaccus' ekphrasis of the doors of the Temple of the Sun at Colchis (*Argonautica* 5. 433–55) operates both analeptically and proleptically: see Hershkowitz (1998), 20–3. Some further examples are collected by Anastasios Nikolopoulos in an unpublished MSt thesis, 'Some Aspects of Ecphrasis in Post-Vergilian Epic' (Oxford, 1995).

7

The Anachronical Structure of Herodotus' *Histories**

Irene de Jong

THE PROBLEM: DISORDER

One of the most memorable scenes in the film *The English Patient* is when Almásy, having left behind his wounded lover Katherine in a cave in the desert, finally reaches a village and asks an English officer for a car so he can go back and save her. When the officer refuses, he desperately begs him to give him a car, any car: 'just give me the fucking car.' Not many viewers will realize that this scene in fact has been subtly prepared for in the first half of the film, during the first meeting between Almásy and Katherine. They are talking about literature, and Almásy claims that he does not need many adjectives: 'A thing is still a thing no matter what you place in front of it. Big car, slow car, chauffeur-driven car—still a car.' These words will acquire a dramatic significance through the events which follow.[1] In view of the important role which Herodotus' *Histories* plays in *The English Patient*, it seems appropriate to reverse the situation and use that story as a lead-in for a discussion of the *Histories*.

This example of subtle preparation in *The English Patient* well illustrates one of the reasons why the film is such a success. The story is beautifully constructed, all details slowly acquiring their significance, just as the identity of the English patient is gradually revealed. Measured against this standard Herodotus' *Histories* would seem to cut a poor figure, with its numerous digressions and

* I wish to thank J. V. Morrison and S. R. van der Mije for their comments, and Mrs B. A. Fasting for her correction of my English.

[1] I owe this observation to Susanna Morton Braund, who also kindly provided me with the exact wording (from *The English Patient: A Screenplay by Anthony Minghella* (London 1997), 24–5 and 148–9). The link between the two scenes is not found in Ondaatje's novel.

its lack of a clear structure. This has created a 'Herodotean question', almost as hotly debated as the famous 'Homeric question'. (The Homeric parallel, invoked here for the first time, will reappear as a leitmotif throughout my entire paper.) In the case of the historian, too, we have on the one hand analysts like Jacoby, who contend that Herodotus developed from a geographer and an ethnographer into a historian, and that his work consists of a series of independently conceived *logoi*, and on the other hand unitarians like Pohlenz, who claim that from the very beginning Herodotus aimed at writing a history of the confrontation between Greeks and barbarians, and that the various *logoi* were written as parts of that whole.[2] In 1971 Fornara cut the Gordian knot by suggesting that in fact both positions are valid: 'The unitarian view provides a proper estimate of Herodotus' skill at the final stage of his career. It is the necessary complement of a developmental hypothesis such as that of Jacoby and his followers whose purpose is to diagnose the problematic features in Herodotus' work. The one describes what we possess; the other attempts to explain how what we do possess could have come into the world.'[3]

But even a unitarian critic who merely sets out to describe 'what we possess' (without at the same time making claims, as Pohlenz does, about 'how it came into the world') is still faced with the problem of the structure of the *Histories*. In his admirable introduction to Herodotus, Gould graphically describes the situation as follows: '. . . to confront the detail of Herodotean narrative, to attempt to grasp its scale and shape and see order in the mass, is a mind-blowing and overwhelming experience. The first impression one has is of being buried under an avalanche of facts and at the same time utterly lost in a landscape bewilderingly criss-crossed and looped by stories without discernible paths or sense of structured connection.'[4] In other words, Herodotus, consummate storyteller where the individual stories are concerned, appears to have failed on the level of the story of his *Histories* as a whole.

Of course, numerous attempts have been made to find method in the madness of Herodotus' material. Gould himself suggests that the stories are connected via 'personal relationships' (kinship, revenge, obligation, guest-friendship, and so on).[5] To take one

[2] Jacoby (1913), Pohlenz (1937). A summary of the debate in Fornara (1971), 1–23 and Cobet (1971), 14–44.

[3] Fornara (1971), 12–13.

[4] Gould (1989), 42.

[5] Ibid. 42–62.

example, when Thrasybulus, tyrant of Miletus, is helped by Periander, tyrant of Corinth, the very fact that the latter is the former's *xeinos* (friend) suffices to briefly switch attention to him and insert the story about Arion, which took place during his reign (1. 19–25). Next we have Immerwahr, another important name in this debate, who contends that the *logoi* of the *Histories* are linked by recurrent thought-patterns, for example, that of 'the rise and fall of rulers'.[6] Finally there is Pohlenz himself, who in the course of his unitarian defence of Herodotus lays bare a number of unifying devices.[7] I mention here those which are relevant to the macrostructure of the *Histories*: (1) explicit cross-references (e.g. 'the treasure [of Croesus] was very great, as I have shown in the first of my *logoi*': 5. 36); (2) flashback and foreshadowing (e.g. '. . . Harpagus took over command—the Harpagus who was entertained by Astyages the Median king at an unlawful feast, and who helped to win the kingship for Cyrus': 1. 162); and (3) mention of a detail whose relevance only later becomes clear (e.g., the robbery by the Samians of a Spartan bowl in 1. 40 will become relevant in 3. 47, when the event is seized upon as a reason to declare war).

ANOTHER SOLUTION: 'ORDER'

In this paper I will continue along the lines set out by Pohlenz. For his three devices all have to do with the narratological category 'time', in particular, 'order'. Order is one of the oldest and best-researched aspects of narratology. It goes back to the Russian Formalists, who distinguished between 'fabula' (the material in chronological order) and 'sjuzet' (the material in the order in which we encounter it in the text), was further worked out by the German scholar Lämmert, who discussed various forms of 'Vorausdeutung' and 'Rückwendung', and was brought to near-perfection by the French narratologist Genette, who developed a refined set of concepts to analyse and describe the various ways in which the chronological order of the fabula may be transposed within the story.[8] It is these concepts which I will be using in this paper.

[6] Immerwahr (1966).

[7] See his own summary: Pohlenz (1937), 86–8.

[8] See Ejxenbaum (1971), Lämmert (1955), 100–94, Genette (1980), 33–85 (and cf. Bal (1985), 51–68; I have adopted her terms 'fabula' and 'story').

If we look at the way in which the events of the *Histories* are ordered, we see that by and large Herodotus follows the example of Homer. In the Homeric epics the time-span covered by the main stories comprises some fifty days. However, much larger stretches of time—the ten years of the war before Troy and the capture of that city, and the twenty years of Odysseus' absence from home and the peaceful end of his life—are also included by means of *external* analepses (flashbacks) and prolepses (flash-forwards). Indeed, even events from a more remote past, such as the youthful exploits of Nestor and the adventures of Bellerophontes, are included in this way. In the same way, Herodotus' main story comprises some eighty years: it starts in 560 BC (Croesus' conquest of the Ionian and Aeolian cities in Asia) and ends in 479–8 BC (the Greek capture of Sestus). Through external prolepses and above all analepses, however, the narrator describes a much longer stretch of time, from around 3000 BC (the reign of Min, the first Egyptian pharaoh) up to 430 BC (the execution of Spartan envoys in Athens).[9]

One important difference between Herodotus and Homer is that in the *Iliad* and the *Odyssey* the external analepses and prolepses are almost without exception voiced by characters,[10] while in the *Histories* it is quite often the narrator who goes back or forward in time. In my view, this difference is one of the factors responsible for the chaotic impression which Herodotus makes on us, in contrast to Homer's handling of time, which has been highly praised from Aristotle onwards. In principle, however, the system is the same: whenever the Herodotean narrator feels that his narratees need to be informed about the background of a person or situation, he stops the main story and goes back in time to provide that information. As Waters writes, 'as Homeric heroes state their own antecedents on the battlefield by offering their opponents a genealogical lecture, so must the antecedents of Kroisos be stated'.[11]

But—again like Homer—Herodotus also inserts *internal* prolepses and analepses, that is, retroversions to and anticipations of events falling *within* the time-span of the main story. Compare, for example, a Homeric internal analepsis like *Iliad* 22. 323 (Achilles

[9] Of course, the main story gets the most attention. Carbonell (1985), 139, 142–3 has estimated that 72% of the text is devoted to the period 560–479/8.

[10] Kullmann (1968).

[11] Waters (1974), 5.

looks at 'the bronze armour, the beautiful set, which he [Hector] had taken from Patroclus after killing him') with a Herodotean one at 5. 56–96, the period of Greek history after the death of Pisistratus (514–499 BC), which is inserted at the beginning of the Ionian revolt (499 BC). These examples reveal two important differences between Homer and Herodotus. First, the Homeric analepsis picks up an event which is also recounted by the narrator; in narratological terms it is a *repeating* internal analepsis. The Herodotean analepsis, by contrast, covers a period *not* covered elsewhere in the *Histories*; it is a *completing* internal analepsis. It will be obvious that the second type of temporal dislocation is more difficult to grasp than the first, and again we have discovered a factor contributing to the lack of transparency of the Herodotean structure. Secondly, while most of Homer's internal prolepses and analepses have a length of a handful of lines (the longest, *Iliad* 1. 366–92, takes up twenty-six lines), their Herodotean counterparts are often quite substantial (forty chapters in the example just given). This increase in scale is yet another complicating factor.

It may be instructive at this point to compare Herodotus' order with the chronological order to which we are accustomed in modern times and which is exemplified in Volume 4 of the *Cambridge Ancient History*. As the table of contents shows at a glance, here the Pisistratidae and Cleisthenes (chapters 4 and 5 of Part II) are discussed in their proper chronological place, before the Ionian revolt (chapter 8). Now while Herodotus' order may have the disadvantage of obscuring the chronological order, it is undeniably effective: by the time he resumes his main story (at the point where Aristagoras comes to Athens to ask for help against the Persians: 5. 97, cf. 55), we know much more about the—anti-Persian—atmosphere in the city. In fact, the last sentence of the internal analepsis runs as follows: . . . *σφι ἐδέδοκτο ἐκ τοῦ φανεροῦ τοῖσι Πέρσῃσι πολεμίους εἶναι* ('. . . it was resolved that they should be openly at war with Persia'; 5. 96. 2). After this, it is hardly surprising—although, according to Herodotus, nonetheless foolish—that the Athenians are easily persuaded by Aristagoras to join the Ionian revolt against the Persians (5. 98). This example shows that Herodotus does not insert his historical excursions at random,[12]

12 So Jacoby (1913), 387 ('he was unable to put everything relevant in its proper place and therefore had recourse to the device of the excursus, which pop up *in surprising places* . . .' (my italics; all translations from the German in this paper are

but rather chooses places where they may be expected to produce the maximum effect.[13]

Looking again at the *Cambridge Ancient History*, it is also interesting to observe that the Persian attacks on the Greek mainland are treated in the section on the Greek states, rather than in that on the Persian empire. This is of course historically appropriate, since these events had a greater impact on Greek than on Persian history. In the *Histories*, however, the temporal framework is not that of Greek history but of Eastern history (the succession of the five rulers Croesus, Cyrus, Cambyses, Darius, and Xerxes). The explanations commonly given for this situation are that: (i) no adequate Greek chronography was yet available, whereas there did exist lists of Eastern kings;[14] or (ii) early Greek history was too fragmented.[15] These certainly may have been factors, but I think there is more to it than that. An important issue in ancient as well as modern warfare is the question of who started the hostilities. The one who starts is the one who is morally to blame. We may recall the *Iliad*, in which it is made very clear that it was the Trojans, first Paris and later Pandarus, who began the hostilities. Herodotus devotes the first five chapters of his work to the debate on who was responsible for the enmity between East and West, and then emphatically puts Croesus forward as his own candidate. When he then goes on to devote four books of his *Histories* to the expansion of Eastern imperialism, the message is the same: the barbarians are the aggressors, and the Greeks are fighting a just war to defend their freedom. Therefore, the Eastern chronological framework, far from being a technical *faute de mieux*, actually has ideological undertones.[16]

So much for my general remarks on 'order' in the *Histories*. Upon reflection, it seems only logical to take 'time' as an important—perhaps the most important—structuralizing and unifying principle in a historical narrative. Thus, turning again for a

mine), Fränkel (1960), 86–7, and Von Fritz (1967), 86, 113, 450. Waters (1985), 128 is puzzling: ('it is not possible to deal with this vast sweep of history in chronological order, even if all inessential information were excluded; thus it must be done in parallel logoi, placed in an *arbitrary* but *appropriate* order' (my italics).

[13] Cf. Carbonell (1985), 146–7. Cf. the deliberate placing of descriptive digressions at the moment a people becomes the object of Eastern imperialism.

[14] Pohlenz (1937), 30–1.

[15] Jacoby (1913), 348–9 and Von Fritz (1967), 113.

[16] It must form a counterweight to repeated claims on the part of the Persians that it was the Greeks who started the injustice (cf. 7. 8. 9, 11 *bis*).

moment to Homer, we may recall Schadewaldt's famous *Ilias-studien*, in which unitarian defence of the *Iliad* he also relies heavily on various forms of 'preparation' and 'retrospection'.[17] More generally, the Homeric analepses and prolepses have been amply investigated. In the case of Herodotus, however, we have only stray remarks, such as those of Van Groningen, who notes—but does not discuss—the Herodotean tendency to foreclose the issue of his story in the form of oracles, dreams, or warnings;[18] Hunter, who argues that *logoi* (direct or indirect speeches) often anticipate the *erga* (action);[19] and Waters, who mentions Herodotus' flash-back technique as one of the devices which the historian derived from Homer.[20] Even Pohlenz, who, as we have seen, takes a great interest in anticipation and retroversion as unifying devices, covers only a fraction of the material and the range of effects which can be achieved through these devices.

How to explain this relative neglect of 'time' in the *Histories*? The answer seems to be that scholars have been distracted by Herodotus' apparent weakness where absolute chronology (i.e. dates) is concerned.[21] The following remarks, by H. Fränkel and D. Lateiner respectively, are illustrative:

> In Herodotus, time, as a means to connect the many things he has to say about different countries, is almost completely lacking. This is surprising for a historian, but, as has often been remarked, he has no interest in chronology. You could even say that he, and in general the archaic period to which he partly belongs, has no eye for the ever progressing time, like modern orientals (*sic*). He does not hesitate to stop time . . . He doesn't even shrink from reversing the order of things.[22]

> Chronological order provides the obvious principle of organization for most historians, but not for Herodotus. Chronological research is as necessary for him as for any other historian, but not for the structure of his historical study.[23]

[17] Schadewaldt (1938).

[18] Van Groningen (1953), 39–42.

[19] Hunter (1982), 191–2. She has analysed this phenomenon in great detail for Thucydides, see Hunter (1973).

[20] Waters (1974), 3.

[21] I say 'apparent' because Strasburger (1956) has convincingly shown that Herodotus' chronology is much better than is often assumed.

[22] Fränkel (1960), 85. His formulation makes it clear that he actually criticizes Herodotus for his handling of time. This curious twentieth-centurycentrism a little further on becomes even more glaring: 'Even more acutely we sense the *abuse* of *our* conception of time in Pindar' (my italics).

[23] Lateiner (1989), 114. In fact, Lateiner's position in his chapter on chronology

There is, to my knowledge, only one—brief—plea to take 'time' as the leading structuralizing principle of the *Histories*, by Carbonell: 'It is not space which orders and organizes the *Histories*. It is time which turns it into a rigorously chronological work, even if this rigour demands an apparent disorder.' Though essentially correct, this definition of Herodotus' procedure is not exactly felicitous. Here narratology again comes in handy, since it offers us the term anachrony, coined by Genette to refer to the various types of discordance between the order of the fabula and the order of the story.[24] I suggest that we call the structure of the *Histories* anachronical: its chronological framework is frequently overturned through long and complex—but effective—anachronies.[25]

A SET OF EXAMPLES

I will now look at a set of specific examples. For that purpose I have chosen analepses and prolepses concerning Xerxes' decision to launch the expedition against Athens which is to form the climax of the *Histories*.

The narrative germ for this decision, which will be taken in 7. 5–19, is the moment when Athens, persuaded by Aristagoras of Miletus, decides to send twenty ships to the Ionians of Asia Minor, who are rebelling against the Persians. This moment is highlighted by the narrator through the insertion of an internal prolepsis:

(1) *αὗται δὲ αἱ νέες ἀρχὴ κακῶν ἐγένοντο Ἕλλησί τε καὶ βαρβάροισι.*

These ships were the beginning of misery for the Greeks and the barbarians. (5. 97. 3)

Commentators have pointed out the resemblance to *Iliad* 11.04, *κακοῦ δ' ἄρα οἱ πέλεν ἀρχή*, 'and this was the beginning of his [Patroclus'] downfall', which is the first prolepsis of Patroclus' death. Plutarch, quoted approvingly by How and Wells, took offence at Herodotus calling the Athenian expedition to liberate

is not consistent: on p. 122 he speaks of 'non-chronological order', but somewhat later he states that 'aside from the dramatic placement of the history of Lydia, a generally chronological scheme of the major units obtains'.

[24] Genette (1980), 35–6.

[25] Note that Thucydides also inserts anachronies, for which see Hornblower (1994), but not on such a scale as to obscure his annalistic order and hence deserve the qualification anachronical.

Ionia κακά.[26] This comment is off the mark for two reasons: in the first place, it is more logical that with κακά Herodotus is referring not only to the Ionian revolt, but to the whole chain of events culminating in the Persian wars, which, though ending in victory for the Greeks, will bring them much suffering.[27] Thus—and this is my second point—throughout the *Histories* Herodotus makes it clear that he considers war evil (cf. esp. 6. 98, where he refers to the Persian wars and the wars for pre-eminance between the leading Greek cities as κακά).[28] This conception of war as bringing fame at the cost of sorrow is thoroughly Homeric.

What I find remarkable in 5. 97. 3 is Herodotus' prediction of misery to come, not only for the Greeks but also for the barbarians. In his proem, too, he announces that he will memorialize the glorious deeds of both Greeks and barbarians. Here again he is following the example of Homer, who shows equal compassion and admiration for Trojans and Greeks. (This 'chivalry' displayed by both authors does not, however, prevent them from designating the barbarians as 'the ones who started it', cf. above.)

The highpoint of the Ionian revolt is the sack of Sardes and the burning of the temple of Cybebe (5. 99–102). Again, the importance of this event is marked for us by the narrator through the insertion of an internal repeating prolepsis (not discussed by Pohlenz):

(2) . . . τὸ σκηπτόμενοι οἱ Πέρσαι ὕστερον ἀντενεπίμπρασαν τὰ ἐν Ἕλλησι ἱρά.

which burning the Persians afterwards made their pretext for burning on their turn the temples of Hellas. (5. 102. 1)

Indeed, of the five passages where Persians burn Greek temples (6. 19. 3, 96. 1, 101. 3; 8. 33, 8. 53. 2), there is one (6. 101. 3) which refers back to this place, telling us that the burning was an act of revenge. The detail σκηπτόμενοι in (2) is intriguing. How and Wells reject it as irrelevant: 'the Persians needed no excuse for destroying Hellenic shrines and the accidental destruction of a Lydian temple was clearly not the reason.' This may be historically true, but the detail is of prime importance in Herodotus'

[26] Plutarch, *De malignitate Herodoti*, 24; How and Wells (1928), 57–8.

[27] Pohlenz (1937) 16; Immerwahr (1966), 113.

[28] See Cobet (1986) 7.

(re)construction of events. This is the first of a number of places where either the Herodotean narrator (6. 44, 94, 7. 138) or Greek characters (7. 157) speak of the Persians using pretexts for what is in fact pure imperialism. Their interpretation is 'confirmed' in 7. 8. *β*.3, where Xerxes announces his intention to conquer all Greek cities, both guilty (of acts of war against him) and not guilty.

The idea of Persian revenge, in (2) only adumbrated by the narrator in the *ἀντ-* of *ἀντενεπίμπρασαν*, soon becomes explicit when Darius' reaction to the news of the sack of Sardes is reported:

(3) . . . *πρῶτα μὲν λέγεται αὐτόν, ὡς ἐπύθετο ταῦτα, Ἰώνων οὐδένα λόγου ποιησάμενον, . . . εἰρέσθαι οἵτινες εἶεν οἱ Ἀθηναῖοι, μετὰ πυθόμενον αἰτῆσαι τὸ τόξον, λαβόντα δὲ καὶ ἐπιθέντα ὀϊστὸν ἄνω πρὸς τὸν οὐρανὸν ἀπεῖναι, καί μιν ἐς τὸν ἠέρα βάλλοντα εἰπεῖν· Ὦ Ζεῦ, ἐκγενέσθαι μοι Ἀθηναίους τείσασθαι, εἴπαντα δὲ ταῦτα προστάξαι ἑνὶ τῶν θεραπόντων δείπνου προκειμένου αὐτῷ ἐς τρὶς ἑκάστοτε εἰπειν· Δέσποτα, μέμνεο των Ἀθηναίων.*

. . . he is first reported, upon hearing these things, to have taken no account of the Ionians . . . but to have asked who the Athenians were; and being told he called for his bow, took it, laid an arrow on it, and shot it in the air, praying: Zeus, grant me vengeance on the Athenians. After that he ordered one of his servants to say to him thrice whenever dinner was served 'Master, remember the Athenians' (5. 105. 1–2)

Pohlenz aptly remarks that 'the "master, remember the Athenians" resembles the lightning which announces a thunderstorm. It indicates the direction which both history and Herodotus' story are going to take.'[29] There is, however, more to be said about this passage. This is the place to supplement Genette's typology of analepses and prolepses. I suggest that we need another pair, viz. *true* vs. *false* analepses or prolepses. Darius' prayer to Zeus is a false prolepsis, in that he will never succeed in carrying out his revenge on the Athenians. In fact, one of the pioneers of Homeric prolepsis research, Duckworth, allowed for the phenomenon of 'false foreshadowing': 'In most cases the expressions of hope, confidence, fear or despair are unfounded and cannot be considered as forecasting the future. Nevertheless they serve as a kind of false foreshadowing and so have an important place in the structure of the epic; they keep the interest of the reader fixed on the events in store for the characters, even though he knows the true outcome.'[30] In the case of the *Histories*, too, the readers know the

[29] Pohlenz (1937), 18. [30] Duckworth (1933), 21.

outcome of the story, the defeat of the Persians by the Greeks; being told about the aspirations of the Persian kings adds to their satisfaction with this outcome.

In accordance with his desire for revenge, Darius launches a punitive expedition against the Athenians, led by Mardonius. Its start is marked by a combination of internal analepsis and prolepsis:

(4) . . . *ἐπορεύοντο δὲ ἐπί τε Ἐρέτριαν καὶ Ἀθήνας. Αὗται μὲν ὦν σφι πρόσχημα ἦσαν τοῦ στόλου, ἀτὰρ ἐν νοῷ ἔχοντες ὅσας ἂν πλείστας δύνωνται καταστρέφεσθαι τῶν Ἑλληνίδων πολίων* . . .

. . . they marched against Eretria and Athens. These cities were the avowed goal of their expedition. But their real intention being to subdue as many Greek cities as they could, . . . (6. 43. 4–44. 1)

The mention of Eretria and Athens must suffice to make the narratees recall that these two cities had sent ships to the Ionians and participated in the capture of Sardis (cf. passages 1 and 2). At the same time, we are told that in fact the Persians have set their eyes on the whole of Greece. This is a false prolepsis, since Mardonius returns empty-handed (6. 44–5).

After this fiasco Darius undertakes a diplomatic offensive, asking the Greek cities to give him 'water and earth'. Some, but not all, do so (6. 48–9). He then decides to undertake a second military expedition:

(5) *ὥστε ἀναμιμνήσκοντός τε αἰεὶ τοῦ θεράποντος μεμνῆσθαί μιν τῶν Ἀθηναίων . . . ἅμα δὲ βουλόμενος ὁ Δαρεῖος ταύτης ἐχόμενος τῆς προφάσιος καταστρέφεσθαι τῆς Ἑλλάδος τοὺς μὴ δόντας αὐτῷ γῆν τε καὶ ὕδωρ. Μαρδόνιον μὲν δὴ φλαύρως πρήξαντα τῷ στόλῳ παραλύει τῆς στρατηγίης, ἄλλους δὲ στρατηγοὺς ἀποδέξας ἀπέστελλε ἐπί τε Ἐρέτριαν καὶ Ἀθήνας, . . . ἐντειλάμενος δὲ ἀπέπεμπε ἐξανδραποδίσαντας Ἀθήνας καὶ Ἐρέτριαν ἀνάγειν ἑωυτῷ ἐς ὄψιν τὰ ἀνδράποδα.*

. . . for his servant was ever reminding him to remember the Athenians . . . and also, having this pretext, Darius wanted to subdue all men that had not given him earth and water. He dismissed Mardonius from his command, because he had not been successful in his expedition, and having appointed others (Datis and Artaphrenes), he sent them against Eretria and Athens . . . And he charged them to enslave the Athenians and Eretrians and bring the slaves into his presence. (6. 94. 1–2)

Here we have no fewer than four internal analepses (the sending of ships by Athens and Eretria, cf. passage 1; the scene with Darius' servant, cf. passage 3; Mardonius' unsuccessful expedition, described in 6. 44–5; and the partially successful diplomatic offensive in 6. 48–9),[31] a true prolepsis (the Eretrians will be enslaved: 6. 101–2 and 109), and a false prolepsis (instead of subduing all men who had not given Darius earth and enslaving the Athenians, the Persians will be defeated by the Athenians at Marathon).

When Darius hears about this defeat in 7. 1 he is even more eager to take up arms against Greece; but he dies before he can fulfil his plans, and Xerxes takes over. He will organize the third and last punitive expedition against Greece, led not by one of his generals but by himself; an event which takes up a full two books of Herodotus' *Histories*. In keeping with the significance of the moment, the launching of this third expedition is marked by a particularly large and complex knot of analepses and prolepses (7. 5–19).

It begins surprisingly: after repeated references to Darius' burning desire to march against Greece (7. 1 *bis*), the first thing we are told about Xerxes is that initially he was not at all eager to do so (7. 5), and had to be persuaded by one of his generals, Mardonius, and some Greeks, including the oracle-monger Onomacritus (7. 5–6). One of the functions of this prelude is to rehearse some of the arguments which Xerxes will later use to motivate his plan to launch an expedition (revenge for all the evil the Greeks have visited upon the Persians, and the attractions of Hellas), and to introduce one of his strategies (to build a bridge over the Hellespont).

Just as, in the Homeric epics, major turns in the plot are punctuated by assembly scenes, so at this crucial point Herodotus has Xerxes assemble the Persian nobles to discuss his plan. The first speaker is the convener Xerxes himself, who gives three reasons for his expedition against Greece: revenge, inherited imperialism, and the attractions of Hellas. Let us first take a closer look at the motive of revenge:

(6) . . . *οὐ πρότερον παύσομαι πρὶν ἢ ἕλω τε καὶ πυρώσω τὰς Ἀθήνας, οἵ γε ἐμὲ καὶ πατέρα τὸν ἐμὸν ὑπῆρξαν ἄδικα ποιεῦντες. πρῶτα μὲν ἐς Σάρδις*

[31] Curiously enough, this passage has been overlooked by Jacoby (1913) 337, who remarks that in 6.48 'the history of the first great Persian expedition against Greece starts unobtrusively ("klanglos"), . . . and as if nothing had happened before, with the stereotypical *μετά δὲ τοῦτο*.'

ἐλθόντες ἅμα Ἀρισταγόρῃ τῷ Μιλησίῳ, δουλῷ δὲ ἡμετέρῳ, [ἀπικόμενοι] ἐνέπρησαν τά τε ἄλσεα καὶ τὰ ἱρά·

. . . I will not stop till I have taken and burnt Athens, for the unprovoked wrong that its people did to my father and me. First they came to Sardis with our slave Aristagoras and burnt the groves and the temples; . . . (7. 8. β.2)

To the by now almost trite analeptic argument of the burning of Sardes (cf. passages 3, 4, and 5) a minor detail is added: the Greeks burnt not only the temples (the plural is a rhetorical exaggeration) but also the groves. This detail does not appear in the actual description by the Herodotean narrator in 5. 101. Either Xerxes is simply giving a fuller account or—and this is more plausible—he has invented this detail in order to build up his case against the Greeks. The Persians are very fond of trees,[32] and burning groves is therefore considered a major offence.

A new analeptic argument is Marathon:

(7) δεύτερα δὲ ἡμέας οἷα ἔρξαν ἐς τὴν σφετέρην ἀποβάντας, ὅτε Δᾶτίς τε καὶ Ἀρταφρένης ἐστρατήγεον, [τὰ] ἐπίστασθέ κου πάντες.

secondly, the kind of things they did to us during the expedition of Datis and Artaphrenes, I think you all know. (7. 8. β.3)

Here, for obvious reasons, Xerxes only alludes to this painful event from the past. He even refrains from mentioning the earlier punitive expedition by Mardonius, which was also unsuccessful. What counts is that these events call for revenge, but no Persian likes to be reminded too much of the exact details. However, the 'I think you all know' is also addressed by the narrator to his Greek narratees, who, on the contrary, will only too gladly remember Marathon. Soon we will come across more examples of analepses and prolepses which are interpreted differently by the Persian characters in the story and the Greek narratees.[33]

I turn to the argument of inherited imperialism. Again, Xerxes looks to the past:

(8) τὰ μέν νυν Κῦρός τε καὶ Καμβύσης πατήρ τε ⟨ὁ⟩ ἐμὸς Δαρεῖος κατεργάσαντο καὶ προσεκτήσαντο ἔθνεα, ἐπισταμένοισι εὖ οὐκ ἄν τις λέγοι.

Now of the nations that Cyrus and Cambyses and Darius my father

[32] Cf 7. 5. 3 and Stein's note ad loc.

[33] For this phenomenon, whereby speeches in historiography have different messages for characters and readers, see Macleod (1982).

subdued and added to our realm, none need tell you, for you all know. (7. 8. α.1)

This *praeteritio* functions in the first place within the context of Xerxes' rhetoric; set on persuading his Persian generals to undertake the expedition against Greece, he spends the first part of his speech on making it clear that imperialism belongs to Persia, and therefore that what he proposes is nothing new. But, as in passage (7), his words are also relevant for the narratees. They, too, 'know the nations that Cyrus and Cambysus and Darius added', because they have been told about them by the narrator in the *Histories*. In other words, here we find the *raison d'être* for Books 1–4, which analysts complain have so little to do with Herodotus' main theme, the confrontation between East and West.[34] Simplifying matters somewhat, we can say that Herodotus needed this long run-up to allow this conversation to take place. Only now are the Greek narratees in the same position as Xerxes' Persian addressees, and able fully to appreciate his words. Again, this may be seen as a Herodotean exploitation and expansion of a Homeric technique, in that the Homeric narrator, too, is wont to inform his narratees beforehand, to enable them to understand an ensuing speech. For example, in introducing Andromache he mentions her father Eetion, thereby allowing this character to use the death of her father by Achilles as a powerful emotional argument in her attempt to persuade Hector to remain inside Troy (*Iliad* 6. 394–8, 414–20).[35]

The imperialism of the Persians is, according to Xerxes, actually sanctioned by the gods:

(9) *ὡς γὰρ ἐγὼ πυνθάνομαι τῶν πρεσβυτέρων, οὐδαμά κω ἠτρεμίσαμεν, ἐπείτε παρελάβομεν τὴν ἡγεμονίην τήνδε παρὰ Μήδων, Κύρου κατελόντος Ἀστυάγεα· ἀλλὰ θεός τε οὕτω ἄγει . . .*

As I learn from our eldest, we have as yet never been inactive, ever since Cyrus deposed Astyages and we took over leadership from the Medes. A god leads us this way (7. 8. α.1)

For all its brevity, this last remark contains a wealth of implica-

[34] Cf. e.g. Jacoby (1913), 333–52 and Von Fritz (1967), 113.

[35] A similar small-scale example from Herodotus is 7. 2, where the detailed information about Darius' (two sets of) sons allows us to savour Demaratus' advice in 7. 3.

tions. To start with, if we look back at the expansionism of Xerxes' predecessors, we find no divine motivation. On the contrary, rather mundane reasons play a role, the ultimate being Atossa's request to Darius to conquer Greece because she would like to have some 'Laconian, Argive, Attic, or Corinthian maidservants' (3. 134). When Xerxes now starts talking about a divine mission, he is perhaps inspired by the oracles of Onomacritus, which he had received just before this council (7. 6). Since the narratees know—what Xerxes does not—that Onomacritus had given him only positive oracles, carefully withholding the negative ones, they may already be smiling at Xerxes' trust in the gods. Moreover, knowing that gods usually lead mortals to their destruction[36] (and, of course, knowing the outcome of Xerxes' expedition), they may attribute an ominous connotation to Xerxes' words. Finally, the very next scene will show that Xerxes' claim to be led by the gods has a less pleasant meaning for him, when a series of divine dreams will literally force him to stick to his decision to march on Greece, against his own and Artabanus' better judgement (7. 12–19). (It is, of course, only in retrospect that the narratees can attach this ironic shade of meaning to Xerxes' words.)[37]

Xerxes' third reason is Hellas itself:

(10) *χώρην . . . τῆς νῦν ἐκτήμεθα οὐκ ἐλάσσονα οὐδὲ φλαυροτέρην παμφορωτέρην δέ*

a land neither less nor worse but more fertile than that which we now possess (7. 8. α.2)

Here he is repeating, in a slightly different form, what Mardonius had earlier said to him in private:

(11) *. . . τούτου δὲ τοῦ λόγου παρενθήκην ποιεέσκετο τήνδε, ὡς ἡ Εὐρώπη περικαλλὴς [εἴη] χώρη καὶ δένδρεα παντοῖα φέρει τὰ ἥμερα ἀρετήν τε ἄκρη . . .*

. . . he [Mardonius] would add to this that Hellas was a very beautiful country, one that bore all kinds of orchard trees, a land of high excellence . . . (7. 5. 3)

With regard to passage (11), Jacoby remarks that here Herodotus

[36] Commentators draw attention to Soph. *OC*. 252–4, 997–8 and Xen. *An*. 6. 3. 18.

[37] For the retrospective reinterpretation of earlier parts of a literary work, see Sternberg (1978), 70.

suppressed his habit of inserting a geographical and ethnographical excursus at the point where a barbarian sets eyes on a strange country. In his view, Herodotus' reasons are aesthetic: to interrupt his main story at this dramatic point for a Hellenic *logos* would break the tension.[38] In my view, another consideration may have played a role. Herodotus will later present geographical information about Greece, not in the form of a separate *logos*, but as an integral part of his story; he will use Xerxes' march through Hellas as a framework for a description of that country, in the following manner:

(12) *διαβὰς δὲ τοῦ Λίσου ποταμοῦ τὸ ῥέεθρον ἀπεξξηρασμένον πόλιας Ἑλληνίδας τάσδε παραμείβετο, Μαρώνειαν, Δίκαιαν, Ἄβδηρα. ταύτας τε δὴ παρεξήιε καὶ κατὰ ταύτας λίμνας ὀνομαστὰς τάσδε, Μαρωνείης μὲν μεταξὺ καὶ Στρύμης κειμένην Ἰσμαρίδα, κατὰ δὲ Δίκαιαν Βιστονίδα, ἐς τὴν ποταμοὶ δύο ἐσιεῖσι τὸ ὕδωρ, Τραῦός τε καὶ Κόμψατος.*

Having crossed the bed (then dried up) of the river Lisus he [Xerxes] passed by the Greek cities of Maronea, Dicaea, and Abdera. Past these he went, and past certain lakes of repute near to them, the Ismarid lake that lies between Maronea and Stryme, and near Dicaea the Bistonian lake, into which the rivers Travus and Compensatus disembogue. (7. 109. 1)

Now why does the Herodotean narrator adopt this—unusual, but highly elegant—procedure?[39] I will suggest an answer to this question at the end of my paper.

So much for Xerxes'—largely analeptic—arguments for wanting to march on Greece. His—proleptic—expectations also deserve our attention:

(13) *μέλλω ζεύξας τὸν Ἑλλήσποντον ἐλᾶν στρατὸν διὰ τῆς Εὐρώπης ἐπὶ τὴν Ἑλλάδα, ἵνα Ἀθηναίους τιμωρήσωμαι . . . οὐ πρότερον παύσομαι πρὶν ἢ ἕλω τε καὶ πυρώσω τὰς Ἀθήνας . . .*

I intend to bridge the Hellespont and to lead an army through Europe against Greece, in order that I may punish the Athenians . . . (Therefore) I will not stop till I have taken and burnt Athens . . . (7. 8. β.1)

Like his father Darius (cf. passages 3 and 5), Xerxes wants to take

[38] Jacoby (1913), 349.

[39] We find it on only one other occasion, in embryonic form, in the Scythian expedition. Cf. e.g. 4. 85–7, where a description of the Pontus is integrated into the story through the device of making Darius view it from a high point.

revenge on the Athenians and burn their city. In his case, this is a partially true prolepsis, in that he will burn Athens (in 8. 53), but since he will then be defeated by the Greeks at Salamis, he will not really have his revenge on them.

But, again like his father (cf. passage 4), his aspirations are in fact much greater:

(14) *εἰ τούτους τε καὶ τοὺς τούτοισι πλησιοχώρους καταστρεψόμεθα, οἳ Πέλοπος τοῦ Φρυγὸς νέμονται χώρην, γῆν τὴν Περσίδα ἀποδέξομεν τῷ Διὸς αἰθέρι ὁμουρέουσαν. οὐ γὰρ δὴ χώρην γε οὐδεμίαν κατόψεται ἥλιος ὁμουρέουσαν τῇ ἡμετέρῃ, ἀλλά σφεας πάσας ἐγὼ ἅμα ὑμῖν πίαν χώρην θήσω, διὰ πάσης διεξ-ελθὼν τῆς Εὐρώπης.*

if we subdue those men, and their neighbours who live in the land of Pelops the Phrygian, we shall show the Persian territories to have the same borders as Zeus' heaven, for the sun will not behold any other country bordering ours, but I will make all into one country, when I have crossed through the whole of Europe. (7. 8. *γ*.1)

Xerxes' object is no longer Athens, but Greece, Europe, indeed the whole world. Accomplishing this mission would make him Zeus' equal on earth. For the Greek narratees, simply formulating such a desire is courting disaster, and again (cf. passage 10) they will take these words as ominous.[40] Indeed, this desire will not be fulfilled, and after Salamis Xerxes himself will give up his attempts. Interestingly enough, he will be advised to do so by Queen Artemisia in the following words:

(15) *σὺ δέ, τῶν εἵνεκα τὸν στόλον ἐποιήσαο, πυρώσας τὰς Ἀθήνας ἀπελᾷς.*

as for you, you will do best to march home, since you have burnt Athens, which was the purpose of your expedition. (8. 102. 3)

In an effort to help the great Persian king save face, she focuses on his moderate ambitions of passage 13, tactfully leaving out the much larger ones of passage 14.

The first to react to Xerxes' speech is Mardonius, who is, of course, strongly in favour of the undertaking he himself initiated. He rehearses the points of revenge and inherited imperialism, and

[40] This is the first in a set of passages where Xerxes is compared to Zeus and hence pictured as a man who oversteps his mortal limits and therefore deserves to be punished; cf. 5. 49, 7. 56, and 8. 80.

adds one related to the ineffective way their Greek opponents fight. To back up this last point, he turns to the past:

(16) *ἐπειρήθην δὲ καὶ αὐτὸς ἤδη ἐπελαύνων ἐπὶ τοὺς ἄνδρας τούτους ὑπὸ πατρὸς τοῦ σοῦ κελευσθείς, καί μοι μέχρι Μακεδονίης ἐλάσαντι καὶ ὀλίγον ἀπολιπόντι ἐς αὐτὰς Ἀθήνας ἀπίκεσθαι οὐδεὶς ἠντιώθη ἐς μάχην.*

I myself have experienced their [the Greeks'] worth when by your father's command I marched against them, and I came as far as Macedonia and almost as far as Athens herself, but nobody stepped forward to fight me . . . (7. 9. α.2)

This is clearly a false internal analepsis, since the narrator (6. 45) and Darius (6, 94, passage 5 above) had concurred in branding Mardonius' expedition a failure.[41] Deeming an attack the best form of defence, Mardonius himself boldly broaches the topic which Xerxes had tactfully glossed over (cf. passage 7) and presents the first punitive expedition against Athens as well-nigh a victory. This one example of a false analepsis—and there are many more in the *Histories*—tells us a great deal about the ancient historians' relationship to historical truth: if historical characters can distort the past for their own rhetorical purposes, why should we expect the narrator to act differently? Once more, Herodotus here had a Homeric precedent, since in the epics too we see both characters and narrator 'making the past'.[42]

The third speaker is Artabanus (a specimen of the well-known Herodotean figure of the 'warner'), who alone dares to oppose the plan for an expedition. He too uses analepses and prolepses as arguments, carefully opposing them to those of the previous speakers. He begins by countering Xerxes' point of the inherited imperialism of his forefathers (cf. passage 8), bringing to the fore an expedition which was *not* successful:

(17) *ἐγὼ δὲ καὶ πατρὶ τῷ σῷ, ἀδελφεῷ δὲ ἐμῷ, Δαρείῳ ἠγόρευον μὴ στρατεύεσθαι ἐπὶ Σκύθας, ἄνδρας οὐδαμόθι γῆς ἄστυ νέμοντας· ὁ δὲ ἐλπίζων Σκύθας τοὺς νομάδας καταστρέψεσθαι ἐμοί τε οὐκ ἐπείθετο, στρατευσάμενός τε πολλοὺς καὶ ἀγαθοὺς τῆς στρατιῆς ἀποβαλὼν ἀπῆλθε. σὺ δέ, ὦ βασιλεῦ, μέλλεις ἐπ' ἄνδρας στρατεύεσθαι πολλὸν ἔτι ἀμείνονας ἢ Σκύθας.*

[41] Cf. Solmsen (1982), 84; Pohlenz (1937), 122.

[42] See Andersen (1990). For the rhetoric of historiography, see Wiseman (1970), 27–40 and Woodman (1988).

For I also urged your father, my brother, Darius, not to lead his army against the Scythians, who nowhere have cities to live in. But he, in his hope to subdue the nomad Scythians, would not be guided by me; he led his army and came back after losing many of his best men. And you, king, intend to go against men who are much better than the Scythians. (7. 10. *α*.2)

He uses this internal repeating analepsis of the Scythian expedition (which was recounted by the Herodotean narrator in 6. 83–144) as a dissuasive paradigm in an a fortiori reasoning: if Darius did not manage to defeat the Scythians, what can Xerxes expect from taking on the Greeks, who are much better fighters than the Scythians?[43]

Next, Artabanus turns to Xerxes' plan to build a bridge over the Hellespont (cf. passage 13):

(18) *ζεύξας φῂς τὸν Ἑλλήσποντον ἐλᾶν στρατὸν διὰ τῆς Εὐρώπης ἐς τὴν Ἑλλάδα. καὶ δὴ καὶ συμήνεικε ἤτοι κατὰ γῆν ἢ [καὶ] κατὰ θάλασσαν ἑσσωθῆναι, ἢ καὶ κατ' ἀμφότερα· οἱ γὰρ ἄνδρες λέγονται εἶναι ἄλκιμοι, πάρεστι δὲ καὶ σταθμώσασθαι, εἰ στρατίην γε τοαύτην σὺν Δάτι καὶ Ἀρταφρένεϊ ἐλθοῦσαν ἐς τὴν Ἀττικὴν χώρην μοῦνοι Ἀθηναῖοι διέφθειραν. οὐκ ὦν ἀμφοτέρῃ σφι ἐχώρησε. ἀλλ' ἢν τῇσι νηυσὶ ἐμβάλωσι καὶ νικήσαντες ναυμαχίῃ πλέωσι ἐς τὸν Ἑλλήσποντον καὶ ἔπειτα λύσωσι τὴν γέφυραν, γοῦτο δή, βασιλεῦ, γίνεται δεινόν.*

You say that you intend to bridge the Hellespont and then lead an army through Europe against Greece. Now suppose it would befall you to be defeated on land or on sea, or even on both. For these men are called valiant, and this can be proven, seeing that the Athenians alone destroyed such a large army coming with Datis and Artaphrenes to Attica. Be it granted that they would not be successful on both fronts. But if they would attack us with their ships and defeat us in a sea battle and thereafter would sail to the Hellespont and break your bridge, that, king, would be a real threat. (7. 10. *β*.1–2)

In keeping with his status as warner, Herodotus allows Artabanus to give a fairly accurate prophecy of what will happen: the Persians will be defeated in a sea battle (Salamis) and the Greeks will consider sailing to the Hellespont to destroy the bridge (a plan from which they are only barely dissuaded; cf. 8. 97, 108, 111, 117, 110). This is an instance of the technique, found in both Herodotus and

[43] It is because of this paradigmatic function that the Scythian expedition is recounted in such detail; for the relation between the Scythian and Greek expeditions, see Immerwahr (1966), 106–10.

(especially) Thucydides, whereby one of two speakers in a situation of deliberation predicts exactly what will happen; in this way, the narratees are given a means by which to evaluate the relative merits of the arguments put forward in the discussion.[44] In the course of his prophetic vision Artabanus also weaves in a brief analepsis, the Persian defeat at Marathon, bringing to the fore precisely what Xerxes had preferred to allude to in the vaguest terms (cf. passage 7) and substantiating his own earlier claim that the Greeks are excellent fighters (cf. passage 17), thereby countering Mardonius' falsely optimistic picture of the Greek enemy (cf. passage 16).

To back up his prophecy concerning the dangers of a bridge over the Hellespont, Artabanus returns to the Scythian expedition, when Darius bridged the river Ister, and it was due to the loyalty of Histiaeus and his Ionians that the bridge was not destroyed and the Persians robbed of their return (7. 10. γ.1.2); this is an internal repeating analepsis of 4. 133–44.

He ends his speech with a long and typically Herodotean diatribe on the envy of the gods, which is intended to temper Xerxes' optimism about the gods supporting Persian imperialism (cf. passage 9). Even here we find, couched in general terms, a fairly exact prolepsis of what later will befall the Persian army (e.g. in 8. 37–8):

(19) *οὕτω δὲ καὶ στρατὸς πολλὸς ὑπὸ ὀλίγου διαφθείρεται κατὰ τοιόνδε· ἐπεάν σφι ὁ θεὸς φθονήσας φόβον ἐμβάλῃ ἢ βροντήν, δι' ὧν ἐφθάρησαν ἀναξίως ἑωυτῶν.*

In like way even a numerous host is destroyed by a lesser one, when the jealous god sends panic or thunder, whereby they perish in an unworthy way.

Artabanus shares the fate of most warners in Herodotus, and Greek literature in general, in that his warning is not heeded. In the last speech of this council scene, Xerxes angrily declares that he will carry out his plan to take revenge and thus earn himself an honourable place in his gallery of ancestors (cf. passage 8).

[44] Hunter (1973) 178: 'in major debates later *erga* eventually demonstrate the superiority of one *logos*.'

THE 'KNOWLEDGE IS POWER' MOTIF

It is with regret that I leave Herodotus' story at this point, just as it is about to take a surprising turn in the form of Xerxes' nocturnal change of mind and harsh correction by a series of divine dreams. But I want to return to passage 17. Let us for a moment follow Artabanus in his recollection of the past and see how the narrator described the moment when he advised Darius against the Scythian expedition:

(20) *Παρασκευαζομένου Δαρείου ἐπὶ τοὺς Σκύθας . . . Ἀρτάβανος ὁ Ὑστάσπεος, ἀδελφεὸς ἐὼν Δαρείου, ἐχρήιζε μηδαμῶς αὐτὸν στρατιὴν ἐπὶ Σκύθας ποιέεσθαι, καταλέγων τῶν Σκυθέων* <u>*τὴν ἀπορίην*</u>. *ἀλλ' οὐ γὰρ ἔπειθε συμβουλεύων οἱ χρηστά . . .*

While Darius was making preparations against the Scythians, Artabanus . . . asked him not to make an expedition against the Scythians, summing up the difficulties of handling them. But when he could not persuade him, though his advice was good . . . (4. 83. 1–2)

The argument employed here by Artabanus versus Darius is that the Scythians are difficult to handle (because of their nomadism). Interestingly enough, this very argument has been prepared for by the narrator in the course of his long ethnographical and geographical excursus on the Scythians:

(21) (the Scythians have made one very clever discovery:)
τοῖσι γὰρ μήτε ἄστεα μήτε τείχεα ᾖ ἐκτισμένα, ἀλλὰ φερέοικοι ἐόντες πάντες ἔωσι ἱπποτοξόται, ζῶντες μὴ ἀπ' ἀρότου ἀλλ' ἀπὸ κτηνέων, οἰκήματά τέ σφι ᾖ ἐπὶ ζευγέων, κῶς οὐκ ἂν εἴησαν οὗτοι ἄμαχοί τε καὶ <u>*ἄποροι*</u> *προμίσγειν;*

For when men have no cities or walls, but all are housebearers and mounted archers, living not by tilling the soil but by cattle-rearing and carrying their house on their waggons, how should not these be invincible and impossible to deal with? (4. 46. 3)

I draw attention to the echo *τὴν ἀπορίην* (passage 20)≈*ἄποροι* (passage 21), which underlines the connection between the two passages. We see that a descriptive excursus, the main butt of the analyst school, does in fact have a plot function, in that it provides the narratees with the necessary background information to understand and appreciate Artabanus' argument in passage 20. We are dealing here with the same phenomenon discussed in connection with passage 8: exploiting and expanding what is essentially a Homeric narrative technique, Herodotus provides his narratees with the necessary information—whether geographical, ethnographical, or historical—to understand a speech by one of the historical characters. It is interesting to see that Herodotus' method, in its turn, will be followed by Thucydides, for example, at the beginning of the Sicilian expedition. He first notes that most of the Athenians were ignorant of the great size of the island and the large number of its inhabitants (6. 1), next proceeds to describe size and number in an ethnographic excursus of five chapters (6. 2–5), and only then has his historical characters declare themselves on the subject (6. 11, 17, 20).

Let us consider this phenomenon a little longer, whereby the Herodotean narrator provides information to his narratees, who, armed with that information, can appreciate and evaluate the words of the historical characters in the story. It seems related to an important leitmotif (or 'thought pattern' in Immerwahr's terminology) which runs through the *Histories*: the 'knowledge is power' motif.[45] At many points in the story we hear about characters who lack, desire, or provide information—whether true or false—about their opponent. Thus, when Darius is exhorted by his wife to conquer Greece, he sends spies to gain information about this new object of imperialism (3. 134–8). As the narrator emphatically notes, these spies were the first Persians to set eyes on mainland Greece.[46] Again, Darius has to be told in passage 3 about the Athenians. Mardonius gives Xerxes a brief and—from a military point of view—completely useless description of Greece (passage 11). In the council scene Xerxes relies on Mardonius' false information regarding the Greeks' military capacities and brushes aside Artabanus' correct information. He will only discover his opponents' valour the hard way, through defeat. We can now appreciate why Herodotus chose to present the geographical information about Greece in close connection with Xerxes' march

[45] The leitmotif has not yet been discussed anywhere. Cf., however, Lewis (1977), 148: 'and it seems to me to be a theme of the History that the Persians gradually discover what the Spartans are like.' He discusses 1. 102; 7. 101–5; 7. 209; 7. 234; 9. 48. I owe this reference to Rosalind Thomas. See also Dewald (1985) and Christ (1994).

[46] Other instances: 1. 59, 71, 102, 152; 3. 4, 17–25; 4. 44; 5. 36, 49–50, 73, 105; 7. 101–5, 209, 234; 9. 48.

through that country (cf. passage 12): it shows us the process by which this Persian king gradually gets to know Greece.

One particular instance of this leitmotif deserves special attention. It is found at the moment when the Ionians are deliberating over whether to attack the Persians:

(22) *οἱ μὲν δὴ ἄλλοι πάντες γνώμην κατὰ τὠυτὸ ἐξεφέροντο, κελεύοντες ἀπίστασθαι, Ἑκαταῖος δ' ὁ λογοποιὸς πρῶτα μὲν οὐκ ἔα πόλεμον βασιλέϊ τῶν Περσέων ἀναιρέεσθαι, καταλέγων τά τε ἔθνεα πάντα τῶν ἦρχε Δαρεῖος καὶ τὴν δύναμιν αὐτοῦ.*

All the rest spoke their minds to the same effect, favouring revolt, save only Hecataeus the historian; he advised them that they would best be guided not to make war on the king of Persia, recounting to them the tale of the nations subject to Darius, and all his power. (5. 36. 2)

Once more (cf. passage 8), the narrator allows a character to make a very brief analepsis ('recounting to them the tale of the nations subject to Darius, and all his power'), in the knowledge that he himself has provided the full information in the preceding books. Seeing that this time the speaker is a historian, I suggest that in fact this passage contains a 'metahistoriographical' message; it can be taken to represent Herodotus' justification for his many descriptive and historical digressions (and therefore, in a sense, for his anachronical structure). They are not the result of a biographical accident (that he happened to start his career as an ethnologist), but of his professional conviction that this kind of information is necessary in order to understand history (and his own story). Only people who have correct information about their opponent can take the right decision or give the right advice.[47]

CONCLUSION

In this paper I have tried to approach the problem of the structure of Herodotus' *Histories* from a fresh angle, that of narratology, and

[47] Perhaps we could even go one step further, as both John Moles and Jim Morrison have suggested to me, and add that Herodotus thought that knowledge of the past was necessary in order to take the right decisions in the present. In other words, his *Histories* have a didactical or political function (specifically, they warn imperialist Athens of his own time not to make the same mistakes as the oriental despots portrayed in his text, cf. Moles 1996). Though I find this suggestion attractive, I feel I am not yet well enough at home in Herodotus and Herodotean scholarship to take up a position.

in particular the aspect of 'order'. Even the single sample chosen for discussion, the prolepses and analepses which have to do with Xerxes' decision to march on Greece, shows both the quantity and quality of these devices in Herodotus. Narrators and characters employ them for different reasons (to inform, warn, persuade, and so on) and with very different effects (irony, suspense, and so on). Further research in this field will certainly enrich our interpretation of the text. I am thinking in particular of the many *implicit* prolepses and analepses.[48] To take one example, the mere fact that somebody is called *περιχαρής* (exceedingly glad) in Herodotus in fact signals that he will end badly.[49] This type of research may have a bearing on the even more controversial question of the genesis of the text. Thus I hope that, after my discussion of the dense network of prolepses and analepses in the Persian council scene (7. 5–11), no one will be inclined to agree with the following remark by Fornara: 'VII–IX is a "book" in itself . . . It can even be separated from what precedes without contextual damage.'[50]

[48] This distinction derives from Bal (1985), 65–6.

[49] Lateiner (1977), (1982), Chiasson (1983).

[50] Fornara (1971), 38.

8

The Snares of the Odyssey: A Feminist Narratological Reading*

Lillian E. Doherty

As I began to write the first version of this paper for the Oxford conference on which the present volume is based, I found myself, quite by coincidence, reading a detective novel in which the heroine, a young feminist scholar of American background, is likewise scheduled to speak at Oxford.[1] I should not have expected a detective novel to let the heroine go about her business and give the paper, especially since she is also portrayed as a protégée of Sherlock Holmes (the dramatic date is 1921). But I *was* a bit taken aback when she was kidnapped by a drug lord and forcibly injected with heroin for a week (to make her a de facto addict and discredit her as a witness). This not only prevented her from giving the paper but required her to be rescued by Holmes, whom she improbably agreed to marry by the end of the book. (The novel is a hybrid, being half-romance.) While a part of me was satisfied by the generically appropriate conclusion, another part was dismayed (more so, apparently, than the heroine herself) by the sudden derailment of her scholarly debut. Here I had been counting on her to uphold the honour of the feminists (not to mention the Americans), and instead she had to be rescued herself.

I hope to convince the reader of the present paper that I'm only being *half* facetious in beginning it this way. If one takes narrative seriously, one can't afford to ignore narratives that have broad popular appeal, and one can't, I think, isolate them in a category separate from the 'serious' narratives that make up the classical canon. In fact, it would be unfair to Laurie R. King, the author of the novel I've been describing, to leave the impression that it was

* This paper includes paraphrased material from Doherty (1995), and explores further ideas in Doherty (1991) and (1992).

[1] King (1995).

only good for a laugh. I read it—in fact, I went out looking for it—because I had been so engrossed by the book to which it is a sequel. That first book, *The Beekeeper's Apprentice*,[2] gives a vivid and highly entertaining account of the heroine's growth from a precocious teenager into the assistant and then the full partner of Sherlock Holmes. An interesting side-effect of my identification with her was a strong, if temporary, enhancement of my own sense of competence—not, to be sure, as a detective, but in my own business, that is, as a scholar and teacher. I don't mean to suggest that literature should be viewed as a form of self-help for the reader, like those best-sellers with titles like *The Seven Habits of Highly Effective People*.[3] What I *have* come to believe is that our stories—those we read, those we see dramatized in various media, and those we tell each other—are central to our sense(s) of identity.

In popular psychology and the mass media, 'identity' is usually presented as something highly individual. Without denying that it has important individualized elements, I would emphasize, for my present purposes, its social and ideological dimensions. My own sense of who I am is shaped not merely by my personal history, but by the possibilities held out to me by the society in which I live.[4] While stories lack the overt coercive power of institutions like courts and corporations, they provide models or templates of behaviour that may be all the more powerful for being internalized and even unconscious. *Traditional* stories and story patterns are especially important models, since whatever attractions ensured their survival in the first place are combined with the authority of age and social approval. It might be objected that in the culture of the late twentieth-century West innovation is more prized than tradition; yet the stories disseminated by our most advanced electronic media are often highly traditional. To cite only one of the most successful examples, George Lucas' *Star Wars* trilogy was consciously modelled on traditional heroic myths, including those of the Greeks.[5]

Thus, even a novel like King's, described on its jacket as 'auda-

[2] King (1994).

[3] This is the title of an actual book, an American best-seller by Stephen R. Covey (New York, 1989).

[4] In a post-structuralist analysis, these possible roles or identities are called 'subject positions' (an intentionally ambiguous term, combining the two senses of 'subject': subjected and endowed with agency). See Doherty (1995), 25, n. 38.

[5] See Pollock (1990).

cious'[6] and designed to unsettle the Victorian gender roles that prevail in the original Sherlock Holmes stories, can—indeed must, to satisfy its intended readers—observe the generic imperative of a happy ending involving the defeat of the criminals and (since the book is part romance) the marriage of the two detectives.[7] Is it too far-fetched to see in this popular novel a distant echo of the *Odyssey*? The heroine's competence, which makes her a 'match' for the hero in several senses; the violent men she is incapable of defeating by herself; the consequent need for the hero to rescue her—all these are elements of the *Odyssey* plot as well.

I don't mean to press this unlikely comparison, or to suggest that King was inspired by the *Odyssey*: her plot is also the standard plot of melodrama, which has thousands of avatars in modern fiction and drama. I note the similarity to the *Odyssey* because my response to King's novel can perhaps shed some light on my response to the epic. It may seem to some readers of this volume that to speak of 'my' response is inappropriate, even 'unscholarly'. There is always a danger of self-absorption and solipsism in focusing on one's own reactions to literature; but I have come to believe that *not* to consider these reactions is either to fool oneself (by denying them) or to neglect an essential piece of the evidence at a critic's disposal. If the standpoint of the observer is important in the physical sciences, how much more central must it be to the study of literature!

Let me begin, then, by sketching in outline some of my own history as a scholar, which has led to my current attempts to combine new theoretical perspectives with more traditional modes of literary analysis. While each scholar's formation is in certain ways unique, I think I am not untypical of those classicists of my generation (the post-World War II 'baby boom') who are receptive to the new approaches.

My training, at both the undergraduate and graduate levels, was quite traditional and had three basic components: linguistic, historical, and 'New Critical'.[8] I was expected to learn the morphology,

[6] This opinion is credited to an anonymous reviewer for the *Chicago Tribune*.

[7] Because the earlier book (*The Beekeeper's Apprentice*) was designed as the first of a series, the union of hero and heroine could be deferred; but in the manner of the old serials, the paperback publisher has printed the first chapter of the second book at the end of the first.

[8] 'The New Criticism' is the name commonly given to an American school of formalist criticism that flourished from the 1920s to the 1950s; its influence on the

syntax, and vocabularies of classical Greek and Latin; to grasp the historical framework in which the most important canonical works were produced; and to appreciate the formal and thematic structures of these works by the literary-critical technique of 'close reading'. As an undergraduate, I was a 'double major' in Classics and French, so I also learned to do *explication de texte*, a form of close reading that has much in common with 'New Critical' approaches.[9] As a French major in the early 1970s, I read Foucault and Roland Barthes, but almost incidentally, because they were recommended to me by a charismatic teacher, not because theory was considered an important part of a literary education.

I would describe my training as traditional, not just because the methods taught me were the old 'tried and true' ones (in fact, New Criticism, as its name suggests, wasn't even particularly old). Rather, this was a traditional education because the emphasis was always on preserving and valuing the tradition. Linguistic and historical competence were essential for those of us who would be the guardians and interpreters of the canon, while New Criticism or *explication de texte* would enhance our own appreciation, and that of our students, for the aesthetic perfection of individual works. I should note that this emphasis on appreciation, however tempered by the feminist readings of more recent years, has remained an essential element of my work as both scholar and teacher. I often suspect that the deepest resistance to theoretical approaches may not be a disagreement about methods but a fear that theory is undermining or even 'trashing' the tradition we have been trained to preserve. I have felt some of this resistance myself, and still feel a tension in my work between the critical impulse and the *habitus* of appreciation.[10]

In graduate school I added some anthropology to my repertoire of analytic frameworks, primarily because I studied with James

teaching of literature in the USA is explored in Kenner (1976) and Cain (1982). See also Spurlin and Fischer (1995), with an excellent annotated bibliography by Anna Carew-Miller.

[9] Some examples of handbooks on *explication de texte* designed for the American market are Mermier and Boilly-Widmer (1972) and Katz and Hall (1970). Interestingly, the 1996 edition of Mermier and Boilly-Widmer has a new title (*Analyse de Texte* has replaced *Explication* . . .), but except for an expansion of the canon from which examples are drawn, the book is very little altered.

[10] I will have more to say about this issue below.

Redfield at the University of Chicago.[11] This was during the middle and late 1970s, when Lévi-Strauss was inspiring French classicists like Vernant, Détienne, and Vidal-Naquet to apply structuralist analysis to Greek myths and social institutions. Yet, in spite of my exposure to these developments, I did not change my own approach, which was still firmly anchored in the close reading I had done as an undergraduate, I was, after all, a student of literature, as I told myself, and I wrote a very traditional literary thesis, a study of the characterization of Achilles and Odysseus and their deployment as foils for one another in the Homeric epics.

It was not until I was out of graduate school and trying to establish my credentials as a scholar by publishing that I began to look more seriously at new theoretical frameworks. I had not received a very thorough 'socialization' as a scholar, for a variety of reasons, including, I think, the generation gap between myself and my professors, who had gotten their jobs in times when jobs were plentiful. I was fortunate to have a good friend of my own age who was more fully initiated by her own mentors into the mysteries of sending abstracts, attending professional meetings, and writing for publication. This friend, whose field is feminist theory, also convinced me that *whatever* approach I took as a scholar, there was a theory implicit in it. That is, I had implicit assumptions about the structure of knowledge, and about the structure of society, that shaped what I saw when I looked at a text. I set about uncovering at least some of these assumptions—to bring them to consciousness, if that were possible, in hopes of clarifying and justifying my work. At the same time, I was learning that to write for publication was to enter a conversation far wider than any to which I had yet contributed. This seemed to me (and to the readers of my early papers) to require a greater familiarity with contemporary theory.

With the benefit of hindsight, I can describe this phase in my own career as one of *bricolage*, to use a term proposed by Lévi-Strauss. I spent a long time 'tinkering' with a variety of theories and methods, borrowing what I found helpful from each. I was never so powerfully affected by a single thinker or school as to become a 'follower' or 'true believer'. But I did get my bearings, as

[11] As the son of anthropologist Robert Redfield, he had observed his father's fieldwork at close range, and eventually sought to apply anthropological concepts to his study of classical texts. Though his linguistic training was traditional, he once told me he had a hard time persuading other classicists that he was 'one of them' and not an 'outsider', i.e. an anthropologist.

a scholar and simultaneously as a teacher. In what follows, I sketch by way of example two of the theoretical paths I have taken, before returning, in my conclusion, to the ways in which my traditional philological and literary training still informs my work.[12] On one level, I see these theoretically informed approaches as paths through the text of Homer. At the same time, they are paths through the terrain of contemporary scholarship.

The first path, that of narratology, is more properly a method than a theory, though it is grounded in linguistic theory. The second path, which I have labelled feminist in my title, is not only theoretical but political, in a broad sense of that term.[13] Let me emphasize here that mine is only one of many available feminist approaches. I do not presume to speak for all feminist classicists, much less for all those who would call themselves feminists.

Despite its somewhat forbidding name and nomenclature, narratology is not an arcane science but a straightforward method of analysing narratives. Like any method of research, it involves posing a set of questions, and I turned to it because the old questions I had been asking of the Homeric text no longer seemed productive to me. The answers seemed too pat, too predictable, even—dare I admit it?—boring. So I was looking for new questions. Narratology may have been an unlikely choice for a Homerist, since it was invented by the French scholar Gérard Genette for the analysis of modern prose fiction—specifically, the work of Proust. But by the time I came across it in the early 1990s, it had been systematized by Mieke Bal and, more importantly for my own work, applied to the Homeric text by Irene de Jong.[14]

The remarkable thing about a new set of questions is that it can make one see with new eyes a terrain covered a hundred times before. The new questions I began to ask, prompted by de Jong and Bal, were these: in any given line of the Homeric text, who is speaking, and to whom? More subtly, whose perspective informs the way the story is told? To use the narratological term, who *focalizes* a given piece of narrative? These proved to be highly productive questions, especially when posed of the *Odyssey*, with its

[12] In what follows, I summarize two strands in the argument of my book (Doherty 1995).

[13] I should note that there are narratologists who do not see their method as compatible with feminism. See the exchange between Lanser (1986 and 1988) and Diengott (1987) in the journal *Style*.

[14] See especially Bal (1985) and de Jong (1987).

elaborate narrative framework. Clearly, there is a single 'primary' narrator, the epic narrator who frames and orchestrates the work as a whole; but there are also many characters who serve as internal, or 'secondary', narrators, and who at times contradict each other. Some of these secondary narrators report the words of yet other characters, who can be seen as narrating on a third level; an example would be the sea-god Proteus, whose words (in direct discourse) are reported to Telemachus by Menelaus. All narrators are also focalizers; that is to say, their perspectives on the action inform the accounts they give of that action. But characters who do not narrate may also serve as focalizers if their perspectives are emphasized in passages narrated by others. I see traces of this 'embedded' focalization in a number of scenes, including the so-called 'catalogue of heroines', the account of famous women whom Odysseus meets in the Underworld (11: 235–329).

From this analysis a kind of narrative hierarchy emerges, in which some positions have greater weight than others. I see two distinct, if related, elements that contribute to the narrative hierarchy: the space allotted to different narrators and focalizers, and the degree to which each is 'authorized'—that is, identified as reliable—by the structure of the epic as a whole. Space alone is not enough to assure a narrator of authority; but without space in which to elaborate her version of the story, a character's authority remains hypothetical. Queen Arete, for example, is presented as both powerful and honorable, a decisive figure whose approval of Odysseus makes the last leg of his journey possible. Yet she narrates a total of only twelve lines,[15] and there are few traces of her focalization in passages narrated by others. Whatever power is attributed to her, it cannot be the power of narration, the power to control the shape of the story. By contrast, the epic narrator and, after him, the hero assume the highest places in the narrative hierarchy because they narrate and focalize the greater part of the story. In so doing, they provide the controlling perspectives from which it is told. Of course, the perspective of a narrator can be undercut or qualified by other elements of a work, including the conflicting testimony of different narrators. For the most part, however, my research has convinced me that Odysseus and the epic narrator of the *Odyssey* are being presented as reliable narrators. Moreover, they reinforce each other's authority, since

[15] 7. 237–9, 8. 443–5, 11. 336–41.

Odysseus is described as a skilled bard and himself praises the performances of bards within the poem. The epic narrator even allows his hero to take over the narration of one-fourth of the poem, that is, Books 9 to 12, with only a short interruption in Book 11. This structural detail, I believe, only reinforces the symbiotic relationship between the epic narrator and his hero.[16]

The other element on which narratology focuses is the recipient of narration, the narratee. While recognizing that the term 'audience' is less precise, I tend to use it in preference to 'narratee'. My aim is not to appease those who reject such precise terms as jargon—though I am myself somewhat put off by Mieke Bal's formidably specialized terminology. I choose the term 'audience' because it can readily be applied to real, historical persons—actual audiences—as well as to internal narratees. While I think it is essential to differentiate between these two types of audience, I also want to consider the relationships between them. Here I depart from narratology proper and borrow—in my *bricolage*—from what is variously called reception theory, reader-response, or audience-oriented criticism.

Within a narrative text, each narrator has his or her own audience. An internal narrator like Odysseus has an internal audience—or rather, a series of such audiences for his various tales—while the epic narrator addresses an audience at his own narrative level, that is, a hypothetical audience that stands outside and 'above' the level of the internal narrators, and is therefore in a position to grasp and judge the narrative as a whole. Various terms have been proposed for this hypothetical audience: the purely descriptive narratological term is 'extradiegetic' (that is, 'outside the narrative'), while reader-response critics have spoken of the 'implied', 'intended', or 'model' audience. Let me emphasize that this is not an actual audience, composed of living human beings. Like the epic narrator who addresses it, this hypothetical audience is purely fictive. It might almost be called a persona, but it is more elusive than most characters because it is characterized only indirectly, by the ways the narrative addresses it.

In my book on the *Odyssey*, I used the term 'implied audience',

[16] There are, of course, important differences between the perspectives of Odysseus and the epic narrator; but though the latter sees more, he does not seriously undercut either Odysseus' reliability as a narrator or his centrality as a focalizer. See Doherty (1995), 164 and 173–4.

despite my reservations about the work of Wolfgang Iser, from whom I borrowed it.[17] I believe it is possible to speak of an implied audience for the *Odyssey* because of the wealth of *internal* narration it features. The repeated episodes of storytelling, with their elaborately characterized narrators and audiences, allow the epic narrator to establish norms or precedents for the reception of stories that in turn suggest the kind of audience he is himself addressing. Often, stories-within-the-story are implicitly framed to please particular members of the internal audience—as the tales of Helen and Menelaus are framed to please Telemachus—so that we can already speak of an implied audience at the level of the story. As there are privileged internal narrators, who are allowed to narrate and focalize large portions of the epic, so there are privileged internal audiences, to whom important pieces of it are addressed. When considered together in their mutual relations, these privileged narrators and audiences make up an interpretive hierarchy within the epic that models the epic's own reception. I believe that this internal hierarchy of narrators and audiences can have a seductive effect on actual audiences, who may not realize that certain responses are being modelled for them.

Let me add two cautions at this point. I do not mean to suggest that the modelling I describe was deliberate or even necessarily conscious on the part of the poet. I am concerned with the effects of the narrative and not with the conscious intentions of its author, which are in any case inaccessible to us. Secondly I would not only admit but insist that *actual* audiences are capable of resisting the responses modelled for them. But I believe such resistance is more difficult than is generally admitted, precisely because the mechanisms are largely unconscious and related to the situations we ourselves occupy within a hierarchical class and gender system.

It should be clear by now that I am not satisfied with narratology as a purely formalist approach. Here I must get back to that sticky (*not* to say dirty) word, 'political'. Like New Criticism, narratology as a method could rather easily be assimilated to a traditional classics education because it can present itself as apolitical. But is it possible to *be*, and not merely seem, apolitical? Or, as my friend in feminist theory insisted, do we really have a theory all along, without exploring or even acknowledging it? I

[17] See Iser (1978). My reservations about his approach are summarized in Doherty (1995), 19, n. 29.

would argue that we do, and that for most of us it consists of an implicit ideology I would call liberal humanism. For many people, the notion of 'implicit ideology' is a contradiction in terms; to them, ideologies are overt plans to remake society, such as the various forms of socialism or feminism. By 'implicit ideology' I mean those ways of thinking that we take for granted to the point of unconsciousness. Such unconscious assumptions are sometimes referred to as the 'dominant ideology' within a society at a given historical moment.[18]

For the sake of clarity, let me give a specific example that may seem—at first glance—wholly unrelated to the *Odyssey*. A major element in liberal humanist ideology is the concept of individual choice as the primary mechanism at work in history and indeed in everyday life. (The very term *liberal*, which has become oddly taboo these days, at least in American political discourse, derives from its Latin root an emphasis on freedom and autonomy that is inseparable from the notion of choice.) In the economic sphere, advertisers and business executives insist that the free market gives us a choice of products to buy and investments to make. In the political sphere, elections are meant to be the expression of 'the people's choice'. In private life, we are urged to 'choose' our careers, our sexual partners, and our 'life-style'. Failure in all these areas is attributed to 'bad choices'.

But this implicit ideology of choice leaves out—or represses—a mass of evidence that our choices are severely limited by the structure of society and by the places we occupy within it. We cannot 'choose' to elect a political leader who is too poor to afford the mass-media campaigns that prevail in current elections. We cannot 'choose' a career in a field where there are no jobs. And a person born into the underclass cannot, except by the most heroic and exceptional effort, 'choose' the education that would make escape from that class possible. In the face of all this evidence, why do we persist in emphasizing choice, and in castigating those who 'choose' badly? Because choice is central to our implicit ideology—to our mental map of the world. We repress or deny the evidence that does not fit this map; hence, I have argued that ideology has an unconscious dimension.

What does any of this have to do with Homer? Can't we enjoy

[18] The post-structuralist critique of ideology, which informs my work, is well explicated by Weedon (1987), 27–32, who also traces its Marxist origins.

and celebrate the formal beauty of the poem, or the *mêtis* of its hero, without taking a political stand? I would argue that ultimately we cannot, because the *Odyssey* itself has a political dimension. If we simply affirm the value of the poem without examining that dimension, we risk ratifying the status hierarchies, including gender and class hierarchies, which the poem embodies. If that is what we want and mean to do, well and good; but I for one do *not* wish to validate those hierarchies.

So I use narratology not simply as an end in itself but also as a means to understand the workings of ideology. Let me add that I do not for a minute think I have myself escaped from ideology or am able to view it objectively from without. I am enmeshed in it, and my critique of it is necessarily imperfect. But I believe that it is more honest to admit my position—as I understand it—and take it into account than to try to ignore it. I think we will produce better scholarship in the long run if we put all our cards on the table.

Using narratology, then, I have arrived at the notion of an interpretive hierarchy within the *Odyssey*, composed of privileged narrators and privileged audiences. From a feminist perspective, the most interesting feature of this hierarchy is its relationship to gender hierarchy and to the dynamics of gender relations, both inside and outside the epic.[19] The *Odyssey* has understandably attracted much attention from feminist critics as one of the ancient works that gives most scope to its female characters.[20] I too have always been impressed by the strong and vivid characterization of figures like Nausicaa, Helen, Circe, and of course Penelope. At a certain stage of my research I began to ask, 'Do the *Odyssey*'s female characters have equal access to the privileges of narration and focalization and to the kinds of control over meaning that these represent? Does the epic include women in its implied audience, and if so, does it address males and females differently?'

My first set of findings concerned the internal female audiences and their relationship to the implied audience of the epic as a

[19] In my book I also touched briefly on the class dimensions of the interpretive hierarchy (see Doherty 1995, 158–9). Related issues have been treated by Rose (1992) and Thalmann (1998).

[20] The feminist-inspired work on the *Odyssey* is now too extensive to summarize adequately in a footnote. A few of the studies I have found most illuminating are Felson-Rubin (1994), Foley (1984), Murnaghan (1986), and Winkler (1990). These may be consulted for further bibliography.

whole. A survey of the contexts in which stories are told within the poem led me to divide them into two basic categories: performances for groups and stories told to individuals. The performances for groups are usually by bards, but other characters, and notably Odysseus himself, take the bard's role at times. The normative audience for these bardic performances, I found, is a group of aristocratic males with at most one aristocratic female—the mistress of the house—in attendance. If present, she is accompanied by her female slaves, but they play no part in the action of the scenes.

In two of these scenes the mistress tries to act like a full member of the audience by responding to the bard. In Book 1 Penelope asks Phemius to change the theme of his song, on the grounds that she is grieved by it. In Book 11 Arete asks the Phaeacians to increase the gifts they are giving 'her' guest, Odysseus, presumably as a reward for the excellent performance he has just given. But in each of these scenes the mistress is then told, in terms which include an identical formula, that it is up to the men to decide what the bard may sing or what reward he will receive. Telemachus tells his mother:

> . . . μῦθος δ' ἄνδρεσσι μελήσει,
> πᾶσι, μάλιστα δ' ἐμοί· τοῦ γὰρ κράτος ἔστ' ἐνὶ οἴκῳ.
>
> . . . Speech will be the men's concern,
> All men's, but mine especially, for mine is the power in the household.
> (1. 358–9)

In the case of Arete, two males in the audience agree with her proposal, but insist that it is the king's role to implement it. Alkinoos, in terms identical to those used by Telemachus, ends his speech with:

> . . . πομπὴ δ' ἄνδρεσσι μελήσει,
> πᾶσι, μάλιστα δ' ἐμοί· τοῦ γὰρ κράτος ἔστ' ἐνὶ δήμῳ.
>
> . . . His escort will be the men's concern,
> All men's, but mine especially, for mine is the power in the land.
> (11. 352–3)[21]

[21] The most famous occurrence of this formula is at *Iliad* 6. 492–3 (Hector to Andromache). For a different interpretation of its implications in all three places, see Martin (1993), 236–7.

It would seem that the normative pattern being portrayed is one in which women do not belong to the implied audience of the bard. Yet, in the case of Arete, there is evidence that Odysseus, in his bard's role, has deliberately included her in his own implied audience. What is the purpose of his lengthy account of the famous women he saw in the Underworld? He has no personal connection with these women, yet he describes his meeting with them in great detail, immediately after the meeting with his mother. He then chooses this point in his narrative to interrupt, giving the audience a chance to respond, and it is Arete who responds first. It is worth noting that he has been told not once but twice that Arete's support will be crucial to the success of his appeal to the Phaeacians.[22] I see the 'catalogue of heroines' as his implicit compliment and appeal to her.[23] He has included her in his implied audience.

Likewise, at the end of Book 23, after his reunion with Penelope, he tells to her alone the full story of his wanderings, and in so doing reverses her exclusion from the audience in Book 1.[24] I see an important connection between Arete and Penelope in their role as privileged recipients of Odysseus' tale. Both are portrayed as intelligent as well as honourable; and both are won over by Odysseus, persuaded to accept the role of his ally and helper. They are not alone in this; Calypso, Nausicaa, Circe, and even Helen are portrayed as listening to the hero and being won over by his words. But Arete and Penelope are singled out as narratees for his story as a whole, and therefore, I believe, as model female narratees for the epic itself.

Thus, the implied audience of the *Odyssey* does include women; but the epic is addressed to them as individuals, not as a group of peers like the males who listen together to Odysseus' tale, as to those of Phemius and Demodocus. Female members of the implied audience are invited to identify with the figures of Arete and Penelope, and to accept the roles[25] of chaste wife and loyal

[22] By Nausicaa (6. 310–15) and by Athena, disguised as a young Phaeacian girl (7. 53–77, esp. 75–7). It is interesting that female characters attest to the power of Arete.

[23] After reaching this conclusion on my own, I found it had been anticipated by several previous commentators, notably Stanford (1958–9), i. 381.

[24] Critics have commented on the apparently otiose length of the paraphrase at 23. 310–41 of Odysseus' tale; one possible function of this paraphrase would be to indicate that Penelope hears the full version, as it was told to the Phaeacians in Books 9–12.

[25] Or subject positions (see n. 4 above).

helpmate. As Odysseus flatters his female listeners within the poem, the poem itself flatters and woos its implied female audience—and any members of the actual audience who accept the roles thus offered them. These seductive effects are the 'snares' of the *Odyssey* to which my title refers, its 'Siren songs', to reverse the gender valence of that powerful cliché.

In a second phase of my research I turned to the role of narrator, and compared male and female characters who fill that role. To get a clearer sense of possible differences between them, I examined several pairs of internal narratives that match or juxtapose female with male narrators: Helen with Menelaus, Circe with Odysseus, Penelope with Odysseus. I also considered the fact that Eumaeus, the faithful male slave, is allowed a leisurely exchange of stories with his master, while Eurycleia, the equally faithful female slave, is placed in a position in which she must be brutally silenced lest she 'betray' Odysseus' identity. I found that, on the one hand, the epic narrator clearly allows selected female characters to narrate and thus to focalize portions of the epic. Yet, when compared with male narrators, the females tend to be portrayed as more dangerous, and the stories they tell are contained within larger narrative frameworks that do not allow them the last word. Helen's tale in Book 4, claiming she helped Odysseus when he came as a spy to Troy because she had had a change of heart, is undercut by Menelaus' account of how she later tried to entice the Greeks in the Wooden Horse to reveal their presence. Even Penelope, who is portrayed as faithful by the epic narrator, is treated with suspicion by Odysseus, the most important internal narrator and focalizer. She enjoys a brief period of narrative autonomy, in which she rejects the disguised Odysseus' predictions, sets the contest of the bow, and even resists the revealed Odysseus until he passes her more intimate test of the bed. But once she has taken him back and exchanged stories with him, she has no more to say. Odysseus has the last word, not only in their exchange of stories (23. 300–43), in which his comes second and is far longer, but in the poem as a whole, where he leaves Penelope with instructions to remain in the house and say nothing to anyone. He does not add, *ποινὴ δ' ἄνδρεσσι μελήσει*[26] but he might as well.

The Sirens are perhaps the most obvious and extreme example

[26] 'Vengeance will be the men's concern.'

of female narrators whose voices must be cut off or at least ignored lest they cause the destruction of the male hero. Not only is their direct speech limited to eight lines, but Odysseus is put on his guard against them and given elaborate instructions for avoiding their snares by Circe, herself a formerly dangerous goddess who has been converted into a helper.

What danger does the female narrator pose, and what does her fate suggest about the implied female audience of the epic? In the cases of Helen and the Sirens, and of Circe in Odysseus' initial encounter with her, the danger is presented as one of seduction through falsehood, whose ultimate aim is the betrayal and destruction of the male who listens and believes. Yet who is the most prominent seducer in the poem? Arguably, it is Odysseus himself, yet he is never described by the epic narrator as wilfully misleading or 'betraying' his female listeners. There is a double standard, I submit, in the poem's evaluation of narrators. I would further argue that the real danger of a female narrator, in a genre so heavily focalized by male figures, is that she will take over the focalization and remake the story with herself at its centre. This might indeed derail the hero's plans for his homecoming; at the same time, it might seriously alter the patterns of audience identification and response. The *Odyssey* thus offers to members of its implied female audience the roles of narratee and honoured helpmate, but warns them against the subversive role of narrator. Of course, it is possible for female members of the actual (external) audience to identify with Odysseus; but because of the poem's narrative double standard, this means identifying with a role they are being warned *as women* not to attempt. In identifying with Odysseus, then, they are on some level 'identifying against themselves'.[27]

How does my traditional classics training inform the research I have outlined here? In the first place, I continue to insist, as did my teachers, on a thorough understanding of the Greek text, and on scrupulously accurate translations of any quoted passages. (I include translations with Greek quotations because my own implied audience includes non-classicists.) I never rely on the translations of others but give my own in order to assume full responsibility for the readings I offer.[28] If a word, phrase, or

27 The expression is that of Judith Fetterley (1978), xii.

28 When the point of a quotation is to emphasize the artistic effect of a passage, I sometimes cite an existing translation on which I do not think I can improve.

formula is central to my interpretation, I search the lexicons and concordances to learn the range and nuances of its usage.

My choice of narratology as a method may well have been influenced by my literary training, for the 'New Critical' emphasis on the formal and structural properties of a work prepared me to accept a focus on narrators and narratees as formal, constitutive elements of the epic. In retrospect, I can see that the formalist approach of New Criticism meshes well with the insistence in classics on the priority of the text. Even when adopting the reception-theorists' concern for audience response, I began with internal audiences, that is, audiences who are identified as such by the work itself. The reflexive dimension of the *Odyssey*, I have argued, gives us 'licence' to speak of an implied audience whose responses are modelled by the internal audiences. My notion of a narrative hierarchy, while obviously related to the feminist critique of gender hierarchy, is also grounded in an analysis of the narrative *structure* of the epic as a whole. Finally, I describe the reading of the *Odyssey* presented in my book as a 'closed' reading—that is, one that seeks determinate patterns of meaning in the formal 'redundancies' between narrative elements and between explicit judgements of different narrators.[29] Although I acknowledge the existence of 'openings', or indeterminacies, in these patterns, I surmise that my preference for the closed reading is traceable to the formation I have described. I find myself still 'wedded', as we say—revealingly—to the text.

Nor have I lost my admiration, or my love, for the text. At the risk of stretching the marital metaphor too far, I might add that I don't want a divorce. I still consider myself a Homerist, and I teach my own students to admire the artistry and sheer beauty of the epics. I noted earlier that I would by no means claim to have freed myself from the prevailing ideology of my own time and place: I am still a liberal humanist. I value 'free choice' as an ideal, however circumscribed its scope in actuality. I even value Penelope's 'choice' to remain faithful to Odysseus, and his to return to her. At the same time, my formerly unconscious identification with the figure of Penelope has been complicated and unsettled as a result of my research. I still see her (and describe her to my students) as a clever and brave figure who is portrayed as exercising what control she has over her situation. But I also see

[29] For this use of the term 'redundancy', see Doherty (1995), 10 and n. 3.

(and describe to my students) her subordinate status in the poem, and the danger that a woman's identification with her may contribute to the acceptance of subordinate status in a 'real-life' gender hierarchy. Finally, I realize that the epic, by facilitating audience identification with its aristocratic heroine, also deflects sympathy from the slave women who are so harshly punished for a sexual 'choice' Penelope narrowly avoids having to make.[30]

These are some of the elements of my work that I would describe as political, in a broad sense of that term. For me at least, recognizing the political or ideological dimension of literature has been like opening Pandora's jar: it is not possible to return to the *status quo ante*. I would not claim that to be valuable, all criticism must have an explicit political focus. But to ignore the political ramifications of one's research is, I believe, potentially to mislead oneself and others.

To return to the question of identity, with which I began: as a feminist classicist, I find myself involved in a contradiction. I have learned to value the artistry and humanity of texts that, by their very artistry, can circumscribe my self-understanding and that of my students. My response is not to reject these texts but to take them for what they are—for *all* that they are, in my apprehension—and to supplement them with a variety of other texts, old and new, that together offer a wider range of *imaginative* possibilities to readers, be they female or male.

[30] It remains an open question whether their 'crime' should be seen as a choice. Though Melantho is rebuked for it by Penelope (19. 91–2), and the women as a group are described as going gladly to meet their lovers among the suitors (20. 6–8), Odysseus also accuses the suitors of 'sleeping with the slave women *by force*' (22. 37).

Genre

9
Introduction

Susanna Morton Braund

Just as it is hard to imagine a world without gender—we have to turn to science-fiction writers like Ursula le Guin for that—so I find it hard to imagine a literary world without genre. Yet it was not always so. Once upon a time (but not so long ago), there were philologists who preferred to dispense with abstract notions such as genre, doubtless in this case assisted by the obvious Frenchness of the word. Happily, the arguments in favour of 'genre' have been put so forcefully that the arena of debate has now shifted to focus upon the precise model of genre that is invoked. That is reflected in the two papers in this section of the book, which take for granted the usefulness of 'genre' as a critical tool and proceed to debate the adequacy and implications of different formulations of 'genre'. To this extent, the debate on genre is perhaps less polarized than the debates on other areas which feature in this volume. At the same time, because genre is so central to our attempts as moderns to begin to grasp the literature of the ancients, it becomes crucial to interrogate our preconceptions of what is entailed in genre. The two papers which follow provide marvellously complementary challenges.

Alessandro Barchiesi returns to a concept of genre promulgated in German scholarship of the 1920s, Kroll's 'crossing' of genres. He distinguishes the rigidity and essentialism of this idea from our current concerns with impurity and instability: he finds both models wanting. In his conclusion he asks what kind of literary history is still viable in the face of postmodern destabilizations of accepted categories such as 'author' and 'genre'. Marcus Wilson takes the specific case of the interpretation of Seneca's *Letters*. He attacks the inadequacy both of the category 'essay' as applied to the *Letters* in the past and of the recent theories inspired by New Historicism and postmodernism. Both contributors, then, are well versed in 'traditional' approaches and in contemporary 'theory', and both present themselves as sceptical of some of the implications of post-structuralist analysis of ancient texts.

The term 'genre' is a latecomer, although the lines of Accius inevitably cited in discussions such as this, *nam quam uaria sint genera poematorum, Baebi, | quamque longe distincta alia ab aliis, nosce* ('For learn, Baebius, how diverse the kinds of poems are, and how far some are distinct from others'), seem to represent the idea. No one, of course, wishes to deny that the ancients found ways of classifying their literary artefacts: it is clear that the Hellenistic scholars, developing Aristotle's systems of classification, devoted huge amounts of time and energy to precisely this. But it is also the case that we find ancient theories of classification wanting. It seems that the place of what we would recognize as a theory of genre was taken by theories of *imitatio*, which set specific texts in a relation of dependence to specific earlier texts. This system of ideas plugs into the metaphor of *genealogy*, according to which the critic can construct a stemma which explains the pedigree of the text under study. This emphasis perhaps reflects the enormous significance of questions of inheritance and genealogy in antiquity generally.

I suggest that the metaphors which we moderns devise under the rubric of genre are similarly a significant reflection of our central concerns. Before looking at some of the dominant metaphors in modern scholarship, let me first comment on our need and desire to devise such models of analysis. Presumably this arises from our sense of *aporia* when faced with alienness of ancient texts. Systems are formed to control bodies of material. A complete body of material might allow a closed system. What is so threatening about the ancient material is its palpable incompleteness. Yet it is also worth asking to what extent we subject the products of contemporary arts to the same kind of systematization. When I go to Twentieth Century Flicks to rent a video, I get to choose from Action/Arthouse/Cartoons/Classics/Comedy/Drama/Film Noir/French/Gangster/Gay/Horror/Musicals/Science Fiction/Thrillers/War/Weepies/Westerns (to name just some of the categories). But we all know that these labels are hints rather than definitions. So how are we to figure a system of genres for ancient literature? Do we see genre as descriptive or prescriptive? Based upon deduction or induction?

Hypostasization is, in my view, inevitable. That is, whether we start from particular texts or from an idealized form or formula, it is hard to resist the idea of separation, of something *more* than 'just' texts. But what I think matters most is not the fact of separation but how precisely we view the relationship between text and genre.

One central metaphor is that of *biology and genetics*. This is the image interrogated by Barchiesi in his exploration of Kroll's 'die Kreuzung der Gattungen'. The focus here is upon the production of texts. On Kroll's view, either texts are pure or they are hybrids produced by parents of two different genres. Such cross-fertilization can, of course, be rich and productive: it resists the dangers of generic 'endogamy', whereby incest will ultimately produce throwbacks (rather as genetic engineering might produce clones). 'Exogamy' is clearly necessary, to provide 'new blood'. At the same time, it is important to acknowledge the potential here for implicit value-judgements about generic purity and impurity.

Another model sees genre as a *recipe* which offers formulae for the production of literary works. The set combinations of *topoi* entailed in this view might ultimately connect with computer-generated literature. That is, if genre were simply a recipe or formula, then computer-generated lyric or epic or satiric poems would be conceivable. But anyone who has heard computer-generated Bach or Mozart will be aware that something vital is missing. This model runs the risk of producing mindless reiterations which do not enrich the stock, as Quintilian saw with clarity when he impugned painters who copy others' work with ruled squares.

One of the most persistent images is that of *mapping*. According to this image, the critic is involved in mapping the works of literature onto a two-dimensional 'descriptive grid'. If you get the coordinates right you can locate any texts onto this matrix. This has its uses as well as its limitations. One of the most provocative 'maps' of genres known to me is contained in Northrop Frye's *Anatomy of Criticism* (Princeton, 1957). He uses the seasons to organize literature into a system consisting of two opposed pairs, perhaps like a two-dimensional disc divided into four quadrants: Mythos of Spring—Comedy; Mythos of Summer—Romance, Mythos of Autumn—Tragedy; Mythos of Winter—Irony and

Satire. This map of literature captures the potential for the development of genres as they situate themselves at and across the boundaries between the 'seasons'.

I am inspired by the striking frequency with which ancient authors offer programmatic statements couched in travel imagery to propose another image of genre which intersects with mapping imagery, but which renders it more dynamic. My image would accommodate three or, better, four dimensions, that is, movement in three planes and movement through time. The closest analogy that occurs to me is that provided by computer games where you become a character in a story and play a part in 'writing' that story from the narrative components that are offered, and may easily find yourself moving in all directions and not only forwards but also backwards in time. Genre, on this model, is the *interactive computer programme*: while it allows and precludes certain possibilities, there is no predicting which decisions will be taken in your particular game.

So far my focus has, perhaps inevitably, been upon texts as objects. We need to bring authors and audiences back into the frame. I don't want the death of the author. But at the same time I am reluctant to heroize him. Extrapolating from the metaphors above, he might be a marriage-broker or a genetic scientist or a cook or an explorer. Or she might be a computer hacker. This last opens up the possibility of illegality: if a system has 'rules', then that is an invitation to break them. It seems to me that any theory of genre has to allow for genre to be taken to and through the limits. This in turn raises the question of 'genre-cide'. Some genres are long-lived. Epic, for example, which currently extends from Homer to *Omeros*. Some are described as short-lived, for example, Latin love elegy. But who killed elegy? Who pronounces the death of a genre? It is not yet clear whether authors or audiences are more responsible in this sphere.

Audiences clearly have a role. We are right, I think, to focus upon the first performance or reading, which is so different from re-performances and rereadings. This is an occasion inevitably tense with the frisson of the unknown. The audience/readers become detectives in search of clues. That the text constructs its audience in the sense that it creates a literary competence in its readership presents an ideal, one articulated by Wordsworth, which is not invariably realized. What if the author has pushed the genre unrecognizably beyond its boundaries, beyond the competence or tolerance of his audience? There might be experiments that fail. And in this relationship between authors and audiences it is crucial to be able to imagine both parties as fallible.

Finally, then, a call for dialogue—and not just the dialogue between author and audience which takes place during performance and reading. We need not be reduced to a stark choice between seeing genre as description or prescription or as a process of either deduction or induction. What is happening is always a dialogue, both synchronic and diachronic, between the actual texts and the hypostasized genre, a contextualized version of Saussure's intersection of *langue* and *parole*. Whichever model or metaphor we use, genre always involves a balance between consistency and innovation, framework and deviation. That is why a study of genre is always concerned with boundaries. And that means that the richest texts for generic studies are not the supposed archetypes (though these we also need) but those which explore the boundaries—texts like Virgil's tenth *Eclogue* and Ovid's *Heroides*. That explains Barchiesi's focus on the 'crossing' of genres and Wilson's choice of a problematic type of literature for scrutiny. And just as the issue of gender-bending is significant for gender studies, so the study of genre into the twenty-first century must be prepared to focus, above all, on genre-bending.

IO

The Crossing

Alessandro Barchiesi

'The Crossing' in my title is the crossing or cross-breeding of literary genres: the implications of this abbreviation will be explained later.

My talk today[1] is influenced, as is obvious, by my own research on Latin poetry and on the impact of literary theory on the study of Latin poetry, but also, less obviously, by my participation in an interesting seminar on genre organized in 1996 by Mary Depew and Dirk Obbink, and hosted by the Centre for Hellenic Studies in Washington DC. I gratefully acknowledge the many ideas I have learned from most of the participants. The proceedings of the conference will present what could be seen as a 'play-book' of generic approaches in the 1990s.[2] To avoid duplication, I will try to focus both on a distant past, late positivistic scholarship in the 1920s and on a near future, the crisis of postmodern culture that many of us are beginning to experience.

That would be enough as an introduction to the present paper, but considering that my panel organizer Susanna Braund has an interest in the two, related I think, issues of persona and the personal voice, I hope she will forgive me if I don the mask of sincerity and briefly sketch the history of my personal involvement in this new conference. Initially I thought that I liked the project very much, except that the stress on 'working together' was perhaps too pacifist: in my generation, quarrel and tussle, ancients versus moderns, scholarship versus theory, has been an indispensable stimulus (towards ideas, and careers). I am not yet ready for a world of co-operation—but then I noticed with relief that the cliché 'working together' was being used by the re-elected Bill

[1] I accept the suggestion of an anonymous referee that my text should be kept as close as possible to the oral version. I am grateful to Susanna Braund, Michael Silk, Michael Reeve amongst conference attenders and to H. U. Gumbrecht (Stanford) for their comments.

[2] Depew–Obbink (2000).

Clinton in a protreptic to the still Republican-dominated Congress. So there is still room for tension and confrontation (and collusion and blackmail . . .) even in a 'working together' era, I think.

I then started to muse on how far theory is relevant to classical scholarship, and I came up with the impression that in one respect at least theory *is* basic to classical scholarship: viz. in its Greek ancient meaning of *theoria* = ritual procession. Classical scholars have a regular habit of imagining themselves caught in a long and slow procession: what changes is their way of reacting to that feeling of being latecomers in a long, unified parade of predecessors, but the feeling is, I think, a shared experience. Now I realized that this shared imaginaire entailed, among other unspoken assumptions, one that should be spelt out from the start: the preconception that the *theoria* of classical philology has a mainstream, or a hard core, which is made of, precisely, scholarship—hard facts, textual criticism, the old *OCD*,—and a mobile and fickle fringe, where external pressures are perceived and accommodated; that pressure comes from 'modern theory', a changing discourse which is by definition irradiated from elsewhere—France, Lithuania, women's studies, anthropology, Freud, multiculturalism, East, South, and other exotic places.

My business today is with a conservative approach to this construct: the idea that contemporary scholarship is a successor to a mythical age when there was no issue of being over- or under-theorized, and scholarship was based on itself. Most of us would agree that this myth of origins has a place and a time: pre-war Germany. When I realized this sense of rift and disjunction, I made a desperate attempt at the most trite of novelistic devices, the time machine. I started daydreaming of sending back in time a young graduate student from a progressive department, like Southern California or Bristol. In my project, the time-traveller would pop up unannounced in a session of the Berliner Akademie der Wissenschaften, in Wilhelmine Germany, and try to tell them how their work was based on unspoken theoretical assumptions. Contrary to my expectations, the visit was not ill received; Diels seemed a bit annoyed, but Usener even took a few notes about post-structuralist anthropology. The picture was less unified than it seemed from a distance. Some despised philosophy, but Heinze, for example, was the son of a professor of philosophy. The first experiment went well, but the next night feedback invaded my dreams, with a vengeance: I saw myself teaching rudiments of textual criticism and metrics to my undergraduates in Verona, and then I was chilled when I saw among them Paul Maas, with an enigmatic smile.

So I unplugged the time machine and turned to the subject of my present discussion. I decided I would try to squeeze out some theory, not from contemporary scholarship but from early twentieth-century Germany, and see how it still underpins our present era of cloudy theorizing and perpetually new ideas. My choice is a conceptual tool which has gone relatively unexamined for a long time, *Die Kreuzung der Gattungen,* familiarly The Crossing, and I will include references to the individual voice of its inventor, Wilhelm Kroll. This man is not the main focus of my paper, but I must admit that he would repay more interest. His scholarship was built on hard work and *Realien,* yet he has produced one of the few tags which are still in currency, after seventy years, in literary interpretation of the classics: his idea of the cross-breeding of genres is still quoted as an authority in the new *OCD* and in books like Simon Goldhill's *The Poet's Voice*,[3] not exactly a nostalgic repository for positivistic scholarship, and in a major paper of the 'working together era', Daniel Selden's *Genre of Genre*.[4]

Kroll's book, *Studien zum Verständnis der römischen Literatur*, came out in 1924: the preface is dated from Breslau, modern Wrocław, the first sentence of the book the heavy-handed allusion 'The father of this book is the War', and the preface acknowledges a mysterious financial benefactor from Missouri. When I asked a famous literary historian about *Die Kreuzung der Gattungen,* the first response was that to him this title spells out disarray, the cosmic confusion and disorder of post-war *Mitteleuropa*. My informant, Sepp Gumbrecht, is the author of a book called *In 1926*, so I thought it was a meaningful reaction.

[3] (1991), 285, 'the construction of new and hybrid poetic forms—what Kroll calls . . .' (yet Kroll is absent from the bibliography and confused with his friend J. Kroll in the Index . . .). Note also Cameron (1992), certainly a very innovative paper, especially in respect of Rossi's (1971) standard treatment of genre in Callimachus, but ready to accept the 'crossing of genres' as a convincing model of explanation. Contra see recently Depew (1992), 314–16; Barchiesi (1997), 65–7; Hunter (1997). Dirk Obbink now promises a critical reassessment for Alexandrian literature.

[4] Selden (1994), 41, 'the hallmark of Hellenistic letters became the crossing of literary kinds', with reference to Kroll in an endnote.

Some will react with greater nervousness. Although *Gattung* is not a term specific to twentieth-century racism, *Kreuzung* can be translated not only as cross-breeding but as miscegenation. It is important to see the biological model at work in this concept: a recent Italian translation of the chapter-heading *L'intreccio dei generi*, intertwining,[5] shows how the metaphor in Kroll's title still invites emendation and disinfection. According to Hannah Arendt, the vast, diluted area of positivist jargon contributes, in a post-Darwinian and post-South African era, to a shared language of racial confusion and irretrievable purity, which forms the necessary basis for totalitarianism. Yet there is little point in accusing a marginal German professor who directed the greatest part of Pauly-Wissowa (and wrote, among many others, the entry 'kiss') of making a significant contribution to Nazism. When Kroll died in 1939 a man who had nothing to fear from the new regime, Hans Drexler, wrote a strange obituary in *Gnomon*:[6] he pointed out that Kroll was a bit of an eccentric, a relativist, without any positive *Weltanschauung*, a sceptic who lived in a time of crisis, and even attributes *Liberalismus* to him. In the late 1930s, Kroll was not perceived as a man fit for *Kulturkampf*. I am not setting up a straw man in Nazi uniform when I talk about his ideas.

And yet *Die Kreuzung* must be understood as a specific idea of the 1920s, as specific as transatlantic ships, the rise of Argentina, and Russian aristocrats driving taxicabs. It should be clear from the start that *Kreuzung* recapitulates a theory on how new genres are produced; not simply, as in our appropriations of the tag, the localized perception of generic and programmatic impurity or instability. *Kreuzung* of genres creates new genres who participate in the nature of their parents: Ovid's *Heroides*, for example, are a *Kreuzung* of two genres, rhetorical epistle and elegy. A modern equivalent of the idea, similarly related to contemporary obsessions, would be *generic engineering* (a pun I owe to Michael Haslam).

So a discussion of *Kreuzung* should include at least a reference to that masterplot of European generic theory, the recurrent biological paradigm. A prehistory of the paradigm has been traced by J.-M. Schaeffer as far back as Aristotle, but I am not sure he is

[5] *Aevum Antiquum*, 4 (1991), 15–38 (translation and preface by L. Belloni).

[6] Drexler (1939). Two aspects of Kroll's 'liberalism' as a German academic of his age are, I suspect, his pioneering interest in ancient sexuality and his unwillingness to expel Jewish contributors from the Pauly–Wissowa team.

right when he constructs from the *Poetics* what he calls an essentialist position on which the biological paradigm is based: 'man is endowed with a generic nature, because man generates man. The same model of generation must be postulated for genres:'[7] for Schaeffer, the genetic and generic are close to each other, and since they have an internal *dynamis,* genres are being assimilated to natural entities, not to artificial objects. Be that as it may, I would certainly welcome new studies on Aristotelian zoology and biology, in the hope that they can illuminate analogies and differences with Aristotelian classifications of poetic individuals and species. However, Schaeffer is clearly right when he points out a new intensity of the biological paradigm in the Romantic era, and presents as messenger-boy for this nineteenth-century trend the French theorist Ferdinand Brunetière: for Brunetière literary history is a post-Darwinian drama of struggle for survival and adaptation among fiercely competitive species, that is, genres. In 1898 generic Darwinism triumphs in Brunetière's *Histoire et littérature,* and in the same year a Paris classicist, Legrand, publishes the closest forerunner of Kroll's *Kreuzung der Gattungen,* the chapter 'La Confusion des genres' in his *Étude sur Théocrite*. However, the German word *Gattung* is closer to ideas of generation than French and English 'genre', although the new entry *genre* in the post-modern *OCD* is elegantly framed by the entries *gens* and *genos*. The German version of Ortega y Gasset's defence of generic essentialism against Croce sounds familiar: 'Jedes Dichtwerk gehört zu einer Gattung wie Jedes Tier zu einer Spezies.'[8] In the German-speaking community of the 1920s Mendel must have been even more important than Darwin,[9] and they even had a fashionable word, *ausmendeln*; *Gattung* is a close relative to generation (*begetten*), and German literary criticism in the 1920s is turning to experiments in 'generational' literary history, which still have an influence on our contemporary handbooks of literature and their periodization.[10]

[7] Schaeffer (1992), 21.

[8] Krauss (1968), 6.

[9] Michael Reeve is doing important work on the theory that shared innovations indicate a closer relationship within a family—a path which crosses historical linguistics, textual criticism, and natural science: the emergence of this paradigm can be located in the third quarter of the nineteenth century.

[10] For some reason, people who care about the history of *Altertumswissenschaft* tend to be interested and involved either in biography (especially interpersonal relationships) or in a reconstruction of political positions; yet the subject of literary

I mention this cluster of ideas because it seems important not to mistake *Die Kreuzung* as an essay on generic impurity and programmatic instability, which is very much the way we are all framing the subject in the 1990s. What Kroll means by *Kreuzung* is clearly the *production* of new literary species by means of cross-breeding; not just confusion (Legrand) or mixing (Deubner). Our lack of interest in late positivistic scholarship becomes dangerous when we recycle old labels without reading the small-print warnings.

People who understand Kroll's idiolect better are not hard to find, even in post-war Germany: here, for example, is Otto Weinreich explaining the birth of the novel to readers of Heliodorus: the text was printed in 1970 and is still quoted by some novel experts with evident relish. The ancient novel 'represents the result of a cross-breeding between two narrative genres: epic and moralistic history', and

> the Greek erotic novel was the result of a liaison [=*Kreuzung*] entered by aging epic with the capriciously attractive Hellenistic historiography. The bastard was an attractive offspring, deriving a strong vitality from his young mother, and received several godparental presents from the Muses of drama and love poetry. In his youth [the *Roman* is a male] he used to read Münchausen stories and exotic travel adventures, and he learnt something useful from the schools of rhetoric. But the stain of his illegitimate birth was, nevertheless, so strong, that no ancient *Ars Poetica* dared to admit the lively mongrel into the exclusive society of literary history.[11]

There is, I agree, something—perhaps involuntarily—delightful when Weinreich turns the birth of the novel into an eighteenth-century novelistic plot, or even a classical pastiche of Marthe Robert's *Roman des origines et origines du roman,* but it is not just political correctness which makes me uneasy about the bastard and the lively mongrel: this is a scholar who still writes from the standpoint of generic essentialism, and in the 1990s gifted classicists like

taste and implicit literary theory is important too. Kroll ends his most ambitious paper on the evaluation of Roman literature with a curious revelation that he is having problems in accepting Sudermann as a true poet. Some of those mythical 'pure scholars' were reading contemporary literature, and reacting to the literary debate. For an interesting analysis of the link between Decadentism and revival of Callimachus see Fantuzzi (1988), pp. xxviii–xxx.

[11] Weinreich (1970), 340 (my emphasis).

Holzberg and Zimmermann are still serious in debating on whether the Cyropaedia is a true novel or not.

So the first stage of my argument is that the biological model reinforces and sustains generic essentialism, and that metaphors used by the critics are not innocent. Not only is the emphasis on biological generation an influential and theory-laden metaphor being carried over from Kroll's work; so is the *implicit evaluation* of genres thought to be generated by Kreuzung. We may not like it, but Kroll intended his *Kreuzung* as an approach to decadence, not decadence in *Mitteleuropa* but in Hellenistic and Roman literary culture. Here I like to start from a paper published in 1900, his 'Studies on the Composition of the *Aeneid*'. As a literary critic, young Kroll had decided to give Vergil another try, starting from a clear bifurcation: traditional classicizing admiration for Vergil; traditional Romantic distaste for Vergil. He proclaims that he is treading a third route, an objective approach, objective analysis of contradictions and problems; *je ne propose rien, je ne suppose rien: j'expose*. Unfortunately for him, after three years Heinze comes out with a monograph which is accepted as objective analysis and yet encapsulates a much bolder *Rettung*, a vindication of Vergil as a master of epic. Heinze's book must have been a giant stumbling-block on Kroll's itinerary. Kroll ended up being recontextualized with the reactionary Paul Jahn and *fin-de-siècle* Vergil-bashing, while Heinze travelled triumphantly towards post-war neo-Humanism and a positive fetishization of Augustan culture. Kroll produced (1905) a curiously reluctant appraisal of *Virgils epische Technik*: to him, Vergil was *fleissig* and *feinsinning*, but not the Roman poet par excellence; Heinze, in parallel, had produced a *sorgfaltige Analyse*. Hard-working and accurate himself, Kroll had been courting disaster in his 1900 *Studien*: he states that the *Aeneid* had no plan at all, *planlos* like no other poem in the history of epic; he notes that Vergil is driven by his sources and unable to think of a narrative project beyond the span of short sections; he seriously maintains that it is a blunder when Aeneas protests to Venus 'why do you confuse your son so many times (*totiens*) with false images?' (1. 407–8)—because there are no other similar tricks in the plot to explain the force of *totiens*.

Those are not simply interpretive shortcomings that we can easily discard: Kroll had seriously thought that classical philology was split between technical work on metrical niceties and subjective verdicts on aesthetic value; and that a Latinist had to face the basic truth that the Romans were inferior because they were imitators, not try to idealize their achievement. Precisely those two frustrating dilemmas were going to spark the breakthrough in people like Leo, Norden, and Heinze, and later Fraenkel; and Kroll was marginalized, although he immediately suggested[12] an orthodox historicizing platform for the study of Roman literature: since for the Romans literature was imitation, it only makes sense to pass a judgement on them according to their own standards. But Kroll was already being beaten at his own game.

This is the precedent against which we should measure Kroll in 1924: he had lost the war about the *Aeneid*, as always the Alsace-Lorraine of Latin studies, and only one side of his programme remained feasible: the idea of writing about Roman and Hellenistic literature as a professional activity, a culture of poetic composition based on shared techniques, buzzwords, and programmatic strategies. An interesting programme, and well suited to Kroll's mentality: a collectionist, a curious, a magpie mind, with a wise feeling for the limits of knowledge, as in his decision to skip Hellenistic poetic theory because Philodemus didn't look solid enough in those pre-Obbink and Delattre years.

To secure a wide selection of examples, Kroll is not fussy about where his genres come from and how they are constructed: *Kreuzung* includes new combinations of content and form (e.g. mimes in hexameter) but also mixing of pre-existent genres, no matter what their status is: combination of *letter* and *elegy* to form Ovid's *Heroides* presupposes that 'letter' and 'elegy' are (can be described as being . . .) on the same footing qua genres; describing the *Satyricon* as a *Kreuzung* of pre-existing genres leads Kroll to accept the *Satyricon* as an instance of the genre 'novel'. Of course we could change the approach[13], mindful of the wise motto[14] DISTINGUE FREQUENTER, and say that the *epistolary* genre is a transhistorical genre based on a communicative act; *elegy* a genealogic genre, based on a reconstructed hypertextual class; 'novel' an analogic genre, based on the observation of typological similarities. For an individual text, it really makes some difference whether it is

[12] Kroll (1903).

[13] For genres as (i) kinds of communication acts, or (ii) genealogies, or (iii) analogies, see Schaeffer (1992).

[14] A favourite with Carlo Dionisotti, one of the heroes of Italian scholarship.

studied as product of a communicative intention (e.g. letter) or as invested by a tradition (e.g. elegy)[15] or as linked to a network of time-free analogies (e.g. novel).

But the idea of *Kreuzung* is simply part of a project which tends to study ancient poetry as a professional activity held together by shared *imaginaire* and practice—except that, as we shall see, this how-to approach incorporates a great deal of evaluation and prejudice. (A worthy project, anyway: the closest analogy which springs to mind is Francis Cairns' approach in his *Generic Composition in Greek and Roman Poetry* (Cairns 1972), but Cairns will not be invited to my trip from 1920s Slesien to present-day Oxford, not because he does not repay discussion—in fact his preference for 'inclusion' instead of 'generic mixing' is a serious improvement on previous scholarship—but because his idea of genre flies in the face of modern usage. The genres reconstructed by Cairns are in fact types, thematic patterns, and pragmatical choices; only lately, after some negotiation with the UN, has he agreed to label his own area 'genres of content', thus legitimizing everybody else in continuing with their own traditional terminology of genre.)

As for my own traditional idea of genre, I choose two basic tenets plus a refinement. The tenets are that people are inclined to imagine genre as something that straddles two oppositions, (i) content versus form,[16] and (ii) literary texts versus society, discourse, institutions. I don't see much point in the whole debate if genres are not used to bridge those oppositions. The less obvious qualification is that 'genre' can be used so as to reconstruct the productive conditions of a text or a tradition; to re-create, at the point of reception, some impression, or imagination, about the setting in which the text was originated and performed.[17]

This last aspect will raise for us the problem of how texts

[15] In fact when we call the *Heroides* 'letters' we are being less specific than when using the name 'elegies': the text owes to 'elegy' not only formal but ideological features, while 'epistolarity' only describes the communicative structure. Both descriptions are helpful, but they don't seem to belong together.

[16] e.g. the wise operative distinction in Reed (1997), 6–7, 'We need a terminology to reflect the different traditions being perpetuated in this poetry, so in this study "bucolic" refers to the tradition *signalled by formal features* [my emphasis], "pastoral" to themes of herdsmen and rustic life . . . It typically includes pastoral or rustic themes, but also others that for one reason or another its pratictioners saw fit to arrogate or assimilate to their poetic line. It excludes pastoral literature that is not *formally* [his emphasis] marked as part of that line, e.g. Longus . . .'

[17] I owe this formulation to discussion with Dirk Obbink.

thematize their own relationship to genres, but for now the idea of origins brings us back to Kroll and to the invention of *Kreuzung*. Because Kroll thought he had found out how genres were generated: in classical Greece they sprang out of society and communal needs, or, in the mood of those Pan-Germanic and Pan-Slavic years in *Mitteleuropa*, 'vom Boden der Landschaft': later on, when literature was severed from community and unity, they were created out of older genres, through *Kreuzung*. From the third century onwards, individual authors make new species out of cross-breeding. Two issues are crucial here: those authors work for success in book form, not performance; those authors work for patrons, especially autocrats, not for audiences of fellow-citizens and patriots. This is my last occasion for reminding you that the *Kreuzung* model incorporates a negative or at best apologetic stance about everything which was produced after the birth of Alexander the Great. It is not by chance that the first text Kroll mentions in his chapter as an exemplary half-breed is a freak, that curse of a poem[18], the *Carmen Saeculare* of Horace.

The only recent paper to have a comparable influence in this area, Rossi (1971) on written and unwritten laws of genre, overlaps Kroll in updating and revising views on Theocritus and Callimachus,[19] but leaves the Romans entirely in the grip of the *Kreuzung* model. This gives the false impression that there is no big difference between Rossi's Callimachus—generic laws are written down for experimental transgression—and early Roman literature as a peak time of *Kreuzung der Gattungen*. Yet Scevola Mariotti, who did so much to connect Republican Rome with Hellenistic literature, had wisely observed that there is a basic difference between Ennius and Callimachus:

> Greek Alexandrianism had an ideal of cultural variety as a ratio of the variety of artistic creation. Callimachus . . . had been working with taste and erudition in the most different genres of poetry; yet he was still substantially respecting . . . the distinctions among literary genres. Every genre kept style, metre, even dialect which were historically appropriate. Ennius moves on, and he practises the Alexandrian principle of variety on genres which had a very ancient and fixed tradition (*Annales*) and even

[18] Probably the least popular text of Augustan poetry in the years between Mommsen and Fraenkel.

[19] Rossi (1971). And of course Kroll presupposes Legrand and Deubner on Theocritus but writes before much of our present-day Callimachus is available.

creates a brand new genre whose main law is mutability (*Satura*). So he is both an Alexandrian poet and a very bold innovator.[20]

A complementary revision of Rossi's approach for Callimachus and Theocritus is now available in recent work by Cameron (1992), Depew (1992), and Fantuzzi (1995). They all accept genre as a relevant issue—so they are all closer to Rossi and Kroll than, for example, to Wilamowitz—but they raise various problems with the *Kreuzung* model and even more with Rossi's approach postulating laws written down to enable better infraction. What Kroll describes as contamination, a scientific experiment in an ivory laboratory, could be functionally a strategy for survival (Darwin keeps coming back, you will notice . . .). Writing epinicians in hexameters is a response to the screening out of lyric metres from the literary system and from performance, not a challenge to a normative poetics. Hymns in elegiacs had existed long before Callimachus. The *Iambi* are not an experiment in generic *polyeideia*, but a self-conscious text which presents itself as pure *iambos*—second word, *Hipponax*, first (and no less important) word *listen to*—then problematizes its Ionian and performative roots. The reference in *Iambus* 13 to writing in different genres and in mixed dialects does not equal ideas of contamination and *Kreuzung*. Callimachus' opponents may be straw men, but they don't think in terms of *Kreuzung*. As for the transgressive nature of *Hecale and Aitia*, Cameron rightly points out many stylistical differences, for example, in *presque-homérique* style and use of simile, which show Callimachus to be very preoccupied indeed with the border between modern epos and modern elegy.[21] Theocritus may turn out to be another counter-witness; the poems we call bucolic have significant metrical differences[22] from the poems we perceive as encomiastic or narrative, and the effect of 'confusion des genres' arises from the first-century collection in book form, not from the generic impurity of the original project.

The most crucial difficulty at this stage of the argument is

[20] Mariotti (1991), 82: translation mine, with slight adaptations. The passage is opportunely quoted by Fantuzzi (1993), 50, n. 42.

[21] Ironically, the *Blut und Boden* problem so persistent in modern criticism of Callimachus had been forestalled by the author in fr. 203, 12–14 and 64–6—major treatments are Depew (1992) and Hunter (1997)—where apparently the critics are figures of fun.

[22] Fantuzzi (1995), 244.

how we decide to assess the impacts of performance and book on generic identity. The *Kreuzung* approach requires classical Greece to be a land of implicit generic obedience and decadent Hellenism to be a territory of unruly experiment. This dichotomy somehow survives through Rossi's approach. But other approaches would be possible right now. First of all, one would like to see a wide-ranging discussion on how the book, including its materiality (presentation of metre, collections and complete works and anthologies) affects issues of generic impurity. Secondly, it should be possible to make forays from the ivory tower into fourth- and fifth-century poetry and show that transgeneric texts are older than Rossi and Kroll would allow them to be. Lutz Käppel's reading[23] of a hymn by Philodamos of Scarpheia shows a fourth-century performance poem interrogating itself on whether the generic boundaries of the paean allow a cult song for Dionysos, not Apollo. Peter Parsons[24] uses Simonides on Plataea to continue and cap the famous deconstruction of differences between late classical and Alexandrian initiated in Dover's introduction to Theocritus. (By the way, Simonides' Plataea also confirms that the generic approach per se should not be jettisoned; because, heuristically, it works: working on archaic elegy as a genre has certainly helped Ewen Bowie to predict some features which the new fragment, however tantalizing, confirms . . .).[25]

Four provisional points may be made here:

(i) Is perhaps the dominance of Athenian theatre over other kinds of literature (a dominance in terms of prestige and visibility) narrowing down our perception of mid-fifth- to early fourth-century, an age that starts with the late Simonides and includes generic innovators like Herodotus, Plato, and Timotheos?

(ii) Are we encouraged to construct an age of generic purity as a foil precisely because we work too hard on the *Kreuzung* model in Alexandrian literature? Is respect for genre always a 'good old days' feature, as Plato wants us to believe when his agenda is indicting generic anarchy in the *Laws*? Useful alternative provocations have been contributed by Derrida, who notes that quotation and recontextualization make change simultaneous with the law of genre: 'what if there were, lodged within the heart of the law itself, a law of impurity or a principle of contamination?' (quoted (yes)

[23] Käppel (1992). [24] Parsons (1992), 12. [25] Bowie (1986).

and translated by Kennedy (1989), 209–10, and similarly by Genette (1981), 71: even mixing of genres and generic insubordination can be constructed as genre.

(iii) Is the historicizing link with political institutions really useful here? Kroll made no secret that for him generic respect ends with the end of free *poleis* and their 'Blut und Boden' atmosphere. For Plato, unruly democracy killed respect for the rules of generic purity. Is this the approach we like to foster today?

(iv) A new discussion should also focus on how and why a divide between oral performance, and written culture affects the need for some kind of generic theory. One might start from a useful provocation in a footnote of G. Nagy's,[26] which suggests that genre is in fact a post-mortem of performance, because it is necessary only when performance fades away and no longer guarantees the *Sitz im Leben* of the text. Of course this is a sly provocation, and Nagy has revised this opposition in a forthcoming paper; he now takes his cue from a blues singer saying 'when I play the blues I don't necessarily have to feel blue', and shows that the issue of re-performance blurs the distinction between performance and generic convention. Starting from here, we might want to explore genre as a conceptual device fit for re-creating and re-enacting performance.

I imagine that many of you will ask who exactly is doing all this job of thinking genres? The poet, the critic, the audience, and what audience? I must say that my own opposition to generic essentialism is weakening as time goes by. Most of us would agree that genres are not natural objects, but theory-related constructs, and yet I agree with Stephen Hinds in a forthcoming paper that some degree of vestigial essentialism is unavoidable in all critical positions about genre. Just think about how many delicate steps are involved in generic interpretations: we construct one or more ideal audiences with their own horizons of expectations; they make guesses for us on the poet's positioning within genres; the poet is now constructed as author and enters into a dialogue with a generic matrix. This is all very complicated, and some are tempted to jettison the whole issue, but then we hear Horace's voice lamenting 'I decided to write satire because I was not good enough at war epic, bucolics, tragedy, and comedy', or Callimachus, 'who

[26] Nagy (1990), 360, with n.

has decided "you must compose elegiacs, you heroic lines, you were assigned by the gods to tragedy . . ." ',[27] and we are back in the same arena.

Of course the main change in the *Kreuzung* issue from the 1920s to the 1990s has been to shift attention from genres as begetting genres to texts as mobilizing genres. This approach does justice to several problems raised but not solved by Kroll when dealing with Roman literature, while astutely softening the sharp edges of generic essentialism and naturalism. The focus now is on how texts construct and invoke genres, and re-create a genealogy, not on how literary species transmute and survive.

In spite of his well-chosen project of a generalizing but culture-specific poetics of Hellenistic and Roman culture, Kroll had shown little interest in the way poets signify and advertise their own negotiations with genre. His chapter on imitation derives from Moriz Haupt the same old examples which are now familiar from the work of Conte, the Ovidian Ariadne and the Ovidian Mars and their memories of Catullus and Ennius, but Kroll apparently considers those as signature episodes of a culture of imitation, not as paradoxes of reflexivity.[28] What is especially lacking, in hindsight, are examples of how we are to deduce generic positions and revisions from the texts themselves, and read thematizations of genres in the fabric of individual texts.

The growth industry in the 1970s and 1980s has been, of course, programmatic interpretation. Bramble, Conte, Hinds, and Gregson Davis have been able to analyse whole texts—not just proems and manifestoes—as metaliterary dramas, involving generic confrontations and revisions.[29] It should now be clear why this perspective differs from the originary model of *Kreuzung*. We could generalize their approach by saying that in Roman literature genres are not just matrices of new texts, but actors in a programmatic display. When we study Ovid's *Fasti* as a dynamic confrontation between epic and elegy, we don't mean to say that we can access the laboratory of the author, where epic and elegy are being used to create a new genre; what our reading is trying to get at is the literary space

[27] Call. fr. 203. 30–3; Horace, Sat. 1.10. 40–9.

[28] He derives from a neglected paper by Ziehen on Statius an occasional formulation, 'eine Art von Zitat unter dem Gesichtspunkt der Poetik' (p. 177), which sounds like a prophecy of a non-*Quellenforschung* approach.

[29] Bramble (1974), Conte (1986), Hinds (1992), Davis (1991). Wilson Nightingale (1995) shows that there is much to do in the area of Platonic dialogue.

in which genres are being talked about—'"genre"' not used—'genre'.

Kroll had collected a mixed bunch of maverick and freakish new genres, bucolic mimes in hexameters, iambus crossed with elegy, armchair lyric poems, and miniature epic. But his genetic approach actually spoils the dynamics of the process, well captured in a Roman buzzword for genre, *opus*; texts are viewed by him as results, not as operations. It is legitimate to describe Lycophron's *Alexandra* as the result of a mixture of epic narrative and dramatic speech; but this genetic explanation has the effect of naturalizing the surprise effect, which is also great fun, when the messenger says 'Forgive me, sir, I have to report a long and uncommonly obscure utterance'; and it also makes the two genres of epic and drama monolithic and separate, while the *Alexandra* is also a commentary on their traditional interference; stylistically, messenger speeches had always been a bit closer to epic than the rest of a tragedy. Kroll uses the anaphora at the beginning of Catullus 64 to show that for Catullus epic mixes with other generic influences, but today a critic would rather focus on the repeated *Tum Thetis* . . . as a freeze-frame where the prospect of an Argonautic epic is literally blocked by the intrusive authorial voice. Therefore the *Crossing* in my title alludes not to the imagery of cross-breeding and generation but to an idea of reading as a linear progress complicated by intersections and deviations; crossings are viewed from the viewpoint of the reader, not from that of the literary historian.

Kroll also had to occlude the revivalist aspect of Roman poetics. Roman poets not only avoid advertising *Kreuzung*, they tend to stage programmatic respect to a traditional genre, precisely to be able to dramatize their work as deviation or genre-bending; the whole process is a part of the semiotics of poetry, not a disinterested confession or the disclosure of a true laboratory. To this end, they need genres to be perceived as strong, pure, and sufficiently unmixed; they practise a reconstructive approach to genre, not a capricious reshuffling. Some of the poetic books interpreted by Kroll as *Kreuzungen* in fact demand a quite different approach. He seems to think that Horace's *Epodes* is a test case of generic impurity, and points out metrical *poikilia* and the importation of elegiac and lyrical traditions. Yet from the point of view of metre Horace is practising what he is preaching: bringing

Archilochus back; most, possibly all, of the epodic patterns are now attested in Archilochus;[30] the avoidance of choliambs and phalaeceans suggests a 'back to the roots' effect, bypassing (respectively) the Hipponactean Callimachus and the Catullan revolution; and the treatment of iambic trimeter similarly spells out 'pure Greek' in opposition to Latinate approaches and Republican senarii. From a thematic point of view, Kroll is wrong when he says that Epode 11 'could just be an elegy'; as often, Leo had anticipately improved on his approach by stating that Epode 11 is an *elegia iambis concepta*; Leo's formulation is dynamic and dialectical, while Kroll misses the contrast between the physical energy of iambus and the languid powerlessness of the elegiac lover. Far from bringing variety into the book by breaking iambic uniformity, Epode 11 enhances generic identity by staging generic impurity.

Often Roman texts are projecting a hyped, exaggerated alias, which includes memories and imaginings of how genres had been in their pure, uncompromised origins:

- Lucretius' frightening *opus* of empowering natural knowledge as an alternative to the reduced and defensive teaching of Vergil's *Georgics*;
- extremist views of love poetry—back to the torture chambers of Meleager and Propertius and to the inner conflicts of Catullus—as an alternative to Ovid's own approach, the soft approach to elegy (irony, relativism, seduction);
- epic imagined in lower genres as super-epic, gigantomachy;
- iambic poetry in the vein of Archilochus and Hipponax threatening to burn out the brakes put on by Horace;
- archaic comedy and *onomasti komodein* as the hard core of satire;
- lyric imagined at the point of origin as live performance, impossible to repeat, since Horace cannot become a civil-war bard or a love-obsessed *puella*.

These are not issues of generic purity or impurity: the authors are not presenting their new work as a *Kreuzung* but as an evolution or devolution of a generic matrix which needs recalling; the recalling of origins identifies the new work in the literary space but also suggests a drama of appropriation and legitimization.

[30] Cavarzere (1992), 27.

When, to the contrary, in a smaller number of situations, *Kreuzung* is bandied about, it deserves to be read not as a disclosure but as a part of a discursive strategy. The well-read narrator in Martin Amis' *The Information* (1995, 53) revisits a weary conversation locus ('there are no typical seasons any more') then links it with Northrop Frye's grand theory of the literary genres as seasons. As a result, the trite topos 'we keep waiting for something to go wrong with the seasons. But something has already gone wrong with the genres. They have all bled into one another. Decorum is no longer observed', now implies a meditation on the traditional poetics of the novel as impure, serio-comic, unlawful, warped. The narrator-cum-author Woody Allen Königsberg in *Deconstructing Harry* faces a traditional Jewish grandma accusing Harry/Woody: 'you with your Chinese girlfriend . . . no wonder pure Jewish is disappearing from this country'; we can see the issue of ethnic diversity both as a manifestation of political self-consciousness (the NY intellectual constructing and deconstructing his Jewish background) and as an analogy for the movie, generically restless and exogamic. Lucian in *Bis accusatus* (33) impersonates Dialogue, his own mixed prosimetric dialogue, accepting the (somewhat exaggerated) accusation that he has a dual nature, is a hippocentaur[31] of a genre. In Derek Walcott's West Indies, in Heliodorus' *Aethiopian Tales*, the problem of reconstructing origins connects poetics and geopolitics.[32] But these are marked examples precisely because they are flaunted, not a revelation of a hidden formula.

So we can decide to discuss genres in terms of authorial self-consciousness and negotiations with the reader, and get rid of the animal species as genres. But this change of visual field is not the end of all problems. What will happen when the whole of Roman literature is mapped this way? If generic theory is the interface between poetics and literary history,[33] what kind of literary history is still viable? We will probably have an excellent history of Roman literature as a sum of author-centred retrospective readings of traditions, genres, and programmes: and we will be at loss about doing

[31] The dimorphism of the word nicely matches the imputation.

[32] On the function of classical memories in Walcott see Farrell (1997); on hybridization and genealogy in Heliodorus, Whitmarsh (1998).

[33] As in the wise remarks of Todorov (1978), 43–61, on genres growing by encoding 'discursive possibilities'. On the nexus between intertextuality and genre see Suerbaum (1985), 59–77.

what came naturally to previous generations, that is, teleological, narrative, forward-oriented literary history. This is probably not bad news at all for many of us, but there is a danger that the whole field of literary history will be marginalized—and that means re-cycling of old handbooks, since there will be a market anyway—or that new historicizing approaches will simply drop programmatic close reading as useless and accuse that school of occluding social and cultural contextualization.

I look forward to our discussion today, but may I try to suggest a few mediations?

(i) Literature is not the only area where similar dilemmas are posed, and I consider promising the rather eclectic approach of some art historians, like the Cambridge (UK then USA) professor Norman Bryson: he apparently manages to combine some revised version of traditional art-historical narrative—with its ideology of perpetual struggle of styles and techniques—with close readings centred on programmatic self-consciousness.[34] This latter approach corrects the heavy teleology of the former.

(ii) I will come back to the accusation of formalism in a moment, but first let me concentrate on the mainstream idea of genres as a 'space of inter-textuality'. This seems to be uncontroversial for many critics now, both as a reaction to essentialism, and as an interpretive tool. So far so good. Yet authors and presumably readers too, especially in the classical world, essentialize or reify genres . . . Does their objectivist *imaginaire* matter? Even generic impurity could be recuperated this way.

(iii) One is free to think that interpretive communities are still a possible avenue, but here the state of our evidence for classical times is lamentable. At the risk of sounding too positivistic, I like to think that lack of secondary evidence[35] for the reception of literature is a major difficulty. Think about Callimachus and Apollonius. Here we have two major poets working more or less simultaneously on two different responses to what looks like a crisis of traditional epic. The two approaches available to modern research have been respectively (a) believe in the biographical construct of the Quarrel, based on no good ancient evidence, or (b) discard biography and try to distil programmatic implications from stylistic and thematic parallels. Yet there is at least a third

[34] Cf. Bryson (1984).

[35] Not that this is the only problem with Fishian logic: Martindale (1993), 16.

meaningful question, that is, how would different interpretive communities react, in a time-span from late third century to first century, to a retrospective contextualization of *Aitia*, *Hecale*, and *Argonautica* which is presumably not simply a modern bias? Ahuvia Kahane is right to ask this question,[36] which does not entail biographical constructs and authorial agendas, but then he circularly produces an implausible reading of a description of a river delta in Apollonius and claims that this is a self-conscious response to the Assyrian river in the *Hymn to Apollo*. Of course he has no ancient testimony for this interpretation.

Yet in Hellenistic and Roman culture readers *are* interested in the evolution of epic, and some readers have names like Catullus, Vergil, and Ovid, people who react to both Apollonius and Callimachus and try to elaborate their own response to the crisis of epic narrative. The absence of secondary sources makes me very doubtful again, but Ovid could be an interesting witness: in the *Metamorphoses* he gives a speedy résumé of the *Argonautica*, plus a detailed account of Medea's role in the poem; Medea steals the action from the heroes, who are stuck in a suspiciously muddy river,[37] the Phasis; then Medea takes leave of the *Argonautic* by an aerial route, flies over a number of Greek places, including the Rhodes of the Telchines,[38] and lands right in the first episode of Callimachus' *Hecale*. Does this imitation count as a testimony about the Quarrel? No, but perhaps it counts as a reaction in a late-Alexandrian interpretive community where the evolution of epic is felt as a problem. Circular reasoning again, but at least about someone who demonstrably read Callimachus and Apollonius and had the competence and vested interest to contextualize and reposition them with reference to the poetics of epic. Echoes of the *Aitia* prologue and the *Hymn to Apollo* in the Roman world regularly show a connection with the poetics of epic; of course I don't agree with Alan Cameron (1995) that, by producing a highly

[36] Kahane (1994), 121–33.

[37] Ov. *Met.* 7.5–6 *multaque perpessi claro sub Iasone tandem | contigerant rapidas limosi Phasidos undas* (Bömer ad loc. discusses the geography of the Phasis and concludes that the epithets are interchangeable stereotypes). Note also 7.2 *perpetua . . . nocte*.

[38] 7. 365–7 *Phoebeamque Rhodon et Ialysios Telchinas | quorum oculos ipso vitiantes omnia visu | Iuppiter exosus fraternis subdidit undis*. I owe this observation to Andrew Zissos. On what is known about Telchines and Rhodes see Young (1987), 152–71: he makes the important point that the Rhodian link must be post-Callimachean.

subtle and articulated interpretation that decentres attention from epic to catalogue elegy, he can persuade *the Romans* that he is right; he might persuade *us* about Callimachus, but the Romans, it seems to me, had different agendas, and their position cannot be affected by Cameron's claim that they must have had the intellectual honesty to read the *Aitia* prologue just as he, Alan Cameron, does.

And yet the cleansing of the genre issue operated by programmatic criticism is not a definitive simplification. I can see reasons for an imminent return of the repressed.

If we simply stick to a vision of genre as text-immanent we will have to face a severe swing of the pendulum: back to history and society. The backlash will not be a gentle one. The intensive use of Bourdieu, Foucault, and Greenblatt can easily lead to a restoration of approaches which have been with us classicists for a long time: here is how I would imagine the paragraph on the *Aeneid* in a New-Historicist history of Roman Literature in 1999 California: 'A young provincial from Mantua succeeds in fashioning himself as a great singer of Roman identity by appropriating and adapting epic and conquers the capital with a new cultural capital . . .' Yet this overreaction to formalism is not unavoidable if we think that the programmatic approach is not necessarily a reduction of literature to itself. Some of the inspirers of this trend, like Bramble and Henderson, have always been very keen on politicization of poetic imagery, and wary of narrowing down their readings too much. Perhaps the obvious answer to New Historicist questioning of formalism is that good formalism had always insisted, not on separation of metapoetics from a neglected referential level, but rather on a kind of *circulation* inside the poetic text. When Roman poets rephrase the *Aitia* prologue as a *recusatio* of epic, they are interested in revisiting the Parthian Euphrates as the Assyrian river of the *Hymn to Apollo*. So one should not write a history of epic poetics without facing the politicization of the imagery. When Propertius thanks Augustus because 'now we can walk safely on the black sands of Euphrates' (4.6. 83–4), one has a sense that a good historical reading cannot dispense with a good formalistic reading of this image. And vice versa.

So I finally come back to our main problem, that of different constructs of genre. We have seen that the problem cannot be solved either by a single modern theory or by a confident act of historicization. But it should be possible to project, as a partial and tentative response, a new history of genre imaginaire, where the outlook has to combine implicit and explicit evidence and find a cautious approach to this combination. In spite of so much activity in the field of genre, from classical to postmodern, we still don't have a comprehensive account of imagery *about* genre, a map of generic ideology and iconology which should be able to cross, and criss-cross, the border between programmatic *écriture* and ancient criticism, between praxis and theory. Such an account will have to face the problem of how modern imagery affects the historical picture it seeks to recover; and it should find interesting things to say about some basic fields for generic imagery, both as specific to the ancient world, and as reinvented in modern culture: the most recurrent imagistic approaches I can think of are class, law, the body, procreation, food, the circulation of waters, gender, and social hierarchy. But this will require improving our approach to programmatic enunciation as well as our approach to explicit documents of literary criticism.

Two first steps are necessary. On programmatic aspects, it is important to realize that this is just a way of looking at the semiotics of poetry, and there is no secure way of fencing metaliterary aspects from references to extratextual reality.[39] *Circulation*, as I said, should be the catchword. Finally, we should decide whether we like to account only for genres which are already explicitly recognized by the participants in a given historical context. This is a difficult decision, because there are obvious advantages in sticking to the generic imaginaire of that particular community. Yet this approach (when it succeeds) is only able to visualize retroactivity in literary history, and we would have to forfeit literary history as a kind of dynamics and a forward-looking process:[40] in simulating operative horizons, we would be at a loss over how to respond to change and accommodate innovation. Dr Watson shows us the way, when he says to Holmes: 'You remind me of

[39] About explicit sources for literary criticism, a delicate negotiation is needed, as Feeney (1995) recently reminded us. (Broadening our sources will be important too, and late antiquity should be included: recent work on authors like Claudian and Nonnos shows that they can give important contributions to a history of generic *imaginaire*.)

[40] In reading Plato, one would be free to present lyric and tragedy as genres, but there could be little tolerance for the 'philosophical dialogue' as genre: this kind of historicization occludes transformations of the literary system.

Edgar Allan Poe's Dupin':[41] *A Study in Scarlet* builds on short stories which Poe himself had gathered in a mixed section of his works labelled 'Tales of Ratiocination', but it also advocates (through this reflexive allusion) a growing autonomy and visibility for the not-yet-existing genre which now hosts both Dupin and Holmes.

To strike a generational note for the last time, I started my career writing a thesis on Vergil and Homeric scholia, and being exposed to more literary theory than any Italian classicist of previous generations. Although I have not found answers to many problems in this field, I am glad that two positions I always found untenable are now being marginalized: the first is considering ancient theory as a mere curiosity; the second, forbidding one's pupils from using words and tools because they have no precise classical counterparts (concepts like point of view, the unconscious, and so on . . . even *Kreuzung*, perhaps). I am still convinced that the answers, better, the questions I am looking for exist somewhere in between those two time-honoured mistakes.

[41] Conan Doyle *A Study in Scarlet* (1887), ch. 2.

11

Seneca's *Epistles* Reclassified

Marcus Wilson

I

Seneca's *Epistles* have been particularly subject to theoretical redefinition. This opening statement raises a problem of its own, for it suggests that there is a particular category or genre to which the *Epistles* incontrovertibly belong. Few, I think, would want to argue with the proposition that the *Epistles* are, at least ostensibly, epistles. Not only are they collected under that title, but each text opens with a greeting framed in accordance with the standard epistolary protocol (*Seneca Lucilio suo salutem*) and ends with the conventional formula of leave-taking employed in Roman correspondence (*vale*). Those who have sought to reclassify the epistles have not attempted to deny their epistolary form, for to do so is impossible. Rather, they have treated it as a purely artificial device which does not so much alert us to the true character of the texts as disguise it. Given, then, that the *Epistles* are at least formally epistles, it seems legitimate to enquire whether the reclassifications stand up to scrutiny, and whether they enhance or impede a better understanding of Seneca's literary technique and philosophical position. In this essay I look at three prominent strategies that have been used to dethrone the 'epistolary' as the defining mode of Seneca's texts, by reconceptualizing it as 'essayistic', 'hortatory', or 'pedagogical'. I test these hypotheses against two specific epistles (nos. 27 and 33), and illustrate from the examination of those texts some features of both individual epistles and the movement of the correspondence as a whole that will need to be embraced by any adequate theoretical account of the *Epistles* that may be put forward in future.

The view that the *Epistles* are really essays is a reclassification that has enjoyed quite a remarkable run. This, when you think about it, involves an astonishingly radical redirection, one that shifts the ground away from under you if you had been so naive as to start thinking about the epistles in terms of their kinship with ordinary letters. Yet, at least in the English-speaking world, this was the first step of interpretation enjoined on every new reader by the near-unanimous opinion of the experts through most of the twentieth century. Duff told us that 'the opening for Seneca was to create the Latin philosophical essay'.[1] Rose observed that 'most of them, though they may pretend to be letters and have been really sent as such, are short essays'.[2] Coleman, in his otherwise excellent article of 1974, reminded us that 'Seneca's letters are a series of carefully organised essays on specific themes'.[3] Quinn, in 1979, stated bluntly that 'Seneca's letters are moral essays, not real letters', eliminating at one stroke the generic distinction between the *Epistles* and the dialogues, popularly referred to as 'moral essays'.[4] Such views were picked up and repeated in the work of non-classicist scholars and more populist writers and translators. Williamson, in *The Senecan Amble*, wrote of 'Seneca's practice of writing essays as epistles', as if the essay had been already an established genre in the first century AD and Seneca had gone out of his way to pretend that he was writing something else.[5] Likewise, in the introduction to the Penguin translation the conventional wisdom continues to be transmitted to new generations of readers: 'The *Epistulae Morales* are essays in disguise.'[6] Instrumental in institutionalizing this approach to the *Epistles* was Summers' edition and commentary on *Select Letters*, in which, despite his title, the more essay-like the epistle, the more likely is it to have been included, while others that are more polythematic are represented only in thematically unified fragments and all selections have been gratuitously endowed with Baconian titles.[7] They have been processed for modern (or, at least, mid-twentieth-century) consumption; converted into the genre they were said to resemble. The degree of distortion involved is effectively concealed. Concealment was less successful, though, in the Loeb edition,[8] which retained

[1] Duff (1964), 184. [2] Rose (1949), 369. [3] Coleman (1974), 288.

[4] Quinn (1979), 213. The same conflation of the epistles with the 'moral essays' occurs in Grant (1964), 77: 'In these epistles—a variant of his philosophical essays . . .'

[5] Williamson (1951), 194.

[6] Campbell (1969), 21. [7] Summers (1910). [8] Gummere (1917).

the device of essay-like titles, but unwittingly highlighted their inaptitude when divorced from the freedom to anthologize.

No one, I suspect, thought of the 'epistle as essay' equation as a specifically theoretical position. For Bacon, it had been a means of validating his own creative practice, by citing a classical precedent for a novel form of composition: 'For Senecaes Epistles to Lucilius, yf one marke them well, are but Essaies; That is dispersed Meditacions, though conveyed in the forme of Epistles.'[9] The role of the equation in more modern times was different. It became, as it was not for Bacon, an *interpretative* hypothesis, a preliminary reorientation, undertaken prior to analysis, which had the effect of restricting the parameters within which the texts were read; which tried to associate the *Epistles* with a more familiar class of texts with which they had something in common. It sought to contextualize them in terms of a modern hierarchy of literary forms; to establish a continuity of identity and tradition between materials and texts belonging to different eras and distinct cultures. It was, in other words, an unrecognized theoretical presupposition about genre. There is still something to be said for the equation. A few of the more thematically unified epistles (for historical reasons the best-known ones, like no. 47 on slavery) are very close to being what we would call essays, 'dispersed Meditacions', as Bacon describes them. Informal structure, conversational tone, the use of literary quotation and historical anecdote, the focus on the self, the exploratory approach to ethical and philosophical issues are all features of the *Epistles* that look ahead to Montaigne who, of course, quotes Seneca continually.[10] Though the *Epistles* are not themselves essays, their influence on the eventual formation of that genre is undeniable. Even Addison distinguishes between two types of composition, those, on the one hand, which 'are written with regularity and method', for which he claims Cicero as his model, and, on the other, those 'that run out into the wildness of those compositions which go by the name of *essays*'; 'Seneca and Montaigne', he writes, 'are patterns for writing in this last kind'.[11] The analogy between the epistle and the essay did at least recognize some of the qualities of the former, and might be partially defended on the grounds of the greater familiarity of

[9] See Kiernan (1985), 317.

[10] For Seneca's influence on Montaigne see Cancik (1967), 91–101.

[11] *Spectator* 476, 4 Sept. 1712.

the essay to the modern reader, who might, via the analogy, be led to a recognition of some features of the Senecan texts that would be obscured were they to be described simply as 'letters'. For Seneca's epistles are, in some respects, even less like ordinary letters than they are like essays. It might be argued that it was the very lack of a developed theory of epistolarity that allowed the essay equation, in the absence of any competitor, to rule Senecan criticism for so many years.

Modern theoretical approaches to the essay do offer some insights that seem applicable to Seneca's *Epistles*, particularly with regard to the fundamental difficulty of clarifying the relation of the personal to the philosophical. Like essays (and the models here are pre-eminently Montaigne and Bacon), the *Epistles* eschew the systematic and ground themselves in personal experience rather than fixed dogmas or a prescribed philosophical methodology. Each new epistle resituates the author differently in a new time, a new mood, sometimes in a new place. Neither the author's self nor the context in which he writes is fixed.[12] He offers a record of his temporary accords with the world and, as it were, rediscovers his philosophy through different situations, as you might learn or relearn a language not from a grammar but by living in a foreign country and improving by trial and error, always coping with an element of uncertainty, sometimes needing to improvise, sometimes getting things partly right, recognizing that you will deal with that particular problem better next time. The comparison comes from Adorno.[13] Later epistles do not cancel out earlier ones but revisit the ideas in new circumstances and combinations. It is never exhaustive, never definitive. An analogy with musical composition is instructive: throughout the collection philosophical ideas as motifs are explored through a series of inversions and reversals, in dissimilar moods, in concordance or discordance with other ideas.[14] Or to shift suddenly (in Senecan manner) to another image, one that also has roots in the theory of the essay,[15] the *Epistles* are prismatic, refracting the author's life and character, his moral and philosophical condition, his soul, in the light of different circumstances.

[12] At *Ep.* 6. 1 Seneca claims to be undergoing a process of transformation; in a number of epistles he seems to be travelling, e.g. 12; 51–7; 70; 86; 87.

[13] Adorno (1984), 161.

[14] Good (1988), 19.

[15] Prisms is the title chosen by Adorno (1981). See Good (1988), 24; 28.

Nevertheless, the essay model proved unsatisfactory. Why? First, it elides the role of Lucilius, by suggesting a more direct and unmediated relation between Seneca and the reader. This most obvious of epistolary features becomes an embarrassing encumbrance to the clean essayistic intimacy of author and reader by intruding an unwanted and redundant third party between them. Secondly, it ignores the ambivalent private/public character of the correspondence, ostensibly personal, but on open display to all. Published essays do not usually purport to have been written originally as a private communication to a particular individual and to have been conditioned by that recipient's peculiar circumstances. Thirdly, it discourages the reading of the collection sequentially, because essays are independent productions, demarcated by thematic boundaries, able to be read in any order or selectively. Consequently, the arrangement of the epistles in Books is downplayed in importance and the reiteration of themes and motifs across widely separated parts of the collection is allowed to pass unnoticed. Fourthly, it marginalizes those epistles at either end of the spectrum that are either too narrowly epistolary, too bound up with Lucilius and his specific concerns to register as essayistic, or so wide-ranging, so varied in theme or urgent in tone as to jar with the usual sense of how an essay should read. The later epistles, for instance, are more often polythematic, and the remarkable evenness of tone evident in the early Books is abandoned in the latter part of the collection. Lastly, the essay is not itself an entirely stable generic marker. It depends very much what kind of essay we think of when looking for something that corresponds to the Senecan epistle. In the Renaissance there was a clearer analogy, for Montaigne was engaged in an exploration of his own interiority[16] in a way that has much in common with Seneca's project in the *Epistles*. Today, the essays likely to be most familiar to those studying Seneca are academic in content, technical in language, impersonal in voice. The modern essay, that genre upon which we project so much cultural value, which we expect every student to master as a test of intellectual proficiency, bears almost no resemblance to an epistle of Seneca.

Probably the most far-reaching consequence of the 'essay' hypothesis was its unarticulated rejection of the 'epistolary' as a literary modality in its own right. This paved the way for more recent

[16] On self scrutiny in the *Epistles*, see Misch (1950), 417–35; Edwards (1997).

attempts to cast the *Epistles* into a new definitional framework. In the 1990s scholars are far more self-conscious about the theoretical foundations of their interpretative procedures, but while the specific analogy with the essay has lately been abandoned, the underlying assumption behind it, that the epistolary is not itself a category to be taken seriously in discussion of Seneca's work, seems to lurk beneath much current critical discussion. Attempts to produce a more theoretically engaged criticism of the *Epistles* seem to me to have been mostly unsuccessful. I would like to discuss two of these. The first is the article called 'An Aristocracy of Virtue: Seneca on the Beginnings of Wisdom', by Tom Habinek, in the volume of *Yale Classical Studies* devoted to the topic of *Beginnings In Classical Literature*;[17] the second is the contribution to the *Reflections of Nero* volume[18] by Yun Lee Too, entitled 'Educating Nero: A Reading of Seneca's *Epistles*'. While quite different in interpretative detail, these two articles have much in common methodologically in their theoretically charged vocabulary and bibliography; in their taking history rather than the texts as a starting-point; in their emphasis on the political rather than the ethical reading of the *Epistles*, in other words, their focus on issues of power; in their use of interpretative concepts (like ideology and hypocrisy) that limit the significance of Seneca's ideas and language to the way in which they serve his own interests personally or those of his particular social class; they are both extremely unsympathetic to Seneca (even hostile); they are both selective in the epistles or parts of epistles they choose to highlight as indicative of his practice, Habinek emphasizing Epistle 90 and Yun Lee Too the end of Epistle 108. However, I shall try to restrict myself here to considering the way they both attempt to reclassify his texts, with the result that aspects which do not fit the new classification are interpreted as failures of consistency or honesty, and the complex three-way relations between Seneca, Lucilius, and us, the reading public, is simplified and misrepresented.

Habinek's theoretical inspiration seems to come from the New Historicism. His argument is that all Seneca's philosophical works reflect the ideology of the Roman aristocracy and perpetuate its sense of its own superiority; that Seneca reproduces in the ethical domain the same class difference one finds at Rome in the economic domain. Seneca and Lucilius are building up their cultural

[17] Dunn and Cole (1992), 187–203.

[18] Elsner and Masters (1994), 211–24.

and ethical capital in a way that excludes the masses and asserts a new kind of pre-eminence over them. An ethical elitism reflects and reinforces social elitism. The question of genre is one he effectively bypasses, lumping all Seneca's writing into a single broad category, the *hortatory*. 'The literary point of departure for the Senecan literary project', he writes, 'is the upper-class Roman tradition of exhortation. The social function of such exhortation is both to transmit the dominant ideology in readily comprehensible form and to correlate specific instances of ethical choice with the general principles it prescribes' (p. 188). Thus, the reclassification of Seneca's work turns it into an 'aristocratic mode of control over thought, word and action' (p. 189). Two more claims of Habinek are worth noting: the first is that 'the standard rhetorical strategy of the opening of a Senecan treatise' is 'the claim to privileged knowledge' (p. 191); the second is that Seneca's relationship with his addressee excludes us as readers. He speaks of 'the absolute irrelevance of the external reader . . .', and asserts that 'Seneca's enstrophic play of *tu* and *ego* creates an inaccessible dialogue, inward directed and self-sustaining' (p. 199). He privileges the relationship of Seneca with Lucilius to such a degree that it becomes a closed correspondence that ignores and disowns outsiders like us.

This position cannot stand up to the kinds of objections a traditionalist scholar might bring forward. Habinek's classification of Seneca's writings as hortatory is impossibly reductive, ignoring their rich generic variety: it glosses over the differences between the consolations and the other 'Dialogues'; between the longer and more leisurely and comprehensive works like the *De Beneficiis* and shorter, more intense reflections on a theme like the *De Providentia*; between short monothematic epistles and long polythematic ones. Nor is it true that Seneca is consistently hortatory, especially in the *Epistles*. Habinek, having defined Seneca's aim as exhortation, interprets the absence of the hortatory in large stretches of his texts as a flaw in Seneca's literary competence: 'Seneca struggles to develop a dogmatic approach within a hortatory framework' (p. 190). Habinek's hypothesis is contradicted by ancient epistolary theory which took the epistle not as an opportunity for exhortation but as a substitute for conversation;[19] by Seneca's own

[19] Demetrius *On Style* 225; Malherbe (1988), 17; Russell and Winterbottom (1972), 211.

confirmation that he too regards the epistle in that light (22. 2; 38. 1; 40. 1; 65. 2; 67. 2); and by Seneca's own distinction between the *submissiora verba* ('low-toned words of conversation', 38. 1) with which he addresses Lucilius and the *contionibus* ('harangues') with which others sometimes need to be prompted.

Equally unpersuasive is Habinek's attempt to restrict Seneca's implied readership to his named addressee (and perhaps other Romans of similar social status and culture). If this presupposition were extended to other ancient texts we would have to admit that a large percentage of classical literature was calculated to repel readers: Lucretius' exclusive relationship with Memmius would convey the message that we are not meant to read the *De Rerum Natura*. Horace's fourteenth ode of his second Book would be for Postumus' eyes only. Seneca, of course, tells us, in Epistle 8. 2, that he is writing for posterity and, in Epistle 27. 1, that besides his other readers he is also speaking to himself.

Habinek's insistence that Seneca's standard opening strategy is 'the claim to privileged knowledge' runs into the immediate textualist objections, first, that he consistently denies that he is a *sapiens* (6. 1; 8. 2; 57. 3; 71. 30, 35–7; 75. 16–18; 79. 11–13; 87. 4–5), and secondly, that the *Epistles* rarely open with philosophical material at all, but usually with diaristic observation. Seneca makes it clear that he is himself learning and growing in the understanding of his philosophy at the same time as Lucilius.

If I move now to the recent interpretation put forward by Yun Lee Too, we find that she claims inspiration for her approach in the third volume of Foucault's *History of Sexuality* and in the book edited by Barbara Johnson entitled *The Pedagogical Imperative: Teaching as a Literary Genre*.[20] The gist of her interpretation is that the *Epistles* are primarily *pedagogical* in character. Seneca is instructing Lucilius in the philosophy of Stoicism, and therefore this relationship re-creates the philosopher's earlier role as teacher of Nero. Tied to this is an emphasis on what she regards as the established historical fact that hypocrisy was the ruling principle of Seneca's character; as she sees it, hypocrisy becomes the main lesson he taught Nero and the main feature of his self-presentation in the *Epistles*. 'Power and domination are the programme of Senecan pedagogy', she writes (p. 212). 'Nero learns well the lesson enacted by his hypocrite pedagogue' (p. 213);

[20] Johnson (1982); Foucault (1986).

and on the *Epistles*: 'Now Seneca rehearses and revises his prior relationship with the boy-emperor' (p. 213). She takes Seneca's insistence that the philosopher's words should be matched by actions not only as a strong, but insincere, repudiation of hypocrisy but also as an 'attempt to cancel out the traditional rhetorical opposition between word and deed . . . to squeeze out words altogether' (pp. 214–15). She then claims that certain features of the correspondence, such as Seneca's admission that he is also writing for himself and the signs that the correspondence may be fictional, do not fit the pedagogical model. These become, therefore, further evidence of hypocrisy, a calculated violation of his 'moral principle that one must enact one's language' (p. 215). Seneca employs a textual metaphor in writing about his own philosophical identity and that of Lucilius; yet at the same time he rejects (she wrongly believes[21]) the 'figure of metaphor as a whole' (p. 219). His highlighting of his own hypocrisy she sees as somehow representing himself 'as being able to disempower the state' (p. 222).

Again, traditional scholarship will easily unbalance this shaky interpretative edifice. Leaving aside the historical assumptions and concentrating just on the questions of generic classification and the role of Lucilius, the pedagogical character of the *Epistles* is never established in the article in the first place.[22] It is no less reductive and unsatisfactory than Habinek's 'exhortation' theory, and is contradicted both by Seneca's refusal to adopt the role of sage and his insistence on the reciprocal advantages for both parties in a situation of philosophical tutelage.[23] Likewise, it would seem to be incompatible with Seneca's acknowledgement of an intended readership beyond his immediate pupil and declaration that he is also talking to himself (8. 2; 27. 1). Ms Too, of course, has the answer to this: every such objection is just further proof of an all-pervasive hypocrisy. But a concept of hypocrisy that encompasses fictionality itself and other literary effects, including the adoption of a *persona*, is one that has lost all precision of definition and critical value. It makes much more sense to admit that the original hypothesis that the *Epistles* are quintessentially pedagogical is hopelessly inadequate.

[21] See *Ep*. 59. 6; Wilson (1987), 102.

[22] In support of her principal contention she refers only to 22. 1; 23. 1–2; 34. 2; 37. 11, 'and so on' (213).

[23] See e.g. 34. 2; 109. 12.

Her interpretation effectively erases the role of Lucilius by making him a cipher for Nero. He is simply a fictional substitute for the real pupil and addressee. The analogy that she asserts is a spectacularly imprecise one. Nero was a 12-year-old child when he came under the philosopher's tuition. Lucilius, on the other hand, is represented in the *Epistles* as resembling Seneca himself more than an imperial schoolboy. He has already entered upon old age (19. 1) and is suffering from the diseases of age (96. 3). He is mature in experience (an equestrian, made procurator of Sicily, currently involved in litigation), a writer (8. 10; 24. 19; 46; 79. 5–7), interested in and informed about philosophy, responding to Seneca's letters with his own examples, criticisms, enthusiasm, and requests for books. The terms in which this relationship is conceived are quite incompatible with that which Seneca had with Nero: one of affinity rather than difference in age, tastes, interests, and attitudes. It is also possible to demonstrate from the text of the *Epistles* that Seneca made a sharp distinction between giving, on the one hand, philosophical advice to grown men and, on the other, pedagogical instruction to youth (33. 7; 36. 4).

By pointing to the weakness of these interpretations according to traditionalist scholarly criteria, it is not my aim to imply that there is something wrong with theoretical approaches generally. The two articles I have discussed seem to me to be equally disappointing on theoretical grounds. Their theoretical frameworks seem borrowed and to have been forced upon uncongenial texts. All they succeed in doing is translating the age-old accusation against Seneca, that his life is in contradiction of his philosophy, into the language of postmodern critical discourse. They do not ask what theory is appropriate for this material. By opting for ready-made categories like the hortatory and the pedagogical, they *evade*, in my view, the real theoretical issue of epistolarity.

The approaches to Seneca's *Epistles* of Habinek and Yun Lee Too are unlikely to satisfy many Senecan scholars, especially those who are more sympathetic to him as a writer, philosopher, and historical figure than they appear to be. Few will be prepared to accept the proposition that one epistle or group of epistles can be singled out as more important than the rest and so offer an unparalled key to the significance of the collection as a whole. What we need is a theoretical scheme that encompasses the Senecan epistle in all its variety; which has explanatory value for the short letters as well as the long ones; for Epistle 1 and Epistle 100. Similarly, we must resist the privileging of any one mode of writing or tone of voice. Seneca, it seems to me, never indicates that he seeks to place his epistles in a fixed category like the 'hortatory' or the 'pedagogical', but his writing embraces both these modes along with many others: the familiar and intimate; the autobiographical; the satirical; the consolatory; the analytical; the literary critical. The first thing to notice about his epistolarity is that it is characterized by frequent modulation. What is needed is a theory that is custom-made; not one that has been bought off the shelf.

II

It is illuminating to make the attempt to relate these broad reclassifications to one or more individual epistles. Towards the close of the third Book Seneca replies, or purports to reply, to a challenge raised by Lucilius to his credentials as philosophical adviser. 'Are you giving me advice?', you say, 'Have you already advised and perfected yourself? Is that why you've got time on your hands to correct others?' (27. 1). As is often the case, the epistolary relationship is reiterated in the opening of the epistle where a query or doubt about something in an earlier letter is raised by the recipient. Lucilius is not represented as a passive addressee but as one who actively collaborates in determining the range of issues to be discussed. In effect Lucilius asks: 'So what qualifies you to act the part of the wise man?' In his answer Seneca has recourse to the common analogy between philosophy and medicine, but with a modification. He does not see himself as a physician diagnosing his patients, but as a fellow patient in the same hospital ward talking about a disease from which he also suffers and the efficacy of the various remedies he has tried. In this manner Seneca denies any claims to the status of *sapiens*. What he says next takes this even further: he is really talking to himself (*sic itaque me audi tamquam mecum loquar*); Lucilius is invited to listen in on his internal dialogue (*in secretum te meum admitto et te adhibito mecum exigo*); to become a witness to the debate going on inside Seneca's mind. This introduces a passage of direct speech purportedly addressed by Seneca to himself (*clamo mihi*, 2). At this juncture there is a conspicuous change of tone, from relaxed and conversational to vehement and demanding. The first word of the speech is an imperative: 'Count up your years' (*numera annos tuos*). He urges himself to put aside those pleasures that only disturb (*dimitte istas voluptates turbidas*) and look for some enduring good (*bonum mansurum circumspice*). He contrasts transient pleasures with the lasting and dependable joy that comes only from virtue (*virtus praestat gaudium perpetuum, securum*).[24] He simultaneously concludes the speech and effects a transition back to a more moderate tone by means of a simile likening interruptions to this *gaudium perpetuum* to clouds that pass beneath but never diminish the brightness of the sun (3). Returning to Lucilius again, Seneca encourages him to aspire to this state of permanent felicity, but warns that he must reach it by his own efforts. It's a thing that can't be delegated (*delegationem res ista non recipit*, 4). Most of the remainder of the epistle (5–8) is taken up with a series of anecdotes about a wealthy freedman, Calvisius Sabinus, who did, in fact, try to delegate to his slaves one of his mental functions, his memory. He acquired slaves specially trained to memorize Homer, Hesiod, and the Greek lyric poets so they could supply him with apt literary quotations on demand. This story does not illustrate the main point Seneca is making (that you cannot in philosophy deputize others to think for you), but the less important contrasting point that some people have, in some non-philosophical contexts, relied on the minds of their subordinates.

The account of Calvisius is elaborated to a length and richness of detail far beyond what is needed for the argument. It seems to be related more for its own sake than to serve as illustration. It is, furthermore, the most memorable part of the epistle, differentiated because of its humour from the more sober mood at the beginning and end. This whole central section has affinities with no other genre so obviously as with satire, and it shares with satire some of its typical motifs: incredibly rich but ill-educated freedmen, dinner parties, and literary pretentiousness. We learn about Satellius Quadratus, who shared Calvisius' food and entertainment but disparaged his learning (*adrosor . . . adrisor . . . derisor*, 7), making jokes at his host's expense, suggesting he train philologists to pick up the crumbs (*ut grammaticos habent analectas*) and that he take up wrestling, since he owned so many slaves of athletic appearance (8). The Calvisius digression is closed off with a return to the theme that introduced it, encapsulated in a

[24] This foreshadows the more detailed treatment of the same subject in *Ep*. 59.

sententia: a healthy mentality is not available for rent or purchase (*bona mens nec commodatur nec emitur*). The conceit that *bona mens* (a deity in Roman religious tradition) can be imagined (preposterously) as a tradable commodity is then expanded into two further statements connected by word repetition (*emitur* . . . *emptorem* . . . *emitur*). The first statement is hypothetical: if it were on sale no one would buy it. The second surprisingly reverses the emphasis on the impossibility of purchase and leaves the reader to grapple with a paradox (one that seems to reflect back on the example of Calvisius): mental dis-ease is purchased on a daily basis.

Throughout his first three Books Seneca draws each epistle towards closure by providing Lucilius with a quotation (almost all of them from Epicurus) on which to focus his reflections. A prime function of this device is that the voice of philosophical authority is displaced from Seneca onto the broad philosophical tradition. Seneca merely transmits the wisdom of Epicurus and other philosophical forerunners. He is himself, like Lucilius, a beneficiary, not the inventor, of these ideas inherited from the past. In Epistle 27 this is especially appropriate because it matches Seneca's role, as he described it in the opening, as a fellow patient sharing remedies with others recuperating in the same ward. Another common function of the closing quotation is to effect a shift in the epistle's theme (and often tone), and that is the case here. Epicurus' maxim fails to echo the main thematic concerns of the rest of the epistle, such as Seneca's repudiation of the role of sage, his contrast between ephemeral pleasures and the lasting joy attendant upon virtue, and the impossibility of pursuing philosophy by surrogate; though it does relate to an incidental feature of the character sketch that introduced Calvisius, namely his wealth (*fuit dives*, 5). Epicurus' idea, which he put in different ways at different times (*dicit Epicurus aliter atque aliter*), is expressed by Seneca as a paradox and a *sententia*: 'Wealth is poverty arranged to accord with the law of nature' (*divitiae sunt ad legem naturae composita paupertas*, 7). This theme of the definition of true wealth is new to this epistle, though not to the *Epistles* as a collection.[25] Another of the quote's functions is to recall earlier epistles and remind the reader that this text is not wholly self-sufficient but part of a sequence. Epicurus' axiom, according to Seneca, warrants repetition and can never be learnt thoroughly enough. Epistle 27 ends, characteristi-

[25] See e.g. 2. 6; 4. 10; 16. 7; 17. 11.

cally, with Seneca adding his own twist to the thought borrowed from Epicurus, a twist designed to throw open a new perspective, to restart rather than close off the train of thought in the reader's mind. Seneca introduces a distinction between two types of people who need to be approached philosophically in different ways. This he expresses as an antithesis: 'for some the remedies only need pointing out; for others they need to be forced down their throats' (*quibusdam remedia monstranda, quibusdam inculcanda sunt*, 9). His employment of the therapeutic metaphor (*remedia*) recalls the opening section of the epistle, and so in imagery, if not thematically, he brings it full circle. Seneca is back in the hospital room discussing with his companions the merits of the various treatments available.

To portray a text like Epistle 27 as intrinsically essayistic, hortatory, or pedagogical is simplistic and inaccurate. It does embrace something of each of these modes but, by the same token, it might be styled just as convincingly 'satirical', since that is the strongest impression it conveys for much of its length. Viewed as an essay, it has no unifying theme. The titles that have been imposed upon it seem arbitrary in their selection of one thematic strand as dominant over the others. Summers chose to elevate into a title the proposition advanced at the end of section 4, that philosophy cannot be delegated: 'Wisdom Not Won By Proxy.'[26] Motto, along with Gummere in his Loeb edition, disagrees. They pick as the controlling theme the thought found in section 3, that only virtue produces enduring happiness: 'Virtue Alone Gives Everlasting Joy'; 'On The Good Which Abides'.[27] All these titles suggest a thematic continuity that is not there and a consistency of seriousness which in the epistle is cut away by the Calvisius anecdotes that occupy half the text. They all gloss over the 'wealth as poverty' theme introduced in the closing stages and Seneca's deliberations on his stance as philosophical counsellor with which the letter began. Is the epistle hortatory or pedagogical? Both propositions assume a dominating authority exercised by Seneca over his reader of a kind which the epistle goes out of its way to deny. Rather than the language of teaching, Seneca uses that of healing; and even then defines himself as a patient, not a doctor. Lucilius' opening question raised the issue of Seneca's pedagogical

[26] Summers (1910), 26.

[27] Motto (1985), 97; Gummere (1917), i. 193.

and philosophical authority, to which his reply is that he makes no claim to authority of the kind assigned to him. There is one part of the epistle where an explicitly hortatory attitude and style are adopted (2–3); but here Seneca has self-consciously adjusted the relation of speaker to addressee by formally presenting it as a speech to himself. He has studiously avoided direct exhortation of the reader. There is one part of the epistle that is openly didactic (9): the reader needs to learn (*numquam satis discitur*) the lesson that 'wealth is poverty brought into accord with the law of nature'. But here too Seneca successfully distances himself from the didacticism by transferring pedagogical authority onto the shoulders of Epicurus; that is, by adjusting once more the relation of speaker and addressee. He makes himself, like the reader, part of Epicurus' audience, one of his pupils.

Epistle 27 includes instruction, exhortation, 'dispersed meditacions', social satire, self-portraiture, and responses to a reader's queries and concerns.[28] Any classification of such a text ought to allow for all of these and the thematic and tonal transitions necessary to bring them into confederation. This is what the Senecan epistle is, a fluid form characterized by a controlled volatility of mode. To reclassify it generically in terms of one of its constituent modes is easy to achieve by selective quotation, but severely reductive and theoretically crude.

The reclassifications of the *Epistles* I have been considering here all fail on one further test: that of structure. Epistle 27 is not structurally like an essay (since it lacks consistency of theme); nor does it bear any resemblance to the form of a speech according to the rhetorical handbooks; nor to a didactic treatise or any other recognized pedagogical model. The freedom of form is not out of keeping, though, with the nature of a personal letter between friends. With its juxtaposition of contrasting moods, manipulations of voice and addressee, and unexpected thematic transitions, Senecan epistolary structure also appears to have much in common with the structure of poetry. The Calvisius section of Epistle 27 is a kind of satirical *ecphrasis*, a description of a scene engraved in Seneca's memory (and concerned with the theme of memory), intended to separate and contrast with the philosophical material that precedes and follows it. A cyclic pattern is traced naturally by

[28] For other readings of *Ep.* 27 see Maurach (1970), 104–6; Hachmann (1995), 198–202.

all letters in that the epistolary conventions are most in evidence at the beginning and the end. The effect is enhanced in this epistle because, as noted above, the therapeutic language (*remedia*), used conspicuously in section 1, is reintroduced in the last lines. This kind of poetic (or even 'musical') approach to structure can be understood as a feature of Senecan epistolarity,[29] but is quite alien to the alternative classifications that have been advocated.

III

In his second epistle Seneca recommended to Lucilius his own custom of taking daily a quotation from one of the great philosophers of the past and making it a focal point for reflection (4–5). This established a ground-rule, observed throughout the first three Books, that each epistle will contain one or more quotes from Epicurus or some other philosopher which Seneca passes on to Lucilius for his edification. At the start of Book IV Seneca drops this by-now familiar feature. In the fourth letter of that Book he discusses that change of practice. In fact he devotes this whole letter (no. 33) to commenting on his own handling of epistolary form and, in particular, his reason for eliminating this most consistent and identifiable feature of his correspondence so far. He indicates that Lucilius himself has requested that the quotes be reinstated: 'You want some quotations (*voces*) from our chiefs included in these letters as in the earlier ones' (1). With this request Seneca refuses to comply. The discoverers of philosophy were not themselves preoccupied with 'choice blooms' (*flosculos*). Where individual utterances stand out there must be an unevenness of quality. The sayings of Epicurus are not uniquely Epicurean but public property, and belong also to Stoicism (2). They appear striking in Epicurus' writing because you don't expect robust sentiments

[29] Some of the prose reads like a kind of poetry, as in *Ep.* 27's last lines, best illustrated by typographic re-arrangement:

> Hoc saepe dicit Epicurus
> aliter atque
> aliter, sed
> numquam nimis dicitur
> quod
> numquam satis discitur;
> quibusdam remedia monstranda,
> quibusdam inculcanda
> sunt.

from a thinker popularly considered to be unmanly, though Seneca thinks otherwise. Unlike the Epicureans, who ascribe all their key ideas to a single founder figure, the Stoics are not under the shadow of a king (*non sumus sub rege*, 4) but look back equally to Zeno, Cleanthes, Chrysippus, Panaetius, and Posidonius. 'Put aside any hope you have that you can get a taste of the thought of the greatest men by reading extracts; it needs to be examined in its entirety, studied in its entirety (*tota tibi inspicienda sunt, tota tractanda*, 5). Seneca comes up with a surprising analogy, one more redolent of the literature of love[30] than the literature of moral instruction: a woman is truly beautiful not because of the excellence of any single feature such as her legs or arms, but because her overall appearance eclipses the attractiveness of the parts.[31] If Lucilius still insists on receiving quotes, Seneca can deal them out in profusion (6).

But he does not do so. Instead, he challenges Lucilius to make a leap in philosophical maturity. Proverbs and maxims that are learned by heart are suitable to children and novices, but it is disgraceful (*turpe est*) for a man who is well started on the road to philosophy 'to chase after choice blooms' (*captare flosculos*, 7). The reader is asked to abandon passivity and formulate maxims rather than memorize them (*dicat ista, non teneat*, 7). '"Zeno said this." "But what do you say?" "Cleanthes said that." "But what do you say?"' Lucilius should assert himself; he should not lie down under the weight of the philosophical tradition but exercise command over it; he should be a producer instead of a mere consumer of wisdom (*impera et dic quod memoriae tradatur*, 7). He needs to stop thinking of himself as a learner and become a teacher (*quousque disces? iam et praecipe*, 9). Let there be a difference between him and the books he reads (*aliquid inter te intersit et librum*, 9). Seneca outlines the dangers inherent in always following the opinion of one's forerunners (10). Of these the worst is that one gives up the attempt to discover anything new. At the end of the epistle Seneca shifts to the first person and asserts his own philo-

[30] e.g. Catullus 86.

[31] This epistle is particularly rich in comparisons: consistent writing is like a forest where no tree stands out above the rest (1); like Epicurus, the Persians, despite their effeminate dress, are sometimes warlike (2); the maxims of the Epicureans are like a shop-window display (3); the Stoics are not like Ovid's poor man counting his flock (4); the independent thinker is like a man who builds his own road (11).

sophical independence: 'I'll follow the old path, but if I find a route more direct and less steep, I'll build my own road' (*ego vero utar via vetere, sed si propiorem planioremque invenero, hanc muniam*, 11). His predecessors he will treat as guides but never as masters (*non domini nostri sed duces sunt*). Truth lies open to all and much of it still awaits explorers of the future.

As in the case of no. 27, attempts to view Epistle 33 as essayistic, hortatory, or pedagogical condemn themselves to gross simplification. While the letter is unified thematically, it is not self-sufficient and only makes sense in relation to other letters in the first three Books, in which the customary inclusion of a quotation was scrupulously observed. In other words, this epistle is too dependent on the epistolary sequence to stand independently in the manner of an essay. The author and addressee are strongly individualized and especially prominent because of their disagreement (Lucilius wants quotes; Seneca refuses) and because of the author's self-assertiveness in the conclusion.[32] The content reinforces the sense of the interconnectedness of this epistle with the wider collection, since it concerns the necessity of reading an author's work as a whole rather than selectively.

> Give up any idea you might have that you can get a taste of the thought of the greatest men piecemeal. It needs to be examined in its entirety, studied in its entirety. Its success lies in its continuity, for such works of intellect are interwoven with their own characteristic qualities so that no part can be subtracted from the whole without destroying it.

> Quare depone istam spem posse te summatim degustare ingenia maximorum virorum: tota tibi inspicienda, tota tractanda. ⟨Continuando⟩ res geritur et per lineamenta sua ingenii opus nectitur ex quo nihil subduci sine ruina potest. (5)

It is difficult to read this without inferring that it is also meant to apply to the *Epistles* themselves.

The language of Epistle 33 is, in many parts, hortatory. Yet the persuasion is not part of some strategy of control.[33] On the contrary, it is an exhortation to independence. Lucilius is urged to become self-reliant (*sibi iam innitatur*) to take command (*impera*), to originate something of his own (*aliquid et de tuo profer*, 7).

[32] Note the emphasis on the first person in s. 11: *non ibo per priorum vestigia? ego vero utar via vetere, sed si propiorem planioremque invenero, hanc muniam.*

[33] As Habinek (1992), 189 portrays it.

Those who fail to do so are criticized as lacking in nobility (8) and easily misled, doomed to consume but never to invent philosophical ideas (10). Similarly, there is some language suggestive of pedagogy here, but only insofar as it is used to encourage the reader to discard the role of student: 'How much longer are you going to stay a learner? It's time to be a teacher!' (*quousque disces? iam et praecipe*, 9). Seneca specifically contrasts the sort of pedagogical activities suitable to youth with the kind of intellectual autarky he enjoins on his adult readers.

> And so we give children sayings to learn off by heart and the sort of thing that the Greeks call 'chria', because the childish mind—which can't cope with anything more demanding—is at least capable of grasping them. For a man who has assuredly progressed some way, to chase after choice blooms is disgraceful, propping himself up with short, commonplace quotations, and relying on his memory.

> Ideo pueris et sententias ediscendas damus et has quas Graeci chrias vocant, quia conplecti illas puerilis animus potest, qui plus adhuc non capit. Certi profectus viro captare flosculos turpe est et fulcire se notissimis ac paucissimis vocibus et memoria stare. (7)

The letter rejects as un-Stoic the authoritarian pedagogical model for philosophical training. 'They are merely guides, not masters, who tackled these subjects before us' (*qui ante nos ista moverunt non domini nostri sed duces sunt*, 11); 'We're not subject to a king: we each lay claim to our own freedom' (*non sumus sub rege: sibi quisque se vindicat*, 4).

'You must be a slave to philosophy', wrote Epicurus. In Book I Seneca borrowed Epicurus' advice and passed it on to Lucilius (*Philosophiae servias opportet*, 8. 7). A certain passivity, it seems, is requisite at least in the early stages of philosophical initiation. The use of quotations in Books I–III reflects this. They are nuggets of wisdom for Lucilius to digest (*concoquas*, 2. 4). They summon him to an effort of understanding. Perhaps the most astonishing thing about Epistle 33 is the vehemence with which Seneca repudiates the approach he previously advocated.[34] Through those earlier Books he had emphasized the seriousness of the exchange of quotations by speaking of them as if they were down-payments

[34] If the correspondence is 'fictional', Seneca need not have raised the issue of his dropping of the quotes at all. He seems to have gone out of his way to make the point that he is reversing his former practice.

on a debt (e.g. 7. 10; 9. 6; 18. 14; 19. 10; 29. 10). Now, in Epistle 33, such quotations are pejoratively described by the diminutive *flosculos* (1, 7). The serious business transaction is redescribed as trifling, a plucking of flowers.[35] The authors of the quotes were previously 'proven authorities' (*probati*, 2. 4); now in Epistle 33 Seneca's tongue is in his cheek when he refers to them as 'chiefs' (*proceres*). It is disgraceful (*turpe est . . . turpe est*, 7) to prop oneself up with other people's sayings, to possess wisdom only in the form of a commonplace book. Seneca's condemnation of the use of quotations is so vigorous, so uncompromising, that he seems implicitly to be undermining the whole basis of the philosophical progress achieved in the first three Books. Epistle 33 could not, for instance, be relocated out of sequence into, say, Book I without destroying the effectiveness of all the letters in Books II and III. At the very least, Seneca is redefining retrospectively Books I–III as more purely preliminary and protreptic than they previously appeared to be.

One might be inclined to interpret this as evidence of an inveterate hypocrisy (along the lines suggested by Yun Lee Too) or as indicating a 'faultline' between Seneca's doctrinal content and hortatory style (along the lines suggested by Habinek); but there is too obviously some attempt being made here to mark a turning-point in the collection and in the relationship of both Seneca and his reader to the philosophical ideas with which they are engaged. The rejection of reliance upon philosophical maxims and the insistence on reading works in their entirety are not the only changes to be noted in the early epistles of Book IV. Surrounding Epistle 33 are letters that put much emphasis on Lucilius having attained considerable progress in his studies (31. 1; 32. 1–2; 34. 1). In Epistle 33 itself there is introduced for the first time a strong contrast between Stoic and Epicurean approaches to philosophy,[36] between manly (*virilis*, 1) and unmanly (*mollitiam*, 2) ethical codes, that is out of keeping with the concentration on areas of common ground between the two schools that prevailed in the preceding Books. From here on, Seneca's stance towards Epicureanism

[35] This makes a mockery of the claim by Habinek (1992), 193–4, that the commercial language used in describing the exchange of quotes amounts to a commodification of philosophy. Seneca does not maintain the practice. After the first 29 epistles the quotes are cancelled and redescribed in no. 33 in anti-commercial terms.

[36] On this aspect of the epistle, see Maso (1980).

becomes far more negative. This shift was heralded in Epistle 30, the first of Book IV, in which Epicurus' views on death were presented through the medium of Bassus (14) who, being a Roman and himself standing on the brink of death, can speak with the greater *auctoritas* (7). There is a new mood of assertiveness in Book IV associated with a move away from Epicurean sources in addition to the renunciation of borrowed sayings. Seneca's echoing of the opening injunction of Epistle 1 ('Reclaim yourself for yourself', *vindica te tibi*) at 33. 4 (*sibi quisque se vindicat*) seems designed to underscore the impression that he is, in some sense, starting afresh.[37] He returns to his original impulse, imbuing it with new connotations, a new energy. What Seneca is doing is no mere recycling of standard Stoic doctrines. He is putting his own spin on them. The distinguishing feature of Stoicism, he suggests in Epistle 33, is its allowance of intellectual adventure, its emancipation of the *proficiens* from the burden of submission to past ideas. Stoicism is re-imagined as an uprising against despotism (*non sumus sub rege*, 4); a reclaiming of personal autonomy (*sibi quisque se vindicat*, 4); an assertion of individual freedom (*non domini sed duces sunt*, 11).

Again, the question of structure is overlooked by alternative classifications of the Epistles. The 'structure' that most matters in the case of Epistle 33 is that of the collection rather than that of a single letter. Much of the effect of Seneca's *Epistles* depends on their sequence. A collection of letters, even fictional letters, contrasts with a collection of essays, for instance, in its relation to time. Though Seneca's letters don't carry dates, it is clearly implied that their order reflects the order of composition or, more importantly, the order in which they purport to have been received and read. In other words, they are arranged chronologically.[38] It is

[37] *Ep.* 33 also contains echoes of other letters in Bks. 1–3: e.g. the idea in 33. 2 that the quotes from Epicurus are common philosophical property recalls the end of Book 1 (12. 11), the last epistle of Book 2 (21. 9), and the last of Book 3 (29. 11). It also occurs elsewhere in those Books (e.g. 16. 7).

[38] References in the text to the changing seasons offer a coherent sequence: Griffin (1976), 400. Specific references forward and backwards between letters, while uncommon, can be found, as when at 57. 1 Seneca humorously declines to return to Naples by sea, an obvious allusion to his miserable bout of sea-sickness in no. 53. Through the collection there is an unmistakable increase in the average length of the letters and the complexity and detail of the philosophical discussions. The theme of retirement from official duties (*otium*) is much more prominent in the first half of the collection (e.g. 19; 22; 36) with the emphasis subsequently switching from the need to retire to how to behave once one has retired (68; 82. 1–4). For the

also the case that the implied reader of the *Epistles* is delineated in unusually explicit terms. His name is Lucilius. He can only have read the letters in the order in which they arrived, the order observed in the collection. To apprehend the intended effect of the *Epistles*, it seems obvious that we should aim to duplicate Lucilius' experience by reading them in the same sequence; not just as a collection but as a series.[39] 'A letter may be regarded as one of the two sides in a dialogue', wrote Demetrius,[40] but he does not discuss the possible generic affinities of a whole correspondence directed to a single addressee. Instead of the 'dialogue' model it is perhaps more fruitful to conceptualize 'serial epistolography', if I might introduce that term, in relation to narrative. Narrative I take to be not only a mode of representation but also a mode of understanding and argument.[41] Individual Senecan epistles are not narrative in form; nor does the collection, even when read sequentially, construct a narrative in the usual sense of the word, since there is no narrator, little physical action, and it is punctuated by continual interruptions of continuity. Yet reading the *Epistles* is analogous in some respects to what one experiences in reading an epistolary novel. They tell a story of the growing relationship between the writer and the recipient and the developing depth and resolve of the philosophy of both. The underlying narrative scheme is one of moral and intellectual progress. In the absence of a narrator, it is left to the reader to interlink the letters, to discern the shape, the direction, the rationale of the correspondence. Seneca's self-description as a *proficiens* rather than a *sapiens* has literary as well as philosophical ramifications. The former, in contrast to the latter, is on a journey. The role implies movement, change, development. Early in the series Seneca declares that he is being transformed by the process upon which he and Lucilius have embarked (6. 1). We are led, both by this and the many references to Lucilius' advancement,[42] to expect some maturation in both their characters and some enrichment of their (and our) understanding. Seldom does Seneca try to argue his philosophical position in

charting of Lucilius' progress, see n. 42 below. At 106. 3, Seneca's words imply that his order of exposition has its own proper sequence (*illa serie rerum cohaerentium*).

39 Contra Misch (1950), 428.

40 Demetrius, *On Style* 223. Russell and Winterbottom (1972), 211.

41 In accordance with the views advocated by White (1978); Mink (1987).

42 See 2. 1; 5. 1; 13. 1; 16. 2; 19. 1; 20. 1; 31. 1; 32. 1; 34. 1; 41. 1; etc.

traditional philosophical or logical terms. In fact he wages a long campaign against logic.[43] On the contrary, the persuasive power of the *Epistles* seems to me very much bound up with the draw of its surreptitious narrative. Of the existence of a progression in philosophical approach and epistolary technique, the early epistles of Book IV (and no. 33 in particular) furnish ample demonstration. When readers approach Seneca's *Epistles* in an anthologizing or selective manner, they seem to me to have failed to grasp the plot.

IV

Viewed in literary terms, the epistle is not so much a genre as a cluster of genres. Some are private, some public; some hover in the no-man's-land between. The subject-matter may range from the personal to the political to the religious or philosophical or a mixture of any of these. In manner they may be commendatory, apologetic, consolatory, didactic, and even vituperative. Groups of epistles may have a single addressee or many, and may be arranged by type, addressee, in chronological order, or by theme. They may be in verse or prose. Although vastly superior to the 'essay' or the 'hortatory' or the 'pedagogical' as a starting-point for trying to understand the nature of Seneca's *Epistles*, the 'epistolary' is itself an inexact and slippery critical category. But that protean quality, so awkward for scholars and critics intent on tying down the character of a text is, in part, the reason why the form is so uniquely serviceable for artful writers in the mould of Seneca. It was, in all probability—for there can be no proof—the publication of Cicero's *Letters To Atticus* (to which the earliest references are in the *Epistles to Lucilius*)[44] that offered Seneca the immediate inspiration for a series of letters addressed to a single correspondent. What more suitable vehicle could be found for conveying an intimate sense of the author's character and communicating a high estimate of the value of friendship? Both these concepts were manifest in the Atticus correspondence and seem to have been accepted by the theorists, such as they were, as innate to the epistolary genre.[45] Cicero's *Letters To Atticus* were not composed

[43] See 45. 5–13; 48; 49. 8–10; 82. 8–10; 83. 8–12; 85; 87. 41; 88. 42–5; 102. 20; 106. 11; 111; 117. 18–20.

[44] See Shackleton Bailey (1965), 61. 118. 1–2.

[45] Demetrius *On Style* 225, 227; Malherbe (1988), 17–19; Russell and Winterbottom (1972), 211.

in order to produce a coherent collection, but arose out of a process of collection and publication after their author's death that saw their separation from the rest of his epistolary output.[46] Seneca discerned in this collection a potential new genre: a life and personality reflected in a series of (apparently) personal letters.[47] As to content, however, he rejected Cicero's gossip about political manoeuvres and scandals,[48] and drew instead on the tradition of philosophical epistolography as represented especially by the example of Epicurus, whose works he read during the composition of the early Books.[49] In both philosophical and literary spheres he challenges the achievements of Greek philosophical epistolography. In doing so he draws upon another Roman source, which he discovered in the verse epistles and satires of Horace,[50] with their humour, ethical commentary, and skilful manipulations of persona and voice. What Seneca creates is a new branch of epistolography, one that is distinctive and sophisticated in its literary affiliations. No simple generic definition can possibly embrace this level of variety and complexity.

It ought to be possible, though, to overcome the most misleading consequence of the term 'epistle', which is that it averts attention from the sequentiality of the collection. Therefore, as indicated above, I take the view that the proper genre to which Seneca's *Epistles* should be assigned is that of 'serial epistolography', recognizing at the same time that any such designation must in the nature of things mark a compromise between the irreconcilable demands of brevity and accuracy.

[46] If Seneca was indeed moved to write his *Epistles* by the example of Cicero, this lends weight to those who maintain that they were designed from scratch for publication; because it was only as a phenomenon of collection and publication that Cicero's *Letters To Atticus* have an independent existence.

[47] An analogy between his own relationship with Lucilius and that of Cicero with Atticus is suggested at 21. 4.

[48] See 118. 1–2.

[49] See 8.7: 'I'm still working through Epicurus, whose saying I read today' (*adhuc Epicurum complicamus, cuius hanc vocem hodierno die legi*). For further evidence see Griffin (1976), 418, n. 5.

[50] Seneca quotes or alludes to Horace's works several times, e.g. at 86. 13; 119. 13; 120. 20.

Historicism

12

Introduction

Historicism and History, or Beauty and the Beast

Simon Swain

Historicism, a term that may be applied to history but which is today mainly appropriated by literature, has many tentacles and many of these are mutually offensive.[1] One way or another it concerns itself with the interpretation of a text written in the past and the possibilities of reading that text both in the present and—for historicists are without any conception of their mortal limitations—in the future. In every case 'knowledge' of the past is about redeeming the present and finding hope for what is to come. Historicism should not be seen simply as a way of making literary critics look respectable. It is also a sign of the extraordinary relationship of doubt that intellectuals in all disciplines have with the past, be it a past of two millennia or two years. But the self-conscious popularity of the concept today—in the form of the *soi-disant* New Historicism—is one of the most audacious strategies yet for dignifying the literary academy.

To a historicizing mind there are two broad (historical, i.e. chronological) divisions of historicism to take note of. First, the (very) old: the set of beliefs which cluster around the assumption that Nature and Human Nature are constants that have remained unchanged since time immemorial and will continue to do so, and in all parts of the globe. This appealing notion of the progress of

[1] See the definitions in Moles, below, pp. 195–219, with comprehensive bibliography, to which add Pelling (2000). For what follows here neophyte readers may find help in Hamilton (1996), Thomas (1991), Veeser (1989), Dylan (1968). For Vico and Nietzsche see respectively Vico (1984) and Nietzsche (1997). Of the innumerable works on Foucault readers may enjoy Miller (1993) and Halperin (1995; 'As far as I'm concerned, the guy was a fucking saint'). For Geertz see Silvermann (1990); the same volume also contains essays on Derrida and Foucault from the theoretical archaeology school. For Greenblatt see Greenblatt (1980) and (1988) and for McGann see McGann (1983).

history, the gradual fulfilment of rational potential, leading to the present was typical of the seventeenth- and eighteenth-century confidence of the Enlightenment. The global expansion of European civilization turned up what was hoped for: other worlds looking like Judaeo-Christian Europeanism.

It is not surprising that the intellectual oligarchy should want to find the world made in its own image. Nor that some of its members, driven by competition, careers, and time, should break ranks and question the consensus. Their historicism, the progenitor of much of today's term, was characterized above all by relativism and subjectivism. Many current New Historicists worship as their ancestor in this regard the early eighteenth-century Neapolitan philosopher Giambattista Vico, who revitalized history as a science and postulated different evolutionary cycles with correlating changes in mentalities. Here literary interpretation and historical explanation went hand in hand. But it was left to the great G. W. F. Hegel at the start of the nineteenth century, and his idea of History as a process of continuities and discontinuities, to set us once and for all against the old certainty of cause and effect (which of course only the philosopher Hegel could supersede). Thus was all possibility of general law made void. As a tool of literary criticism (and therefore of class war) this historicism was brilliantly wielded by Marx to expose the mystifications of all teleological history, which was the wagging tail of the bourgeois dog. Friedrich Nietzsche's mad wit, again, aimed a devasting blow at the teleological consequences of historicism (though not historicism per se), as he railed against the comforting reading of the past–present nexus that justified the Prussian empire. And he and Wilhelm Dilthey, the late nineteenth-century philosopher, critic, and psychologist, who brought to literature the approach of *Geistesgeschichte*, are the older immediate ancestors of today's fashion.

Dilthey's *Geistesgeschichte* (effectively, 'culture-history') was a reaction against positivist interpretations of literature. Not surprisingly, its origins lie in early nineteenth-century German *Romantik* and its concern to place individuals in their society (see, famously, Goethe's *Wilhelm Meisters Lehrjahre*). The result was a reaction against literary 'genius' in favour of exploring common characteristics and backgrounds. The pathway to the darling of today's historicists, the philosopher-historian Michel Foucault, is not hard to plot. The difference is that Foucault took dialectic confrontation out of the arena of meaning into that of power. The different epochal modes of signification, Foucault's 'epistemes', were revealed by contradiction—and revealed in turn a 'Thucydidean' unitary 'systematics' of power. It is down the byways of the mastertext that Foucault travelled to uncover his epistemes. He was master of the anecdote, the vignette, the scene, a genius at recovering what is juxtaposed just when it seemed mimetic and familiar. For Foucault the past was no liberation; yet to some academics it has been quite appealing to be assured that the 'microphysics' of eighteenth-century punishment (cf. *Discipline and Punish*) were much the same as those of their twentieth-century classrooms. The twenty-first century will be no different.

Add to this Foucault a strong dash of Clifford Geertz's self-speaking anthropological descriptions of Indonesia and Morocco, add a touch of Derrida, and you end up with the Shakespearean subversions of Stephen Greenblatt, the Romantics in Jerome McGann, or the privileged post-colonial and post-female *romans-à-clef*. The present of the past: the always present past is an engaging idea often explored by these recent historicists. It is important in the texts that follow here. For both Thucydides and Polybius, as commentators on the present (they are not historians), were aware of previous readings of the same—and of their own supersessions. In this volume Thucydides/Moles has no pretensions to be called a historicist critic—he just reads the text as a simple scholar. No byways here; but Thucydides is a fit subject for (t)his type of enquiry because on one level he/Moles (re-)presents *avant le mot* an Enlightenment view of progressively sophisticated human integration through which there operates a constant law of Human Nature, a mechanism of prediction that allows for interpretation of past, present, future; *and* at the same time his chosen mastertext—the power of Periclean Athens—is constantly undone by the juxtaposition of episodes like the Plague and the Sicilian Disaster. Thucydides' notion of the 'always present' is *the* challenge to every generation's criticism, and Thucydides, in Moles' words, emerges as the 'proto-historical-historicist' who 'textualized' a war as case work for his all-too-human dialectics.

It is part (but only part) of historicism's remit to study texts of no worth and no interest (*Geistesgeschichte* again). Polybius (the man who 'lived a lot' or had 'many lives', as a conference-goer chirped) is one such. He is only 'interesting' to students of Roman expansion. Yet he is a perfect byway for historicist enquiry, which is what Henderson cunningly pursues, kicking off appositely from a fragment of Derrida. Polybius resembled but rivalled Thucydides, with a bigger story with an ineluctable quasi-Stoic conclusion: we all get the Roman Empire we deserve. But a true historicist does not stop with the obvious: that is, post-colonial history before colonies. A bytext to end all bytexts, a spurious autobiography of Polybius' modern historical commentator, Frank Walbank ('FWW'), is Henderson's 'anecdotal' reserve to illuminate the contradictions of the original, most of which was lost long ago. But there is danger too—we may be witnessing the implosion of the sacred rite. For another way of reading these pages is to believe in Walbank's words and to curse Henderson for subjecting us to the most classical of all: the history of classical scholarship.

13

A False Dilemma: Thucydides' *History* and Historicism*

John Moles

THE PROBLEM

For a laboratory on historicism, Thucydides, greatest and most influential of ancient historians, yet still today an immensely controversial figure, seemed an appropriate case-study. This participant had only murky notions about 'historicism', and consultation of a range of colleagues elicited two (and only two) responses: 'Historicism? I'm confused'; 'Historicist? That's what Don Fowler calls people he disagrees with.' Nor are such reactions confined to the ignorant. E. H. Carr complained that 'Popper uses the word historicism as a catch-all for any opinion he dislikes', and as late as 1988 John Cannon dismissed historicism as 'a confused and confusing word, which should be abandoned, since it obscures more than it illuminates'. Such typically British poverty of response to theory was fecund ground for the conference's educative work.

Necessarily brief immersion in writings about historicism[1] brought inchoate illumination.

The German *historismus* was first translated into English as 'historism', later as 'historicism', which has prevailed. Historicist thought concerns all aspects of human life, but 'historical' and 'literary' historicism may be usefully, if artificially, distinguished.

* I thank the conference organizers and, as readers, Simon Hornblower, Damien Nelis, Peter Rhodes, Malcolm Schofield, and Tony Woodman.

[1] Dictionary entries: Iggers (1973); Cannon (1988); McCanles (1993); Fowler and Fowler (1996); guide: Hamilton (1996); works on/including, 'historical' historicism: Meinecke (1936/1972); Aron (1938); Lee and Beck (1954); Popper (1957); *History and Theory*, Beiheft 14 (1975); Momigliano (1977); Cameron (1989); Le Goff (1992); Jenkins (1995); Evans (1997); 'literary' historicism: Greenblatt (1980) and (1988); Veeser (1989); Thomas (1991); Perkins (1992); Martindale (1993); Hawthorn (1996); Ryan (1996); Fowler (1999), introduction, whose writings and talkings have done so much to educate British classicists.

Historical historicism was originally an assertion of the supreme importance of historical explanation. Diverse developments followed:

- The belief that history is a human product (hence rejection of divine agency in history);
- The necessity of establishing history *wie es eigentlich gewesenist* (Ranke)—history as it really happened (facts, chronology, etc.);
- The application of so-called scientific method to the study of history;
- The belief that, like the sciences, history exhibits laws and principles;
- The belief that explaining the past enables, by extrapolation, prediction of the future;
- A genetic or teleological view of history;
- Emphasis on understanding the particular historical context;
- Denial of the Enlightenment proposition that all history is essentially the same;
- Insistence on distinctive differences between different periods and cultures, precise historical circumstances greatly influencing or even dictating human attitudes and behaviour;
- Changes of moral attitude to the study of history, older claims for its universal moral value being replaced variously by moral relativism, exculpation of the past (understanding the past on its own terms), or denial of the relevance of any moral response;
- The belief that if historical circumstances condition human behaviour, this must equally apply to the historian, who is 'always already' implicated/complicit in history and its discourses and hence must study the past either through his own cultural presuppositions or through those of the period studied or in recognition of the futility of either of these projects;
- Denial that history can be scientific or predictive.

Literary historicism similarly views texts as human products, with, again, many diverse developments:

- The claim that literary texts are products of their culture or period;
- The claim that the meaning of literary texts can be delimited by the establishment of the cultural presuppositions of the writer and his contemporary readers;

- The claim that literary texts are products not simply of their culture and period but of their formal structures (which may be intrinsic and timeless or themselves products of their culture) or of their codes (which are intrinsic to their cultures and therefore require cracking by later readers);
- The claim that texts are products not simply of their culture and period and of their formal structures and/or of their codes but of the creative originality of the individual writer;
- The claim that 'literary' texts are no different from non-literary texts in being the products of their own cultures;
- The claim that literary and other texts are producers as well as products of their cultures, and therein bridge the gap between internal (formal) and external (cultural) factors in their production;
- The claim that literary texts are simply one element of the plethora of different media which comprise human verbal productions and which constitute the general 'discourse' of a culture or its particular 'discourses' about specific areas of life.

This last definition, characteristic of the 'New Historicism' of the 1980s onwards, may involve: (a) insistence that texts' historical context (in the broadest sense) overrides their formal aspects; (b) the idea that all culture is essentially 'textual'; (c) the downgrading of literary texts within the overall contextualized culture (no particular kinds of texts being particularly worthy of study); (d) interest less in the contents of texts than in the discourses that produce them; (e) transference of the idea of authorship from individual texts to the discourses that constitute the culture; (f) contextualization of individual texts within the context of all other texts which constitute the culture (hence elision of the distinction between text and external cultural factors); (g) contention of radical decentring (arising from sharp and unpredictable cultural shifts); (h) definition of historical context in terms of hierarchies of power (of gender, race, or class); (i) investigation of whether literary texts within a culture tend to subvert or (even when apparently subverting) to collude with those hierarchies of power; (j) use of literary study to subvert contemporary hierarchies of power. These various perspectives tend to bring historical and literary historicism together.

Although context determines the precise application of the term 'historicist', two questions remain fundamental: the extent to which a period/text can be understood within its own historical context, and the extent to which later interpreters can bridge the gap between their own context and that of the period/texts they are studying.

THE INTERACTION OF THEORY AND PRACTICE

Thucydides can be viewed under three aspects: as historian writing the past; as textual product of the past; as text whereby *we* try to write the past. All three aspects interact with historicist concerns. The sequel therefore correlates these concerns with major Thucydidean problems.

While Thucydides' preface[2] justifies his choice of the Peloponnesian War by its supreme greatness (1. 1. 1–3), it is an important sub-claim[3] that only contemporary history can be done properly: he wrote up the war, *beginning immediately it started* (1. 1. 1); *to discover clearly* the things before it and the things *still more ancient was impossible because of the quantity of time intervening* (1. 1. 3; cf. 20. 1); such 'things' can only be discovered by means of 'indications' (*tekmeria*, 1. 1. 3; 20. 1; 21. 1) or 'signs' (*semeia*, 21. 1), 'sufficiently' (21. 1) to establish that they were not great (1. 3), but necessarily less accurately inasmuch as they are 'ancient things' (21. 1). By contrast, rigorous scrutiny of eyewitness testimony (22. 2–3) makes it possible to discover 'the deeds themselves' of 'this war' (21. 2).[4] Thus Thucydides' choice of contemporary history collapses one of historicism's key dilemmas: the gap between

[2] Moles (1993a), 98–114, here revised and redirected; valuable observations in Hornblower (1991), 3–66 and Marincola (1997), *passim*.

[3] Wrongly denied by Woodman (1988b), 149 ff.

[4] This summary immediately invalidates Shrimpton's radical claims ((1997), 45–6, 198) that (a) 'in this system there can be no conceptual distinction between historical facts and their description . . . [and] no room for a sophisticated historical method': 1. 1. 1 *xunegrapse ton polemon* is proleptic of chs. 22–3 and the 'identification' of the war with the *History* Thucydides has composed *incorporates* the methodological rigour of 1. 2 and 23. 5–6; and (b) '*heurisko* cannot mean "find out by investigation or enquiry" . . . [but] evokes the ancient, rhetorical concept of *heuresis*, which means the discovery . . . of the appropriate narrative procedure'; note especially the contrast (n. 15) between 22. 3, 'things were discovered with much labour' and 20. 3, 'so unpainstaking for most people is the search for the truth': unlike 'most people, who merely seek without pain', Thucydides 'takes pains' and 'finds'. (All the extremely literalist translations in this paper are my own and essay verbal relationships customarily ignored.)

historian and period.[5] Yet this contemporary history 'is set down as a possession for always' (22. 4). There could be no more radical challenge to historicism in any of its forms.

The seemingly endlessly discussed 1. 22 remains crucial for Thucydides' conception of history and his *History*. There is no interpretative consensus, and existing treatments are error-strewn (largely through neglect of the organic complexity of Thucydides' argument) and insensitive to his densely brilliant language and literary allusion:

> [1] As for all the things that each side said in speech [*logos*], either when they were going to war or when they were already in it, it was difficult both for me in the case of the things that I heard myself and for those who reported to me from various different places to remember completely the accurate content of the things that were said. But as it seemed to me, keeping as closely as possible to the general drift of what truly was said, that each speaker would most say what was necessary concerning the always presents, so I have rendered the speeches. [2] But as regards the deeds of the things that were done in the war, I did not think it a worthy procedure to write by asking for information from the person who chanced to be present, nor just in accordance with what seemed to me to be so, but both in the case of things at which I myself was present and of things which I learnt about from others, by going through them in each case with accuracy as far as possible. [3] They were discovered with much labour, because those who were present at each particular deed did not say the same things about the same things, but in accordance with the individual's sympathy for one side or the other or his memory. [4] And perhaps the lack of the *muthos* element in my *History* will appear rather unpleasing to an audience, but if those who wish to look at [*skopein*] the clearness [*to saphes*] both of the things that happened and of those which, in accordance with the human thing, are going to happen again some time like this and near the present ones, should judge it useful, that will be sufficient. It is set down as a possession for always rather than as a competition piece for present hearing.

How *can* the *History* be 'a possession set down for always'? This is the single most important question about Thucydides, from which all other questions flow. The claim follows the statement that the *History* covers 'both . . . the things that happened and . . . those which, in accordance with the human thing, are going to happen

[5] Ancient discussions of the pros/cons of contemporary history: Marincola (1997), 66–95.

again some time like this and near the present ones'. And from the perspective of the preface's architecture, the apparently strongly closural 'it is set down [*xugkeitai*] as a possession *for always* rather than as a competition piece *for present hearing*' rings with 1. 1. 1: 'Thucydides . . . wrote up [*xunegrapse*] the war between the Peloponnesians and Athenians, how they waged war on each other, *beginning immediately it started and expecting that it would be* great and more worthy of record than those *which had happened before it*', this ring reinforcing the work's timelessness.[6]

Interpretation of the claim of timelessness involves the prior concept of 'the clearness', which has itself been variously interpreted: 'the (clear) truth' (the traditional view), 'a clear picture' (Hornblower), 'a clear account' (Rhodes), 'a realistic view' (Woodman).[7] But simple logic[8] excludes anything less than 'the truth'. First, if Thucydides does not provide the truth of the things that have happened, he cannot make his case that 'this war will . . . from the deeds themselves reveal itself to those who look at it to have been greater than preceding wars' (1. 21. 2). Secondly, the use of *saphes* picks up and contrasts with *saphos* in 1. 1. 3: periods before the Peloponnesian War 'cannot be discovered clearly'. But Thucydides has 'discovered the clearness' of the Peloponnesian War. So far from the concepts of 'clearness' in 1. 1. 3 and 1. 22. 4 being different, as Hornblower states, they are the same.[9] *To saphes*, 'the clear truth', as visually verifiable, comes from the rigorous assessment of eyewitness testimony on which Thucydides has just insisted (1. 22. 2–3).[10]

Enter the proto-historical-historicist, the oft-hailed 'Thucydi-

[6] Then, after 23. 1–4 on the war's supreme greatness, 23. 5–6 treats Thucydides' 'pre-writing' of the causes of the war: 23. 5 *prougrapsa* < 1. 1 *xunegrapse*.

[7] Traditional: e.g. Lesky (1966), 459; Ste. Croix (1972), 31; Dover (1973), 43; Hornblower (1994b), 102; (1991), 61; Rhodes (1988), 5 (and subsequent commentaries); Woodman (1988a), 11, 62, n. 162. 'Clarity' (Marincola (1997), 117) is suitably visual but insufficiently explicit. 'Clearness' could underlie a mnemonic system based on 'clear images' (cf. e.g. Cic. *De orat*. 2. 358 *locis . . . illustribus*, Liv. 6. 1. 2 (perhaps also *Praef*. 10) with Kraus (1994), 85 (cf. *Rhet. Her*. 3. 32), a possibility unexploited by Shrimpton (1997), 192–8 in his argument for Thucydidean mnemonics, but this argument is already untenable (n. 4).

[8] Moles (1993a), 107; (1993b), 15.

[9] Hornblower (1991), 7, 58. Precisely, they are the same in relation to periods before the Peloponnesian War (there unattainable) and to the Peloponnesian War (there attainable); the 'clearness' of similar future events will necessarily be more generalized (p. 212).

[10] The 'second preface' (5. 26) restates the truth claim: Marincola (1997), 133–4.

des, the scientific historian' ('scientific' in its traditional, positivist, sense).[11] This impression is supported by the implicit parallel between Thucydidean and Hippocratic method,[12] and by Thucydides' omission of 'the *muthos*-element' (since on any interpretation *muthos* implies some sort of 'story', and some modern historicists claim that history is effectively the 'stories' that we tell about the past, a claim which would have been anathema to the first historicists).

But what *exactly* is 'the *muthos*-element'? Scholarship divides: 'the storytelling element' (of Herodotus, logographers, and historical romance generally); 'story pattern' (in contrast with Thucydides' own year-by-year, summer–winter, narrative); 'the mythical or legendary element'; 'the fabulous element'; 'the sorts of patriotic stories that please audiences'.[13]

Precise analysis is needed. Thucydides' exclusion of 'stories' reinforces the truth of his account, an implication that is strengthened by his use of *to muthodes* in 1. 21. 1:[14]

But anyone who considered from the aforesaid indications that things

[11] Cf. e.g. Cochrane (1929); Gomme (1954); Romilly (1990), 105–37; Shrimpton (1997), 104.

[12] Controversial as to extent and implications; certainly, 1. 22. 4, 23. 5–6 (n. 58) and 138. 3 (p. 215) ~ 2. 48. 3 (aetiology, diagnosis, and prognosis of the plague), 'so let each individual, doctor or layman, speak about it as he knows: from what origin it was likely to have arisen and what causes of so great a change he considers to be sufficient to have the power for change [note the ambiguous dismissiveness]. But I, having myself fallen sick and having myself seen others suffering, shall reveal what kind of thing it was and the things by which anyone looking and knowing them in advance might most be able not to be ignorant of it, if it should ever again befall' ~ e.g. *Epid.* 1. 11 (2. 634–36L), 'tell what has happened before, know the present, foretell the things to be: study these things', cf. also 3. 82. 2 (*stasis* like ravaging disease), 6. 14 (statesman as doctor), 8. 97. 2, etc.; discussion: Cochrane (1929); Weidauer (1954); Ste. Croix (1972), 29–32; Hornblower (1994b), 110–12, 131–5; (1991), 61, 320–1; Swain (1994); Morgan (1994); on the possibility, but unlikelihood, that 'what kind of thing it was' inspired Ranke's 'wie es eigentlich gewesenist': Hornblower (1991), 321 with bibliography; on the medical analogy in Herodotus: Thomas (1997).

[13] Storytelling element: Gomme (1945), 149, influentially; story pattern: Shrimpton (1997), 266, 285; mythical/legendary element: Woodman (1988a), 11; Moles (1993a), 104; fabulous element: Rhodes (1988), 5; patriotic stories: Flory (1990), accepted by Hornblower (1991), 61; Marincola (1997), 117–18 formally accepts Gomme but effectively endorses 'the mythic(al)'.

[14] Woodman (1988a), 8, 10, and 51, n. 47 emphasises that 20–2 are not a single passage on 'method', as many have misinterpreted (and, despite Woodman, still do): 20–1 cover method *re* pre-war events, 22 method *re* the war. Nevertheless, 22 receives increased definition from a series of parallels and contrasts with 1 and 20–1 and 23 further redefines 22 (p. 204).

were more or less what I have described would not go wrong, neither trusting what the poets have eulogized about them, embellishing them for the purposes of exaggeration, nor what the prose-writers have put together for the purpose of enticement to the audience rather than the truth, things that cannot be checked and the majority of them having won out owing to time untrustworthily to the point of *to muthodes*, but believing that they have been discovered from the clearest signs sufficiently in so far as they are ancient things.

Thucydides asserts the superiority of his version of pre-war events and of his historical methods in reconstructing them to those of the poets and prose-writers.[15] As in ch. 22, the *muthos*-element implies audience-pleasing and suspect historicity (the stories being 'uncheckable'). But such material has acquired a spurious authority (having 'won out'). Translations such as 'the storytelling element' or 'the fabulous' are thus excluded. Thucydides explicitly links such material to the passage of (considerable) time. Hence he must be referring to myths or legends (*some* of which would of course be 'patriotic stories'). Chs. 21–2, therefore, distinguish between 'myth' (more or less in our sense) and history, as Livy (among several later historians) interpreted Thucydides.[16] Moreover, Thucydides points the paradox that qua old, myths or legends from the past can be viewed alternatively as authoritative or as suspect.[17] But there is a further paradox:[18] these stories only become 'myths' or 'legends' when 'put together' by the logographers: there can be 'myths' or 'legends' about contemporary events, which (as it were) overleap their proper chronological context and immediately acquire spurious authority. Thus the absence of 'mythical' material from the *History* need not be due only to Thucydides' writing contemporary history: he rigorously excludes *that kind* of 'uncheckable' material as *generically* incompatible with the quest for truth: further proof, seemingly, of his Rankean credentials.

But another problem arises: how does Thucydides' 'clear truth'

[15] Primarily Herodotus and 'logographers', also encomiastic orators: Marincola (1997), 21; also certain sophists (~ 22.4).

[16] *Praef*. 6 (cf. 5. 21. 9) *Quae ante conditam condendamve urbem poeticis magis decora fabulis quam incorruptis rerum gestarum monumentis traduntur* (Moles (1993c), 149); the general distinction: Marincola (1997), 117–27.

[17] Tony Woodman discerns similar paradox in *prisca fides facto, sed fama perennis* (*Aen*. 9. 79).

[18] Found in later historians: Liv. 5. 21. 9 (with Moles (1993c), 148); Tac. *Ann*. 4. 10–11 with Martin and Woodman (1989), 123–5, 127–32; Wiseman (1997). Cf. our 'a legend in his own lifetime'.

relate to the phrase 'those [things] which, in accordance with the human thing, are going to happen again some time like this and near the present ones'? That phrase cannot simply gloss 'the things that happened' (Rhodes/Hornblower),[19] because, as Woodman insists,[20] it is 'the clear truth' *both* of 'the things that happened' *and* of 'those which, in accordance with the human thing, are going to happen again some time like this and near the present ones'. Thucydides will provide both the clear truth of the events of the Peloponnesian War and the more generalized truths which underlie both those events and the similar events of the future,[21] hence in his narrative the pervasive tension between documentation of a mass of particulars and the need to generalize (illustrated, for example, by representative figures, recurrent patterns, avoidance of merely repetitive detail, use of short-cut formulae).[22] Not that ch. 22 itself concedes selectivity:[23] for present purposes the great war and the great *History* must seem one (Thucydides relaxes later: 3. 81. 5, 90. 1; 4. 23. 1).

How do these various tensions relate to historicist concerns? The criterion 'in accordance with the human thing', that is, 'given that human nature is constant',[24] parallels historicist insistence on

[19] Rhodes (1988), 5; Hornblower (1991), 61.

[20] Woodman (1988a), 24.

[21] Moles (1993a), 107–10.

[22] Moles (1993a), 108; Hornblower (1994b), 34–44.

[23] 22. 2 cannot mean 'the *erga* which I have chosen to describe' (thus, reluctantly, Hornblower (1994b), 37; cf. also Swain (1993), 40; Shrimpton (1997), 45–6, 196–8): (a) the Greek discourages this; Parry's claim ((1957/81), 92, cf. Shrimpton (1997), 45, 197) that 1.17 *eprachthe . . . ouden . . . ergon axiologon* makes an *ergon* necessarily an *axiologon prachthen*, i.e. *ergon* = 'factual report/reported event', logically fails (1.17 concedes the existence of non-*axiologa erga* and makes *no* distinction between *erga* and *prachthenta*; cf. also 23. 1. 'of the deeds before, the greatest that was done'); nor does 1. 17 entail selectivity in 1. 22: the *Archaeology* is necessarily selective; (b) the parallel formulation about *logoi* is comprehensive; (c) 'the deeds' picks up 21. 2 and is picked up by 23. 1 'of the deeds before', both of the *raw* deeds, otherwise Thucydides' argument for the war's supreme greatness fails; (d) 22. 2–*fin*. suggests detailed comprehensiveness (Hornblower (1991), 60); (e) other literary devices imply total coverage (n. 50); (f) in 'the deeds of the things done', which Shrimpton interprets as 'the factual reports arising from the things done', 'the things done' can be explained either as genitive of definition (strengthening the contrasts with 22. 1's *logoi*) or (better) as glossing 21. 2 'the deeds themselves' (Gomme (1945), 139); (g) 22. 4 'the things that happened' are 'objective' yet gloss 21. 2 'the deeds themselves' (readers 'look at' both).

[24] Rival interpretations: 'human nature': Ste. Croix (1972), 29–33; Swain (1994) (constancy of human nature and Hippocratic 'prognosis'); 'human condition' or 'situation' (including its uncertainties): Stahl (1966), 33 followed by Hornblower (1991), 61. But Ste. Croix (p. 32) correctly argues that 22 requires 'a factor making

history as a human product, conceding little or nothing to divine agency.[25] It might, however, seem incompatible with historicist claims that different cultures and periods produce, and are produced by, distinctively different types of human behaviour. Yet *kinesis* ('upheaval', 'change') is endemic to Thucydides' world,[26] and he recognizes and explores differences of period, race, and culture. Such variation can be accommodated within a basic model of the constancy of human nature provided that constancy is defined in sufficiently broad terms. So in 21. 2: 'people always judge the present war to be the greatest': different wars, different periods, the same basic human reaction.

Ch. 23, however, does deepen the conception of 'in accordance with the human thing':

[1] Of the deeds before, the greatest that was done was the Median war [the Persian war of 481–79], yet this had a speedy decision through two naval battles and land battles. But in the case of this war, its length advanced to a great size and also it happened that disasters [*pathemata*] occurred to Greece during it such as did not otherwise occur in the same space of time. [2] For neither were so many cities captured and made desolate, some by barbarians, some by the people themselves as they waged counter-war (some also changed inhabitants when they were captured), nor so many exiles of people and killing, some of it in the war itself, some because of civil strife. [3] And the things that were before this were said by hearsay, but rather rarely substantiated in deed, were established to be not untrustworthy—about earthquakes, which held sway over a very great part of the land and were at the same time most powerful, and eclipses of the sun, which occurred more frequently by comparison with what was remembered from former times, and there were great droughts, and from them both famines and that which did most damage and which did not least destroy: the plaguey sickness. For all these made a simultaneous attack along with this war. [4] The Athenians and Peloponnesians began it after dissolving the thirty years' truce which they had made after the capture of Euboea. [5] As to why they dissolved it, I have pre-written

for constancy'. I suspect interaction with Herodotus' 'things done by men' (*Praef.*), with Thucydides characteristically 'trumping' Herodotus by his limitless time frame (and equally characteristically, unfairly, since Hdt. 1. 5. 4 is just as limitless as 1. 22. 4).

[25] That Thucydides makes *some* concessions is argued by Oost (1975), Marinatos (1981), Dover (1988), 65–73, Swain (1994), 313, and Cawkwell (1997), 4; contested by Hornblower (1991), 206–7; (1992); Rutherford (1994), 63–4 (the better emphasis). Cf. n. 28 and further discussion in the text, p. 205.

[26] Moles (1993a), 100.

first the causes [*aitiai*] and the differences, so that no one need seek from what so great a war as this came upon the Greeks.[6] The truest pre-cause [*alethestate prophasis*], though least apparent in men's speech, I believe to have been the fact that the Athenians, becoming great and making the Peloponnesians fearful, compelled them towards going to war. But the causes said in the open on each side were as follows, as a result of which they dissolved the truce and came to the war.

First, while man can be active, performing 'deeds' (*erga*), he can also be passive, 'suffering disasters' (*pathemata*); the latter are of two types: man-made (history is a human product but the product of interaction of different humans) and natural (earthquakes, etc.). The interplay of active/passive, human/natural is pointed by the metaphor 'for all these made a simultaneous attack along with this war' (23. 3), and by the variation between 'so great a war as this *came upon* the Greeks' (23. 5) and 'they *came to* the war' (23. 6). Secondly, while man strives to be rational, the world contains gigantic forces of irrationalism (both in man and nature). The contrast between chs. 22 and 23 is not only between active and passive but between reason (*logos*) and unreason (*pathos*).[27] Ch. 23's multiple perspective might seem pessimistic by comparison with certain sorts of historicism, and indeed informs the great 'Thucydides, optimist or pessimist?' debate,[28] but the perspective is, rather, realistic, and it allows significance to human *response* to 'disasters' (e.g. the Athenians' irrational response to the plague and Pericles' rallying of them: 2. 51. 4–54. 5; 59. 1–64. 6).

How does the idea of 'the things which, in accordance with the human thing, are going to happen again some time like this and near the present ones' (22. 4) relate to historicist assertion or denial of history's predictive power? Thucydides eschews the crudities of cyclical history, but 'in accordance with the human thing' entails similar things happening in the future; the medical parallel has similar implications; Thucydides' own narrative contains some repeated patterning[29] and many temporal contexts which evoke later ones (the *Archaeology* at once explanatory and programmatic, the Themistocles and Pausianias narratives anticipatory of Alcibiades

[27] *Pace* many scholars, 23. 3's eclipses, triggers of human irrationalism, do not make Thucydides himself superstitious; discussion in Stephenson (1999).

[28] e.g. Romilly (1963), 357; Ste. Croix (1972), 31; Rutherford (1994), 54.

[29] Cf. e.g. Rawlings (1981) (the second half of the *History*, from 5. 25, in some respects reprises the first).

and Lysander, the Funeral Speech at once 430 and 403, Athens' defeat in Sicily proleptic of her fall, and so on;[30] and for Thucydides foresight is a pre-eminent political virtue.[31] On the historicist divide between predictive and non-predictive history Thucydides compromises intelligently, leaning towards the predictive but avoiding crudity. He also (like Herodotus, but unlike Marx or Fukuyama) avoids the fatuity of teleological historicism: 2. 64. 3, 'all things naturally decline.'[32]

Underlying everything thus far is Thucydides' profoundly historicist concern with the relationship between different periods of time: past, present, and future. This relationship is pointed by repetition, and variation in application, of the term 'always': 21. 2, *ton paronta aiei*; 22. 1, *ton aiei paronton*; 22. 4, *es aiei*: there are repeated presents, there are always different presents, and since Thucydides' work covers both, it is an always possession. Moreover, 22. 4 echoes the profound musings of the poet Hesiod on beginnings, linear time, timeless time, and his own transcendental poetry:[33] *Theog.* 31–4, '[The Muses] breathed into me a divine voice | that I might celebrate the things to be and the things before | and they bade me hymn the race of the blessed ones who are for always | and always to sing of themselves first and last.' But Thucydides' 'possession . . . for always' 'caps' Hesiod's claim for the immortality of his poetry (*aiei/aeidein*). Thus 22. 4 compares Thucydides' timeless project with those of poets (including Hesiod and Homer),[34] seers,[35] doctors,[36] sophists,[37] and logographers (including Herodotus),[38] and asserts its 'divinatory'

[30] Space precludes validation of these claims here.

[31] Ste. Croix (1972), 30, 177.

[32] Like Herodotus, Thucydides propounds biological models of growth and decline: Hornblower (1991), 6, 339.

[33] Moles (1993a), 109 f.

[34] *Xugkeitai* (of literary composition (*LSJ* II. 2)) < 1. 1. 1. *xunegrapse* but also (*xug*)*keitai* with *ktema* (in contrast to *-chrem*) suggests 'to be stored up' (*LSJ keimai* III), hence *ktema* . . . *xugkeitai* 'trumps' Homeric property phrases such as *ktemata keitai* (*Il*. 9. 382), figuring the *History* as a 'free inheritance' for all generations; discussion in Moles (1999).

[35] Besides Hesiod, cf. *Il*. 1. 70 (Calchas 'knew what is, what will be and what was before').

[36] Cf. n. 13.

[37] 'Competition piece' must *include* allusion to sophistic performances (cf. 3. 38. 7 (p. 217)), which implied venality (n. 39) reinforces.

[38] That 'competition piece for present hearing' (< 'enticement to the audience', just as *xugkeitai* < 21. 1 *xunethesan*) attacks logographers generally and Herodotus particularly is well understood (n. 16); but also, given the 'property' imagery

superiority to them all. Thucydides' *History* is *the* work, which 'synthesizes' (*xunethesan*) and 'compounds' (*xugkeitai*) *all other relevant* works.[39] And, importantly, it is a *text*: 'set down as a possession for always rather than as a competition piece for present hearing.' Although 'rather than' does not absolutely exclude oral delivery and aural reception, it privileges 'looking' over 'hearing', and 'looking at' (what else?) a text and its contents. Moreover, the earlier phrase, 'those who wish to look', evokes the formula 'for anyone who wishes to look' used in Athenian inscriptions,[40] with further implications for authority, textuality, openness of access, and permanence. While there had been texts and readers before Thucydides, he is the first to insist on the intellectual superiority of engagement with a great written text to oral performance and aural reception.[41] This insistence can be viewed alternatively as historicist—in its advocacy of a potentially major cultural shift—and unhistoricist—in its elevation of a reading text over other verbal productions.

The Hesiodic intertext conveyed by the play on 'always' introduces the problem of Thucydides' speeches.[42] The links between 22. 1 and 21. 2 and between 22. 1 and 22. 4 bind 'the always presents' (=the immediate presents)[43] into a conceptual relationship with other types of time: the repeated presents of 21. 2 and the 'always' transcendental time of 22. 4. Thucydides implies that the content of the speeches he attributes to the various speakers is less close to historical fact than is the content of the 'deeds' he records.[44] This relative unhistoricity operates in the sphere of 'the

(n. 35), *to parachrema* glosses *chrema* = 'money' (one 'hears' *para* separately (n. 50)), underscoring Herodotean and logographic venality in contrast to Thucydides' timeless munificence (n. 35).

[39] Fifth-century claims of various professionals to a secularized form of 'divination': Lloyd (1979), 45; the general 'agonistic' culture: Lloyd (1987), 58–9, 85–91, 97–101. Thucydides' simultaneous acknowledgement of, and claim to transcend, his agonistic culture finds parallels in Livy *Praef*. 2 (Moles (1993c), 144) and Tac. *Ann*. 4. 32. 1 (Martin and Woodman (1989), 169–70). Note how Thucydides' singular *ktema* 'trumps' the Homeric plural *ktemata* (n. 35), thereby implying the *comprehensiveness* of Thucydides' *singular* text.

[40] Examples (already fifth century) in Thomas (1989), 61, n. 151; discussion in Moles (1999).

[41] Havelock (1964), 53–4; Hunter (1982), 287–96; measured dissent in Marincola (1997), 21 and Hornblower (1991), 60–1; here and in Moles (1999) I hope to have strengthened and refined the Havelock/Hunter position.

[42] This discussion seeks to short-circuit the enormous bibliography.

[43] Not 'the always present things' 'the constants' (Moles 1993a, 105; 1993b, 15 f.), which *hekastoi* undermines (cf. e.g. 1. 2. 1).

[44] Cf. esp. Rusten (1989), 12.

necessary things' (*ta deonta*), a term which has been interpreted in two main ways: 'the rhetorically appropriate' and 'the objectively best arguments'. To dismiss the latter interpretation on the ground that some speeches come in opposed pairs[45] is fallacious: Thucydides never writes *ta deonta, tout court*, but *ta deonta* superimposed on what individual speakers actually said. 'The best arguments' finds strong support in the use of *ta deonta* at 1. 138. 3, where Themistocles is 'the best at improvising what was necessary' ('improvisation' includes both action and speech), and at 2. 60. 5, where Pericles is 'inferior to none in both knowing and expounding what is necessary'.[46] The Themistocles parallel will prove decisive for this interpretation of *ta deonta*.[47]

Thus the latitude that Thucydides claims for his speeches is due partly to the difficulty of remembering the detail, partly to a positive need to make individual speakers say the necessary things about the relationship between particular presents and generals and universals.[48] The fact that not all the speeches reflect on universals matters little: sometimes the connection between immediate circumstances and universals may legitimately be nil. It is also true that 'universals' are 'always already' deconstructible, but this too is part of the dynamic debate. Moreover, human beings are circumscribed in space as well as time: *paron* covers both dimensions, and while 22. 1, *ton aei paronton*, interacts with the temporal implications of 21. 2 and 22. 4, it *also* interacts with the spatial implications of 22. 2–3, *paratuchontos*, *paren*, *para* and *parontes*; note also 1. 1. 3, *epi makrotaton skopounti*, where time is imaged spatially and Thucydides approaches historicist conceptions of the past (for example, Robertson's 'what we call the past is, in effect, a series of foreign countries inhabited by strangers').[49]

[45] Ibid. 13. Gomme's different objection ((1945), 140) is met in n. 49.

[46] Similarly 1. 139. 4, 'most able both in speaking and acting', Thucydides' Themistoclean description of Pericles (Ste. Croix (1972), 178; Hornblower (1991), 223), echoing 1. 138. 3 particularly; also Isocrates 13. 8 and Demosthenes 6. 1: other politicians neither speak nor do 'the right things'.

[47] See p. 215 below.

[48] There is no self-contradiction (*pace* many): 'keeping as closely as possible . . .' and providing 'the necessary things' are in tension: *both* are *needed*, the former to ground the speeches historically, the latter to maximize the best arguments for the case of the particular speaker; *both* are *subject to variables*: the former to the difficulty of precise remembrance and the need to supply 'the necessary things'; the latter to the need to maintain a historical basis and Thucydides' own (presumably considerable) difficulty in supplying what *he* thought 'the necessary things'.

[49] Also *paron* = 'be present to/at' (21. 2, 22. 2, > ch. 23 [active ~ passive]), *para* = 'at'/from' (22. 2), 22. 4 *paraplesion* ('things near the present ones') and 22. 4

The speeches' role, therefore, is to bridge the gaps between different circumstances, contexts, periods, and times, thereby constructing the 'always-ness' of Thucydides' *History*. To the extent that the licence claimed by Thucydides for his speeches reflects the information deficit of a predominantly oral society, it supports one historicist claim. To the extent that the licence is exploited by Thucydides, it is incompatible with the conception of history as it actually happened, but the speeches' predominant fictionality subserves profoundly historical and historicist purposes. For modern historians who wish to use the speeches as evidence for what was actually said there is one ironic consolation: where speakers argue badly, this is historical.

The speeches also involve Thucydides' discussion of causality (23. 5–6), a basic historicist concern. The essential distinction here is between the various 'causes', 'differences', and 'accusations' that triggered the war, which were publicly stated and have some explanatory force, and the much more important, longer-term, psychological, hence 'truest', cause, which was very little stated.[50] But three aspects of Thucydides' wording remain undervalued. First, the clamant intertext with Herodotus on the *causes* of Greek–barbarian enmity: 1. 5. 3, 'This is what the Persians and Phoenicians *say*. But I am not going to say that these things happened this way or otherwise, rather I shall indicate the man whom *I myself know to have begun* unjust deeds towards the Greeks.'[51] This intertext, itself only one element in Thucydides' sustained imitation of, and rivalry with, Herodotus throughout the preface,[52] the Homeric imitation/rivalry also present in ch. 23 and also sustained throughout the preface,[53] and the Hesiodic echo of 22. 4 again point the question of ancient historiography's extensive intertextuality within itself and with other literary genres, a ques-

para/chrema (n. 39). Hence 22 is totally comprehensive (n. 24) both horizontally and vertically: words, deeds (including *hekasta*), *opsis*, *akoe*, participation, Thucydides and others, space and time (past, present, future).

[50] Ste. Croix (1972), 50–63, Hornblower (1991), 64–5, Derow (1994), 80, and Cawkwell (1997), 20–2 are variously flawed; better Gomme (1945), 152–4; Heath (1986); Rood (1998), 208–10; I hope to have advanced understanding of 23. 5–6 in a forthcoming paper entitled 'Narrative Problems in Thucydides Book I'.

[51] Richardson (1990), 160–1; Moles (1993a), 114; not in Hornblower (1991), 65 or (1996), 19–38 ('Thucydides and Herodotus'), 122–45 ('Thucydides' use of Herodotus').

[52] Moles (1993a), 98–114; also nn. 16 and 39.

[53] Moles (1993a), 98–114; also n. 35.

tion hugely challenging to the concept of 'history as it really happened'. Second, the paradoxical application of *prophasis* (often 'stated cause', even [false] 'excuse')[54] to 'true cause little stated', paradox sharpened by verbal clashes (*alethestaten/aphanestaten, phasin/aphan/phaneron, phasin/logoi/legomenai*):[55] language inverted as what should have been public becomes private and truth un-uttered. Thucydides exposes and ruthlessly probes the gap within public discourse between signifier and signified.[56] Third, the continuing medical analogy in the 'diagnosed causations',[57] which again deepens Thucydides' 'scientific' approach.

In the rest of Book 1 the various *aitiai* loom large in the speeches,[58] while the *alethestate prophasis* is mentioned twice in Thucydides' own historical analysis (1. 88 and 118. 2) and repeatedly in the speeches, whether explicitly (by the Corcyraeans: 33. 3, 'if anyone among you thinks that the war . . . will not happen, he is mistaken, failing to realize that the Spartans desire war through fear of you', and the ephor Sthenelaidas: 86. 5, 'do not allow the Athenians to become greater'), or implicitly (in the two Corinthian speeches and in the Athenian speech). This seeming discrepancy with 'the truest cause least apparent in speech' is a problem *only* if Thucydides' speeches are historical documents. In reality, the *emphasis in the speeches* on the 'truest cause *least apparent in speech*' exemplifies the things which the historical speakers did not say (or hardly), but which *Thucydides thinks a necessary* element of the situation which speakers *ought* to have mentioned; Spartan fear of Athenian imperialist expansion was one of the constants of the *Pentecontaetia* and should have been discussed 'on particular occasions' by speakers alert to the interplay between those particulars

[54] Thuc. 3. 82. 4, 86. 4, 111. 1; 4. 47. 2; 5. 80. 3; 6. 8. 4, 33. 2, 76. 2; 8. 87. 5.

[55] *Prophasis*: e.g. Pearson (1952); (1972); Rawlings (1975); Heubeck (1980); Richardson (1990); Hornblower (1991), 64–5; demarcation of the 'true' derivation (*prophemi/prophaino*?) cannot repress the verbal clashes.

[56] Cf. 3. 82. 4 'they changed the accustomed evaluation of words to deeds in self-justification'; interpretation: Wilson (1982); Worthington (1982); Hornblower (1991), 483; Swain (1993), 36–7. Moles (n. 51) probes the intricate wordplays of Thucydides' analysis of causality.

[57] Guaranteed by (i) the available medical resonance of *prophasis* (Rawlings 1975); (ii) the verbal parallel with 2. 48. 3 (n. 13); note the irony: Thucydides applies medical aetiology to the war but decries its usefulness in the medical context; (iii) the parallel distinction between necessary and concomitant causes and recognition of double causation in medical writings (Swain (1994), 318); (iv) the parallel medical distinction between apparent and un-apparent processes (ibid. 316); (v) the contextualization of the war among disasters which include plague.

[58] Rhodes (1987), 154–6; Heath (1986), 104–5; Rood (1998), 208 ff.; Moles (n. 51).

and that constant. Hence the Corcyraeans' allegedly public proclamation of the *prophasis* in the first full speech of the narrative is at once unhistorical and profoundly historicist, boldly transcending 'history as it really happened' in order to underline deeper historical causation.

Inherent in chs. 22–3 is Thucydides' intense interest in language, its possibilities, limitations, and distortions.[59] Besides the discussion of the speeches and the problematics of *alethestate prophasis*, there is stress on the inadequacy both of ordinary *logoi* as purveyors of fact (22. 3) and of Thucydides' own language in comprehending the natural disasters which accompanied the war (23. 3).[60] Chs. 22–3 begin and end with discussion of *logoi*. Ch. 22. 1 contrasts what, as it *seemed to Thucydides, should* have been said but *was not* with what *truly* was said; 23. 6 contrasts what *was very little said* but what *Thucydides believed* to be *truest* with what *was* said but was relatively unimportant. There is truth and Truth. Only *Thucydides'* speeches can properly explore the *True* issues of a particular situation. If, as most commentators hold, the speeches exhibit profound and wide-ranging political analysis and thought, the latter are *Thucydides'*.

Everything said so far credits ch. 23 with historical profundity. But ch. 23 is a main weapon of Woodman's attack on the concept of 'Thucydides the scientific historian': the emphasis on disasters and sufferings reflects the perspective of epic and tragedy, hence Thucydides' continuing evocation of, and rivalry with, Homer; the emphasis is sustained throughout the *History*; and it prefigures the manner of later 'tragic'[61] historians; Thucydides deploys extensive rhetorical 'amplification' to 'prove' the war's supreme greatness; both content and style subserve the 'pleasure' (for Woodman, 'entertainment') which Thucydides had only ambiguously disclaimed in 22. 4, and contrast markedly with 'scientific history'.[62]

Individually, these claims are correct and important. Nevertheless, the resultant picture of Thucydides is one-dimensional. First,

[59] Loraux (1986); Swain (1993); Moles (n. 51).

[60] Moles (1993a), 113: 'these tremendous events seem to defy historical canons and the historian's attempts to impose order on them. This is very different from the "clear truth" of ch. 22. Here historiography ruefully contemplates its own inability to comprehend reality.'

[61] Still a useful term (with ancient justification), provided (a) it acknowledges the influence of tragedy throughout ancient historiography; (b) it does not entail a 'school'. That is, 'tragic' historians *take to extremes a general tendency* of ancient historiography.

[62] Woodman (1988a), 28–32; cf. also nn. 26–7.

it neglects the 'scientific' elements of ch. 23 itself (the chronological precision, rigorous causality, deepening conception of 'the human thing'). Secondly, it radically fissures 'literature' and 'history': there is no recognition that 'the literary' (the echoes of Homer in 23. 5 (~ *Il.* 1. 6–7) or of Herodotus in 23. 6) can function as a vehicle for the historical, and 'pleasure' (an indispensable element of reader response even to tragic narrative) degenerates into 'entertainment'. Thirdly, it ignores Thucydides' preoccupation with the problem of finding language—and different sorts of language—which will encompass the war in all its different facets. Thucydides' conception of history-writing is far richer and profounder than either the 'literature' or 'scientific-history' model, and includes both. Even rhetorical excess is double-edged: while it may produce unjustifiable exaggeration (for example, the claim that the Peloponnesian War was greater than the Persian), it may also convey the sheer impossibility of representing extreme things adequately in language. *Logos*/language can express *logos*/reason: unreason (*to alogon*) is 'logically' inexpressible.[63]

Some of these points become clearer when we return yet again to the marvellous complexities of 22. 4. For the crucial phrase 'to look at the clearness' was understood by later ancient historians such as Duris and Livy, as implying that Thucydides' *History* would be an as far as possible unmediated *mimesis*.[64] This understanding seems right, explaining alike the general ancient emphasis on Thucydides' unparalleled 'vividness';[65] the narrative start (1. 24. 1, 'there is a city Epidamnus . . .'), with its present tense, insider/outsider figure (*espleonti*), and asyndetic prologue-feel; the very high proportion of speech-material; the strong influence of drama and tragedy, both in tragic patterning (the plague narrative of Book 2, the Nicias-focused narrative of Book 7, whose obituary (7. 86. 5) so startlingly anticipates *Poetics* 13), the use of dramatic dialogue (Melos), and tragic vocabulary, tragic emotions, and internal audience in Book 7.[66]

[63] Cf. 2. 50. 1 'the form of the disease was *kreisson logou*' ('stronger than language/reason').

[64] Duris fr. 1; Woodman (1988a), 25 and 59 n. 140; Morgan (1993), 184–5; Walker (1993), 356–7; Leigh (1997), 34–6; Liv. *Praef.* 10 with Moles (1993c), 154.

[65] D.H. *Thuc.* 15; Plu. *De glor. Ath.* 347a; historiographical *enargeia* generally: Woodman (1988a), 25–8, 59–60, 89–90; Davidson (1991); Walker (1993); Leigh (1997), 10–15, 30–40.

[66] Moles (1993a), 112 with bibliography; Rood (1998), 198–9.

The device of the effectively unmediated *mimesis* has major consequences. First, on narrative organization, not only tragic patterning, but also the various narrative dislocations and omissions in Book I documented and discussed by Badian and Hornblower.[67] For Badian these are cunning ploys to minimize evidence detrimental to Athens in the question of war-guilt; for Hornblower they are narratologically intriguing but remain duplicitous. In fact, however, they illustrate the drip-feed, as-and-when release of information necessitated by unmediated *mimesis* (cf. drama):[68] again not history as it actually happened but something tighter and more economical (nearer Aristotelian notions of unity).[69] Second, if only contemporary history is properly doable, what more appropriate vehicle than the unmediated *mimesis*, the time-machine whereby Thucydides transports his own and every succeeding generation into a contemporary world? Here is an excellent practical answer to historicism's central dilemma (even though it was abused by the 'tragic' historians). Third, the unmediated *mimesis* raises the external audience's, or reader's, role.[70]

The roles of reader and historian are both separate and complementary; truth is 'clear truth', what has been 'seen' by the historian or eyewitnesses (1. 1. 3, 22. 2–3) and rigorously sifted. The historian also 'looks' (1. 1. 3, 22. 2–3), and then constructs his *mimesis*, at which the reader 'looks'. 'Seeing' is prior, 'looking' involves contemplation and understanding. The correct response by the reader is suggested by Thucydides' description of his own behaviour at the start of the preface—he 'sees' and works from 'indications' (1. 1. 1)—and by various 'internal readers', for example, at 7. 42. 3:

> Demosthenes, *seeing* how things were and *considering* that it was impossible to delay and suffer what Nicias had suffered (—for Nicias, *an object of fear* when he *first* arrived, when he did not *immediately* attack Syracuse but wintered in Catana, was despised and Gylippus anticipated him by arriving from the Peloponnese with an army, which the Syracusans would not have sent for if Nicias had attacked *immediately*. For thinking that they were sufficient of themselves they would simulta-

[67] Badian (1993), 125–62; Hornblower (1994a), esp. 140–6.

[68] Moles (1995).

[69] For qualification of the much-invoked Aristotelian parallel see p. 214 below.

[70] Fourthly, presumably, the so-called *mise en abyme* problematizes seeing, reading, interpretation, text etc. (Walker (1993), 361–3), but that is later in the process.

neously have realized that they were weaker and been walled in, so that, even if they had sent for it, it would no longer have helped them to the same degree)—Demosthenes, then, *examining* these things *thoroughly*, and realizing that he himself *also* was *most formidable* to their opponents on *the first day above all* . . .

Demosthenes begins by seeing in a quasi-literal sense (*idon*), then moves to 'considering', then to 'insight' (*anaskopon*), and the bracketed narrative summary (of events from 6. 50ff.) is simultaneously 'objective' and focalized by Demosthenes. His analysis' 'authority' derives from his being (one) 'author' of the summary.[71]

A key question now arises: how is the *History* 'useful' for the reader (22. 4)? There are two views: it promotes purely theoretical understanding of political affairs;[72] or it promotes such understanding as a prerequisite of competent participation in politics (so already Polybius, Livy, and Lucian).[73]

We need first to understand the business of understanding. Readers 'look at the clearness both of the things that have happened and of those which are going to happen'. Subject to broad historical fact, speakers within the text say 'the necessary things' about the relations between past, present, and future, between present and more remote circumstances, between particulars and universals. The time-frames of the narrative evoke future contexts. Foresight, commended within the text, is promoted by its very organization. Thucydides' concern with universals and particulars is a scholarly commonplace, but is Thucydides' concern with deriving universals from particulars or is it, rather, with the interaction, or dialectic, between the two? The latter emphasis is preferable. If particular truths are in themselves trivial and uninformative (*Poetics* 9), universal truths are little better. It is the dialectic between the two and between all the gradations in

[71] *Contra* Hornblower (1994a), 134–5, with bibliography. Dover's argument, ambiguously endorsed by Hornblower, that the nominatives and finite tenses of the summary exclude Demosthenes from being the one (more precisely, one of the two) 'who sees' is theoretically inconclusive: examples in classical literature of 'deviant focalization' (where things said by the narrator contain focalization by figures in the text (Fowler (1990)), are legion.

[72] e.g. Gomme (1945), 149–50 (slightly ambiguous); Stahl (1966), 15–19; Macleod (1983), 101–2, 146–7.

[73] Ste. Croix (1972), 29–33; Hornblower (1994b), 133–4; (1991), 61 (formulations muddied by the introduction of the question of 'morality', which is important but 'here' subsidiary); Polyb. 3. 31. 12; Liv. *Praef.* 10 with Moles (1993c) 154; Lucn. *Hist. Conscr.* 42. Rutherford (1994) sidesteps the question.

between which matters. So 1. 22 implies, and the interpretation is confirmed by the most perspicuous and successful of all the 'internal readers':

[1. 138. 3] Themistocles most clearly revealed the strength of natural ability and was particularly worthy to be admired in this respect, more than any other man: for by his native intelligence and neither having learned anything in advance towards it nor having learned afterwards [sc. neither like Prometheus nor like Epimetheus], he was both the *best knower of things present* by means of the least deliberation, and the best conjecturer of *the things that were going to happen*, to the greatest extent of *what would be*; and the things which he took in hand he was able to expound and the things of which he had no experience he did not fall short of *judging* appositely;[74] and the better or worse course in what was yet obscure he *foresaw* the most. To sum up, by power of natural ability and by brevity of study this was the best man at *improvising what was necessary*.

The conceptual frame echoes 1. 22: past, present, future, immediate things, action/speech; there are verbal echoes: *ton mellonton* ~ *ton mellonton, tou genesemenou* ~ *ton genomenon, krinai* ~ *krinein, ta deonta* ~ *ta deonta*. Themistocles' special skill (*autoschediazein ta deonta*) mediates everything: all the different types of time, action, and speech. He instantiates the full programme of 1. 22: understanding, judgement, forethought, excellence in both speech and action, the ability to bring different time-scales and contexts into the right perspective and thus at any given moment to speak and implement the necessary things, his achievement the more remarkable because he 'studied' little (Oxford *melete* would not have benefited him).[75]

Many scholars interpret the medical analogy negatively: Thucydides diagnoses the problems but offers no cure. Of course, brute 'human nature' is 'incurable' (3. 82. 2). But the prescription of rational thought and behaviour in politics and warfare as represented by Themistocles, Pericles, Hermocrates, Demosthenes

[74] 'Fall short of' and 'appositely' essay the Greek's spatial imagery.

[75] *Pace* Macleod (1983), 146; Rutherford (1994), 63; Hornblower (1991), 223 describes the portrait as sophistic; but its dismissal of Promethean sophistic cleverness and of the influence of Mnesiphilus, 'a kind of proto-sophist' (Ste. Croix (1972), 177), and its concession that *melete* is not absolutely indispensable make it anti-sophistic—appropriately (n. 38); on the metaliterary implications of Themistocles' lack of education see p. 217.

(partially), and so on *is* a cure; the ideal is itself a constant, universally applicable, but in any given situation entailing a complex balancing-act between varying temporal and spatial perspectives. Yet the context of individual politicians, even brilliant ones like Themistocles who instantiate the political ideal, is necessarily limited by their particular time and circumstances; hence the text must give the reader a representative collection of case-studies, to illustrate the full range of the mix of temporal and spatial perspectives which may confront individual politicians at particular moments. The reader: *any* reader at any time. For if political competence resides in juggling *genomena* and *mellonta* to decide what to do *now*, the *genomena* of the Peloponnesian War and their interaction with universals have timeless illustrative value. Again Thucydides seems at once to recognize the key historicist dilemma and at least partially to resolve it. Such complex interaction does not diminish the war's distinctive greatness: understanding and judgement require discrimination about the relative greatness and significance of things. The haphazard subjectivity of 21. 2 ('people always judge the present war to be the greatest') must yield to the informed judgement of 22. 4 and 138. 2.

This analysis already makes purely theoretical understanding an implausible goal. What would be the point of Thucydides' insistence that ideal politicians such as Themistocles and Pericles possessed not only understanding and forethought but the ability to express them persuasively and to enact them? Competent internal readers are particularly eloquent cases: they not only see and interpret, they act, rightly. Similarly Thucydides himself: he sees, makes inferences, acts (in writing his *History*, and indeed in participating in it—(in 1. 22 and elsewhere *pareimi* can cover not only witnessing but participation and experience).[76] Relevant also is Thucydides' stress on his position vis-à-vis the plague—both 'participant' and 'eyewitness' (n. 12)—and on his own CV in 5. 26. 4–5,[77] where he almost becomes his own 'internal reader'. Similarly, the device of the unmediated *mimesis*, ancient theory of which makes readers not merely onlookers but imaginative participants.[78] And whatever theory of tragedy one adopts, it will surely be one implication that contemplation, even, in a sense, experi-

[76] As e.g. 1. 29. 1.

[77] Marincola (1997), 133–4.

[78] Demetr. *Eloc.* 216; Liv. 10. 31. 15; Sen. *De ira* 2. 2. 3–6; Plu. *Art.* 8. 1.

ence, of suffering teaches the audience endurance of the sufferings of life.[79] The effects on the reader of ch. 23 and 7. 71 (the famous depiction of the emotional reactions of the non-combatants on both sides to the decisive sea-battle) cannot be confined to intellectual understanding. Here too the *History* straddles both its own and any other time. Thucydides, then, wrote his *History* primarily to teach his readers how to become competent politicians.

To the question: 'why doesn't he say so?' (with the usual deadening implication that because he doesn't, he can't mean it), Fats Waller gave one good answer. Asked by an earnest woman musicologist: 'What is this thing called swing, Mr Waller?', he riddlingly replied: 'Lady, if you gotta ask, you ain't got it' ('gotta'/'got', 'got' = 'need', 'possess', 'understand'). Even to ask certain questions is stupid: the artistic representation itself questions the reader's response. So Thucydides leaves a gap for readers to fill. He gives some help, by emphasizing the supreme importance of the Peloponnesian War and by stressing its unprecedented 'disasters', thereby reinforcing their 'wish' to 'look' and providing an 'enticement' that parallels, but in its moral and intellectual seriousness far surpasses, the 'enticements' of the logographers (1. 21. 1); but readers have to work out for themselves what it is all for. By bridging this gap within the text, readers are set on the process of bridging the gap between the 'act' of reading and political action outside the text. The same point is implicit in the piquant irony that Themistocles, most perspicuous of Thucydides' internal readers and the embodiment of the full programme of 1. 22, achieves this status 'by his native intelligence . . ., by power of natural ability and by brevity of study' (= without reading Thucydides). The usefulness of even a text such as Thucydides' varies from individual to individual, according both to innate ability and political position.[80]

But there is another good answer. In the Mytilene Debate Cleon is made to attack specious oratory (3. 38. 3–7): 'as a result of such oratorical *competitions* the city gives the prizes to others but herself assumes the dangers. You are the cause, running the competition badly, you who customarily become *spectators of speeches and hearers of deeds, looking on* the possibility of *the deeds that are going*

[79] Macleod (1983), 11–12; Gribble (1998), 51.

[80] Cf. 2. 40. 2 (Pericles (with Rusten (1989) 154)); 6. 39. 1 (Aristagoras); 3. 38. 3–7 (text); Gomme (1945), 443.

to happen from the point of view of those who speak well, and *the things that have already been done,* not taking the deed seen with your eyes as more trustworthy than the one which you have heard of, from the point of view of those who are clever verbal critics . . . Simply put, you are overcome by the *pleasure of listening* and resemble seated *spectators of the sophists* rather than decision-makers for the city.'

However misguided his present policy, however unattractive an internal reader, 'Cleon' warns against misreading, against 'mis-seeing', the *History*: it is *not* a sophistic 'competition piece', a source of 'mere pleasure'; 'looking' requires active discrimination, not passive acceptance of other people's focalizations; readers have to *think* about the relations between past and future, to *act*, not just *sit back*.

CONCLUSION

Many-headed historicism provides useful practical approaches to traditional Thucydidean interpretative problems. But more significantly, the supreme ambition of Thucydides' project *entails* multiple engagement with historicism's fundamental concerns. As 'a possession set down for always', whose utility consists in promoting understanding of, and competent participation in, political processes, Thucydides' *History* must:

(a) persuade his contemporaries of the pre-eminence both of the theme (the war's supreme greatness) and of Thucydides' treatment of this kind of material; hence the sustained intertextual relationships with Homer and Herodotus and the agonistic attacks on various groups and individuals, the aim of which is to establish Thucydides' superiority both to comparable authors/texts of the past and to various contemporary rivals. This superiority partly derives from the superior intensity of engagement permitted by a reading text. From this perspective, Thucydides' *History* is 'of its time', and his multiple literary allusions do not so much align historiography with other genres as appropriate those genres, thereby establishing his own 'authority';[81]

(b) persuade all readers of the war's greatness (for contemporary readers, supreme greatness; for later readers, supreme greatness up to Thucydides' own time), since, for various obvious reasons,

[81] Cf. Marincola (1977), 226–7.

'great things' promote greater understanding of 'the human thing';[82]

(c) provide both contemporary and later readers with a scrupulously accurate account of the 'things that happened' in the Peloponnesian War as the solid historical case-work base of the dialectic across the full range of spatial and temporal perspectives, that base constituting not 'history as text' in the sense of 'merely text', but 'history as text' in the sense that Thucydides has textualized the war in such a way as to incorporate rigorous historical method and suggest comprehensive treatment (the war 'becomes' the text), thereby allowing readers to concentrate undistractedly on the business of understanding;

(d) create various mechanisms (especially the speeches) to engage the case-work base in those wider dialectics, which extend throughout space and throughout time;

(e) put readers (all readers) inside the text, so that that text is always in a sense contemporary and they see and experience the problems, as they unfold, for themselves;

(f) in contrast to (a), harness the language and techniques of epic, tragedy, and formal rhetoric for various purposes: generalization of material; readers' emotional arousal and imaginative participation; linguistic and literary diversity mimetic of a many-faceted war;

(g) create a gap between the text, its own context and all possible contexts, so that the wider dialectic will include dialectic precisely between text and context(s).

Whatever its practical deficiencies, therefore, Thucydides' *History* is brilliantly conceived as a text for any context,[83] or, as another contributor to this collection might say: a productively proleptic ekphrasis within the text or texts of life.[84]

[82] Moles (1993a), 109.

[83] Of course, if the *History* is so conceived (both by Thucydides and his readers), some of the usual criticisms of Thucydides will necessarily be misconceived.

[84] One might add that Thucydides' many-layered conception provides (never more relevantly than at a time of IT and Internet revolution) a powerful defence of 'the book' as supreme vehicle for the exploration of the human condition.

14

Polybius/Walbank*

John Henderson

> The archive: if we want to know what that will have meant, we will only know in times to come. Perhaps.
>
> (Derrida (1996), 36)

Fortune cast the life of Frank W. Walbank in stirring times.[1] He was hard at work on Polybius' *Histories* for well over half of the twentieth century. His great commentary itself took up the thirty-four years between the engagement in 1944 and completion ready for publication of the third and final volume in 1979; and supplementary extensions and revisions of his thinking continued to appear through the next two decades, fortified by retirement, by relocation, and by the changing conceptualizations of ancient history and Ancient History brought about by successive realignments of Scholarship with Theory. In *Hypomnemata* (1992) FWW also wrote up the first instalment of his memoirs, from his earliest recollections ('from about 1914 onwards': born 1909) up to appointment to the Chair of Latin in the University of Liverpool (i.e. 'around 1946').[2]

We don't know how long Polybius took to work on *Polybius*, we don't possess his memoirs, and indeed grasping the historicality of the authorship of the *Histories* is (very likely) the fundamental

* This essay celebrates what Frank Walbank has done with Polybius' *Histories*; and remembers George Forrest, too, inspirational—irrepressible—historicist.

[1] *After* Shuckburgh (1889), i. p. xvii.

[2] (1992), 1: Dorothy Thompson kindly lent me her own copy; and Frank Walbank talked over with me the 'moments' of his scholarly life in memorable conversation, and then penned a generous response to my TS (= 'pers. comm.' below; see. esp. n. 22). Does FWW think his first name has played a significant part in his own self-conception and -construction? 'Certainly not consciously: but subconsciously who can tell . . .' As for me, once a 'First Period' Greats person for Roman History, always one: I spent ages trying to learn to think political history and historicism with FWW, with WGF.

challenge of his writing, but on anyone's reckoning he must have had less time to complete his forty books than FWW to ponder their excerpted remains. More melodramatically, we could say that it took Rome less time, according to Polybius, to achieve world hegemony—fifty-three years—than FWW has had to polish off the *Histories*.[3] The (dodgy) story we are given that *Poly-bios* lived up to the macrobiotic overtones in his (he says unique) name (= 'Plenty in/of life'), by reaching the age of 82 before a fatal fall from his horse, has traditionally served to open wide the possible span of his composition; but why be so mean? FWW produced his memoir at *that* milepost, and he has had a whole string of new essays written since.[4]

The massive *Historical Commentary* (originally planned for two volumes: in the out-turn, 2,355 pages) represents 'post-war' classical Scholarship at its grandest-finest. If anyone should ever suppose there really was a time (perhaps a Golden Age heyday of Scholarship) 'before Theory', and there are good reasons why that sort of idea, however daft as put, should have featured at the level of sloganizing and lobbying, at given moments of action and fashion, of faction and fraction, then Walbank's *Polybius* is the best place for them to go settle down for a rethink. Here I shall first set out the main lines of what FWW has had to say about his monumental lifework. Then I shall look at a particular problem of interpretation that lurks at the heart of our comprehension of Polybius' monumental lifework, and (plucking up courage/in all temerity) dust off a reading ruled out and rejected by FWW, at a key point in the *Histories* where Polybius is, precisely, handing out the main lines of what he has to say about his project.

The point will be to indicate 'the logic of the supplement' at work in Polybius' Walbank: but there will be no need to decide just what *that* might amount to (neither fish nor fowl), since FWW's understanding of Polybius' work has always turned on the assumption that the life and times of the history-writer must interactively engage with the production of the work, in an ongoing

[3] To make a point or two about historicality, FWW observes (pers. comm.) that 'I made virtually the same comment myself in a paper [of 1997]' (= 1998, 46): 'I have been interested in this book [i.e. Book 6] for over fifty years—as long as it took the Romans to rise to world dominion!'

[4] Ps.-Lucian *Macrobii* 22. Plutarch *An seni sit gerenda respublica* 791 f. (= Polyb. 36. 16. 11) must note that 'Polybius records that King Massanissa died at ninety, leaving a four-year-old child of his own'. On the unique name: 36. 12. 5.

dialectic between the thesis that enframes and is affirmed by the *History*, and the necessarily constant adjustment of its conceptualization, verbalization, and definition, produced in the course of its production—produced not least by the impact made on its author by the process of composition, within the changing environments experienced by the historian. Whereas Polybius is indeed the most vociferous and energetic of ancient historians in providing explicitation of his procedures, to the point where the construction of the narrator and his narration are virtually thematized as *the* story of the *Histories*,[5] FWW by contrast abides by the depersonalizing regime of the commentary within the ascetic order of Scholarship. Lets Polybius do the talking, wants us to learn through Polybius—as *he* has, and does. And Walbank's 'historical' (non-'philological') Polybius is (emphatically) caught up in revisionary flux and repositioning, a dramatic site where ancient Theory and Scholarship work together in unmissably high profile as the narrative strives to fix events, while events keep retroactively fixing the narrative. So is Polybius' Walbank, too, only he doesn't write that out for you, not even retrospectively. No. To see how reading Polybius has figured for FWW, you need to supplement his own modulated but determinedly reticent accounts with your own (pragmatic) Theory of modern Scholarship: even the *Commentary* does tell, and is out to tell, what Polybius can do for 'us'—but only if you can tune into the rhetoric, and 'find' your FWW.

This essay is about the FWW that *I* found in his Polybian work when I looked back from 1997, through what I think I thought back in the late 1960s, to the inception of the project back in those days of The War. *Autres temps, autres moeurs*. If the question 'Why Polybius?' today *demands* that we include the further question 'Why Walbank's Polybius?', and if this *sort of* question today forces itself onto the agenda, close to the top,[6] then clearly we need to Theorize this sea-change in (classical) Scholarship, as a pressing issue in our self-comprehension. The critical point is not that clas-

[5] Marincola (1997), *passim*. 'Polybius actually trumpets his reflections on the historian's role as culture hero (custodian, bearer and wielder of all the power of the intellect, of rhetoric, of moral didaxis) as the very essence of his project. . . . [T]he *folies de grandeur* . . . —the portentous bluffing and fetching self-delusion that make [the ancient historian] such a high-rolling con-artist. . . . [T]he jostling, the posturing and the foul play in the critical antics of these antique critics.' (Henderson 1998, 26).

[6] e.g. Hallett and Van Nortwick (1997); cf. Henderson (1999), pp. x–xiii.

sical research has been struggling to personalize its voices, but that it remains so difficult, for all the Theory there may be, to locate the personal and the pragmatic in writings as they are displaced by the shifts of history, particularly where resistance to the paternal texts of our anxiety interferes with receptivity and obstructs reception. For now, I merely propose to insist that this is an (irresistible) opportunity to recognize how directly politicized and historicized our paradigmatic classical Scholarship took itself to be, ideally, all along—however tight the lips were sealed, however outlawed overt self-regard: *more suo*.

I

WHY POLYBIUS, FRANK?

> No reason to get excited, the thief he kindly spoke.
> (Dylan (1968), 'All Along the Watchtower')

First, the answer of hindsight, from the memoir (with *my* scissors-and-paste).[7] On the same page, the Bradford schoolboy of the early twenties comes upon Oxbridge Colleges and British Universities as collected sets of cigarette cards, and gets to reflect on the mixing of social class and its linguistic badges: 'Usually these separate worlds were kept decently apart' (1992, 42). At the Grammar School, he 'opted for the classical side owing to a complete mis-understanding of what was involved . . . I now know, however, that chance and error play a great part at all times in shaping one's life and I do not regret at all that my parents' ignorance turned me into a classical scholar.' (p.68). The classics teachers saw their boys were 'made to feel that we were an élite, enjoying the rare privilege of learning Greek' (p. 77) and 'were all indoctrinated with the cyclical views of [Spengler's] *The Decline of the West*' (p.79). One of them managed to get approved

> a special period of Roman History for our school alone . . . 200–133 B.C.; and this led to a piece of initiative on his part, which was to be decisive for my whole life's work—little though either he or I could have foreseen this at the time. Pointing out that the main Greek source for the period we were to study was the second century Achaean historian Polybius, he produced a small, rather grubby German school edition of this author (I do

[7] Excerption is, of course, *the* Polybian process: what Polybius did, and what he suffers.

not know to this day what edition it was) and instructed another boy . . . and me . . ., to translate and make a précis of it . . . for the rest of the form. . . . To read chunks of Polybius in the original (I forget now how far down we went) and to set out the gist of his account, including the constitutional section in Book 6, was a very enlightening experience, and, as I have said, fired me with an interest in that author which was later to bear unexpected fruit. (p. 80)

When the time came, after a nerves-ruined shot for Oxford, this (*soi-disant*) medium flier targeted his Cambridge application for 'what I later realized were very unsubstantial reasons. From a set of cigarette cards . . . I had discovered that the oldest college in Cambridge was Peterhouse, founded in 1284. I knew absolutely nothing of its reputation or who would be teaching me, should I go there' (p. 88). In the second year, 1930, four Mediterranean cruise places were offered as an essay prize, for Oxbridge undergraduates and public-school boys—'I was not at the time so struck by the appalling social and sexual bias implied . . . as I am now. What interested me was the first subject, "Federalism in the Greek World", and I at once decided to have a shot at it' (p. 107).[8] After joining the Socialist Society and the League of Nations Union and getting a good First Class, including a History paper on the Second Punic War, the new graduate was asked if he'd 'care to stay on for a fourth year and do a "piece of research"'; the Delphic Oracle was said to be too worked over, but 'I had a better idea. In my essay on Greek federalism for the Hellenic Travellers' Club competition, I had come across an Achaean statesman called Aratus' (p. 113).

The thirties are remembered as the time when the Universities were politicised . . . I had been a Labour sympathiser since at least 1926, when I felt strongly on the side of the miners . . . I think the first theoretical work which influenced me was Bernard Shaw's *Intelligent Woman's Guide to Socialism*, which I read while at Cambridge. . . . While I was in Jena . . . I had become very conscious of the dangers presented by the Nazi movement. (pp. 125f.)

Getting engaged, typing out the book on Aratus, teaching for a year in North Manchester High School, getting married, FWW in the early 1930s became 'increasingly interested in politics. . . . We

[8] Cf. Walbank (1985), 20–37 (repr. from 1976/7).

read a lot of left-wing books, including Palme Dutt's *Fascism and Social Revolution*, which we found persuasive; today with hindsight it looks very different' (p. 133). *Aratos* got him a job in Liverpool, just, and Mary Walbank, the activist of the team, joined the Communist Party first.

> In the summer of 1934 Mary and I had another holiday with political overtones—or at any rate that is how we saw it . . . in the Spanish Pyrenees. . . . When the Civil War broke out in 1936 we both felt very strongly committed to the republican side. (pp. 139f.) . . . I took on the Honorary Secretaryship of the Merseyside branch of the National Council for Civil Liberties, which had not very much to do until the Blackshirts became more active. . . . With the outbreak of the Spanish Civil War this political work rocketed. . . . We saw everything in a rather over-simplified way, with too many blacks and whites, and we accepted the Communist Party line. . . . We were to some extent naive, but surely not so naive as those solid citizens who thought they could save us from war by concessions to Hitler and Mussolini. (pp. 149f.)

Running the Left Book Club in Liverpool had them put up Koestler, fresh from a Franco jail but off Stalin: 'He remarked that we should probably report his political deviation to the Party (he was by this time somewhat drunk). We were all indignant at such a suggestion, which I think shows clearly that we were none of us true communists at heart, but basically liberals! A real communist would have shopped him without compunction' (p. 152).

'In some ways my academic life, teaching and research, and our joint political activities at this time seemed almost like two separate forms of existence' (p. 158). In 1938 they took in an illegal entrant to the UK, a Sudeten German Czech wounded fighting in the International Brigade in Spain, and—as was learned later—a (pragmatically?) converted Fascist prisoner: 'I had always shied at doing anything against the law, but this seemed a case where one could not say no. . . . "Turn him in", they [the CP] said' (pp. 167f.). 'Meanwhile work in the University was going on much as usual. . . . In November 1939 the two worlds I was living in were temporarily brought together, when we put up Professor Benjamin Farrington. . . . He was a Marxist and . . . was to be responsible for my writing my most controversial book, *The Decline of the Roman Empire in the West*' (pp. 171f.). Though the whole business now sounds rather absurd and a storm in a teacup, it was extremely worrying at the time', when the Walbanks were prosecuted and fined for aiding and abetting the alien/refugee (p. 179).[9]

Meantime, the first baby, and post-natal troubles—and the bombshell of the Molotov–Ribbentrop pact: on the instant, 'the Communist party now began to speak of the imperialist war. Seen in retrospect this seems so ludicrous and absurd that one wonders how anyone could have taken it seriously. But at the time . . .' (p. 180).

FWW was told he must resign from the Home Guard, 'no reasons given . . . C. P. Membership was now damning' (pp. 181 f.). He 'remained at the University for the rest of the war', serving on the Fire Watch and lecturing to soldiers, not least on 'Campaigning with Alexander' (p. 186). Shortly before the war *Philip V* was finished, and in 1943 he contacted OUP with the idea of a commentary on Tacitus' *Histories*; Syme—somewhere in Anatolia—was supposed to have bagged that, and by the time he 'relinquished' it, the 'alternative project' had taken hold: 'little did I realise then that Polybius was going to occupy the next thirty-four years of my life . . . I appreciated their having undertaken such a book in war-time, when the future was still uncertain (though indeed by 1944 it was pretty clear that the pendulum had swung decisively in our favour)' (p. 195)

By then (in 1943) *The Decline* project had been devised: I was still a Marxist (of sorts) though I had split decisively from the C. P., whose shifts of policy made it contemptible. (For when Hitler attacked Stalin, the war had in their view once more become a just one and to be supported.) Moreover, especially during the early war years, I was often worried by the problem of reconciling the subject of my work with the world we were now living in—that constantly recurring problem of 'relevance'. This book . . . seemed to offer an opportunity to make a statement about how I saw the present and the future. It was going to be a tract for the times . . . By the time the book appeared in 1946 the war was already over and the atomic bomb had been dropped on Japan. . . . My concern with the relevance of the classics also surfaced in . . . a short article published . . . in June 1943, 'Is our Roman history teaching re-

[9] FWW (pers. comm.) points out my lapse in historicality here: 'How natural to assume that when a couple have taken a refugee into their home to stay illegally, they should both be charged. But no; to the official mind of 1938 such an action could only have been that of the "head of the household" (*sic*!)'. The *Memoir* always keeps one eye duly trained on the experience of being married to Polybius.

actionary?' . . . My other political effusion was . . . in 1944 . . . entitled 'The causes of Greek decline'. . . . In May [1945] came VE day—8 May. . . . I was talking . . . on 'Is history bunk?' Shortly afterwards came the dropping of the atom bombs on Hiroshima and Nagasaki. (pp. 196–200) 'The rather strange subsequent history of this small book [*The Decline*]' has a 'Japanese larger version' (1963), republished by Liverpool in a 'new English edition' as *The Awful Revolution* (p. 197)—just when *I* was pitching into Polybius' Walbank in 1969.

With 1946 and (as ever chance-ridden) election to the Chair of Latin, the memoir firmly closes: '. . . 1951 . . . until I retired in 1977. But that is another story' (p. 204).

Now this skeleton précis suggests accurately enough how the memoir is written, with virtually no indication whatever of the method of production of the record (as between memory, diaries, public records, research, consultation, revision in the light of consultation and readerly responses . . .), as is the way with memoirs; and on the other hand, correlatively, with the firmest supervision from the authorial present, invading the narration with controlled apologetics for the excesses, misprisions, false steps, and naiveties of the past, and coolant irony for the actor-self's efforts to string together a chosen path toward a settled goal or rational objective, as they get discomposed and replaced by the vagaries of a contingent world of lunacy, mayhem, and horror laced with the mundane dance of ordinary crises, opportunities, and routine.

Our narrator allows himself to speak only parsimoniously of the inner life of his (un)hero, and not at all of his own. So this is a steady record of the successive phases of a life pegged to its own specifics: the plain stylistics that personify dispassionate perspective. Shorn of frustrations, resentments, or regrets, as of satisfaction, jubilation, and preening. Even *anti*-snobbery (the most likely chink in the armour) gets severely rationed. Above all, FWW good as marries into a (relatively brief—but relative to *what*?) political radicalism that implodes before it can charge up a crusade, and instead ends up depriving him of a war, of all the histrionic rush and the proving of self. His (substitutive) efforts to mobilize historical writing and classics get neatly mocked by the planetary enormities of thermonuclear detonation: 'Is history bunk?' The scale of events beggars the mere person, as *The Decline of the West* ushers in an unimaginable future history of devastation in the Far East.

Polybius is fully accounted for in *Hypomnemata*, as another matter-of-fact happenstance: the teacher's random assignment; the chance of a free holiday; the Tripos syllabus; the second-best idea for somewhere to start playing at research; in the event, the second-string proposal for something to pass the time with, it-could-should've-been Tacitus', not Polybius', *Histories*: 'I wrote several articles rather than embark on a large project while the future seemed so uncertain. But in 1943 I began to feel the need for something more substantial' (p. 194). Thirty-four years on it, and FWW is surprised to find retirement is upon him! But no, this was not, after all, a strange obsessionality, let alone a charismatic vocation or destiny: just an unglamorous trajectory through a catena of options and constraints, threaded on a line in liberalism, if you like, but no hint of a mission. The popularizing historicist who dared read out the lessons of Antiquity—'Fascism is not inevitable' (1946, 79); 'authoritarian repression and the caste state are not the inevitable fate in store for us' (1969, 120)—would scarcely have agreed with the tepid analysis which now speaks for him, now the walls are down and the USSR bosses no imperializing Comintern. The origins of the *Commentary* in the will to integrate a self and make sense amidst the uncertainties of World War, however easily all this can be sensationalized, are proof against their retrospective reduction in the memoir to the humdrum status of an 'occupation' for an academic.

Any reader acquainted with the outmanoeuvring of Polybius by superpower-driven ructions that engulfed his life and his country, wrong-footing and compromising him with political U-turns and doublethink, before delivering him, eventually, to the unforeseeable serenity of a secure and lengthy later life in the study, will find the young FWW's tenacious attachment and self-dedication to his unfashionable chosen field of professional expertise pellucid. The politics of federalism and its Achaean heroes speak clearly to the thirties Europe of the League of Nations, just as Later Macedon's Balkanized intrigues with neighbours, clients, and satellites before the lightning supervention of implacable Rome typologized the present menaces of *Machtpolitik*; right-minded political loyalties twisted and turned absurdly cock-eyed, sidelining the patriot in another Polybius—*you*; and Carthage and Corinth, the obliteration of whole cities and populations by blitz, lived next door in the total war of Liverpool bombing raids—and others.

The popularizing historicist Polybius' lessons for the future surely won his devotee with his very special brand of irresistible 'relevance'—that wearisome wor(l)d of reproach for classics. Scholars have not generally been in the habit of thrusting their motives on readers; and the passage of time dissipates the significance of the originary impulse before the proliferation of contexts in which the achieved monument functions, as the significance of it becomes that of a realized edifice interacting with new receptions. Smoothing away obsolescent and lapsed investments and intellections—'the theme of "I have not changed", of emotional permanence and intellectual continuity'—naturally supervenes in the retroaction-pledged discourse of authorial apologia.[10]

2

FWW: WHY POLYBIUS

Past events make us pay particular attention to the future, if we really make thorough inquiry in each case into the past.

(Pol. 12. 25. e6, trans. Paton (1922–7), *cit.* Walbank (1946), p. xiii = (1969), 9)[11]

The 'Preface' to the *Commentary* (1957–79, I. pp. vii–x) is the soul of brevity. Two sides define the project; then one-and-a-bit append 'A word on the frontispiece, [which] portrays our only surviving representation of Polybius'. The 'more than life size' relief shows 'a young man', though it must belong to Polybius' later life, 'and may have been set up after his death'. This is 'a Polybius idealized . . . in the role of a hero of Arcadia'. Before this, the

[10] Genette (1997), 256: cf. 252 on the 'Olympian appraisal' of serene 'next-to-last-thoughts'. FWW (pers. comm.) agrees—'100%'—that the *Memoir* plays up '*tyche* with a small "t" ', and plays down 'the social and personal conditions of the early forties', in narrating the emergence of the *Commentary*. He made the point himself, in a paper on 'The Problem of Greek Nationality' given to the Classical Association AGM of 1951 (=1985, 1–19, at 19): 'Though the historian is apt to believe that the subject he has chosen to study is one which he came to by chance, or because it seemed to have been neglected, or because it arose out of some earlier work, or for some other wholly personal reason, fifty years hence it will be quite obvious that the themes chosen by historians today, and the treatment accorded to them, were directly related to contemporary problems, or, to use De Sanctis' words, "to the spiritual needs of men and women living in the middle of the twentieth century".'

[11] Cf. Hahm (1995), 47 on this. Translation will be taken from well-thumbed Paton except where noted.

Commentary opened, reassuringly, with standard prefatory *topoi* of the genre (*opportunum, necessarium, quaesitum*): 'The last full commentary', he begins, . . . no longer satisfies current needs. . . . [It] is primarily philological; whereas most people who read Polybius today turn to him as the main source for much Hellenistic history . . . Primarily my concern has been with whatever might help to elucidate what Polybius thought and said . . . [The] later development and influence [of ideas and theories on which Polybius draws] have been excluded as having no proper place here. I have also tried to avoid turning the commentary into a history.'

But this canonical austerity and abstemious rigour is, all the same, the peg on which FWW hangs protreptic for the historicizing project latent in his labours. If only we stop and listen. The *tabula gratulatoria* offers 'a special tribute . . . to the delegates of the Clarendon Press, who gave encouragement to the scheme for this commentary in 1943, when the future prospects for scholarly work were obscure', after stressing that his 'work . . . has straggled over most of the last twelve years'. When he began by gently settling 'The last full commentary on Polybius' into well-respected retirement, he actually underlined that 'Schweighaeuser published [it] during the French Revolution; but his eight massive volumes . . . are fundamentally untouched by the stirring events going on at the time—except that in the last two the author, hitherto described as *Argentoratensis*, has suddenly grown conscious that he is also *Franco-Gallus*. The work appeared between 1789 and 1795, and the *Lexikon Polybianum* followed the next year. It is in essence a product of eighteenth-century scholarship.'[12]

Those 'people who read Polybius today' in fact 'turn to him . . . above all, as the first man who really came to grips with the problem of the rise of Rome to world empire—which is equivalent to saying that his readers today are pre-eminently those who share his own interests'.

So scholarly historicism here centres on the orientation within historical writing toward the present,[13] as this *Preface* economically

[12] FWW (pers. comm.) points out to me that 'the danger of too readily assuming a scholar's philological aloofness from his work' is well illustrated by Schweighaeuser's note on 6. 57. 7, where he 'pictures the [French] revolution in the guise of the goddess Philosophia making her epiphany to live in France and there regulate and control men's lives' (1995b, 218, n. 94).

[13] Hamilton (1996) is a useful and provocative explication of historicism(s); Ryan (1996) neatly maps out new historicism vis-à-vis cultural materialism. Walbank

thrusts the (theory-laden) proposition on the reader that 'we' are 'today' self-reflexively alive to the Revolutions, the stirring events, the problem of world empires, which entitle us to claim to share Polybius' interests, and will, through Polybius, think 1943–56 politically, along with FWW. To 'satisfy current needs' is, to be sure, nothing other than this proposition (in polar opposition to a Philology that had perversely taken the *Histories* out of history, and vice versa). Why else read Polybius?

3

POLYBIUS' PLAN

in rebus magnis memoriaque dignis consilia primum, deinde acta, postea euentus exspectantur.

(Cicero, *De oratore* 2. 63: *lex historiae*)

Polybius' *Histories* are a traditional theatre for 'unitarian versus analyst' disputation. Attempts to tie chunks of material to particular phases of composition as a preliminary to, or confirmation of, stages in the author's mutating intellection of his project have taken the form of a more-or-less routine or imaginatively circular search for dates *post quos* and *ante quos non*, for statements and suppositions that are period-bound, and for views and perspectives which (should) belong to temporally distinct Polybian selves.[14] For all that his work survives mutilated in excerpts and compiled citations, particularly after the first Olympiad of his chosen epoch and the appended excursus on the Roman polity (I–V + VI), this 'contemporary' historian is particularly eloquent on the structuring, economy, parameters, horizons paraded by his elaborated narrative. It is uncontroversial to suppose that he continued to be every bit as talkative in editorial signposting and guidance in the grievously lacerated later books.

(1985), 283 ('Polybius Between Greece and Rome', repr. from Geneva in 1974) lets past a very rare flash of overt contemporaneity: 'Men like Cephalus moved to the right . . . while others, like Polybius, became more cautious and so in effect moved to the right.'

[14] I would countenance 'ethnographic presents', even about an extinct Carthage or a disbanded (or aetiolated) Achaean League, thus abandoning most of the alleged 'dates' for early (because obsolete) strata of text: cf. Erbse (1951), *pace* Walbank (1957), i. 292 f. (cf. n. 41 below. At (1995a), 278, n. 46, FWW reverts to an open verdict on the Achaean chs. 2. 37–70).

The Theory that materializes in Polybius' overture is powerfully presented and re-inforced at the outset and at the end of Book II + the proem to Book III. The scope of the *Histories* will 'begin' from the 140th Olympiad (220–16 BCE). But before we are ready for this ἀρχή, a preliminary account of the antecedents is required: this προκατασκευή takes two books. The 'real' start to the narrative proper will be from III onwards. By then, the crucially interwoven subjects of causality and the ordering of strands of narration have been prototypically explored in the preliminaries; and Polybius has shown how he (was) meant to become the one and only genuinely universal historian, both because the ascent of Rome to world hegemony 'in fifty-three years' handed him perfect fusion of form with content and because he had the Scholarly/Theoretical nous to shadow history in his mimesis. As we read on through his pages, the several histories of the rival power-blocs (Carthage, Macedonian Hellas, Rome, and subsidiaries) progressively interlock, and are then subsumed by conquest within the history of cosmopolis: Rome—or 'mondialatinization'.[15] All previous lives and their archives debouch in this grand plot of 'Zusammenhangstiftung' (συμπλοκή).[16]

History 'works together' through the many synchronisms that set off the period that opened Rome's Second Punic, or Hannibalic, War, the Social War in Hellas, from the era brought to a close by the historical narrative of Polybius' and FWW's hero, Aratus, just out of reach of direct eyewitnesses for Polybius.[17] In the first Olympiad of the main narrative bloc (III–V), Polybius and his readers must look lively and hop intricate patterns around the Mediterranean, as the several theatres of action are dealt round in their own place, as in the preliminary sketch, but begin to tend πρὸς ἓν τέλος ('toward one end', 4. 28. 3 f.).[18] Thus the schematic triangulation between Rome, Carthage, and Macedon/Hellas

[15] Derrida's neologism for 'the hegemony of Latin over the world today, through religion and Roman law'—now with the admixture of 'Anglo-American hegemony' (aka mcdonaldization, or *col*anization) (1996a, 214).

[16] Walbank (1985), 313–24, Meissner (1986), 317 f. Hatched *by* Polybius, Walbank (1972), 58 reminds us; dramatized and explicated by the editorial mouthpiece Agelaus at 5. 104. 1–11, cf. Champion (1997). From the prim(ev)al imagery of 'political weaving in Greece': Scheid and Svenbro (1996), esp. 9–34.

[17] *Hist.* 1. 3; 4. 2. 2. Synchronisms (in Books 4–5): Walbank (1985), 298–312.

[18] Cf. Walbank (1972), 103; the continual round of 'orderly' (τεταγμένως) self-interruption is still being explained, and championed, at 38. 5 f., esp. 6. 3 (FWW (1985), 318 f., Boncquet (1982–3), 284).

steadily emerges as the spine of the story: triumphs over Hannibal at Zama and over the last king of Macedon at Pydna frame the world conquest, as the contest for subordination of all rivals is concluded and 'history' brought to an emphatic full stop (in Book XXIX).

Polybius is indeed a byword for systematic holism. He parades teleology, economy, discipline—with unwavering seriousness, chalcenteric concentration on detail, and earnest explicitation of values. Traditionally valued for the plain factity of his privileged insider view through much of his narrative, and as such *tolerated* in classical Philology despite plodding prose, trite rhetoric, and second-rate syntactical grip, Polybius' *project* makes him a historiographical gem: famously self-named 'pragmatic', 'apodeictic', and precisely, 'monoeidic' and 'somatoeidic'.[19] It is not, therefore, unexpected to find that he has a *Theory* of circumscription (περιγραφή); trite enough at the time, no doubt, and close kin to mainstream (narratological) 'guff' in Rhetoric. Listen to this:

> διόπερ οὐχ οὕτως ἐστὶ φροντιστέον τῆς αὐτῶν τῶν πράξεων ἐξηγήσεως, οὔτε τοῖς γράφουσί οὔτε τοῖς ἀναγινώσκουσι τὰς ἱστορίας, ὡς τῶν πρότερων καὶ τῶν ἅμα καὶ τῶν ἐπιγινομένων τοῖς ἔργοις.
>
> Therefore both writers and readers of history should not pay so much attention to the actual narrative of events, as to what precedes, what accompanies, and what follows each. (3. 31.11)

And now this:

> Polybius' tripartite analysis of 'what preceded, accompanied, and followed' the events was a standard item in rhetorical handbooks as a guide to the elaboration of narrative.[20]

In fact Polybius takes his usual crashingly symmetrical stance on the issue:

> ἀκμὴν γὰρ φαμεν ἀνακαιότατα μέρη τῆς ἱστορίας εἶναι τά τ' ἐπιγινόμενα τοῖς ἔργοις καὶ τὰ παρεπόμενα καὶ μάλιστα τὰ περὶ τὰς αἰτίας.

[19] 1. 2. 8; 2. 37. 3; 9. 1. 2; 1. 3. 4.; etc. These are, of course, *all* theory-laden terms: the term 'pragmatic' has come a long way in h/History.

[20] Wiseman (1993), 144, on Pol. 3. 31. 11–13, referring to Hermogenes 16. 22, after Woodman (1988), 108 n. 79. Heath (1989), 80 f. mentions Polybius' organicism (1. 4. 5–11), but just has him 'subsequently revise . . . his plan [with] an extension'.

For I maintain that far the most essential part of history is the consideration of the remote or immediate consequences of events and especially that of causes (3. 32. 6 (Paton): Rather, 'I declare the most essential parts of history to be both the aftermath of events and their concomitant circumstances, and especially the matter of their causes'.)

And it is no surprise to find that he builds this tripartite scheme into the overall structure of the whole plan of the *Histories*, so that the elaborate management of the scene-setting business of *αἰτίαι* prepares for its eventual mirror-image in a post-liminary follow-up to treatment of the events of 220–168 BCE. This, he explains, painstakingly as ever, will handle the epiphenomena, outcome, or *τὰ ἐπιγινόμενα*:

Now if from their success or failure alone we could form an adequate judgement of how far states and individuals are worthy of praise or blame, I could here lay down my pen, bringing my narrative and this whole work to a close with the last-mentioned events, *κατὰ τὴν ἐξ ἀρχῆς πρόθεσιν* ['as was my original intention', as in Walbank e.g. (1985), 330] . . . But since judgements regarding either the conquerors or the conquered based purely on performance are by no means final . . . *προσθετέον ἂν εἴη* ['I must append'] to the history of the above period an account of the subsequent policy of the conquerors and their method of universal rule, as well as of the various opinions and appreciations of their rulers entertained by the subjects, and finally I must describe what were the prevailing and dominant tendencies of the various peoples in their private and public life. . . . So the final end achieved by this work will be, to gain knowledge of what was the condition of each people after each had been crushed and had come under the dominion of Rome, until the disturbed and troubled time *πάλιν ἐπιγινομένης* ['that afterwards ensued']. About this latter . . . *προήχθην οἷον ἀρχὴν ποιησάμενος ἄλλην γράφειν* ['I was induced to write as if starting on a fresh work'] (3. 4. 1–13).

This passage introduces a carefully orchestrated summary of events from 167 to 146 BCE, culminating in the utter destruction of Carthage and, for the final chapter, 'the beginning and end of the general calamity that overtook Greece' (3. 5. 6: *ἅμα τὴν ἀρχὴν καὶ τὸ τέλος ἔσχε τὸ κοινὸν ἀτύχημα πάσης τῆς Ἑλλαδος*). Such is Polybius' plan, he grinds it in, and 'now having given a summary of the most important events, with the object of conveying to my readers a notion of this work as a whole and its contents in detail, it is time for me *μνημονεύοντας τῆς προθέσεως ἐπαναγαγεῖν ἐπὶ τὴν* ἀρχὴν τῆς αὐτῶν ὑποθέσεως ('to call to mind my original plan and return to the starting-point of my history', 3. 5. 9)'. With that he is off, lecturing away for all he is worth on the grind of 'causes' and 'beginnings' of the Hannibalic War.[21]

I have given in Greek several phrases which are misrepresented by Paton's translation. Some of them are cardinal for Polybius' parade of structuration. Absolutely central is

> προήχθην οἷον ἀρχὴν ποιησάμενος ἄλλην γράφειν ('About this ⟨latter⟩, he goes on, I was induced to write as if beginning/starting on a new work', Walbank (1972), 24, (1985), 161, 293, 'as if he were making a new start, that is, as if he were beginning a new work', (1985), 333; 'I was persuaded to write about them and to make them the starting-point of what amounts almost to a new work', trans. Scott-Kilvert (1979), 182: overseen—'selected with an introduction'—by FWW), 'These I designed to make the starting-point of what may almost be called a new work', in Shuckburgh's version ((1889), i. 169f.: 'The plan extended').

In my view, Polybius' editorial here directs us to recognize, not a 'fresh start' on 'extra years',[22] but mirror-image *structural* responsion between the junctions between preliminaries and ἀρχή, at one limit, and between τέλος, and post-liminaries, at the other. τὰ ἐπιγινόμενα are to be set off from the main *History*, marking a '*quasi* second start'.

Similarly, the slogan phrase κατὰ τὴν ἐξ ἀρχῆς πρόθεσιν (together with its two components) is used here, and consistently elsewhere, of the economy of the work.[23] *Not* to indicate that the text he means to present consists of a *first phase* of composition overlain by 'a new start' to a revised conception, continuation, and completion of the extended version, in subsequent departure from an earlier 'original' plan.

However, Polybian Scholarship repeatedly, but incorrectly,

[21] See Derow (1979), 9 f., Meissner (1986), 318f.

[22] Walbank (1957), i. 303 (At (1972), 183, n. 147 (1985), 324, this becomes 'as he says, virtually a new work'); Gabba (1991), 16. FWW (pers. comm.) has not found my analyses of 3. 4 and 3. 31–2 convincing: 'alas no'; in brief, the latter passage concerns the micro-level of 'specific events or groups of events', and the former passage tells us that 'the inclusion of anything after 168 requires separate explanation. . . . I don't think your gallant attempt to assert a unitary view quite comes off'.

[23] Cf. 2. 14. 1, 37. 2, 71. 9, and other passages in Walbank (1957), i. 301. So Derow (1996), 1210, 'Polybius' original purpose was . . . He later extended his purpose . . .'; Luce (1997), 125, 'He originally ended his history in 167 . . . But . . . he decided to add eleven more books . . .'; etc. etc.

deduces from these points in this, Polybius' most expansive editorial, strategically situated at the crucial *incipit* of the Histories, that we are reading a composite preface that retains the first project from 220–168 but interpolates the secondary project of 167–46, which will occupy Books XXX–XXXIX (before the final volume of 'end papers', (XL).

This, the orthodox interpretation, licenses and legitimates, at a stroke, the 'analyst' textual explorations already mentioned; and trying to relate the duplex process of writing to its written product makes for challenging and tortuous adventures in discriminating first wind from second thoughts; and in identifying original copy still retained later (at whatever cost to coherence or referential validity). This is, however, (I propose) to make a mug of the *Theorist* Polybius, just as he is explaining that he would be a dolt if he stopped his work before the job was done: 'since judgements regarding either the conquerors or the conquered based purely on performance are by no means final (οὐκ αὐτοτελεῖς) . . . προσθετέον ἂν εἴη ("I must append") to the history of the above period an account of the subsequent policy of the conquerors and their method of universal rule, etc.'.[24]

'The final end' (τελεσιούργημα) proposed for the finality of this most teleologically rounded of masterworks[25] is a perfectly theorized plan, set over against the likes of abjected Timaeus and Phylarchus, predecessors who (must) lack totalization and (so) analytic seriousness, while our Professor supplies the ideal Theorist and Scholar.[26] He creates orderly narration from the destruction of the world order, he re-creates a Hellenism where his narrative will star as its annunciation. And for him the expansion of Roman power 'had been completed' (ἐτετελείωτο, 3. 4. 6) by Pydna, so we do not await further expansion between 167 and 146, but rather 'the

[24] Cf. πρὸς δὲ τούτοις later in the series of limbs that stretch the sentence (3. 4. 6). At 8. 11. 3 f. Polybius chews over Theopompus for changing horses in midstream: 'No one could approve of the general scheme of this writer. Having set himself the task of writing the general history of Greece from the point where Thucydides leaves off . . . he abandoned Greece and her efforts, and changing his plan decided to write the history of Philip. Surely it would have been much more dignified and fairer to include Philip's achievements in the history of Greece than to include the history of Greece in that of Philip' (cf. Millar (1987), 8). Does it take one to gnaw one?

[25] See the final chapter, of exultation at completion (39. 8. 8: the last words are τῆς ὅλης πραγματείας).

[26] Alonso-Núnez (1990).

development of the policy of the conquerors and the reactions of the rest of the world'.[27]

Now the Polybius we have is so perfectly finalized a text that, for example, an 'excerpt' can tell us of his harvest of *posthumous* honours—a neat trick indeed.[28] Then, for example, chapters in one and the same book can first crown our curtain-raiser of a preface with the recognition that he needs luck for his lifespan to let him complete his plan, though in any case the project won't lapse 'since there are many others who will set their hands to the task and labour to complete it' (πρός τὸ τὴν πρόθεσιν ἐπὶ τέλος ἀγαγεῖν . . . ἐπὶ τέλος ἀγαγεῖν αὐτήν, 3. 5. 7f.), and then go on, nevertheless, to deplore people 'who think that this my work is difficult to acquire and difficult to read owing to the number and length of the Books it contains. How much easier it is to acquire and peruse forty Books, all as it were connected by one thread . . . than to read or procure the works of those who treat of particular transactions' (3. 32. 1–3).[29] It is scarcely difficult, besides such piquant crises for the unitarian, to assume that not every sentence or thought in this massive lifework is compatible with all the rest. Any lengthy composition *must* alter its author, if only by occupying a sizeable chunk of their time passing by. Even a work exclusively devoted to organic coherence and monological consistency.

Informed and imaginative implication of our Polybius within the twists and turns of a h/History that constantly altered the sense of what he wrote as he wrote it, altered the sense of his writing it, and altered the authorial valency of his own authority, dramatizes his writing as a (revolutionary, repressive, . . . whatever . . .) *process* of collaboration with Contingency. Yet as Scholarship has done its damnedest to pinpoint a privileged moment for the inscription of each item or episode of text, it has worked to and fro between the body of the *Histories* and its supposed 'extension', fixating on the watershed as the *definitive* second 'bombshell' in Polybius' political experience.

That 'disturbed and troubled time' between 150 and 146,

[27] Richardson (1979), 2: but accepting a 'revised plan' of continuation past 168.

[28] 39. 5. 4: for the excerption from Polybius (as military handbook), cf. Thompson (1985).

[29] On this passage: FWW (1985), 314, 323f. For supposed late insertions clustering in Book 3, cf. Walbank (1957), i. 296f., Eckstein (1992), 393; on the problematic measurements for Hannibal's march across Gaul at 3. 39. 8, cf. Pothecary (1995): late or interpolated.

culminating in the final suppression of Macedonian autonomy, the razing of both Carthage and, along with its city, the Achaean fortress of Acrocorinth, and the at least temporary dissolution of the Achaean League becomes the rehabilitated former hostage Polybius' ('Molotov–Ribbentrop') mid-life crisis of 'shock'.[30] So it is that the imperfectly adapted preface to the ἀρχή shrivels under FWW's recursive scrutiny, to reveal an ever more ragged set of unconvincing pleas for extending the work by twenty years and ten books, or an extra third of its length. As we estimate (with FWW) when poor Polybius was obliged to confect 'The alleged purpose of the' inevitable 'extension', and work out 'The real purpose of the extension', the *Histories* fray and babble into failure, irreparably holed by history: 'unresolved conflict. . . . Eventually he may have come to feel that his new purpose, clumsily and obscurely set out and difficult to fulfil, was something of an embarrassment'.[31]

But this structural form of the 'extension', or 'continuation', or 'pendant', or *supplement* demands to be generalized throughout reception of the whole mighty project, over all the years of Polybius' writing career.[32] From initial transumption to Rome as Achaean hostage after Pydna, the final captive in Rome's drive to ascendancy, the historian went on to construe the conquest in terms of its out-turn, until return home was granted but interrupted by the call to join his Roman patron sacking Carthage, so that he could only help alleviate Roman reprisals on rebellious

[30] 'Shock induced Polybius to return to his writing-table and to attach a whole new portion to his history' (Gruen (1984), 346: 350, Polybius 'ended with confusion rather than clarity'; denied by Kallett-Marx (1995), 22, n. 45.) FWW (pers. comm.) rightly warns us that 'hostage' in this context is the sort of loose talk that can cost lives: 'the thousand hostages from Achaea, of whom Polybius was one', were, rather, 'detained, by *force majeure*' (quote from Rawson (1989), 463, in *CAH*[2]).

[31] Walbank (1985), 325–43, his/the most devastating critique of Polybius' editorial yet, at 330–4; 341–3; cf. 343: 'This could be why we hear nothing of it in the epilogue with which he wound up Book XXXIX' (= 39. 8: preliminaries; beginning (in 220 BCE), then regularly sectionalized world events; 'until the sack of Carthage, the battle of the Achaeans and the Romans at the Isthmus and the consequent settlement of Greece'). Against FWW's arguments for incoherence, Shimron (1979–80), 97–9, insists that 3. 4 f. are *ex hypothesi* 'late': if Polybius had changed his mind, he would surely have changed this editorial? FWW (e.g. (1985), 294) irreverently supposes the extension was 'because Polybius had material urgently needing to be published'!

[32] Cf. Walbank (1957), i. 302: 'This plan *supplements*, but does not supersede, that enunciated repeatedly throughout the work.'

Achaea in the aftermath of its disaster (thus missing 'his' war). As Hellas settled and Polybius lived on, long, but who knows how long,[33] we can't be sure that he did not drastically re-conceive his entire perspective; we can only speculate on what any pre-146 (or so) drafting, or version, may have looked like.

Ever since 146,[34] hindsight has made the horrific symmetry which shapes the span of Polybius' tripartite narrative so undeniable that the effort to imagine a vision in which the plot was over in 168 becomes a daunting and invaluable exercise in historicizing contingency. For all that the nexus of Cornelii Scipiones and Aemilii Pauli grips together the triad of Punic Wars along with Macedon from early Roman incursions into Illyria to the demotion of the Kingdom at Pydna; that Corinth and Polybius' Megalopolis duetted to disaster between Achaea, Sparta, and the major powers all the way from the acme of Macedon to the domination of Rome; that Luck circuited Polybius the Arcadian federalist cipher between Hellas, Carthage, and Rome so that his apodeictic history could 'not *tell* but *show*' us[35] culture red in tooth and claw.

Historians like to be awkward cusses. Does Polybius hold out for Theory? FWW would have the *Histories* fizzle out in the inconclusive dismay of another *Hellenika*.[36] I think Polybius' invitation to readers to supply their own evaluation of Roman hegemony does chime with Herodotus' (Solonian) drive to 'Look to the end', and so to hand out your own prizes and condemnations.[37] But in pushing the line that in *this* history an event is to be seen as *distinct* from its upshot, but *not complete* or *intelligible* until joined by it, I have specifically had in mind synkrisis with the *Thucydidean* war of interpretation. Admitting three segmented phases to 'his' war, rich in responsions between the 431–421 and 414–404 narratives, but insisting (against the consensus) on its overarching unity, Thucydides must run down the median period of ceasefire, truce, and treaty as mere superficies, or else forfeit the grandeur and

[33] The *terminus post* of *c.*118 depends on a lacunose and corrupt set of road-map statistics in 3. 39 (cf. Eckstein (1992), 390 and n. 15).

[34] e.g. for Pausanias: Arafat (1996), 39, 202 f. On Polybius as our first 'Roman Greek': Henderson [forthcoming].

[35] Davidson (1991), 24. At Carthage, Scipio grabs Polybius' hand and dreads the doom of Rome, at least in prospect; then cries for the next Troy—Rome (38. 21, 22).

[36] (1985), 180: 'It is symbolic that his history should end, like Xenophon's, in years of ταραχὴ καὶ κίνησις.'

[37] Moles (1996), 271–7, esp. 275, '. . . inevitably carries the narrative beyond its formal ending'.

dramatic unity of his lifework.[38] Whereas Polybius the post-Aristotelian Scholar gathers somatoeidic form for his Theorized work by triangulating (1) the study proper with (2) a legion of antecedents organized into a prelude, plus (3) a postlude, compacted from an immediate aftermath that slurs into an accelerando vortex of apocalyptic—settlement.[39] Such at any rate is the grand scheme suggested for the *Histories* by structural comparison with the extant avatars, in line with its key programmatic formula.

Not that we should find 'the truth' of Polybius in *any* favourite editorial flourish. No. *That* is the mistake when those phrases in III are taken for *the* decisive proof of (botched, patchy, irreparable) revision.

Yet this problematic is just how 'Polybius/Walbank' gets real, for me, working together *both* their historicalities. Only, the Scholar, however informed by Theory, needed specific legitimation (from within the text itself) to release a historicist *supplementarity*, whereas this is a general datum, or axiom, in the Theory of contemporary Scholarship (what you live through lives through you).[40] Imagine Polybius working on Book XV by 150,[41] and you'll 'see something of the strong emotional background which coloured his attitudes and probably gave him the impetus to carry through his great enterprise to a successful conclusion'.[42] Imagine Frank Walbank working on Polybius in . . .

Studying history does not mean absorbing the past as if one were drinking coffee.[43]

[38] 5. 26. 2 f., esp. *καὶ τὴν διὰ μέσου ζύμβασιν εἴ τις μὴ ἀξιώσει πόλεμον νομίζειν, οὐκ ὀρθῶς δικαιώσει*, cf. Strauss (1997), 169f. The editorial armature splashes Herodotean, Thucydidean, etc. metahistorical touches all over Polybius.

[39] For division between Books 30–3 and 35–9 as history turns into memoirs, cf. Walbank (1985, 338–43, Marincola (1997), 192. Praise of patrons already starts with elogium for Aemilius Paullus (31. 22–30) and an account of Polybius' acquaintance with Scipio 'as promised in the previous book' (31. 23). Polybius enters the limelight at 36. 11.

[40] Cf. Henderson (1998a) on the lived-through history of Rome living through Livy's history of Rome.

[41] Walbank (1972), 19, Eckstein (1985), 277, 'Polybius' constant reference in books 1–15 to Carthage as an existing state is a strong indication that this past of the *Histories* . . . was already written by 150 B.C.'.

[42] Walbank (1985), 279.

[43] Walbank (1993), 15: 'It is a dynamic, dialectical process involving investigation, selection and interpretation. At each stage the historian interacts with his material. The past is in some sense recreated afresh for each person who concerns himself with it.'

PS

SCHOLARSHIP AND THEORY

It will be no use hiding behind our set of *Journal of Roman Studies*.
(Momigliano (1974), 5: when the ghost of Polybius visits us . . .)

Try this. Take any two polarized projects working together toward co-operative mutual support. Both will be obliged to rewrite their accounts of themselves and each other. It'll be like starting over—they must go back to 'the beginning', to explain how and where their principles are unshaken, and have indeed led to the new initiative, with its attendant need for apologetics; and they must signal what new considerations justify adjustment, novel realignment, fresh partnership. The desiderata: pacific positivity without opportunist trimming; compromise without being compromised; in short: turning to collaboration without turn(coat)ing into collaborators.

'Working together', the Oxford conference where this essay originated, was itself a re-start, working together the achievements of an earlier conference and its own contribution. Participants knew from the beginning(s) that their working together was supplementing, so threatening to supplant, their predecessors'. We knew at the time that what we would tell ourselves later, whenever that might be, would differ *because* of what we thought it might be; and we knew that what we would tell ourselves we had thought would differ *because* we told ourselves it would. What frame regulates the historicality *of this book*?[44]

[44] Capitalized instances of 'Theory' and 'Scholarship' throughout this chapter allude to an earlier title projected for this book. 'The Common Task: Scholarship and Theory in Classical Literature': a historicist tic and supplementary trace for the archive.

Reception/History of Scholarship

15

Introduction

Michael Reeve

If a medieval commentator on the *Thebaid* saw Titus and Domitian in Polynices and Eteocles, what is that to me?

Perhaps I have not met the idea before, and when I follow it up I rather like it. It annoys me, therefore, when Blenkinsop in 1997 (I hope there is no classical scholar of that name) puts it forward as though it were quite new, with no mention of the medieval commentator.[1] I suppose it annoys me for two reasons: I would rather see credit given where it is due, and fresh things to work on are hardly in short supply. The first reason, however, is less intellectual than moral, and the same could be said of the second. After all, neither affects the truth of Blenkinsop's article, if truth was its aim.

On the other hand, perhaps I dislike the idea and would rather forget it, along with other ideas that strike me as false or at best superficial. Before forgetting it, though, I casually mention it to two colleagues. One says 'oh, but it's an important episode in the reception of the *Thebaid*'. The other says 'interpretations come and go, and no doubt 800 or even eight years from now people will be just as unimpressed by yours, which you haven't yet given us, by the way'.

An important episode in the medieval reception of the *Thebaid* it may well be, however medievalists calibrate importance. I am not a medievalist, though; and if medievalists urge me to take an interest at least in what medieval readers of the *Thebaid* wrote in Latin about it, because medievalists themselves are too busy reading medieval vernaculars, then I mutter that any dereliction of duty seems to lie with them, not me. They are offended, and remind me

[1] de Angelis (1997), 106–7. For later occurrences of the same idea (*advertens inter imperatorem Domitianum et Titum germanos seditionem et simultatem ad illorum instructionem Thebanam scripsit historiam*) see de Angelis (1984), 199.

that but for medieval manuscripts there would be no *Thebaid* to read and interpret; if I think I am confronting face to face an epic written 1,900 years ago, I am deluding myself.

How can I disagree? I have spent much of my working life examining and often collating medieval manuscripts, and on occasions when a certain amount of preaching seemed to be called for I have argued that instead of treating manuscripts purely as bearers of readings classicists should try to set them in a historical context, or else they will not do their editorial job properly.[2] If the question arises, for instance, whether a reading could be a conjecture, the answer depends on the aims, resources, and abilities of whoever introduced it, and those in turn depend on historical circumstances. I remember encountering as an undergraduate George Thomson's view that editors of classical Greek texts ought to know the entire history of the Greek language.[3] At the time it seemed a tall order and perhaps even a disguised plea for a shift in priorities, but he was right, at least as regards the history of the language up to the time when manuscripts of classical Greek texts ceased to be written (roughly the time of Stephanus's lexicon, published in 1572). Following such precepts, though, leads to unease, both personal and institutional. I have no training in medieval history and more interest anyway in ancient history, and my Faculty does not want me to teach medieval history (nor does the Faculty of History).

Like manuscripts of classical texts, the foundations of many things that classical scholars nowadays take for granted lie in periods neither ancient nor modern. Not until the fourteenth century was it shown that there were two authors called Pliny.[4] The demonstration could be repeated from what one is tempted to call primary evidence, but evidence conveys nothing outside a framework, and no more than Rome itself was the framework of Roman history built in a day. It is not a bad idea to inspect the foundations once in a while and prod the framework. Demolishing rickety buildings and clearing the ground is a scholarly mode favoured by Alan Cameron for one, and very arresting he makes it.[5] On a small scale we are all aware of the need to practise it.

[2] Reeve (1986), 132–3, (1987), 437–40, (1995), 505–6.

[3] Thomson (1960).

[4] Iohannes de Matociis (Giovanni Mansionario), *Brevis adnotatio de duobus Pliniis*, ed. Merrill (1910), 186–8.

[5] His most recent such achievement is his book on Callimachus: Cameron (1995).

Before repeating someone's assertion that a usage is attested from the early fourth century, one checks whether they had in mind the *Historia Augusta*.

While I have been conducting this debate with my medievalist colleague and making concessions, my other colleague has lost patience. Is the history of scholarship really what people understand by reception?[6] Surely the fundamental question is why, in 1997, anyone should want to receive works composed by ancient Greeks and Romans at all. If you cannot explain what you get out of the *Thebaid* beyond manuscripts to collate, why collate them? Various kinds of reception over the centuries have brought the poem down to us, and if you fail to receive it—appreciate it, react to it, interrogate it—in your own way, then you are telling people to read something else, or to do research in biochemistry or media studies. I object that this is a case not for studying reception but for enacting it; furthermore, if people 800 or even eight years from now are going to look down their nose at my reception of the *Thebaid,* why should I bother to receive it?

My colleague ignores the first part of the objection and replies to the second. In some ways I am in a much better position for interpreting the *Thebaid* than the medieval commentator: I can read the *Silvae* and he could not,[7] I can read Greek versions of the story and he could not, I can read a number of good books on the *Aeneid* that he could not, I have a concordance to Statius and he had not, I can sound out colleagues by e-mail and he could not, and so on. Altogether, I should realize that he was making the best he could of rather limited materials. True, I can read only four lines of the *Bellum Germanicum* and odd bits of Antimachus' *Thebaid,* which by 2797 may both have turned up in full;[8] but I too should do the best I can with the materials available to me.

The medievalist interrupts. Appealing to the *Silvae* and good books on the *Aeneid* is just retreating to equally slippery ground, because the commentator might not have agreed that the books were good or the *Silvae* relevant. Furthermore, materials are one thing, but there is also the wider intellectual context of the time, not to mention the concerns of the commentator himself, no

[6] Godman (1990), esp. 151 and 173, treats as a superior form of scholarship the reception of classical poetry by Peter of Blois and Johannes Secundus.

[7] Reeve (1983), 397–9.

[8] Courtney (1980), 195–200 and (1993), 360; Matthews (1996), 79–206.

nonentity (perhaps) but the subject of a thumbnail sketch by one of his ecclesiastical contemporaries and the author of a datable work *De Regimine Principum* that includes a number of edifying stories from Suetonius. Just as we can see why Mommsen took against Cicero if we read about Mommsen's life,[9] so we can see from the thumbnail sketch and *De Regimine Principum* why the commentator was drawn to the parallel with Titus and Domitian; and we ourselves, even if we have no personal axe to grind (and who has not?), are bound to approach the *Thebaid* with a range of attitudes not formed in the days of Statius.

Reservations greet the second of these arguments. Euripides was barely dead when people started blaming his presentation of murderesses and adulteresses on troubles with the women of his household.[10] Inferring such troubles from his plays and then using them to account for the plays was never a sound procedure, but recent critics of Sophocles have not regarded the story of the sacred snake, hardly made up from the plays, as the key to understanding *Ajax* or *Electra* (though I am less sure about Thucydides' exile and his mining concession in Thrace).[11] It is hardly fair, then, to use against medieval commentators, Mommsen, or ourselves, an argument best summed up in the immortal words of Mandy Rice-Davies: 'he would [sc. say that], wouldn't he?'.[12] More strictly, it is unfair as long as the view expressed by the medieval commentator, Mommsen, or us includes a contention that can be tested against evidence publicly available. Whether Statius did or did not intend Titus and Domitian to be seen in Polynices and Eteocles is a historical question, and the answer does not depend on the experiences and enthusiasms of a medieval commentator.

Of course, Statius did not leave the answer on record in a single sentence for posterity to believe or disbelieve, and the only evidence available, beyond what is needed for establishing that chronology does not rule out the commentator's suggestion, is

[9] Wucher (1956), 92–5, Schmid (1973), 34–6.

[10] *Frogs* 1048.

[11] On the Sophoclean snake, a modern figment, see now Connolly (1998), 10–12. On Thucydides' exile the two lives printed in the OCT take different views: Marcellinus praises him for bearing no grudge over it, whereas 'most have composed histories because of their own experiences, with precious little concern for the truth' (ss. 14–27); the anonymous biographer says that because of it he seizes every opportunity of running the Athenians down (ss. 4).

[12] Jay (1996), 304, no. 8, from the *Guardian* for 1 July 1963.

his poems, above all the *Thebaid* itself, and ancient traditions of literary interpretation. Does the suggestion explain things in the *Thebaid* that had seemed puzzling? Does it reveal things that no one had noticed? In short, where does it lead? Many debates in classical scholarship are caused by loss of evidence that must once have existed, but the evidence that would resolve most debates over literary interpretation—why did Tacitus include this episode? why did Propertius put this poem next to that one? why did Virgil choose that word?—has never existed if one's notion of truth is correspondence to fact. Truth as coherence is the most that one can hope for.

Truth? Evidence? Why not just be grateful for classical works and use them for any purpose that suits us? *Oedipus Tyrannus* comes with no instructions attached, or else conflicting instructions, and the nearest thing to jail that you will finish up in if you use it as an indictment of infant exposure is the pages of *Gnomon*. As the commentator on the *Thebaid* has had a lot to put up with and deserves a rest, here is a passage from a commentator on Horace, taken to be Heiric of Auxerre.[13]

Carm. 1. 2. 41–4:

Sive Mercurius ideo dicitur, quoniam pulcher iuvenis erat, quemadmodum Mercurius pulcher apparet, dum dimissa figura celestium comisatur in terris; et hoc est quod dicit, sive tu ales imitaris illum iuvenem, tu, dico, qui es patiens vocari filius almae Maiae. Hoc hic intellegitur dictum de Augusto, sed in veritate quamquam nescienter loquebantur et quasi prophetabant de Christo, qui in tempore Augusti natus fuit; et Virgilius 'iam nova progenies celo demittitur alto'.

Or he is spoken of as Mercury because he was a good-looking young man, just as Mercury has a good-looking appearance when he lays aside his heavenly guise and revels on earth; and what he means is [? that is what he means when he says] 'Or if you imitate in winged form that young man, you, I mean who are tolerant of being called the son of gracious Maia'. This is taken here as referring to Augustus, but they were speaking in a vein of truth, though unawares, and giving a prophecy, as it were, about Christ, who was born in the time of Augustus; and Virgil says, 'now a new scion is sent down from lofty heaven'.

His stance could have been different: 'you, dear reader, are a

[13] Carlotta Dionisotti mentioned it in the discussion, and I thank her for supplying chapter and verse: Botschuyver (1940), 8.

humble Christian like me, and the only pious thing we can do with this flagrantly secular poem is to read "Christ" for "Augustus" throughout'. Instead, he spoke of truth and made a historical claim, that Horace was talking about Christ. It goes unmentioned in modern commentaries, which instead say things like this.[14]

Our passage seems unusually theological in tone. The normal Hellenistic *σωτήρ* might be a god in heaven, or a man become a god, or even a new god on earth; but here he is one of the old gods become a man. This saviour is to make good the Roman sin (*expiandi*), and his sojourn on earth involves, if not suffering, at least an element of condescension (43 *patiens* n.). One does not wish to press analogies too far, but it would be equally wrong to ignore clear resemblances. Nobody will suppose that Horace was directly acquainted with the writings of theologians and mystics, but it is hard to deny that his language bears some resemblance to certain eastern inscriptions in honour of Augustus (see below). And in spite of all the important differences of emphasis it is not a mere coincidence that the area and age that produced these inscriptions also produced, under strong Jewish influence, Christian theology. See further . . . The identification of Mercury and Octavian is not a pretty fancy of the poet's, but was derived from something that was going on in the real world. This range of ideas belongs to the East, and Horace's words show blurred traces of the eastern belief in a divine saviour.

Is that just how classical scholars in the twentieth century say what Heiric of Auxerre said in the ninth? Be that as it may, there are three claims that he could have made: that by Augustus Horace meant Christ; that Horace's words refer to Christ; and that through Horace someone else (God) meant Christ. He refuses to make the first (*nescienter*) and instead makes the third, which he defends on the strength of coherence: it fits *Eclogue* 4. Could he have refrained from making either and still have made the second? If so, could it have been anything other than a historical claim?

'Cambridge Sustainable City', I learn from its *Newsletter* 3 (December 1997), 'is about working together'. At the 1995 London conference which Stephen Harrison mentions in his General Introduction, the papers of which have now been published as Adams and Mayer (1999), I dimly remember having a notion of who should work together, but my reflections here have plunged me back in doubt. Is it on the one hand those who want to say 'for

[14] Nisbet and Hubbard (1970), 35–6.

Augustus read Christ' or some modern equivalent, on the other those who invoke truth and evidence? Is it people who often disagree about what counts as evidence? Or is there a third party whose existence has escaped me? When I fell to thinking about who might work together over *Rezeptionsgeschichte* in particular (the Germans invented the term, so let them have it just this once[15]), I was not at all sure whether the trendies do it and the fuddy-duddies not or the reverse, or whether some phases of it, like those that involve Mussolini or *Spartacus*, reveal more than others, like the alleged attempt by Geoffrey of Anjou, allegedly successful, to conclude a siege by applying Book 4 of Vegetius.[16] Above all, I hoped to find out, without going to the trouble of searching out Jocelyn on Grafton, or the controversy that William M. Calder III stirred up a few years ago in North America, whether those who urge the study of reception do so for its own sake or because they consider it the only access to Antiquity.[17] That my own mind on the matter is open, not to say empty, will be plain from the amount of μέν and δέ in my remarks here.

[15] The term 'Rezeption' is particularly associated with the series *Poetik und Hermeneutik*, where 'Rezeption' and 'Rezeptionsasthetik' entered the index in vol. 2 (1966) and 'Rezeptionsgeschichte' in vol. 5 (1973). Sceptical remarks of René Wellek's in vol. 5, pp. 515–17, bear the title 'Zur methodischen Aporie einer Rezeptionsgeschichte'. The opening words of Grimm (1977) are 'Die seit etwa funf Jahren als eigener literaturwissenschaftlicher Forschungsbereich etablierte Rezeptionsforschung'.

[16] The story entered Vegetian studies among the *Veterum testimonia* in P. Scriverius's second edition (Scriverius 1633), from *Ioannis monachi Maioris Monasterii qui rege Ludovico iuniore vixit historiae Gauffredi ducis Normannorum* (Paris 1610), 90–5. Scriverius pointed out that nothing in Vegetius corresponds.

[17] I have now gone to the trouble. Jocelyn (1984) reviewed Grafton (1983); Calder (1980–1) drew several responses in the next number of the same journal (75 (1981–2), 120–2, 248–50, 362–6). In one of these Leach (1981–2), 363, says 'classicists who respect primary sources spend far more time with secondary literature than they care to admit; establishing the data by which this literature, much of it influential over several generations, may be objectively evaluated is therefore neither peripheral to nor a substitute for traditional classical scholarship, but at the very heart of the discipline', and in another Ackerman (1981–2) says 'the history of classical scholarship is primarily a kind of history, not a kind of classics'.

16

Giants on the Shoulders of Dwarfs? Considerations on the Value of Renaissance and Early Modern Scholarship for Today's Classicists

Ingrid A. R. De Smet

INTRODUCTION

The list of contributors at the beginning of the recently published *Cambridge Companion to Renaissance Humanism* (1996)[1] reveals three specialists of English, three 'straightforward' historians, and three 'curators or librarians'. Of the remaining six, four are professionally occupied with (respectively) comparative literature, the history of philosophy, Renaissance studies, and Italian. Only the professional description of the last two experts in this alphabetical list points to the discipline of 'classical studies', and in one case indirectly: they are the 'Director of the Warburg Institute and Professor of the Classical Tradition at London University' (Nicholas Mann, who is of course a well-known Petrarch specialist) and a 'Professor of Latin at Cambridge' (Michael Reeve, who needs no further introduction here). Obviously, this list reveals the heterogeneity, widespread appeal, and interdisciplinary potential of the field of Renaissance humanism. It is indeed one of the aims of the volume 'to counter the view that Renaissance humanism was a narrowly philological exercise, concerned only with the technicalities of classical scholarship and with a definable curriculum consisting of grammar, rhetoric, poetry, history and moral philosophy'. In other words, the *Cambridge Companion* does not want to concentrate on the *studia humanitatis* as they were defined five decades ago by Paul Oskar Kristeller in his influential essay 'Humanism and Scholasticism in the Italian Renais-

[1] Kraye (1996).

sance'.[2] Instead, the *Cambridge Companion* wishes to highlight the 'role of humanism as a broad intellectual and cultural movement'. So the input of classicists to this volume is that of a minority, although the *Companion* naturally still abounds with the names of classical authors, and specialist publications in the field assume (as the editor points out) that readers have a solid knowledge of ancient as well as Renaissance culture and 'that they can comfortably handle Latin and Greek'.

What has happened here? Has the opening up of the study of Renaissance humanism and related but seminal fields such as the classical tradition and the history of scholarship ousted classicists from what was a natural extension to their researches? Or have classicists willingly yielded the land they had once colonized because they now equal humanism with 'explication', a form of textual criticism that is now frowned upon? Or are classicists now so preoccupied with their own 'personal voice'[3] that they no longer have the time or urge to listen to the voice of scholars from the past? In other words, has the baby been thrown out with the bathwater?

Admittedly, the study of humanism and of Renaissance scholarship was always a minority interest among classicists, but it was almost uniquely their domain as it sprang mainly and directly from the study of the transmission of classical texts. The trend by which Renaissance humanism and the classical legacy in general are now appropriated by other disciplines goes back at least to the 1960s and 1970s. We find forebodings of it in the 1950s when a scholar such as R. R. Bolgar expressed the hope that his study of *The Classical Heritage and Its Beneficiaries* would contribute to the revaluation of the classical curriculum, which he felt had been under increasing threat since late Edwardian times.[4] However, Bolgar's emphasis on the utility of studying the classical heritage is also the admission of its ancillary relation towards other fields of study.[5] Some twenty years after Bolgar, in 1976, the Romance

[2] Kristeller (1944–5). For a re-examination of the evidence at the base of Kristeller's definition, see Kohl (1992).

[3] See Hallett and Van Nortwick (1996), critically reviewed by Beard (1997).

[4] Bolgar (1977), introduction.

[5] Pragmatic considerations still motivate publications such as Sowerby (1994): 'With the continuing decline of classical studies as a school subject and the growing tendency amongst teachers in English to choose modern authors for study in schools, it is increasingly the case that when students of English are finally faced with earlier literature . . . they are seriously handicapped by unfamiliarity with the

philologist August Buck (b. 1911), while recognizing the contribution of classicists to the study of 'das Weiterwirken der Antike' (the continuing influence of Antiquity), could easily claim that it was too large and complex a subject to be mastered by one single discipline.[6] The appropriation goes hand in hand with a shift of focus and of the way in which questions are formulated: indeed, as Buck pointed out, the emphasis no longer lay on the influencing author or literary work but on the readership and culture influenced by him or it. Since then, it would appear that the scale has continued to tip and that the engagement of classicists with the study of humanism has continued to be solely a matter of individual taste and interest.

Of course, it is not my aim here to proclaim that classicists should try to monopolize or dominate the study of Renaissance humanism once more: anyone who knows my own work will realize that I am a fond supporter of interdisciplinary and comparative approaches. Nor am I blind to the enormous progress that classicists 'proper' have made and are making by their contributions to this field. One may just think of a book such as Julia Haig Gaisser's *Catullus and his Renaissance Readers*, not to mention any examples from the Continent where classics and Renaissance studies are more likely bedfellows. But if I am allowed to play the devil's advocate for a while, then I should first like to voice a few considerations on why classicists should take Renaissance scholarship into account, even those who do not have a passion for the study of manuscripts and dusty old books with regard to the transmission of classical texts, or who have not strayed (like myself) into other pastures. Then, in a second part, I shall advocate a cautious, or if you wish, eclectic use of theory as well as consider what classicists themselves may bring to the study of humanism. But let us begin our first section with a few concrete examples from the realm of satire.

classical tradition underpinning so much of our culture in the Renaissance and beyond. This book . . . has been written primarily with the needs of such readers in mind . . .' (pp. 1–2).

[6] Buck (1976), 7: 'Obwohl die klassische Philologie das Weiterwirken der Antike in den europäischen Literaturen keineswegs außer acht gelassen hat . . . ist die sich hier stellende Aufgabe zu umfangreich und komplex, als daß sie von einer Disziplin allein bewältigt werden könnte.'

CLASSICISTS AND RENAISSANCE HUMANISM IN A DIACHRONIC PERSPECTIVE

Functionality: Two Practical Examples

1. SATURA/SATIRA/*ΣΑΤΨΡΟΣ*

One of the first things we teach our students who take a paper in Roman satire is the etymology of the word *satura*, which we will say means 'replete', 'stuffed', a 'hodge-podge'. A similar statement is also *de rigueur* in present-day studies on Roman satires.[7] For this bit of knowledge we draw directly or indirectly on the outcome of a scholarly debate that started in the early 1910s, when the pages of the learned journal *Classical Philology* were awash with articles on the origins of Roman satire and the etymology and first generic use of the term *satura*, with every contributor trying to outdo his predecessor by offering better, and above all, more testimonia on the subject.[8] The remarkable thing about this debate is that it had taken place before, some 300-odd years earlier. Yet none of these early twentieth-century classicists shows any awareness of this, and that is certainly surprising in the case of one of the participants in this early discussion, Berthold Louis Ullman (1882–1965), for he would later also be a respected Renaissance scholar.[9]

Although it would be churlish to deny merit to these and many later[10] articles on the subject of *satura* on the grounds that their 'bibliography' is incomplete, the fact remains that much of the

[7] See e.g. Braund (1996), pp. x–xi: 'The origins of Roman verse satire are obscure, although various theories are offered by the Romans themselves. What seems clear is that there is no Greek original on which the writers of Roman satire modelled their works. . . . Ancient theories connect the name *satura* with ideas of variety and abundance. Most appealing is the explanation which makes the author of satire a cook serving up to his audience a sausage stuffed full of varied ingredients. Other theories offer possible links with drama. . . . Such ideas, although not necessarily to be accepted literally, are valuable for their emphasis upon the dramatic dimension in satire.'

[8] See Hendrickson (1911), Ingersoll (1912), Webb (1912), Wheeler (1912), Ullman (1913).

[9] See Ullman (1930, 1955, 1963), and with Stadter (1972).

[10] So Martyn (1972) continues the debate of the articles that appeared in *Classical Philology*: though he makes a quick and general reference to Van Rooy (1966) (see below), he does not himself mention any philologists of the Early Modern period. This is all the more significant as Martyn's interests have since moved to the field of Neo-Latin literature. Wiseman (1988) ends his search for the existence of satyr-play in Augustan Rome with the tentative suggestion that satyrs may indeed have been relevant to Roman satire (p. 13).

evidence (from Horace, Varro, Quintilian, Diomedes, Pseudo-acron, and others) had already been considered; certainly, the gist of their conclusion had been pre-empted, since the question of whether 'satire' was derived from the word *satur* or whether it had any connection with the Greek *satyros* had been a philological battlefield throughout the sixteenth century. That debate had involved scholars such as Julius Caesar Scaliger (1484–1558), Petrus Nannius (1496–1557), and Francesco Robortello (1516–1614). The matter was finally settled in 1605 by the learned Calvinist scholar Isaac Casaubon (1559–1614), whose monograph *De Satyrica Graecorum Poesi et Romanorum Satura* demonstrated that *satura* and *satyros* are completely separate.[11]

Because of the self-confessed indebtedness of Dryden's *Discourse Concerning Satire* to the studies of the Continental scholars, the *satyros/satura* question was well known to students of English literature in the 1940s and possibly before.[12] Only in the 1950s, however, was full attention drawn to this Renaissance controversy, not in the pages of a classical journal, but in those of *Bibliothèque d'Humanisme et Renaissance*, by two *seizièmistes* (C.-A. Mayer and John William Jolliffe (1929–1985)).[13] Since then the *satura/satyros* question has been regularly alluded to in a variety of studies concerned with Renaissance scholarship and literature. Van Rooy in the mid-1960s drew on Jolliffe's article in his *Studies in Classical Satire and Related Literary Theory*,[14] but it seems that only two decades ago classicists started to show common awareness of the humanists' debate on satire: Michael Coffey in his book on *Roman Satire* (1976) describes Casaubon's work as 'a thoroughly documented study of the different aspects of Roman *satura* . . . to which the efforts of modern scholars have little to add'.[15] Finally, credit was given where credit was due.

Or was it? Classical studies that single out Casaubon's achievement, tend to overlook the fact that Casaubon did not solve the problem *ex nihilo*: his was just the most complete study that benefited from a good distribution in print and rode on the crest of the Hellenist's established reputation. Moreover, his views were

[11] For a survey of the debate and the more recent literature about it, see De Smet (1996), 32ff.

[12] See e.g. Randolph (1942), 379.

[13] Mayer (1951), Jolliffe (1956).

[14] Van Rooy (1966), ch. 1; Jolliffe (1956) features in the bibliography.

[15] Coffey (1976), 8–9 (at 9).

long opposed and controversial, and that was, as we shall see further on, not without its own consequences.

II. APOCOLOCYNTOSIS

As a second example I would like to mention the Menippean satire which is commonly attributed to L. Annaeus Seneca and generally known as the *Apocolocyntosis*. The title *Apocolocyntosis*, as you will know, has no manuscript authority but is culled from the Byzantine epitome of the historical work by Cassius Dio. Modern-day classical scholars have spent much energy and time debating the legitimacy and meaning of this title,[16] without showing any deference to the scholars of the sixteenth and seventeenth centuries who were concerned with the same question. Indeed, I have demonstrated elsewhere that the seventeenth-century Dutch philologist, Daniel Heinsius (1580–1655), already offered an explanation for *Apocolocyntosis* which is still the most popular: viz., that it is a pun on the word *apotheosis* in which the word θεός is substituted by κολοκύντη or gourd as a symbol of stupidity.[17]

So, one might say that the *praxis* of the history of scholarship (at the micro-level, if you wish) may at least preserve the twentieth- and no doubt also the twenty-first-century classicist from a few lacunae or gaffes. Compared to the ancient grammarians, Renaissance scholars may be *recentiores*, but they are not necessarily *deteriores*.

Reflections: A Larger Historical Perspective

More than that, however, awareness of the history of scholarship (at the macro-level) will reveal to the classicist that he or she is an organic part of a continuous tradition that reaches from Alcuin to Wilamowitz and beyond to our present day. Scholarship of the Renaissance or of any past period cannot be ignored: but unlike the pea under the princess's seven mattresses, the discomfort it may cause cannot be alleviated by removing it; it has to be acknowledged and assimilated properly. Indeed, already at the beginning of the century Sir John Sandys wrote in his magisterial *History of Classical Scholarship*:

> A knowledge of the general course of the history of scholarship in the past

[16] See Bringmann (1985), 885–914 (at 889–92: 'Der Sinn des Werktitels').

[17] I. De Smet (1994), 69–72.

is essential to a complete understanding of its position in the present and its prospects for the future. Such a knowledge is indispensable to the student, and even to the scholar, who desires to make an intelligent use of the leading commentaries on classical authors which necessarily refer to the labours of eminent scholars in bygone days.[18]

This Janus-faced perception of a classicist's 'historical situatedness' is not so different from the sentiment that Petrarch expressed in his *Rerum Memorandarum Libri* (1. 19): there Petrarch claimed that his 'conversing', or interaction, with the ancients made him 'velut in confinio duorum populorum constitutus ac simul ante retroque prospiciens' ('as if set on the border between two peoples, looking to forwards and backwards simultaneously').

The same idea comes back (unsurprisingly) in the theoretical reflections or *Wissenschaftswissenschaft* of classicists in socialist Germany of the late 1970s and early 1980s. Jürgen Dummer and Max Künze thus emphasized how our own interaction with the ancient heritage is never direct but always also involves an interaction with the perceptions or images of Antiquity from both the past and the present:

Die Frage, welche Bedeutung das Erbe der Antike für das Denken und die Vorstellungswelt der Gegenwart besitzt, läßt sich nur beantworten, wenn man sie im Bewustsein der jahrhundertelangen Bemühens um die geistige Hinterlassenschaft der Alten Welt stellt. Der Versuch vollends, unser Verhältnis zur Antike theoretisch zu klären, muß zwangläufig die entsprechende Ansätze aller früheren Epochen in den Blick nehmen: *Auseinandersätzung mit dem antiken Erbe bedeutet immer auch Auseinandersätzung mit vergangenen und gegenwärtigen Antikebildern.* [my italics][19]

The question of the meaning of the classical heritage for the ideas and imagery of the present, can only be answered if we ask this question in the full consciousness of a centuries-old preoccupation with the ideological legacy of the ancient world. In our attempt totally to explain our relationship with Antiquity on a theoretical level, we must necessarily take into account the corresponding relations [with Antiquity] of all earlier periods: *for interacting with the ancient heritage always also implies an interaction with past and present perceptions of Antiquity.*

Much more recently, and in a different socio-intellectual set-up,

[18] Sandys (1903), 13.

[19] Dummer and Künze (1983), 1, 'Zum Geleit'. See also Irmscher (1979).

the same notion has been voiced by Marcello Gigante, who warns that the present-day classicist should not unthinkingly adopt contemporary ideologies or modes of thought; that is: without a consciousness of the place in history of one's own activities as a classicist.[20] The classicist who is aware of his 'situatedness' need not be afraid to reassert what is already known to be valuable, and can progress to new methods of exploration and novel insights:

> . . . rimanendo consapevole della sua posizione nella storia degli studi classici, [il filologo classico del nostro tempo] non dispera di confermare valori già conosciuti e di additare nuove possibilità di conoscenza e d'intelligenza, e nuove vie alla storia.[21]

> [The present-day classicist] who remains conscious of his place in the history of classical studies is not at pains to confirm values that are already known nor to point to new possibilities of knowledge and understanding and [to add] new ways to this history.

RENAISSANCE SCHOLARSHIP IN A SYNCHRONIC PERSPECTIVE

Reception and Intertext

So, hitherto we have reviewed the study of Renaissance scholarship in a diachronic perspective.

The detailed study of Renaissance scholarship also deserves a cardinal place in a more 'synchronic' study of humanism, both in the narrow and broad sense of the word (I use 'synchronic' here on the understanding that when it comes to textual relations, there is always an element of diachrony). There is one caveat, however, as all too often promising investigations result in the sheer enumeration of ad hoc textual material (rather like the arid *Quellenforschung* so maligned by theorists). To amass representative passages from humanist writings which illustrate, say again, the long-lasting

[20] Gigante (1989), 9: 'La prima esigenza fondamentale avvertita dal giovane studioso è quella di crearsi una coscienza del proprio lavoro e della sua posizione nella storia dell'esercizio della sua attività; questa infatti viene a inserirsi nel perenne processo storico che contraddistingue la nostra vita di studiosi. Non è suffiente aderire a un'ideologia o a un indirizzo di pensiero contemporaneo, benché tale adesione non sia stata sempre professata, con grave pregiudizio per gli studi classici, che venivano così a situarsi in una posizione di estraneità rispetto alla cultura e alla storia contemporanea: l'acquisizione del momento storico, in cui si viene a operare, è preliminare alla propria attività o, per essere più esatti, è contemporanea all' attività.'

[21] Gigante (1989), 13.

discussion on the etymology of satire, is a necessary task, but if the evidence is not *interpreted* the study of Renaissance scholarship indeed risks turning into a bland and unappealing antiquarian exercise. It is here that I believe that the literary theories concerned with reception and intertextuality may have a particular merit,[22] as does the equivalent method of contextualization in the history of ideas.[23]

As a recipient of Ancient Literature, Renaissance Scholarship is inevitably coloured (as is our own) by the historical and socio-intellectual circumstances in which it takes place. To return to our prime example: I have already mentioned that it took a long time, in fact several decades, for Casaubon's resolution of the *satura*-question to be generally accepted. One of the elements at play in this delay was the interpersonal relations between the scholars involved. Casaubon's main opponent, Daniel Heinsius, for instance, felt no doubt obliged to promote, at least at the surface, the Greek etymology of *satura* because he had been the protégé of Joseph Scaliger (1540–1609), whose venerated father, Julius Caesar Scaliger, had been a powerful backer of the Greek connection. The Frenchman Nicolas Rigault (1575–1657), in contrast, had no hesitations in accepting Casaubon's viewpoint, because he lived and worked in the same intellectual circles as Isaac Casaubon before the latter went into voluntary exile in England; indeed, Rigault would succeed to Casaubon in his position as the *garde de la bibliothèque du roi* (keeper of the king's library). *Quidquid recipitur, recipitur ad modum recipientis*.[24]

On the other hand, it goes almost without saying, Renaissance scholarship is itself also a creative impulse and powerful intertext for other works of the Renaissance and Early Modern period in

[22] For considerations on, and principles of, intertextuality in Renaissance literature (but equally applicable to Renaissance scholarship), see Schoeck (1984). For a 'case-study' of intertextuality and Erasmus, see Schoeck (1991).

[23] See e.g. Schoeck (1984), 15–16 and Schmitt and Skinner (1988), introduction (where the term 'contextual criticism' is studiously avoided): 'we have sought to identify the ramifications of one particular discipline [philosophy] at a particular period of time. Later ages split up this unity into a large number of different areas of knowledge. The aim of the present History is to join the pieces together again, seeking to furnish a guide to the subject as far as possible in its own terms' (p. 4).

[24] 'Whatever is received, is received in the manner of the receiver', axiom of Thomas of Aquinas, favoured by the School of Konstanz. Quoted by Sotera Fornaro in her introduction on the work of the Konstanz classicist Manfred Fuhrmann (1925–) and its relation to the reception theories of Hans Robert Jauss (Fuhrmann (1992), 16).

which the classical heritage is felt to be present. This has been illustrated, for instance, by Thomas Greene's pioneering study on poetic imitation in the Renaissance, *The Light in Troy*,[25] and by many others who may not always have adopted the exact terminology (or jargon) of modern literary theory.[26]

A pre-condition for recognizing such an intertext, however, is to have a good grasp of the complex history of the rediscovery, transmission, and *availability* of ancient texts. Indeed, only then can we begin to clarify the background to, and the horizon of expectations for, many of the humanists' own creations. Let us return to our second example, the *Apocolocyntosis*. This satirical work by Seneca elicited the scholarly interest of men like Erasmus, Lipsius, and Daniel Heinsius, and it was patently a source of inspiration, an intertext, for their own satirical writings.[27] In the case of Erasmus' *Praise of Folly*, however, particular care has to be taken in the indication of such intertexts, as Erasmus did not know Seneca's satire before he had finished and published the first version of this, his most famous work.[28] It is clear that the work of classicists such as Leighton Reynolds, Nigel Wilson, Michael Reeve, and many others who study the transmission of classical texts is indispensable for such an approach of scholarship and literature from the Renaissance and Early Modern period.[29]

Similarly, Renaissance epitomes and translations (from the Greek into Latin, or from the ancient languages into the vernacular) may be considered as particular forms of scholarship, and they too have left a mark on contemporary literature or thought, a mark that is not yet fully recognized, although much work has been done on individual texts (such as Heliodorus' *Ethiopica* which has greatly influenced the French novel through the vernacular translations

[25] Greene (1982). At the time of the publication of *The Light in Troy* Greene was Frederick Clifford Ford Professor of English and Comparative Literature at Yale University.

[26] See e.g. the well-documented study of McLaughlin (1995); for 'the Classical Background' see pp. 5–7 (and *passim*).

[27] Classical scholars who have studied the transmission of Seneca's satire include, most notably, M. D. Reeve, P. T. Eden, and Renata Roncali. For bibliographical references and a study of the influence and reception of the *Apocolocyntosis* see above all De Smet (1994), as well as, more generally, De Smet (1996).

[28] See De Smet (1994), 54–9.

[29] See e.g. Reynolds (1986) (including contributions by Reeve), Reynolds and Wilson (1991), Wilson (1992).

and a Latin epitome). Literary theorists have suggested that knowledge of both the Urtext and its mediator is desirable for a full appreciation of intertextual relations.[30] Is it not obvious that the linguistic skills of classicists are badly needed in at least this area of Renaissance studies?

To come back to the matter of reception and intertext: not all the beneficiaries of Renaissance scholarship have to be strictly textual, however. The false etymology of satire, for instance, was responsible for the emblematic presence of a satyr-figure on the frontispieces of editions of satires from the sixteenth to the eighteenth centuries. Still further removed from the actual text, there is a seventeenth-century statue of a satyr in Versailles that personifies 'le poème satyrique' and a fresco in the Palazzo Pitti of Florence where satyrs are seen to chase the Muses away from Parnassus (which, incidentally, is another element from ancient mythology that acquired new symbolic or allegorical connotations in the Renaissance mind and was the subject of scholarly treatises[31]). The convenience and ubiquitous nature of the iconographic symbolism of the satyr may in turn be partly to blame for the reluctance of scholars to abandon the Greek etymology. Be that as it may, the intertextual ripples caused by the false etymology can still be felt today, in our own (unthinking) use of the adjectives 'satiric' or 'satirical', and in the appearance of the odd satyr on the cover of scholarly works by classicists who are otherwise utterly 'sensible' about the origins of *satura*.[32]

Wrong But Still Right

This brings us to a further point, viz., that errors or outdated views in Renaissance scholarship are therefore not to be dismissed. Each stage of understanding or misunderstanding a text or philological problem is for its own reasons as significant as any other.[33]

Examples of the value of 'erroneous' scholarship are legion: we could think of the significance of omissions (or expansions) in

[30] See the introductory chapter in Worton and Still (1990), 8.

[31] The Frenchman Jean de Saint-Genies or Sangenesius was the author of a treatise entitled *De Parnasso Libri duo*, first published with his *Joannis Sangenesii Poemata* (Paris, 1654). For a modern study of the Parnassian image in literature as well as the visual arts, see Fumaroli (1989).

[32] See the cover illustration of Braund (1989). It may be noted that Braund (1992) has a bowl of fruit or 'lanx satura' on its cover. Braund (1996) features Roman portrait busts.

[33] See the remarks on 'errori' in Gigante (1989), 13.

translations.[34] Commentaries with allegorical interpretations of Homer, that are now entirely obsolete in Homeric exegesis, similarly prove to be an inexpendable intertext for sixteenth-century poetry, both in Latin and the vernacular.[35] The criticism of false attributions has now also received due attention, with Paul Gerhardt Schmidt's article in the newly published *Medieval and Renaissance Scholarship: Proceedings of the Second European Science Foundation Workshop on the Classical Tradition in the Middle Ages and the Renaissance.*[36]

That does not mean that one cannot be discriminating: Justus Lipsius (1547–1606) and John Barclay (1582–1621) themselves complained in their satires about the readiness with which the textual critics of their own time made unnecessary and unsubstantiated emendations and conjectures.[37] Indeed, Herbert Jaumann's history of practical literary criticism has now clearly demonstrated that scholars of the Renaissance and the Early Modern period were very much aware of the perils of their critical activities.[38] But when Wade Richardson, in his excellent study of the French humanists and their manuscript sources of Petronius, remarks that 'the scholars did not always exercise good judgment' and that their scholarship needs to be evaluated, he tacitly assumes that familiar position of superiority which stems from his own historically defined position in Petronius studies, and which is only justified in the light of his preparations for a critical edition destined for the use of modern-day readers.[39] The value of his book for the understanding of sixteenth- and seventeenth-century (mis)readings and imitations of Petronius is a happy by-product (and far from incidental). In that respect, Richardson's study is a good indication of how mainstream classical concerns may converge with the interests of students of Renaissance humanism.

To conclude: when Petrarch and his contemporaries began to rediscover the texts of classical Antiquity and to see their wealth

34 Jondorf (1996), to name just one example.

35 See e.g. Ford (1995) and Tucker (1996).

36 Schmidt (1997). Note that Mann and Olsen (1997) holds a 50 page 'Bibliography of Classical Scholarship in the Middle Ages and the Early Renaissance (9th to 15th Centuries)'.

37 Kenney (1974), 27.

38 Jaumann (1995), esp. 184–7.

39 Richardson (1993), p. xii.

and range in a new light, the overall feeling was one of awe, but mixed with feelings of self worth and pride. The *locus classicus* to describe this goes back to the proto-Renaissance of the twelfth century, and likens the receiving authors to 'Dwarfs on the shoulders of Giants'.[40] The relation between today's classicists and those of the Renaissance past is more the inverse, as the former tend either to ignore the latter or to feel vastly superior to them. We have seen, however, that the achievements of Renaissance scholars are still of value and that they provide an important filter or interface for our present interaction with Antiquity as well as for that of their own day. The modern classicist, conversely, possesses linguistic and interpretative skills that are indispensable for an in-depth understanding of the Renaissance and Early Modern period. So, is it not time that we cease to be Giants on the Shoulders of Dwarfs? Renaissance studies are booming and classicists may just as well have their share.

[40] Greene (1982), 84, quotes from Peter of Blois, *Epistolae*, in Migne, PL207, 289–90. Mann (1984), 20, culls the image from Bernard of Chartres. For the history of this topos, see Merton (1965).

17

Purity in Danger: The Contextual Life of Savants

Christopher Stray

I

In her anthropological analysis of boundaries and pollution, *Purity and Danger* (Douglas 1966), Mary Douglas redefined 'dirt' as 'matter out of place'. Impurity, she argued, is not a state intrinsic to an object or person, but stems from their being where, according to a particular system of values, they should not be. In a sense I am myself out of place among the contributors to this book, since I write not as a classical scholar, but as a student of the uses of classics by different social groups—including classical scholars. My interest in classical scholarship is thus not in how to carry it out, but in how others practise it: in particular, in how they define their task, and why such conceptions emerge, are reproduced, or contested in different institutional settings. To call myself, in effect, an ethnographer rather than a native is not to claim superiority of insight. The distinction is in any case to be made between roles, not persons: there is no reason why a classical scholar should not also explore the history of his or her field. Yet scholars in other fields also have a legitimate interest in the history of classical scholarship, and bring to its study techniques and perspectives which may enrich our understanding. Here, then, is a collaborative project to be pursued through dialogue between the bearers of different kinds of knowledge, bringing to it a variety of questions and insights. The present chapter, offered as a contribution to this dialogue, springs from the study of disputes between classical scholars who differed in their conceptions of their subject. My hope is that it may help to establish the conditions for the possibility of collaboration: an organic division of labour, in which different perspectives lead to constructive debate rather than to mutual stereotyping.[1]

[1] My thanks in particular to Michael Reeve for his kindly but astringent

Douglas's account of notions of boundaries and pollution is relevant to the theme of the present volume, since the issues at stake in debates between traditional and new-style critics of classical literature include those of the boundaries between text and context, 'literary' and other readings. Behind the debates stands a history of institutional separation in which literature has been set apart from history, archaeology, philosophy, and philology. The location of these boundaries, and the way in which areas of classics have been combined or related, has varied between institutions. For more than a century from the 1850s, the Honour Moderations course at Oxford, which consisted of language and literature, led on to Literae Humaniores, in which ancient history was combined with ancient and modern philosophy. In Cambridge, the Classical Tripos was split into two parts in 1879. Part I, like Honour Moderations, concentrated on language and literature; Part II contained specialized courses in literature, philosophy, history, archaeology, and philology. In both places, teachers and students could be found who sought to cross these boundaries. In Oxford, two successive Regius Professors of Greek, Gilbert Murray and Eric Dodds, tried with limited success to transcend them: through most of his period of office Murray organized a set of contextualizing lectures as a preliminary to the Greats course (the 'Seven against Greats'). In the late-Victorian and Edwardian periods Greats was regarded as the university's premier course, though from about 1890 it was overtaken in numerical terms by the school of Modern History. In Cambridge, in the late nineteenth century, it was the equivalent of Mods which was successful, while Part II numbers remained very small; but literature was treated largely as a linguistic corpus. The high hopes raised in the 1860s, when Henry Sidgwick, Henry Jackson, and their allies began to reform the system of teaching, sank amid the spears and arrows of vested interests.[2] Francis Cornford, whose pioneering book *Thucydides Mythistoricus* (Cornford 1907) brought together Greek literature, philosophy, and medicine, later wrote the elegant satire *Microsmographia Academica* (Cornford 1908).[3] This witty and much-quoted

comments on an abortive draft. Some of the material presented here was discussed more briefly in an earlier paper, Stray (1997a).

[2] Not to mention a financial crisis which severely limited the expansion of university staff and facilities. See Stray (1998b).

[3] For a good introduction to the local institutional background to Cornford's skit, see Johnson (1994).

guide to academic politics was the product of a decade's participant observation of a little world in which it was almost impossible to bring about change. Much of Cornford's inspiration came from his older colleague and friend Jane Harrison, who brought the ideas of Durkheim and Bergson to bear on the study of Greek art, myth, and literature. In the Edwardian years, Harrison's influence on both Cornford and Gilbert Murray led to the placing of Greek literature, especially drama, in a context of ritual and belief. Their work held out the possibility of a fruitful alliance between classics and the emerging study of anthropology, some of whose pioneers were working in Cambridge.[4] By the early 1920s these possibilities had faded away. Harrison had left Cambridge for Paris; Murray, always a half-hearted supporter of 'ritualism', had become disenchanted, and was in any case deeply involved in the League of Nations. Meanwhile Malinowski (who had been interned in Australia by Murray's brother, a colonial administrator) was preaching the gospel of anthropology through intensive fieldwork; his major rival as a disciplinary empire-builder, Radcliffe-Brown, sought to distance the subject from psychology and speculative history and to define it as a specialized natural science. Classics and anthropology went their separate ways; sociology had taken root in London rather than in the ancient universities, and had hardly emerged as a fully grown field.[5]

My subtitle alludes to a recent study of anthropological analyses of Iceland by an Icelandic anthropologist. Gísli Pálsson's *The Textual Life of Savants* (Pálsson 1995) examines the role of his fellow-Icelandic academics and compatriots in the highlighting of linguistic purity and social equality as foci of Icelandic identity. Pálsson's title alludes to Malinowski's anthropological classic *The Sexual Life of Savages in North-Western Melanesia* (Malinowski 1929). It suggests, perhaps, both that anthropologists as a tribe are amenable to the analysis they direct at others, and that the textual sphere is as central to their existence as sex has been seen to be in

[4] The Torres Strait expedition had taken place in 1898 (A.C. Haddon, C.S. Myers, and E. Seligman): see Hurle and Rouse (1998). Harrison went in 1910 to lectures by the young A. R. Brown (later self-hyphenated as Radcliffe-Brown). On the other hand, of the two obvious links between the two fields, J. G. Frazer was reclusive, his privacy guarded by his fiercely protective wife; William Ridgeway was violently misogynist, and Harrison was a pet hate. Henry Jackson (Regius Professor of Greek, 1906–21) planned to give lectures on 'anthropology and classics', but they never materialized.

[5] On its failure, see Soffer (1982).

the life of 'savages'. Pálsson's work on patriotic theorizing is a useful reminder of what the linguist Deborah Cameron has recently discussed in her book *Verbal Hygiene* (Cameron 1995): persisting concerns with linguistic purity stem from much more than a technical or professional concern with linguistic accuracy. These are obsessional concerns with the marking of distinctions felt to be vital to one's personal or corporate self-image. Pálsson's study of the role of scholarship in the ideological defence of linguistic and cultural purity provides a fruitful exemplar for the English cases I shall be discussing.

The twist I have given to Mary Douglas's title is meant to hint at the presence of challenge and response; of a *politics* of 'purity'. The major weakness of Douglas's analysis is that her Durkheimianism leads her to assume that knowledge boundaries reflect logically prior societal forms. This perspective makes it difficult to account for cultural change, for power differentials, and for the role of individuals. None of these are given the analytic autonomy which would enable them to be conceived of as independent variables. There are similar weaknesses in Kuhn's analysis of scientific revolutions. His stress on the workings of 'normal science', massively supported by shared assumptions within a knowledge community until a divergent view reaches critical mass and provokes change, is in many ways enlightening. There are two related problems with this picture of successive states of normal science. The first is that consensus is assumed—dispute and disagreement are residualized. The second is that change is not adequately explained. Kuhnian paradigms, and the normal science they underpin, roll on and on until, suddenly, they roll over; change is a gestalt switch, rather like the Roman Catholic church moving instantly from one state of certainty to another. The politics of knowledge has no place in this picture.

Similar difficulties can be found in the major sociological account of curricular content and structure developed by Basil Bernstein in the late 1960s. Bernstein also drew on Durkheim's work, and was in addition directly influenced by Mary Douglas; but he also took inspiration from the structuralism of Lévi-Strauss. Curriculum is thus seen as a set of units whose contents are not intrinsically significant; what is significant is the pattern constituted by their formal relations, and—here Bernstein goes beyond Lévi-Strauss—the strength with which the boundaries between them are maintained. These factors he calls 'classification and framing'. It is remarkable that the *content* of subjects has no place in this analysis. Bernstein talks of the relative 'purity' of subject contents, but without a theoretical notion of content, purity can have little meaning. 'Pure' subject combinations are those drawn from a 'common universe of knowledge'—the example given is Chemistry, Mathematics, Physics—but this 'universe' is a folk-category which lies outside Bernstein's theory. Similarly, he suggested that the proposed Oxford Human Sciences degree course was a 'relatively pure combination': again, this depends on common-sense judgements external to Bernstein's categorial framework.[6]

The role of a *politics* of 'purity' can be illustrated by reminding ourselves that the idea of scholarly collaboration is not an unproblematically shared notion. It is an assertion of the value of dialogue between practitioners of different styles of scholarship; an assertion that the understanding of antiquity is hindered by the mutual isolation of methodological camps among scholars.[7] In the next section I consider some disputes which erupted among English classical scholars in the second half of the nineteenth century. My concern is to identify their ideological and institutional contexts, and to establish what were the nature and sources of unity and diversity in the academy. As will appear below, notions of 'purity', sometimes explicitly formulated as such, can be discerned in these disputes.

II

In 1851 the Cambridge classicist Richard Shilleto issued a polemical pamphlet entitled *Thucydides or Grote?* His target was the sixth volume of Grote's *History of Greece*, which had just appeared.

[6] The subjects involved were Anthropology, Sociology, Psychology, and Biology. There are further relevant features of Bernstein's analysis which I shall not inflict on the reader. The most convenient source for both his own paper and perceptive comments by A. H. Halsey is Hopper (1971): for the Oxford course, see esp. pp. 189 (Bernstein) and 267 (Halsey).

[7] On a pragmatic level, of course, a 'mechanical' collaboration has been practised in the assembly of a comprehensive work of reference. An early example is provided by William Smith's classical dictionaries. The original plan was for John Wordsworth to write one himself. On his death in 1839, John Murray asked J. W. Donaldson to take it over, but Donaldson declined on the ground that it was 'too large a work for one man to finish. But in collaboration it might be done . . .'. Donaldson to Murray, 16 Apr. 1840 (John Murray Archives).

Most of Shilleto's charges related to alleged misunderstandings of the Greek of Thucydides. But his major complaint had to do with Grote's claim that Thucydides was biased against the demagogue Cleon. This may explain why, though much of Shilleto's pamphlet is taken up with detailed linguistic analysis, it opens in a very different vein. 'I confess', he says, 'that I opened and read throughout Mr Grote's volume with great prejudice against its author—the prejudice of one not ashamed to call himself a Tory against one not (I believe) ashamed to call himself a Republican—of one proud of an Academical Education against one disregarding such a position.'[8] Grote's offence was a double one. In seeking to rehabilitate Cleon, he was at once showing democratic sympathies and challenging the objectivity of Thucydides. This was not the first time that party politics had reared its head in such scholarly disputes. The heady and (to conservatives) alarming atmosphere of Europe in the late 1840s could be paralleled in the 1820s and early 1830s, when reformist proposals were continually being brought before parliament. In 1825, when the Cambridge Greek chair was being filled after Monk's translation to the see of Chester, the two leading candidates were a liberal (Julius Hare) and a conservative (Hugh Rose). The first round of voting was inconclusive, but in the second one of Hare's supporters, Croft, switched his vote to a third candidate, A. F. Scholefield, who was then elected. Rose encountered Croft and Hare the next day, and Croft told him that he had heard that the archbishop of Canterbury was said to have intervened on behalf of Rose: he had therefore 'given his vote in the generous indignation of Whig independence'.[9] The ideological polarization between Hare and Rose seems to have continued, since in 1834 the latter was widely suspected of having had a hand in the expulsion from Trinity of Hare's friend and collaborator, Connop Thirlwall.[10]

[8] Shilleto (1851), 1. The overtones of 'Republican' in mid-nineteenth-century England might be compared with those of 'Communist' in the USA 100 years later.

[9] The account is from the diary of Christopher Wordsworth jr, then an undergraduate; his eponymous father, the conservative Master of Trinity College, was the presumed target of the alleged archiepiscopal intervention. Young Wordsworth is quoting a letter from Rose to his father. (Trinity College Library, Cambridge, O.11.9. Quoted by permission of the Master and Fellows of Trinity College.)

[10] Thirlwall had argued publicly against compelling undergraduates to attend chapel services. He and Hare jointly edited the *Philological Museum*, a journal which countered the Porsonian scholarly tradition in Cambridge by publishing articles from, or influenced by, German scholarship.

Shilleto's introduction of the question on academic allegiances had its ironic aspects. It is true that Grote was a merchant banker without a teaching position. Shilleto himself, however, occupied a somewhat marginal position in Cambridge: his marriage had debarred him from a college fellowship, and he made his living by taking private pupils. This will perhaps have sharpened his antagonism to the views of a successful outsider, at a time when the first inroads into the overwhelmingly linguistic curriculum of the Classical Tripos had just been made with the addition, in 1849, of a paper on ancient history. But it is also relevant that at this time the university was being investigated by a royal commission which was drawing up reformed statutes.[11] The autonomy of the conservative enclaves of Oxford and Cambridge was being threatened by a liberal government in London; and this surely has something to do with Shilleto's sensitivity to Grote's *History*.

Shilleto's pamphlet represents a defensive assertion of the Porsonian tradition of close linguistic study, of which he was perhaps the last representative, against a contextualizing historiography which threatened to outflank it. The Porsonian style, sometimes referred to as 'pure or definite scholarship', was also described as 'narrow and masculine'. Its practitioners not only devoted themselves to understanding the nuances of Latin and (especially) Greek usage, but also used this understanding to compose proses and verses in both languages. In this emphasis, which also obtained, if less strongly, at Oxford, lay the distinctive feature of the classical scholarship practised in the ancient universities and in the public schools. At the same time, the dispute was about several other issues as well: marginal status within academic institutions, political allegiances, and the autonomy of universities vis-à-vis the state. The autonomy of the literary text stands for the autonomy of its interpreters.[12] It is notable that a historical text (Thucydides), which cannot be as easily divorced from historical context as some might, is the object of attention.

Grote decided not to publish a reply to Shilleto, though he did add an appendix to a later volume of his *History*. The cudgels were taken up by his younger brother John, Professor of Moral

[11] The impact of the Royal Commission on Cambridge is described by D. A. Winstanley (1947), 234–69; and by Searby (1997), 507–44.

[12] One thinks of the protective motives behind early twentieth-century Russian Formalism, whose orientation seems to have been affected by the need for *Idiotensicherheit*—making one's public statements proof against the fools in power.

Philosophy at Cambridge.[13] He began his pamphlet by stressing that Shilleto's attack, though 'in itself worthless . . . may be of . . . interest as a specimen of . . . classical criticism'. In his peroration, he argues that 'pamphlets like this of Mr Shilleto's . . . stand in the way of good criticism . . . they convert discussion into recrimination, and controversy into quarrel; they discredit criticism . . . they stop the mouths . . . of many who have truth to utter . . .'. In his peroration he refers to his opponent's 'childishness . . . garrulity . . . senile narrow-mindedness'. Strong language for a mild-mannered cleric; but it illustrates the intensity of Grote's commitment to genuine open discussion. This ideal was carried on after his death by the 'Grote Club', whose members included the Trinity classicists Henry Jackson and Henry Sidgwick.

John Grote's references to Shilleto display a more general concern about constructive criticism and its enemies. This generalizing vein re-emerged ten years later, when he sprang to the defence of William Whewell, the master of his college, with a pamphlet entitled *A Few Words on Criticism* (Grote 1861). The target this time was a dismissive anonymous notice in the *Saturday Review* of Whewell's *Platonic Dialogues for English Readers*. Grote opens by remarking that:

> It is commonly said that ours is in a very special manner a critical age. One may doubt however how far this is really the case. We are fond of *reading* criticism; but a good deal of the criticism we read seems to presume on readers who . . . are . . . incapable of making [a criticism] for themselves. There is one thing that this criticism never seems to have a notion of, and that is, the possibility of criticism on itself.

Grote goes on to claim that 'Latin and Greek scholarship is . . . the only branch of science or literature in which . . . the . . . impertinent assumption' he is attacking in the review 'is ever found . . .'. Part of the problem, he suggests, is the lack of academic journals in which proper discussion could take place.[14] The *Journal of Classical and Sacred Philology*, which J. E. B. Mayor had started in 1854, had ceased publication by the time Grote wrote his pamphlet; its successor, the *Journal of Philology*, did not begin to appear till 1868. The first British classical journal to appear which survives today, the *Journal of Hellenic Studies*, was not founded

[13] Grote (1851). On Grote, see in general Gibbin (1989).

[14] Grote (1861), 3, 41.

until 1880. Grote was thus writing at a time when those standard features of a developed academic community, journals and learned societies, had not emerged. For published articles and reviews, readers were largely dependent on general literary magazines like the *Saturday Review* and the *Athenaeum*. (*JHS*, it should be noted, was doubly specialized, concentrating on Greece rather than Rome, and on archaeological and historical material rather than on language and literature.) Grote raises the question, what are the conditions for successful debate? It is worth noticing that both of those defended by him from criticism were in some sense amateurs. (It was said of Whewell that science was his forte and omniscience his weakness; his major claim to intellectual fame is as a philosopher of science.)

The lack of journals mentioned by John Grote is a symptom of the embeddedness of classics in Victorian England as a gentlemanly pursuit. No professional academic career or community had yet emerged, and indeed had hardly done so by the end of the century. As Grote put it in his essay 'Old Studies and New' in 1856, knowledge of classics constituted a 'bond of intellectual communion among civilized men'.[15] This status began to be eroded in the 1850s by the foundation of new honours courses at Oxford and Cambridge following the Royal Commission of 1850. The foundation of the Oxford Latin Chair was among the consequences of the Commission's report. Reviewing the inaugural lecture of John Conington, the first incumbent, Richard Monckton Milnes declared that the appointment of a Professor of Latin at Oxford was

> in itself a strong proof of the diminution of the classical spirit. This very eulogy of the Latin language reads like a funeral oration over that condition of study, when the colloquialisms of life, the banter of youth, the academic sports . . . the principles of philosophy, and the verities of religion, spoke the great common diction.[16]

THE DEFENCE OF THE PAGE

Next I want to consider a series of statements issued by T. E. Page between 1879 and 1900 in defence of the literary study of classical

[15] Grote (1856), 114.

[16] Milnes (1857), 512. Milnes was a keen student of 'diction'; collections of idiosyncratic phraseology and pronunciation abound in his commonplace books (Trinity College Library, Cambridge, Houghton G 1–16).

texts as a liberalizing activity. His targets were the introduction of specialized courses in the classical tripos; the alleged obstruction of literary appreciation by mechanical scholarship on Horace; and the campaign for the teaching of classical archaeology carried on by Percy and Ernest Gardner.

The full-blown insertion of ancient history into the Cambridge curriculum had to wait until the late 1870s, when the tripos was re-organized into two parts. Part I represented the traditional liberal education model and was devoted to language and literature; Part II consisted of a set of specialized courses, including literature but also history, philology, archaeology, and philosophy. In 1877, during the debates which led up to this reorganization, the Greek scholar Henry Jackson characterized the traditional style of Porsonian scholarship in the following manner. 'I must go back to the old tripos,' he said, 'the golden age of "pure scholarship". What . . . "pure scholarship" meant was this. They read Thucydides, but not Grote; they studied the construction of the speeches, but did not confuse themselves with trying to study their drift. They read the Phaedrus, but had no Theory of Ideas . . .'[17]

The older members of Jackson's audience would have recognized the reference to Shilleto's pamphlet; and indeed Jackson was using 'pure scholarship' to refer to the Porsonian style of work carried on by Shilleto. I have described it as complemented and supported by the practice of composition, which was carried on in the public schools as well as in the ancient universities. The world of the classically educated gentleman in mid-Victorian England included both sectors; but the reform of the tripos took the organization of classical knowledge down a road which the schools did not follow. It is significant, therefore, that the most outspoken attack on the reforms of the late 1870s came from Page, a member of the Cambridge classical board whose active career was spent as a schoolmaster at Charterhouse.

'The proposed scheme,' said Page, 'while making liberal provision for men with *special* knowledge of any of the sections B, C, D, E (in any of which it would be possible to take a high place with but little classical knowledge) absolutely ignores the requirements of perhaps a far more important class of students—the men, who without any desire to pursue any special branch of classical learning, are widely read in classical literature . . . the proposed scheme

[17] Winstanley (1950), 211.

. . . affords men of high *general* attainments no opportunity to distinguish themselves.'[18] 'B, C, D, and E' were the Part II options in philosophy, ancient history, archaeology, and comparative philology. Note that for Page, 'classical knowledge' refers only to knowledge of Greek and Latin.

Page pursued the theme in 1888, in a review of a new edition of Orelli's Horace:

> The editor follows Orelli in treating all English editions since the days of Bentley and Cunningham as if they were non-existent. Probably this is due to the fact that English editors have paid comparatively little attention to spelling, to the scholia, to MSS, and to emendations. An opinion apparently prevails in Germany, and is becoming increasingly prevalent in England, that these things constitute the most important portion of the study of classical literature. It may be so. It may be the odes of Horace . . . can only be properly understood by one who is strictly orthodox on the spelling of *querella*, who has groped for treasure among the antiquarian dustheaps of Porphyrion, Acron and Comm Cruq, who can exactly estimate the evidential value of ABMOSTdy. It may be so; but if it is so, then the study of the classics, long and justly considered a necessary part of liberal education, will not long withstand the vigorous attacks with which it is continually assailed.[19]

And Page goes on to draw a characteristic contrast between 'dry and unprofitable details' of texts as opposed to 'the secret of their living force'.[20] The supersession of 'liberal education' by 'learning' is thus allied to the subordination of teachers to professors.

An attempt by the archaeological brothers Percy and Ernest Gardner in 1900 to promote classical archaeology in schools particularly incensed him. Here the dirt is literally in evidence, material evidence obtruding on what had been a relaxed world in which one read Plato or Thucydides with one's feet on the fender. The kind of visceral reaction such analysis could prompt is suggested in the words of Housman (an advocate of physical responses to literature), in his denunciation of the encroachment of the 'miry clay of the nineteenth century . . . the horrible pit of the twentieth' on 'the library of Apollo on the Palatine'.[21] This is dirt as matter out of place, indeed. Even more pungent, and self-

[18] Ibid. 221.

[19] Page (1888). Porphyrion *et al.* are ancient commentators and scholiasts; ABMOSTdy are manuscript sources for the text of Horace.

[20] Ibid.

[21] Housman (1969), 35.

revelatory, is the remark by Gilbert Murray's pupil, Isobel Henderson, that Jane Harrison's work had 'tipped [the study of Hellenism] over to the slimy side'.[22] Page was more restrained, but something of the same theme is evident in his sarcastic counter to Percy Gardner that 'he who would walk with Plato must neglect ideas and tread the solid soil of the Academy'. He went on to claim that 'the living, imperishable value of the classics is almost entirely independent of [archaeology]', and that 'education is being much injured by professors . . . they live in a world of theory, and from it, they hold out a guiding hand to men in hourly contact with hard facts'.[23]

Page's remarks summarize a reaction to shifts both in curriculum content and in the social organization of scholarship: the marginalization both of the learned schoolmasters who had formerly shared a common world with their university colleagues, and the literary texts whose eternal value they had revered. Page had shared second place in the classical tripos of 1873 with Verrall; in the competition for the Chancellor's Medal, of which two were awarded annually, they and S. H. Butcher, who came first, were so close that, uniquely, three medals were awarded. Butcher and Verrall went on to academic careers, Page taught at Charterhouse till he retired. Barred from a headship by not being ordained, prevented from seeking the Cambridge Latin Chair by his wife's refusal to move there, he had some cause to be resentful. As an organized academic field gradually emerged in late nineteenth-century Cambridge, we can see the beginnings of a division of labour, the staking of claims to their authors by scholars working within a single institution. One thinks of Jebb's Sophocles, Verrall's Euripides, Headlam's Aeschylus. The apostrophes hint at possessiveness. Alongside this pattern, from the later 1860s there emerges a collaborative attempt to provide organized teaching on an inter-collegiate basis. The initiative of the Trinity dons Jebb, Jackson, and Currey, it was followed up by the young F. M. Cornford, a leading light in the Cambridge Classical Society. This was founded to do what a faculty would have done had it existed. In the late 1920s, when yet another royal commission led to the establishment of the Classics Faculty, it dissolved itself. These

[22] Henderson, in J. Smith and A. Toynbee (eds.), *Gilbert Murray: An Unfinished Autobiography, with Contributions by his Friends* (London, 1960), 140.

[23] T. E. Page, *The Times*, 2 Jan. 1904, p. 10, col. d.

developments had to do with undergraduate teaching, not research, but they arguably encouraged prospective scholars to think of their own projects as something more than private possessions.

The British Academy

The changes Page resisted were pressed by members of a group of academic liberals whose influence was strong in the 1860s, though it waned in the following two decades. They included Richard Jebb and three Henries: Jackson, Roby, Sidgwick. In the late 1890s they were offered a chance to organize intellectual life centrally and to provide, in effect, a map of knowledge, when the British Academy was founded.[24] At this point the academic career was just about established, and of the forty-eight original fellows, thirty-seven had been educated at Oxford or Cambridge and twenty-nine were teaching there. Around half the total were engaged in the study of classical or pre-classical cultures. As one might expect, the naming of sections in the new body was the subject of private negotiation. The language of successive drafts is significantly wobbly. Early drafts seem to have defined 'literature' as 'the sciences of language, history, philosophy and antiquities'; later drafts replaced this with 'modern philology'.[25] Some may be reminded of the recent reorganization of the Academy, which has merged philology and history. Like the original mapping of knowledge, this shows clearly how dangerous it is to read such nomenclature as an unmediated reflection of the current state of an intellectual field. The example of the British Academy illustrates how many classifications of knowledge are the momentary products of processes of negotiation—diplomatic compromises between the rhetorics of opposed interest groups.

The study of English literature was at this point hardly recognized as a serious academic pursuit; the Cambridge tripos was founded only in 1917, and the Oxford English School had only recently been established after long and stormy debates between the advocates of modern literature and those who believed that scientific philology was the only way to approach a text. The bandying of phrases like 'chatter about Shelley' and 'novels about

[24] See Harvie (1976), 215–17; Collini (1991), 21–7.

[25] The reference in an early Royal Society statement (4 June 1901) to '*exact* literary studies' (my emphasis) had already indicated the struggle to place knowledge boundaries in precisely the right location—in this case, to include rigorous scholarship and to exclude 'novels and sunsets'.

sunsets' indicates the fearful contempt felt by opponents of the proposed school. Opposition between philological and literary-critical dons led to a predictable campaign of mutual sniping and stereotyping. Similar results have obtained in more recent disputes on the study of literature. A recent presidential address to the Classical Association by David West opened with the announcement that he intended to 'take [his audience] through a few of Horace's Odes', and that now and again he would introduce 'a little flurry of theory'. West's first sentence was a pointed, and doubtless deliberate, parody of the belletrist phraseology of old. The second phrase I have quoted could be guaranteed, and was surely intended, to infuriate the 'new Latinists' in his audiences. Nor did it fail to do so. Sitting next to a leading deconstructionist scholar, I was able to witness his groans and writhing as 'flurry' succeeded 'flurry'.

The foundation of the Academy ran against a powerful ideological current of decentralized autonomy in nineteenth-century England. Here the dangerous anti-exemplars were at different times the centralized French and the regimented Prussians. Dean Trench, in his celebrated paper to the Philological Society of London in 1857 on deficiencies in English dictionaries—a paper which led to the production of Murray's *New English Dictionary*, now familiar as the *OED*—was typical of this current in denouncing centralized prescription of usage. 'I cannot understand how any writer with the smallest confidence in himself . . .', he declared, 'should consent . . . to let one self-made dictator, of forty, determine for him what words he should use, and what he should forbear from using.' (The reference to 'forty' is to the members of the French Academy, who produced the official French dictionary.) In fact, the origins of the Academy lie in an international academic meeting in the mid-1890s, at which it was found that while the Royal Society represented British natural science, the humanities had no such organization. Within classical scholarship this anti-centralist current was manifested in the glorification of the English style of tasteful, intuitive scholarship as opposed, increasingly, to what was seen as the over-organized mechanical Germanic style ('Dampfmachiner Wissenschaft'). This was a stereotypical contrast which hardened as Germany, Lucifer-like, was transformed from angel to devil, and it reached its apogee, as one might expect, during the First World War (see e.g. Murray 1915). Similar stereotyping was engaged in in the USA (Nimis 1984). The aspect of this English style I want to emphasize is its potential for the discouragement of working together. Where scholarship is a matter of individual taste, scholars are likely to work alone. Against this background, the collaboration practised by Jane Harrison and her friends—the so-called Cambridge Ritualist tendency—was an even more striking development than has been assumed.

The English scholar was a gentleman. In Gramsci's terms, our intellectuals were organic—not critics of the established order, but recruited to its ranks. The result was that, in many cases, a concern with social style hampered the search for truth. Two American sociologists who visited the English universities in the 1930s reported that the objectives of scholarship appeared to be 'to prepare the university man to move easily and urbanely in formal social circles . . . to be in polite society rather than to understand social life . . . men are trained to argue with charm and lofty detachment rather than to investigate with precision'.[26] That opinion was published in 1938. One has to allow for its concern with social science rather than with classics, but the Oxbridge style rather than a specific subject is what is being described. This was, after all, at a time when, as Robin Nisbet has reported, there were only two graduate students engaged in classical research in Oxford. In the same year, Louis MacNeice recalled in his poem 'Autumn Journal' how he 'studied the classics at Marlborough and Merton'. Not everyone, he went on, 'had the privilege of learning a language | That is incontrovertibly dead, and of carting a toy-box of hall-marked marmoreal phrases | Around in his head'. MacNeice catches the mixture of snobbism, pedagogic ritualism, and genuine concern for ideas. 'The boy on the Modern Side is merely a parasite, | But the classical student is born to the purple . . .' but he goes on, 'And knowledge, besides, should be prized for the sake of knowledge: | Oxford crowded the mantelpiece with gods—Scaliger, Heinsius, Dindorf, Bentley and Wilamowitz— | As we learned our genuflections for Honour Mods.' It is worth noting the slightly uneasy disjunction of elite culture and the pursuit of learning: 'and besides . . .' No mention of Liddell and Scott, of Pauly-Wissowa-Kroll, or of any other collaborative projects: the gods are heroic individuals, to be celebrated, emulated, and at

[26] Becker and Barnes (1938, 1961), 794.

that stage, quoted in examinations.[27] Knowledge is a commodity to be prized and guarded in an institutional climate which fosters competition for marks and prizes, not collaboration for learning.

Which brings us back, in a way, to 'purity'. The 'pure scholarship' of Shilleto was a style exemplified by Porson's writings. It was maintained largely within the institutional context of Cambridge, where its narrow rigour was consonant with the rigorous, problem-solving focus of Cambridge mathematics. The motive force which fuelled the maintenance of this ethos was competition: between colleges and between individual candidates for honours. The strains generated by this competition were so great that mental and physical breakdown were not uncommon occurrences. It is difficult to pinpoint detailed effects of this ethos on subsequent scholarly work, but one might suspect that it discouraged the sharing of knowledge in favour of possessiveness. (Shilleto, incidentally, was for long situated at the heart of this ethos. Having vacated his college fellowship by marriage, he became the leading private tutor or 'coach' in Cambridge, cramming his pupils with tips for translation and composition.) This, then is an aspect of boundaries which might well be explored further: between my knowledge and your knowledge. Within a scholarly community, there is here a potential contradiction, since publication, the act which demonstrates how much one knows, is an act of sharing: it makes my knowledge into our knowledge.[28]

III

CONCLUSIONS

The disputes I have considered revolve around the ideological defence of the text against perceived challenges. Shilleto's reaction to Grote's treatment of Thucydides belongs to a period in which the introduction of modern works into discussions of classical authors was often seen as a kind of blasphemy. What is at stake in this case is also a particular style of scholarship. Page's conception was not that of the Porsonians, but nevertheless the threat posed

[27] Few of his contemporaries, one imagines, will have gone so far as to name their residence after their favourite scholar, as has Professor W. M. Calder III, currently resident in the second Villa Mowitz. Students of the history of classical scholarship, especially those with a sense of humour, owe Professor Calder a debt of gratitude for the public listing of his private collection (Calder and Kramer 1992).

[28] A partial resolution is of course found in *prior* publication.

for him by archaeology and by over-professionalized textual scholarship was similar to the threat Grote posed to Shilleto's ideal. They seemed to detract from respect for a repository of ideal and eternal value, and to threaten the integrity and continuation of scholarly practices into which several generations had been socialized. As with the series of nineteenth-century Methodenstreiten in Germany, mostly involving Hermann, the text–context debate is more fruitfully seen as a dispute between absolutist and relativist views.[29] It is worth emphasizing that the absolute invoked was eternity: an exemplary source of value, proof against change and relativity. Texts appeared to speak to successive readers in a way which transcended time—to be absolutely and unequivocally present to them in some essential sense which was not affected by quibbling over the details of individual letters or words.

By 'the contextual life of savants', I mean to refer not just to the contextualizing impact of historicism, but the wider contexts in which scholarship takes place. In Victorian England structural changes in academic institutions and in their social contexts set up challenges to particular conceptions of classics. The introduction of new honours courses after state intervention in the 1850s, the reorganization of the university curriculum after further intervention in the 1870s, the setting up of faculty structures after another wave in the 1920s, all had knock-on effects.[30] Boundaries were created both within classics, between it and other subjects, and between academics and the ordinary world. J. C. Stobart's two books on Greece and Rome (Stobart 1911, 1912) were intended to heal the first and last of these divisions, which Stobart himself, typical of his semi-professional generation, experienced. The asking of large cultural questions about the ideals of Hellenism went out of fashion after the Great War. In Oxford, the home of lost causes, Sir Richard Livingstone carried on the good fight. Alfred Zimmern's *Greek Commonwealth* emerged from Oxford teaching blended with a concern for adult education. The nearest parallel to Zimmern in Cambridge was perhaps T. R. Glover, whose wide range and popularizing concerns sat uneasily with the reigning Cantabrigian ideology of academic specialism.[31]

[29] This point has been stressed by Glenn Most (Most 1997).

[30] Oxford had, however, begun to set up faculties just before the First World War.

[31] There are also parallels with Livingstone: e.g. in Glover's broadcasts on 'The Challenge of the Greek' for the BBC in 1938.

From the 1920s on a cosily fragmented intellectual field was consolidated, buttressed by the succession of compulsory Latin to the throne once occupied by compulsory Greek and, after 1945, by an expansion of secondary education in which a rise in absolute numbers of classical pupils masked the relative decline of the subject in schools. Rigour rather than imagination was at a premium. The typical classical scholar was someone who, in G. S. Kirk's formulation, was 'always looking over his shoulder'—less to see if the ghosts had been aroused by a blood offering, I imagine, than to see if he was about to be stabbed in the back. The staffing of the higher reaches of government and civil service by Oxbridge graduates (mostly Oxford men) provided a cushion,[32] as did the distancing of the British Academy and the UGC from the seat of government. Perhaps this encouraged a complacency about academic freedom which has left British academics ill-equipped to cope with recent bouts of state intervention.

The current debates on methodology follow a weakening of academic boundaries, a blurring of genres, which have eroded some of the bases for self-definition built up since the 1850s. The new, less clearly structured intellectual field is now inhabited by a variety of new totalizing theoretical positions which undercut the old certainties of a positivist 'field coverage' model.[33] The resulting uncertainties are likely to promote a stereotyping of styles which discourages not only working together, but talking together.

All this, together with my earlier strictures on Kuhn, may suggest that his notion of normal science has no mileage left. Is there such a thing as 'normal classics'?[34] If so, what is it? How is it reproduced and propagated? and how is it changed? These are questions worth asking, and answering, as long as we avoid the reification of 'normal classics' into an assumed dominant mode of activity carried on within a single consensual community. The demarcation between schools and universities, dons and beaks, which we now take for granted, should remind us that there is a pedagogic dimension to this subject. What is the relationship between the debates on the study of classical literature and the changing national situation of classics? The declining supply of linguistically trained students, the relative expansion of non-linguistic teach-

[32] For staffing figures at the Board of Education, see Stray (1998a), 238.

[33] For 'blurred genres', see Geertz (1973); for 'field coverage', Graff (1987).

[34] Cf. the remarks of Robert A. Kaster (who uses the phrase): Kaster (1997), 345.

ing, may have brought to an end an era of co-operation between schools and universities. The collapse of compulsory Latin in 1960 led *inter alia* to a honeymoon period in which the universities made contact with schools. They needed to recruit. Now that Oxford and Cambridge are accepting students without Latin or Greek, the honeymoon may be over.

The ancient universities constitute, of course, two of the most secure positions in the academy. The collegiate universities have size, flexibility, and interdisciplinary potential; here London, seen as a federal unit, is the only rival. It does not have the explicitly interdisciplinary tradition of, for example, the University of Chicago; but as the case of Shilleto versus Grote reminds us, the metropolitan university—the godless college in Gower Street—once played an important role as a secular gadfly, teaching new subjects, attracting different kinds of students. The divisions between these few and the larger number of smaller institutions might be bridged by channels of communication which allow for frequent and interactive discussion. The growth of online databases, electronic journals, and internet discussion groups may help to redress the imbalance which would obtain between richer and poorer institutions. They may also promote a genuinely co-operative culture of debate in which criticism, in John Grote's terms, is joined by 'criticism on criticism'.

The disputes I have described can be paralleled by those over Hellenism—another pure essence seen to be under attack. The excavations of Schliemann and the explorations of Harrison cast a shadow on the bright, serene world of Greece which so inspired and comforted scholars like Jebb. Ventris was an amateur, but he had a professional collaborator in John Chadwick with him, and of course his argument was that what was thought to be non-Greek was Greek. This might be thought to have stood in his favour, though there was, I believe, a samizdat literature circulating among his opponents containing scathing references to 'wo wo' and the like.[35] Bernal's *Black Athena* points the other way, which is surely one reason why it has made such a stir. But it has also become bogged down in American cultural politics.[36] Interestingly, however, Bernal has not suffered from the xenophobia which

[35] It is worth noting that the pronunciation of Latin 'v' as 'w' was a major target for conservatives in nineteenth century debates on the subject: see Stray (1998a), 126–30.

[36] For a brief survey, see Stray (1997b).

has informed the internal disputes about scholarship in American classics. This is also a feature absent, as far as I know, from the British debates.

These disputes between adherents of textual/literary scholarship and their opponents are both polyvalent, and—a related point—embedded in social and institutional contexts. They thus raise questions about the bases and connotations of current debates and about the institutional changes which have provoked and fuelled them. In Anglo-American anthropology the study of disputes was for long relegated to the marginal field of the anthropology of law.[37] It has recently been argued, however, that the dispute process may provide an essential key to the disclosure of the socio-cultural order at large.[38] Similarly, the disputes I have discussed serve to illuminate features of the world of learning in which they occur. They reveal its fault-lines, its divisions, its obsessions.

The nature and possibility of co-operation vary according to historical circumstance, institutional structures, and ideological currents. The divisions and differences which obstruct co-operation have been both vertical (class; university versus school staff) and horizontal (textualists versus contextualists; fragmenting specialisms). The disputes which take place across their boundaries offer useful clues to the fault-lines and bones of contention which underlie them. Shilleto's attack on Grote, as we have seen, was motivated by more than a concern for accurate linguistic analysis. The historical contexts which Grote evoked were not just the extra-textual world of the Greeks, but the contested sphere of Victorian cultural politics. Similarly, the opposed views on Icelandic language which Pálsson discusses are powerfully motivated by convictions on class and nation. 'Purity' is all too often a secondary end, enclitic on primary ends which are left unstated. As such, it tends to be the target of concerns displaced from other sites: 'hygienic obsessions.' Purity may be in danger; but there is also a danger in 'purity'.

[37] The study of law remains marginal to the work of students of ancient history. Its insertion in undergraduate curricula usually reflects personal interest; as with the short-lived course in the Cambridge Classical Tripos, 'Group F' (c. 1968–84), instigated by A. H. M. Jones and largely taught, until his retirement, by J. A. Crook. (My thanks to John Crook for information and discussion.)

[38] Comaroff and Roberts (1981).

18

Latin Studies in Germany, 1933–1945: Institutional Conditions, Political Pressures, Scholarly Consequences

Peter Lebrecht Schmidt

I am grateful for the invitation to participate in this colloquium on *Wissenschaftstheorie* and *Wissenschaftsgeschichte*, because it allows me to continue a topic which began to interest me professionally some years ago in connection with a conference on classics in the Germany of the 1920s,[1] and which I plan to treat more completely in a book on Latin scholarship in Germany from about 1850 to about 1950, that is, from Ritschl to Büchner, my own *Doktorvater*. The colloquial format of our symposium allows me to speak more informally and to include, as is inevitable in the case of my topic, some personal memories. One last private remark on a note of gratitude: I came to *Wissenschaftsgeschichte* through W. M. Calder III, and although I disagree with him on a number of points, including some doubts over whether the complete publication of all preserved letters even of such a gigantic figure as Wilamowitz is really called for, I remember fondly the fall semester of 1977 and my stay at the Villa Mowitz 1 at Boulder, Colorado.

My interest in the role of the classics in Nazi Germany coincides with, but is not caused by, a new wave of what Germans like to call *Vergangenheitsbewältigung*, coming to terms with our own national past. Symptoms of this new wave are of course the huge interest on the part of the German public in the book of Goldhagen (1997), as well as an exhibition on the role of the German army, especially on the Eastern Front, which is at present drawing tens of thousands of visitors in Munich and elsewhere. What we are witnessing by way of these (as I see it) symptomatic events is the interest of a new generation. Immediately after the war the contemporaries of

[1] Schmidt (1995), see 179–81.

dictatorship, battle, and defeat simply wanted to forget, and I remember that during my university studies in the 1950s the topic of the role of classics in the Third Reich was hardly raised, and even those of my academic teachers whose uncompromising position towards Nazism was well known to us students, such as Walter Jens, who later defected to general rhetoric, or Karl Büchner, scarcely talked about their experiences before 1945. It simply was not a topic of dicussion in academic circles. The second phase of *Vergangenheitsbewältigung*, or better *Vergangenheitsnichtbewältigung*, that is, the student revolution of the late 1960s and early 1970s used the half-forgotten memories of dictatorship and war crimes as political weapons in the confrontation with the older generation. The third wave, as one may call it, of *Vergangenheitsbewältigung* concerns the children of parents who were born after the war, for whom the Third Reich is, on the one hand, just history, but on the other hand, history of a very special kind, who try to understand what really was going on in the minds and actions of those then living and active. This third generation is not content with general answers involving political or social causes, but is concerned with the question of personal responsibility and guilt, the age-old question of ancient historiography.

What has classics, and especially Latin studies, to do with all this? The first point I want to make is that up to the 1920s and 1930s the cultural prestige of the subject was such that even now one is asked why the influence of the cultural tradition of classics did not help to stop the brown hordes. It is neither the time nor the place to meditate on the possible role of any cultural tradition confronted with outward forces such as a lost war, the breakdown of a political system of high prestige, economic forces such as inflation and war reparations, and the like. The second question is whether classics with its (so to speak) ideological outlook, its individual humanism with strongly conservative undertones, was really very well equipped to brave the tide. Here we are getting increasingly close to our topic: what were the institutional conditions for classical, and especially Latin, scholarship from the 1920s to the 1930s? How did it react to political pressure? And how was research affected by the Nazi ideology, through assent and dissent,[2] and in what way did these reactions continue after the war?

[2] Answers like Kytzler's (1989), 1059 (classics 'followed the twelve years of the Hitler regime largely uncomprehendingly') or Classen's (1989), 172–5, who in a

How was Latin scholarship in Germany, under radically changed political conditions, still influenced by conflicting forces going back to the Third Reich?

These are big questions, and I, of course, can only scratch the surface. They should, however, be raised, even if any answer supplied here can only be imperfect and certainly incomplete. Fortunately we have now two books illuminating the Nazi past of German classics, Volker Losemann's extremely well documented *Nationalsozialismus und Antike* and Cornelia Wegeler's much more personal work, *Altertumswissenschaft und Nationalsozialismus*.[3] One last word on my personal involvement, since, as we all know, there is no such thing as historical objectivity, and personal presuppositions can be subdued but only after having been admitted to oneself or (here) publicly. My father was a Protestant pastor member of the so-called 'confessing church', and my feeling of identity with this anti-Nazi tradition is very strong. That doesn't (I hope) make me blind to the forces with which the generation of the 1920s and 1930s had to cope. Classics was no better, but definitely no worse, than the generality of the humanities.

I

Now to my first main section, that is, the institutional conditions of Latin scholarship in the 1930s. Why, you may ask, the concentration on Latin? One of the aims of my paper given at the aforementioned conference on the classics in the 1920s was to show that the separation of Latin and Greek in Germany was much older than is usually presumed, that it goes back to the academic professionalization of the German universities in the middle of the nineteenth century—in Latin especially through the influence of the school of Friedrich Ritschl—and that this separation became irreversible by way of the school reforms of the late nineteenth century. Since that time it was possible at a *Gymnasium* of a certain type to have Latin without Greek, and the demand for teachers of Latin was in consequence much greater than for those of both

few lines (p. 174) characterizes Drexler, Oppermann, and others as 'scholars without importance', are hardly sufficient, privileging as they do the seemingly unbroken continuity of 'pure' scholarship or admitting only humanistic impulses.

[3] Losemann (1977) and Wegeler (1996); see also Königs (1995); anachronistic exaggerations are noted in the methodologically noteworthy reviews of J. Deininger, *Gymnasium*, 104 (1997), 345–8 and W. Nippel, *Gnomon* 70 (1998), 373–5.

Greek *and* Latin, the so called *Vollphilologen*. Some universities even offered special classes for students who studied Latin but not Greek. Since the 1890s, therefore, the contract of a professor of classics, in Prussia at least, specified that he be responsible for either Latin or Greek, the 'Verpflichtung, das ganze Gebiet der klassischen Philologie', but 'mit besonderer Berücksichtigung des Lateinischen' or 'insbesondere die lateinische Sprache und Literatur . . . zu vertreten'; I am citing the *Berufungsurkunden* of Eduard Norden, called in 1899 to Breslau and 1906 to Berlin, where he was invited 'zur Stärkung der Vertretung lateinischer Philologie'.[4] The split is personified in the pair of professorial colleagues at Göttingen in the early 1890s, namely, Wilamowitz, who often called himself a Hellenist,[5] and Friedrich Leo, who—if I may translate from my article already mentioned[6]—'as one of the oldest pupils of Buecheler and therefore as a second-generation pupil of Ritschl . . . provided perhaps the first and certainly the most effective definition of the study of Latin as *historistische Textwissenschaft*, and thereby began an irreversible process which led to Latin studies as literary scholarship and loosened its connection as a discipline with the study of Greek'.

At the time of the Third Reich classics was represented in all the twenty-three universities of Germany.[7] Ties with the three Swiss-German universities (Bern, Basel, Zürich), which till then had routinely been an integral part of the Academia of the German speaking community—much more so than the three Austrian universities (Vienna, Graz, and Innsbruck)—became naturally less close as a consequence of the political change, after Harald Fuchs, a Berlin pupil of Norden and Werner Jaeger, had left Germany in time to take up a chair in Basel. In Austria the situation changed little, even after 1938. On the other hand, one should not forget the German University in Prague, which functioned till 1945, or (perhaps less well known) that at Dorpat (Tartu) in Estonia, which, after the Russification of the late 1900s, was after Estonia's independence in 1918 revitalized as the academic centre of the German-speaking population of the Baltic states, until Stalin and

[4] Schmidt (1995), 125, 115–16.

[5] Schmidt (1985), 362.

[6] Schmidt (1995), 133.

[7] For the professors and *Privatdozenten* active in 1932/3 see Ludwig (1986), 232–4; for the situation in 1936, Wegeler (1996), 395–7 (where on p. 397 'Erich' should be 'Friedrich', sc. Klingner).

Hitler in 1941 conspired to bring the Baltic Germans 'heim ins Reich'. Finally, the Reichsuniversität of Strasbourg was added in 1941 as an outcome of the successful campaign against France; the other Reichsuniversität, Posen (Poznań), founded after 1939, never, so far as I know, had classics in that period.

The academic teachers and researchers active in these places belonged to three generations, a generation being defined by the criterion of a strong teacher–pupil relationship. After the generation of the pupils of Ritschl, who almost completely dominated the market, the second generation can be defined by the same relationship to Franz Buecheler at Bonn, another pupil of Ritschl's. Chronologically speaking, this generation comprised Latinists born from 1851 (Leo) to 1874, occupying the chairs of Latin from 1883 (again Leo) to 1912, and leaving them by death or retirement from 1912 (Franz Skutsch, the father of Otto Skutsch) to 1939, the retirement of Alfred Klotz, the Livy scholar, at Erlangen.[8] That means that the scholarly activities of the Buecheler school, through personalities like Norden and Richard Heinze, Georg Wissowa and Wilhelm Kroll, were still measurably influential in the 1920s, less so in the 1930s. The Latinists filling the chairs since around 1930 (and that is the main group with which I am concerned) crystallized around pupils of Norden and Heinze, and included scholars born as late as 1905, among them *makrobioi* like Erich Burck (1901–94) and Hildebrecht Hommel (1899–1996)—for example, Hans Drexler and Hans Oppermann, born 1895, Friedrich Levy, later Lenz (1896), Erich Reitzenstein, son of Richard Reitzenstein (1897), Georg Rohde and Hildebrecht Hommel (1899), Harald Fuchs (1900), the Livy and Tacitus scholars Erich Burck and Erich Köstermann (1901; both later at Kiel, and part of my memories as assistant professor in that slightly cool but pleasant North German city), then Ulrich Knoche (1902), Andreas Thierfelder, the specialist on Roman comedy (1903), and the Varronian Hellfried Dahlmann (1905). Most of these names will come up again in the course of my talk. Of the next generation of Latinists, born from 1906 to 1925, which habilitated in the 1930s, I will have little to say on this occasion.

If we look a little more closely at the four universities which since the nineteenth century had dominated German classics, Bonn, Berlin, Leipzig, and Göttingen—in 1933 Bonn, with the

[8] See Schmidt (1995), 126–7.

Latinists Friedrich Marx, an editor of the old school, and Ernst Bickel, of whom I know little, and the Hellenist Christian Jensen, was not nearly so influential as it had been a generation earlier. At Berlin there taught the Hellenist Ludwig Deubner and the Latinist Johannes Stroux, the latter of whom presumably owed his outstanding career, including the chairs at Munich and Berlin, to his personal friendship with Werner Jaeger. The distance of quality and influence from Deubner and Stroux to Eduard Norden and Werner Jaeger and the still-active Wilamowitz in the Berlin of the 1920s can easily be measured. By far the best combination of teachers in both literatures was offered by Leipzig, with Wolfgang Schadewaldt, and later Karl Reinhardt in Greek and Friedrich Klingner in Latin. These seminars had the good fortune of continuity in those politically troubled times, and what that meant can be seen in the different cases of Göttingen[9] and Halle.[10]

On the whole, however, the situation of Latin studies had changed drastically for the better. Whereas until 1931 six Latin chairs in the twenty-three universities were held by Greek scholars, the most prominent being Bruno Snell at Hamburg,[11] there were now enough promising younger scholars available; the lamentable situation in which Wilamowitz had written, in connection with the succession of Schadewaldt, who had held the Latin chair at Königsberg up to 1929, 'Harder [professor of Greek at Kiel] will offer us a Latinist, if there is one', was by the 1930s a thing of the past.[12] And not only that: research in and study of Latin at the universities had regained some of the prestige which it had lost in connection with the quantitative and qualitative pressure of the Wilamowitz school, the nadir being the time of Norden's call to Berlin around 1906; Norden himself, living in Berlin as it were personally under the shadow of Wilamowitz, practised what I have called a 'Latinistik des schlechten Gewissens', Latin studies with a bad conscience.[13] Even at high-school level Latin fared better than Greek, to cite the fascinating new book of Suzanne L. Marchand:[14] during the Third Reich, the *Gymnasien* were not disbanded, but Nazi disdain for non-

[9] See Wegeler (1996), 220–35.
[10] See Losemann (1977), 61–8.
[11] See Schmidt (1995), 148–9.
[12] Ibid. 150, 149.
[13] Ibid. 142, 172 f; see also Schmidt (1985), 390 f., 396–7.
[14] Marchand (1996), 341.

utilitarian education hastened the demise of the classical schools. There were some surprising reversals, as in Reich Education Minister Rust's 1936–37 instructions on the reorganization of the schools which, while closing a number of *Gymnasien*, reinstituted Latin as an obligatory subject for all secondary school students. By 1938, Greek language instruction had been restricted to a few schools.

II

Now to my second topic. How were Latin scholars as individuals affected by the new political situation after 30 January 1933; how did they react to it? My first remark concerns the fact, astonishing at least for me, and for which I have no explanation to offer, that only comparatively small numbers of Latinists were Jewish and as such dismissed or forced to emigrate—namely, Eduard Fraenkel, Kurt Latte, and Eduard Norden (who was forced into retirement in 1935); one should add the *Privatdozenten* Ludwig Bieler and Georg Rohde, who declined to divorce his Jewish wife, and Konrat Ziegler, who was dismissed because of his political activities in democratic and peace organizations before 1933.[15]

For the rest, two extremes of assent or opposition were in theory possible: on the one hand, active participation in the system, including criminal activities; on the other, active opposition. By their profession Latin scholars—by contrast with judges, policemen, or soldiers—were naturally spared the at best difficult and at worst dangerous decisions encountered in the persecution of *Volksfeinde*, officially identified enemies of the people. On the other hand, no Latinist emigrated for purely political reasons or reacted like the Hellenist Kurt von Fritz, who, as Extraordinarius at Rostock, declined to swear the oath of unconditional obedience to the Führer in 1935 if the freedom of teaching was not guaranteed, 'if I am not shown in writing from the highest authority that this oath does not enable demands to be made of me to teach anything contrary to my convictions';[16] he was immediately dismissed and emigrated to the USA, becoming professor at Columbia in 1938, but returning in 1954 to Germany.

The intermediate group of the politically disinterested was—as

[15] See Ludwig (1986) and the list in Wegeler (1996), 373–94.

[16] See Wegeler (1996), 200–1.

it always is—probably the majority. Among the dissenters we may place the so called 'innere Emigranten', giving expression to their position in pointed silence on matters dear to the regime or in verbal doublespeak, the language of slaves, as it has also been called. As we shall see, I would count Friedrich Klingner among this group, which was, of course, judged unreliable by the powers that be. This position was feasible and not immediately dangerous, but of course could harm university careers. For those who assented to the regime, a rough description of the spectrum would include, in ascending order, (i) verbal compromise, (ii) institutional involvement, (iii) ideological proximity, or (iv) active propagandizing for the Nazi ideology.

(i) Verbal compromise, in difference to unthinking imitation of the contemporary political jargon, may be defined as the pointed use of key words of the time like 'Führertum' or other words connected with 'Führer' in prominent places, for example, as a title of a scholarly monograph;[17] work on the special colour found in even academic language of the time should prove useful.

(ii) Much closer to the centre of power and to compromising commitment is, of course, institutional involvement. Membership of the Nazi party comes immediately to mind; as yet, party membership of German classicists is known in a number of individual cases, but it has never been, to my knowledge, systematically ascertained, though the register of party members is preserved in the Berlin Document Centre and therefore accessible, as far as I know, to qualified researchers; I think we should try to fill this gap in our knowledge. On the other hand, party membership, being the key to power in dictatorial regimes, was not freely handed out by the Nazis (nor indeed by the Communists) to possible opportunists, since conviction counted more than quantity. The regime had other chances to discipline and indoctrinate the upwardly

[17] A random selection of titles from 1930 onward and in different fields would include W. Hartnacke, *Naturgrenzen geistiger Bildung. Inflation der Bildung—Schwindendes Führertum—Herrschaft der Urteilslosen* (Leipzig, 1930); H. Gauger, *Persönlicher Besitz als Grundlage von Führertum und Verantwortungsbewustsein in England* (Heidelberg, 1936); M. Pohlenz, *Antikes Führertum. Cicero De officiis und das Lebensideal des Panaitios* (Leipzig/Berlin, 1934); H. Beer, *Führen und Folgen, Herrschen und Beherrschtwerden im Sprachgut der Angelsachsen. Ein Beitrag zur Erforschung von Führertum und Gefolgschaft in der germanischen Welt* (Breslau, 1939), printed with subsidies of the 'Forschungs- und Lehrgemeinschaft Das Ahnenerbe'. The terminological context, ranging from conservative to reactionary concepts, is evident.

mobile of yore. Look at Andreas Thierfelder, for whom even membership of the Nazi teacher union, the *Nationalsozialistische Lehrerbund*, participation at a *Dozenten-Lehrgang* in 1934 and *Dozenten-Akademie* in 1935, and service with the SA in 1933/4 was not enough to get the chair of Latin at Göttingen in 1936,[18] the SA, in contrast to the SS, being seen as an acceptable alternative and therefore as a compromise by the careerists.

Above all, the so-called *Lagerarbeit* (camp work) of the *Nationalsozialistische Deutsche Dozentenbund* can be understood as an opportunity for indoctrination, and a chapter in Losemann's book is instructive on this point.[19] The 'Lager', another 'Un-Wort' of the time and since then stigmatized, seemed to be the apt expression of the new era, combining (in our case) scholarly work and the idea of *Männerbund*; the Latinist Hans Oppermann, one of the leading Nazi propagandists among classicists, likened it perversely to the Platonic Academy.[20] The *Dozentenlager* of Würzburg in 1941, the protocol of which is preserved, however, ironically took place in an hotel. The invitees—according to the protocol of Hans Drexler—were only those 'among whom the national socialist position as such was no longer a point of discussion'[21]—whatever that may mean. The list of participants, in any case, reads like a *Who's Who* of German classicists of the time, including among the Hellenists Hermann Gundert, Richard Harder, Hans Herter, Albin Lesky, and Wolfgang Schadewaldt; the Latinists being—and here I give a complete list—Erich Burck, Hans Drexler, Hildebrecht Hommel, Ulrich Knoche, Hans Oppermann, Otto Seel, and Rudolf Till. Now, I do not want to give the impression that everyone invited was ideologically involved, and obviously there were grades of involvement between *speakers* like Drexler and Oppermann, whose ideological leanings—like those of Knoche and Till—are not in doubt, *participants* in the discussion, and *mere listeners*. It must, however, be stated, that Burck, Hommel, and Seel, on the surface less involved, must have been considered as promising material for indoctrination by the organizer Drexler. Missing names—for example, that of Bickel, who in 1933 had praised Werner Jaeger as a leading opponent of the 'Verjudung der Philologie'[22]—may indicate

[18] See Wegeler (1996), 227–8.
[19] Losemann (1977), 94–108.
[20] See ibid. 95 and, on Oppermann in general, Malitz (1998).
[21] Losemann (1977), 97.
[22] See Wegeler (1996), 186.

ideological distance, or be explained by personal aversion or biographical accident.

Even closer to the centre of power was the *SS-Forschungs- und Lehrgemeinschaft*, 'Das Ahnenerbe' ('ancestral heritage').[23] The *Reichsführung SS* was planning to reconstruct the so-called Germanic heritage, offering research opportunities for classicists too, for example, in the evaluation of ancient authors and texts. The plan was to use the results of this enterprise in the schooling of SS officers. Heinrich Himmler himself was personally involved, and between 1937 and 1938 a special section was founded to explore ancient Greece and Italy 'in the Indogermanic and Aryan context'.[24] The Latinist Rudolf Till, habilitated in 1936, was chosen as head of the department, and was at the same time enrolled in the SS with the rank of *Untersturmführer*; in 1938 Till was promoted to Extraordinarius at the University of Munich. The research activity of the *Ahnenerbe* was split up into sections for ancient history, Greek, and Latin philology, the Hellenist being Franz Dirlmeier, after the war Ordinarius at Mainz and Heidelberg, the ancient historian Franz Altheim, from 1950 Ordinarius at the Free University of Berlin.

Now, as much as it irritates me whenever I use Till's facsimile of the Tacitean Codex Aesinas (now at the Biblioteca Nazionale at Rome), which has an introduction by Himmler, it must be admitted, as stressed by Losemann, that the actual scholarly work done by the *Ahnenerbe* classicists was remarkably free of Nazi ideology and Nazi propaganda, a facsimile of a Latin manuscript being, perhaps, not the ideal place for such statements. Till was, as Losemann has it,[25] even more restrained concerning verbal compromise than Dirlmeier, whose 'preparedness to make concessions in the area of terminology was more strongly marked'. The primary motivation, however, of Altheim, Dirlmeier, and Till was to use the chances of professional advancement and the excellent research facilities, travel grants, and access to Italian manuscripts and excavations the SS could offer, and even though the line of Matthias Claudius, 'wer Pech anfaßt, besudelt sich' ('he who touches pitch defiles himself') is quite true, the extremely difficult situation of the humanities under the Nazis, and especially in wartime, should be reckoned with. The different later fate of the three *Ahnenerbe* classicists is interesting: Till, perhaps as a

[23] See Losemann (1977), 118–23. [24] Ibid. 118. [25] Ibid. 122–3.

member of the SS, was dismissed in 1945 and had to wait till 1958 to regain professorship in the forgiving atmosphere of the 1950s and at the 'deep brown' Classical Institute of the University of Erlangen (as Karl Büchner called it in private conversation). Neither Altheim's nor Dirlmeier's career seems to have been affected by that touch of the brown brush.

Our third point of involvement was ideological proximity, which will be touched upon in the third section of my talk. Looking at the possible or probable activists—category (iv)—and starting with the group of the Würzburg *Lagerarbeit*, the composition of which is certainly no coincidence, the grading of participation in ascending order should be: Burck, Till, Knoche, Oppermann, and Drexler; of Seel, who was instrumental in calling Till in 1958 to Erlangen, I have no precise information to offer at the moment, and Hommel stayed in the background until 1955 anyway, when he emerged to get the Latin chair at Tübingen at the age of 56.

Erich Burck, however, is an interesting case: in Losemann's book we meet him a second time at the Berlin '*Fachtagung Altertumswissenschaft*' in April 1941, again, among others, together with Schadewaldt and Knoche.[26] Burck had collaborated with Oppermann already in the book on *Probleme der augusteischen Erneuerung* (Frankfurt a.M. 1938), published in the series 'Auf dem Wege zum nationalpolitischen Gymnasium' for which the National Socialist teachers' union and the *NSD-Dozentenbund* were jointly responsible; other monographs in the series are by confessed Nazis like Drexler, the Hellenists Hans Bogner and Wolf Aly, and the ancient historian Hans Berve. So, one gets the impression of a closed circle of persons, of opportunities for publicity and topics within which Burck moved; the 'augusteische Erneuerung', about which Oppermann spoke at the Würzburg Conference, being, with its political overtones, an obvious pet topic for Nazi classicists. There can be no doubt, in my opinion, that Burck was what in German is called a *Mitläufer*, a fellow-traveller. On the other hand, when the venerable Friedrich Münzer, ancient historian at Münster till 1935, was deported to Theresienstadt in 1942, Burck did not hesitate to travel to Berlin to contact the relevant officials and obtain certain alleviations for his former colleague at Münster (since 1928), that is, the permission to write and to receive letters

[26] Ibid. 230, n. 158.

and the use of the contents of his suitcase, including texts of Herodotus and Tacitus.[27] During the *Endlösung* it definitely needed courage to stand up for a deported Jew. I met Burck in the 1960s at Kiel; he was an enormously active and energetic man, with a love of sport and an urge to move and influence things. He belonged to a group of classicists—among them Victor Pöschl at Heidelberg, Franz Beckmann at Münster, and Josef Martin at Würzburg—who after the war were enormously important for the revival of their universities through their authority and through not being too much tainted by the past. On the other hand, personalities like Burck, with that urge to be in the swim, were, if not dedicated Nazis, in danger in the 1930s and early 1940s of forgetting that the better alternative could and perhaps should have been a determined distance and the sound of silence.

It is interesting to note that quite a number of Burck's articles in the 1930s, as we shall see, are thematically much closer to official ideology than those of Ulrich Knoche,[28] who joined the party in 1937, having in 1936 been passed over by the dean and rector of Göttingen University in the procedure to fill the chair of Kurt Latte, Knoche's earlier works being too close to the 'third humanism' (about which later). His time-serving flexibility was rewarded with the chair of Ernst Kapp at Hamburg in 1939, thereby ending the 'Latinist' phase of Snell's teaching. At Hamburg[29] Knoche was active in the *NSD-Dozenzentenbund*, looking for contacts among other Nazi members of the faculty, an activity which correspondingly led to isolation in the seminar. I have heard a story that in 1945 Snell said to Knoche: 'Was wollen Sie denn noch hier?'; but Knoche successfully appealed against the decision of the denazification committee to prohibit him from teaching, while Kapp was only allowed to return in 1954 to teach as Emeritus; such are the vagaries of a *Rechtsstaat*. In comparison to Knoche's, Till's career after the war was interrupted for a longer time, as we have seen. Hans Oppermann,[30] the only declared anti-Semite of the group,[31] was so to speak demoted: he became the principal of one of the

[27] Kneppe and Wiesehöfer (1983), 141–3, see 135.

[28] For his career see Wegeler (1996), 225–9.

[29] See Lohse (1991), 784–7, 790–2, 801–2.

[30] On him see now the detailed study of Malitz (1998).

[31] In the 'Schriftenreihe zur weltanschaulichen Schulungsarbeit bei der NSDAP' he published a pamphlet *Der Jude im griechisch-römischen Altertum* (Munich, 1943); see Wegeler (1996), 43 and 280, n.103.

prestigious *Humanistische Gymnasien* at Hamburg, the other being also under the sway of a former Nazi.

Hans Drexler, about whom we have now a very instructive chapter in the book of Wegeler,[32] having in 1933 become Extra-Ordinarius only eight years after his habilitation in 1925, seems to have opted for the Nazis very early, like Knoche, for career reasons, with the result that in 1935 he was chosen as the successor of Wilhelm Kroll at Breslau; Drexler became, like Knoche, a party member in 1937. Moreover, coming from a fundamentalist Protestant family, he seems to have transferred his beliefs too. At Breslau he organized a discussion group which aimed at a scholarly and scientific foundation for Nazi ideology, although in 1939 the dean of the Göttingen faculty, the Hellenist Karl Deichgräber, himself a party member since 1937, had to confess: 'he will not succeed in his efforts to break through to a wholly clear conception of the problems.'[33] However, Drexler was chosen in 1940 for the Göttingen chair of Latin, becoming in 1943 rector of the university, so that he had to put aside research as well as teaching. Drexler, working at the same time for the SD (*Sicherheitsdienst*) of the SS, was doubtless a more than willing instrument of the regime, and it is again symptomatic of the generous and forgiving atmosphere of the post-war time that the faculty opted for his dismissal not because of his Nazi activities—he was seen as a 'good Nazi' (whatever that may be)—but because after the assassination attempt against Hitler in 1944 he submitted a list of fifteen colleagues 'standing far aside from National Socialism' to the authorities.[34]

III

Finally, how was Latin scholarship as such, that is, teaching and research, affected by the momentous change which took place after 1933? Not much, as the concluding section of Losemann's book,[35] at a first glance, seems to imply. The institutional infighting of the diverse Nazi bureaucracies, which allowed Hitler to keep his dogs on the leash, could be used either by clever university politicians or by the younger generation of academics, insofar as they were willing to follow the rules of verbal compromise, *Sprachregelung*.

[32] Wegeler (1996), 244–63.

[33] See ibid. 247.

[34] Ibid. 253–4.

[35] Losemann (1977), 174–81.

One has to keep in mind that the Nazis had only six years till the beginning of the war, which drastically changed priorities, and even communist Germany, with a centralized and much more effective political party after the founding of the GDR in 1949, needed twelve years before things really began to move. It is only individuals like Drexler, the ideologist, and Oppermann, the propagandist of the system, whose work was visibly affected; or on the other hand isolated topics like the *Germania* of Tacitus, which seduced people like Köstermann, to whom Norden—of all people—was writing in 1933: 'Den Steuermann Hitler liebe ich, trotz allem, wie sie.'[36] So it seems that the real change was connected with the loss of the scholars who had to leave their positions or even Germany for so-called racial reasons. For those remaining it was business as usual, especially as the system of values of the so-called *Bildungsbürgertum* remained by and large intact. Even a unified effort such as the *Fachtagung* of 1941 organized by the ancient historian Helmut Berve, later enlarged by written contributions and published as *Das neue Bild der Antike*,[37] disappointed the converted like Fritz Schachermeyr, who complained that a common denominator such as the concept of race was missing.[38]

On the other hand, if one steps back for a moment from everyday business, the overall picture of the 1930s is clearly different from that of the 1920s. To understand this one has to look back at the series of paradigms which had dominated German classics since the beginning of the nineteenth century: *Altertumswissenschaft* in the first generation, textual criticism in the second, historical interpretation in the third, and literary interpretation with humanistic emphasis in the generation since around 1900. This generation, influenced especially by Werner Jaeger and his so called 'third humanism', showed the prevalence of literature over history, Greek over Latin, poetry over prose, and the classical epochs over the non-classical, later, or even Christian periods of ancient literature. Seen in this light, the recurrence of interest in Latin prose, Cicero (Pohlenz, Knoche, Pöschl), Varro (Dahlmann), Sallust (Pöschl), Livy (Burck), and Tacitus (Köstermann) in the 1930s is remarkable, whereas in the work of Latinists of the 1920s, like Heinze, Norden, and Fraenkel, poetry had clearly

[36] See Mensching (1992), 122.
[37] 2 vols. (Leipzig, 1942); see Losemann (1977), 108–15; Lohse (1991), 791–2.
[38] See Losemann (1977), 111, and Lohse (1991), 812, n.72.

dominated. No immediate connexion with Nazi ideology can be discerned in the new stress on Latin prose authors; but in the new atmosphere, to work on writers with more overt political potential was not only not an obstacle in one's career, but on the contrary, could actually advance it.

There certainly was no clear change of paradigm, as demanded by Drexler in his polemics against the third humanism,[39] but there were elements pointing in that direction—the special interest, as we have seen, in *augusteische Erneuerung*; the continuity of research into *Romerwerte*, that is, the key concepts of Roman tradition culminating in Augustus the leader; the attempt of the Tübingen Latinist, Otto Weinreich, to link *Volkskunde* and history of religion to the concept of race;[40] and so on. Compared with the linguistic interests of Eduard Fraenkel and Richard Heinze, emanating from work on the *Thesaurus linguae Latinae*, there is now clearly a change of emphasis in the research on *Römerwerte*, even if Fraenkel already in 1925 had recommended Roman literature not as an aim in itself, but as a means on the way to the 'tiefe Gehalte des Römertums' (the profound values of Romanity).[41] The *Kleine Schriften* of Richard Heinze were published by Erich Burck in 1938 under the title *Vom Geist des Römertums*, meaning national character and ideology (as we would call it), symbolized by the *Römerwerte*.[42] Burck's own papers of the 1930s[43] implement, as it were, this programme: (1) *Livius als augusteischer Historiker*; (2) *Staat, Volk und Dichtung im republikanischen Rom*; (3) *Altrömische Werte in der augusteischen Literatur* (4) *Altrom im Kriege* (of 1940); (5) *Die altrömische Familie*; (6) *Das Bild der Karthager in der römischen Literatur*—'Karthager' meaning, of course, the arch-enemy as such. Klingner's collection of essays published in 1943, already through this title *Römische Geisteswelt*—not 'Römertum'—and by means of his preface stressing 'Geist, Kunst, Schönheit, Bedeutung, Gedanke, Wort', and, as we would call it, the potential of reception,[44] clearly formulates a pro-

[39] Drexler (1942).

[40] Cancik (1982).

[41] Schmidt (1995), 175–7.

[42] Heinze (1938), republished 1939 and (with a new preface by Burck without his comments of (1938), p. 278–94), 1960.

[43] Nos. 1 and 5 have been republished in Burck (1981), 144–80, 7–48; for the publication dates of the rest, the offprints of which were not accessible for study by the general public in my time as assistant professor at Kiel, see Burck (1966), 431–2.

[44] Klinger (1943), pp. ix–xi.

gramme which, in sharp contrast, unmasks the dangerous tendencies inherent in the concept of *Römertum* defined in a romantic and nationalistic spirit.

This tendency partially explains why, after 1945, the focus of the third humanism—literature, Greek, poetry, and classicism—came back with a vengeance, one onesidedness supplanting another. In the attempt to re-establish politics and culture in the spirit of the time before 1933, conservatism, restoration, and classicism formed the political as well as the cultural backbone of the society of West Germany in the generation before 1968/9. It was again the time of the Hellenists, through figures like Bruno Snell, whose moral authority was well deserved, through *revenants* like Kurt von Fritz and Rudolf Pfeiffer, or through Wolfgang Schadewaldt, whose tactical behaviour of the 1930s and early 1940s has, as far as I know, never been discussed in detail. Latin studies had suffered through the expulsion of Fraenkel, and suffered again now through demotion and dismissal, the ideologically involved, if they kept their positions, being silent for a while or losing their nerve for ever—as in the case of Knoche and Till. Research on *Römerwerte*, having lost all reputation, survived in collections of articles published by Oppermann,[45] who, through his old Nazi companion Ernst Anrich as publisher, had found a refuge in the *Wissenschaftliche Buchgesellschaft*. Klingner, with his aesthetic interpretations of quasi-autonomous poetry at some distance from history and politics, was at the height of his influence, and things began to change only through the influence of Karl Büchner and his school. But here, of course, I must stop, not only because my time has run out, but also because I would be speaking *pro domo scientifica*.

[45] See the list in Malitz (1998).

Bibliography

ABRAMS, M. H. (1953), *The Mirror and the Lamp: Romantic Theory and the Critical Tradition* (New York).

ACKERMANN, R. (1981–2), 'Further Reflections on the Calder Controversy', *CW* 75: 364–6.

ADAMS, J. N. and MAYER, R. G. (eds.) (1999), *Aspects of the Language of Latin Poetry* (Oxford).

ADORNO, T. (1981), *Prisms* (Cambridge, Mass.).

—— (1984), 'The Essay as Form', *New German Critique*, 32: 151–71.

ALONSO-NÚNEZ, J. M. (1990), 'The Emergence of Universal Historiography from the 4th to the 2nd Centuries B.C.', in Verdin *et al.* (eds.), 173–92.

AMIS, M. (1995), *The Information* (London).

ANDERSEN, O. (1990), 'The Making of the Past in the *Iliad*', *HSCPh* 93: 25–45.

ANDERSON, W. S. (1957), 'Vergil's Second *Iliad*', *TAPA* 88: 17–30; repr. in Harrison (1990).

ARAFAT, K. W. (1996), *Pausanias' Greece: Ancient Artists and Roman Rulers* (Cambridge).

ARON, R. (1938), *Introduction à la philosophie de l'histoire* (Paris).

Ars Narrandi (1996) = *Ars Narrandi. Scritti di narrativa antica in memoria di Luigi Pepe* (Naples).

ASTIN, A. E., WALBANK, F. W., FREDERICKSEN, M. W., and OGILVIE, R. M. (eds.) (1989), *The Cambridge Ancient History, VIII: Rome and the Mediterranean to 133 B.C.* (Cambridge).

AUERBACH, E. (1965), *Literary Language and Its Public in Late Latin Antiquity and in the Middle Ages* (Princeton).

AUSTIN, J. L. (1980), *How To Do Things with Words* (Oxford).

AUSTIN, R. G. (1955), *P. Vergili Maronis Aeneidos Liber Quartus* (Oxford).

—— (1977), *P. Vergili Maronis Aeneidos Liber Sextus* (Oxford).

AXELSON, B. (1945), *Unpoetische Wörter* (Lund).

BADIAN, E. (1993), *From Plataea to Potidaea: Studies in the History and Historiography of the Pentecontaetia* (Baltimore).

BAKHTIN, M. (1981), *The Dialogic Imagination: Four Essays* (Austin).

—— (1986), *Estetyka twórczoœci slownej* (Warsaw).

Bakula, B. (1994), *Czlowiek jako dzielo sztuki* (Poznań).

Bal, M. (1985), *Narratology: Introduction to the Theory of Narrative* (Toronto).

Barchiesi, A. (1984), *La traccia del modello. Effetti omerici nella narrazione virgiliana* (Pisa).

—— (1994), *Il poeta e il principe: Ovidio e il discorso augusteo* (Rome).

—— (1997a), *The Poet and the Prince* (Berkeley—Los Angeles).

—— (1997b), 'Endgames: Ovid's *Metamorphoses* 15 and *Fasti* 6', in Roberts *et al.* (eds.), 181–208.

—— (1997c), 'Vergilian Narrative Ekphrasis', in C. Martindale (ed.), *The Cambridge Companion to Virgil* (Cambridge), 271–81.

Barthes, R. (1974), *S/Z* (New York).

—— (1977), *Image—Music—Text* (London).

—— (1988), 'Introduction to the Structural Study of Narratives', in *The Semiotic Challenge* (Oxford), 95–135.

Bartsch, S. (1989), *Decoding the Ancient Novel* (Princeton).

Beard, M. (1997), 'Not You'=review of Hallett and Van Nortwick (1996), in *London Review of Books*. 19.2, pp. 10–11.

Becker, A. S. (1992), 'Reading Poetry Through a Distant Lens: Ekphrasis, Ancient Greek Rhetoricians and the Pseudo-Hesiodic Shield of Heracles', *AJP* 113: 5–24.

—— (1995), *The Shield of Achilles and the Poetics of Ekphrasis* (Lanham, Md.).

Becker, H. and Barnes, H. E. (1938, repr. 1961), *Social Thought from Lore to Science* (London).

Benjamin, A. (ed.) (1988), *Post-Structuralist Classics* (London).

Benveniste, É. (1971), *Problems in General Linguistics* (Miami).

Bernal, M. (1987), *Black Athena*, 2 vols (New Brunswick).

Beye, C. R. (1969), 'Jason as Love-Hero in Apollonius' *Argonautika*', *GRBS* 10: 31–55.

Blänsdorf, J. (1991), 'Interpretation psychologique de l'autarkeia stoicienne chez Sénèque' in Chevallier and Poignault (eds.), 81–96.

Bolgar, R. R. (1977), *The Classical Heritage and its Beneficiaries*, 5th edn. (Cambridge).

Boncquet, J. (1982–3), 'Polybius on the Critical Evaluation of Historians', *Ancient Society*, 13–14: 277–91.

Botschuyver, H. J. (1940), *Scholia in Horatium . . . quae ab Heirico Autissiodorensi profecta esse videntur IV i* (Amsterdam).

Bowra, C. M. (1967), *Greek Lyric Poetry: From Alcman to Simonides* (Oxford).

Bramble, J. C. (1970), 'Structure and Ambiguity in Catullus LXIV', *PCPS*, NS 16: 22–41.

—— (1974), *Persius and the Programmatic Satire* (Cambridge).

BRANHAM, R. B. (1995), 'Inventing the Novel' in Mandelker (ed.).

BRAUND, S. M. (1989), *Satire and Society in Ancient Rome* (Exeter).

—— (1992), *Roman Verse Satire, Greece & Rome*: New Surveys in the Classics, 23 (Oxford).

—— (1996), *The Roman Satirists and their Masks* (Bristol).

BRINGMANN, K. (1985), 'Senecas "Apocolocyntosis": Ein Forschungsbericht 1959–1982', *ANRW* II, 32.2: 885–914.

BRINK, C. O. (1985), *English Classical Scholarship* (Cambridge).

BROOKS, C. (1947), *The Well Wrought Urn: Studies in the Structure of Poetry* (New York).

BROOKS, P. (1984), *Reading for the Plot* (New York).

—— (1994), *Psychoanalysis and Storytelling* (Oxford).

BRYSON, N. (1984), *Tradition and Desire: From David to Delacroix* (Cambridge, 1984).

BUCK, A. (1976), *Die Rezeption der Antike in den romanischen Literaturen der Renaissance* [Grundlagen der Romanistik], 8 (Berlin).

BÜHLER, K. (1934), *Sprachtheorie. Die Darstellungsfunktion der Sprache* (Jena).

BURCK, E. (1966/1981), *Vom Menschenbild in der römischen Literatur*, 1/2 (Heidelberg).

CAIN, W. E. (1982), 'The Institutionalization of the New Criticism', *MLN* 97: 162–72.

CAIRNS, F. (1972), *Generic Composition in Greek and Roman Poetry* (Edinburgh).

CALAME, C. (1986), *Le Récit en Grèce ancienne. Énonciations et représentations des poètes* (Paris).

—— (1988), *Il racconto in Grecia. Enunciazioni e rappresentazioni di poeti*, (Roma–Bari).

—— and KRAMER, D. J. (1992), *An Introductory Bibliography to the History of Classical Scholarship Chiefly in the XIXth and XXth Centuries* (Hildesheim).

CALDER, W. W. III (1980–1), 'Research Opportunities in the Modern History of Classical Scholarship', *Classical World*, 74: 241–51.

—— FLASHAR, H., and LINDKEN, TH. (1985) (eds.), *Wilamowitz nach 50 Jahren* (Darmstadt).

CALLEBAT, L. (1968), *Sermo Cotidianus dans les* Métamorphoses *d'Apulée* (Caen).

CAMERON, A. (1992), 'Genre and Style in Callimachus', *TAPA* 122: 305–12.

—— (1995), *Callimachus and His Critics* (Princeton).

—— (ed.) (1989), *History as Text: The Writing of Ancient History* (London).

CAMERON, D. (1995), *Verbal Hygiene* (London).

CAMPBELL, M. (1991), *Moschus: Europa* (Hildesheim).

CAMPBELL, R. (1969), *Seneca: Letters from a Stoic* (Harmondsworth).

CANCIK, H. (1967), *Untersuchungen zu Senecas Epistulae Morales* (Hildesheim).

—— (1982), 'Antike Volkskunde 1936', *Der altsprachliche Unterricht* 83.2: 80–99.

CANNON, J. A. (1988), 'Historicism', in id. (ed.), *The Blackwell Dictionary of Historians* (Oxford), 192–4.

CARBONELL, C.-O. (1985), 'L'espace et le temps dans l'oeuvre d'Hérodote', *Storia del Storiografia*, 7: 138–49.

CARNAP, R. (1960), *Meaning and Necessity. A Study in Semantics and Modal Logic*, 3rd edn. (Chicago).

CAVARZERE, A. (1992), *Orazio, Il libro degli epodi* (Venice).

CAWKWELL, G. (1997), *Thucydides and the Peloponnesian War* (London).

CHAMPION, C. (1997), 'The Nature of Authoritative Evidence in Polybius and Agelaus' Speech at Naupactus', *TAPA* 127: 111–28.

CHEVALLIER, R. and POIGNAULT, R. (eds.) (1991), *Présence de Sénèque* (Paris).

CHIASSON, C. C. (1983), 'An Ominous Word in Herodotus', *Hermes* 110: 115–16.

CHRIST, M. C. (1994), 'Herodotean Kings and Historical Inquiry', *CA* 13: 167–202.

CLARE, R. J. (1996), 'Catullus 64 and the *Argonautica* of Apollonius Rhodius: Allusion and Exemplarity', *PCPS* NS. 42: 60–88.

CLASSEN, C. J. (1989), 'La filologia classica tedesca 1918–1988', in A. Destro, *Atti delle giornate delle nationes* (Bologna).

CLAUSEN, W. (1994), *Virgil: Eclogues* (Oxford).

COBET, J. (1971), *Herodots Exkurse und die Frage der Einheit seines Werkes* (Wiesbaden).

—— (1986), 'Herodotus and Thucydides on War', in I. S. Moxon, J. D. Smart, and A. J. Woodman (eds.), *Past Perspectives: Studies in Greek and Roman Historical Writing* (Cambridge), 1–18.

COCHRANE, C. N. (1929), *Thucydides and the Science of History* (London).

COFFEY, M. (1976), *Roman Satire* (London and New York).

COHAN, S. and SHIRES, L. M. (1988) *Telling Stories: A Theoretical Analysis of Narrative Fiction* (New York and London).

COLEMAN, R. (1974), 'The Artful Moralist: A Study of Seneca's Epistolary Style', *CQ* 24: 2276–89.

—— (1979), *Vergil: Eclogues* (Cambridge).

COLLINI, S. (1991), *Public Moralists: Political Thought and Intellectual Life in Britain 1850–1930* (Oxford).

COMAROFF, J. L. and ROBERTS, S (1981), *Rules and Processes: The Cultural Logic of Dispute in an African Context* (Chicago).

Conacher, D. J. (1996), *Aeschylus: The Earlier Plays and Related Studies* (Toronto).

Connolly, A. (1998), 'Was Sophocles Heroised as Dexion?', *JHS* 118: 1–21.

Conte, G. B. (1986), *The Rhetoric of Imitation* (Ithaca, NY).

—— (1994), *Genres and Readers* (Baltimore).

Cornford, F. M. (1907), *Thucydides Mythistoricus* (Cambridge).

—— (1908), *Microsmographia Academica* (Cambridge).

Courtney, E. (1980), *A Commentary on the Satires of Juvenal* (London).

—— (1993), *The Fragmentary Latin Poets* (Oxford).

Craik, E. M. (1988), *Euripides: Phoenician Women* (Warminster).

—— (ed.) (1990), *'Owls to Athens': Essays in Classical Studies Presented to Sir Kenneth Dover* (Oxford).

Cropp, M. J. (1988), *Euripides: Electra* (Warminster).

Cupitt, D. (1991), *What is a story?* (London).

D'Alessio, G. B. (1994), 'First-Person Problems in Pindar', *BICS* 39: 117–139.

Dällenbach, L. (1989), *The Mirror in the Text* (London).

Danielewicz, J. (1976), *Morfologia hymnu antycznego* (Poznań).

—— (1990), 'Deixis in Greek Choral Lyric', *QUCC*, ns 34: 7–17.

—— (1980), 'Reguly rozpoczynania tekstu w melice greckiej': *Eos* 68: 41–50.

Davidson, J. (1991), 'The Gaze in Polybius' *Histories*', *JRS* 81: 10–24.

Davis, G. (1991), *Polyhymnia: The Rhetoric of Horatian Lyric Discourse* (Berkeley).

de Angelis, V. (1984), 'Magna questio preposita coram Dante et domino Francisco Petrarca et Virgiliano', *Studi Petrarcheschi*, ns 1: 103–209.

—— (1997), 'I commenti medievali alla *Tebaide* di Stazio: Anselmo di Laon, Goffredo Babione, Ilario d'Orléans', in Mann and Munk Olsen (eds.), 75–136.

De Jong, I. J. F. (1987), *Narrators and Focalizers: The Presentation of the Story in the Iliad* (Amsterdam).

—— (1991), *Narrative in Drama: The Art of the Euripidean Messenger Speech* (Leiden).

—— and Sullivan, J. P. (eds.) (1994), *Modern Critical Theory and Classical Literature* (Leiden).

De Man, P. (1972), 'Genesis and Genealogy in Nietzsche's *The Birth of Tragedy', Diacritics*, 2.4:44–53.

—— (1973), 'Semiology and Rhetoric', *Diacritics*, 3.3: 27–33; repr. in Harari (1979).

De Smet, I. A. R. (1994), 'The Legacy of the Gourd Re-Examined: The Fortune of Seneca's *Apocolocyntosis* and Its Influence on Humanist Satire', in R. De Smet (ed.), *La Satire humaniste: actes du Colloque international des 31 mars, 1er et 2 avril 1993* (Brussels and Louvain), 49–75.

De Smet, I. A. R. (1996), *Menippean Satire and the Republic of Letters 1581–1655* (Geneva).

Depew, M. (1992), 'Genre, Occasion and Imitation in Callimachus, frr. 191 and 203 Pf.', *TAPA* 122:313–30.

—— and Obbink, D. (forthcoming, 2001), *Matrices of Genre* (Cambridge Mass.).

Derow, P. S. (1979), 'Polybius, Rome, and the East', *JRS* 69: 1–5.

—— (1994), 'Historical Explanation: Polybius and His Predecessors', in Hornblower (ed.), 73–90.

—— (1996), 'Polybius', in *Oxford Classical Dictionary*[3] (Oxford).

Derrida, J. (1984), *Margins of Philosophy* (Brighton).

—— (1992), *Acts of Literature* (London).

—— (1996a), ' "*As if* I were dead": An Interview With Jacques Derrida', in J. Brannigan, R. Robbins, and J. Wolfreys (eds.), *Applying: To Derrida* (Basingstoke), 212–26.

—— (1996b), *Archive Fever: A Freudian Impression* (Chicago).

Devaney, M. J. (1997), *'Since at heart Plato . . .' and Other Postmodernist Myths* (London).

Dewald, C. (1985), 'Practical Knowledge and the Historian's Role in Herodotus and Thucydides', in *The Greek Historians: Literature and History. Papers Presented to A. E. Raubitschek* (Saratoga, Cal.), 47–63.

Diengott, N. (1987), 'Narratology and Feminism,' *Style* 22: 42–51.

Doherty, L. E. (1991), 'The Internal and Implied Audiences of *Odyssey* 11', *Arethusa* 24: 145–76.

—— (1992), 'Gender and Internal Audiences in the *Odyssey*', *AJPh* 113: 161–77.

—— (1995), *Siren Songs: Gender, Audiences and Narrators in the Odyssey* (Ann Arbor).

Douglas, M. (1966), *Purity and Danger: An Analysis of Concepts of Pollution and Taboo* (London).

Dover, K. J. (1973), *Thucydides, Greece & Rome*, New Surveys in the Classics, 7 (Oxford).

—— (1988), 'Thucydides on Oracles', in *The Greeks and their Legacy* (Oxford), 65–73.

Dowden, K. (1987), review of Winkler (1985), *CR*, NS 37: 39–41.

Drexler, H. (1939), 'Wilhelm Kroll', *Gnomon*, 15: 590–2.

—— (1942), *Der dritte Humanismus—Ein kritischer Epilog* (Frankfurt a. M. 2nd edn.).

Duckworth, G. (1933), *Foreshadowing and Suspense in the Epics of Homer, Apollonius and Vergil* (Princeton).

DUFF, J. W. (1964), *A Literary History of Rome in the Silver Age*, 3rd ed. (London).

DUMMER, J. and KÜNZE, M. (eds.) (1983), *Antikerezeption, Antikeverhältnis, Antikebegegnung in Vergangenheit and Gegenwart: eine Aufsatzsammlung* (Stendal).

DUNN, F. M. and COLE, T. (eds.) (1992), *Beginnings in Classical Literature*, Yale Classical Studies, 29 (Cambridge and New York).

DYLAN, B. (1968), *John Wesley Harding* (Columbia Records, New York).

EAGLETON, T. (1996), *The Illusions of Postmodernism* (Cambridge, Mass.).

ECKSTEIN, A. M. (1985), 'Polybius, Syracuse, and the Politics of Accommodation', *Greek, Roman, and Byzantine Studies*, 26: 265–82.

—— (1992), 'Notes on the Birth and Death of Polybius', *AJPh* 113: 387–406.

EDWARDS, C. (1997a), *Writing Rome* (Cambridge).

—— (1997b), 'Self-scrutiny and Self-transformation in Seneca's Letters' *G&R* 44: 23–37.

EDWARDS, M. W. (1991), *The Iliad: A Commentary V – Books 17–20* (Cambridge).

EJXENBAUM, B. M. (1971), 'The Theory of the Formal Method', in L. Matejka and K. Pomorska (eds.), *Readings in Russian Poetics* (Cambridge Mass.), 3–37.

ELIOT, T. S. (1920), *The Sacred Wood* (London).

ELSNER, J. (ed.) (1996), *Art and Text in Roman Culture* (Cambridge).

—— and MASTERS, J. (1994), *Reflections of Nero* (Chapel Hill and London).

EMPSON, W. (1947), *Seven Types of Ambiguity*, 2nd edn. (London).

ERBSE, H. (1951), 'Zur Entstehung des polybianischen Geschichtswerkes', *RhM* 94:157–79.

EVANS, R. J. (1997), *In Defence of History* (London).

FABER, R. (1991), 'Faschistische Vergil-Philologie: Zum Beispiel Hans Oppermann', *Hephaistos* 10: 111–33.

FANTUZZI, M. (1988), Introduction to K. Ziegler, *L'epos ellenistico* (Bari).

—— (1993), 'Il sistema letterario della poesia alessandrina nel III sec. a.C' ., in G. Cambiano, L. Canfora, and D. Lanza (eds.), *Lo spazio letterario della Grecia antica*, I. 2 (Roma), 31–73.

—— (1995), 'Variazioni sull' esametro in Teocrito', in Fantuzzi and R. Pretagostini (eds.), *Struttura e storia dell'esametro greco* (Rome), 221–64.

FARRELL, J. (1997), 'Derek Walcott's Omeros: The Classical Epic in a Postmodern world', *SAQ* 96: 247–72.

FEENEY, D. (1998), *Literature and Religion at Rome* (Cambridge).

—— (1995), 'Criticism, Ancient and Modern', in H. Hine, D. Innes, and C. Pelling, (eds.), *Ethics and Rhetoric* (Oxford), 301–12.

FELSON-RUBIN, N. (1994), *Regarding Penelope: From Courtship to Poetics* (Princeton).

FETTERLEY, J. (1978), *The Resisting Reader: A Feminist Approach to American Fiction* (Bloomington, Ind.).

FINLEY, J. H., Jr. (1955), *Pindar and Aeschylus* (Cambridge, Mass.).

FISH, S. (1980), *Is There A Text in This Class?* (Cambridge, Mass.).

FITZGERALD, W. (2000), *Slavery and the Roman Literary Imagination* (Cambridge).

FLASHAR, H. (ed.) (1995), *Altertumswissenschaft in den 20er Jahren. Neue Fragen und Impulse* (Stuttgart).

FLORY, S. (1990), 'The Meaning of *to me muthodes* (1. 22. 4) and the Usefulness of Thucydides' *History*', *CJ* 85: 193–208.

FOLEY, H. (1984), '"Reverse Similes" and Sex Roles in the *Odyssey*', in Peradotto and Sullivan (eds.), 59–78.

FORD, P. (1995), 'Jean Dorat and the Reception of Homer in Renaissance France', *International Journal of the Classical Tradition*, 2.2: 265–74.

—— and JONDORF, G. (eds.) (1996), *Life and Letters in the Age of François Ier* (Cambridge).

FORNARA, C. W. (1971), *Herodotus: An Interpretative Essay* (Oxford).

FOUCAULT, M. (1979), 'What Is An Author?', trans. J. V. Harari, in Harari (1979), 141–60.

—— (1986), *The History of Sexuality 1: Introduction* (Harmondsworth).

—— (1987), *The History of Sexuality 2: The Use of Pleasure* (Harmondsworth).

—— (1988), *The History of Sexuality 3: The Care of the Self* (Harmondsworth).

FOWLER, A. (1982), *Kinds of Literature* (Oxford).

FOWLER, D. P. (1989), 'First Thoughts on Closure: Problems and Prospects', *MD* 22: 75–122.

—— (1990), 'Deviant Focalisation in Virgil's *Aeneid*', *PCPS*, NS 36: 42–63.

—— (1991), 'Narrate and Describe: The Problem of Ekphrasis', *JRS* 81: 112–22.

—— (1993), 'Roman Literature' (review column), *G&R* 39: 226–36.

—— (1995), 'Modern Literary Theory and Latin Poetry: Some Anglo-American Perspectives', *Arachnion*, 2 [http://www.cisi.unito.it/arachne/num2/fowler.html].

—— (1996), 'Even Better Than the Real Thing: A Tale of Two Cities', in Elsner (ed.), 57–74.

—— (1997), 'On the Shoulders of Giants: Intertextuality and Classical Studies', *MD* 39: 13–34.

—— (2000), *Roman Constructions: Readings in Postmodern Latin* (Oxford).

—— and FOWLER, P. G. (1996), 'Literary Theory and Classical Studies', in Hornblower and Spawforth (eds.), 871–5.

FRÄNKEL, H. (1960), 'Eine Stileigenheit in der frühgriechischen Literatur', in *Wege und Formen frühgriechischen Denkens*, 2nd ed. (Munich), 40–96.

—— (1962), *Dichtung und Philosophie des frühen Griechentums* (Munich).

FRIEDLANDER, P. (1912), *Johannes von Gaza und Paulus Silentarius* (Leipzig/Berlin).

FUHRMANN, M. (1992), *Antico e moderno* (Bari).

FUMAROLI, M. (1989), *L'Inspiration du poète de Poussin: essai sur l'allégorie du Parnasse* (Paris).

GABBA, E. (1991), *Dionysius and the History of Archaic Rome* (Berkeley).

GAISSER, J. H. (1993), *Catullus and His Renaissance Readers* (Oxford).

GALINSKY, K. (ed.) (1992), *The Interpretation of Roman Poetry: Empiricism or Hermeneutics?* (Frankfurt/Bern/New York/Paris).

GEERTZ, C. (1973), *The Interpretation of Cultures* (London).

GENETTE, G. (1972), *Figures III* (Paris).

—— (1980), *Narrative Discourse* (Oxford).

—— (1981) *Introduzione all'architesto* (Parma).

—— (1982), *Figures of Literary Discourse* (Oxford).

—— (1982), *Palimpsestes. La littérature au second degré* (Paris).

—— (1997) *Paratexts: Thresholds of interpretation* (Cambridge).

—— and TODOROV, T. (eds.) (1986), *Théorie des genres* (Paris).

GERBER, D. E. (1982), *Pindar's Olympian One: A Commentary* (Toronto–Buffalo–London).

GIBBINS, J. R. (1989), 'John Grote, Cambridge University and the Development of Victorian Thought', PhD thesis, University of Newcastle upon Tyne.

GIGANTE, M. (1989), *Classico e mediazione: contributi alla storia della filologia antica* (Roma).

GILL, C. and WISEMAN, T. P. (eds.) (1993), *Lies and Fiction in the Ancient World* (Exeter).

GODMAN, P. (1990), 'Literary Classicism and Latin Erotic Poetry of the Twelfth Century and the Renaissance' in Godman and Murray (eds.), 149–82.

—— and MURRAY, O. (eds.) (1990), *Latin Poetry and the Classical Tradition: Essays in Medieval and Renaissance Literature* (Oxford).

GOLDEN, M. and TOOHEY, P. (eds.) (1997) *Inventing Ancient Culture: Historicism, Periodization, and the Ancient World* (New York).

GOLDHAGEN, D. J. (1997), *Hitler's Willing Executioners: Ordinary Germans and the Holocaust* (London).

GOLDHILL, S. (1983), *Language, Sexuality, Narrative: The Oresteia* (Cambridge).

—— (1991) *The Poet's Voice* (Cambridge).

—— (1995), *Foucault's Virginity* (Cambridge).

Goldhill, S. (ed.) (forthcoming), *Being Greek Under Rome* (Cambridge).
—— and Osborne, R. G., (eds.) (1994), *Art and Text in Greek Culture* (Cambridge).
Gomme, A. W. (1945), *A Historical Commentary on Thucydides: Volume 1* (Oxford).
—— (1954), *The Greek Attitude to Poetry and History* (Berkeley and Los Angeles).
Good, J. (1988), *The Observing Self: Rediscovering the Essay* (London and New York).
Gostoli, A. (1990), *Terpander* (Rome).
Gould, J. (1989), *Herodotus* (London).
Graff, G. (1987), *Professing Literature: An Institutional History* (Chicago).
—— (1997), 'Agonistic: Eight Controversial Propositions on Controversy', *TAPA* 127: 389–93.
Grafton, A. T. (1983), *Joseph Scaliger: A Study in Classical Scholarship I* (Oxford).
—— (1993), *Joseph Scaliger: A Study in Classical Scholarship II* (Oxford).
Grant, M. (1964), *Roman Literature*, rev. edn. (Harmondsworth).
Greenblatt, S. (1980), *Renaissance Self-Fashioning: From More to Shakespeare* (Chicago/London).
—— (1988), *Shakespearean Negotiations: The Circulation of Social Energy in Renaissance England* (Berkeley).
Greene, T. N. (1982), *The Light in Troy: Imitation and Discovery in Renaissance Poetry* (New Haven and London).
Greimas, A.-J. (1983), *Structural Semantics: An Attempt at a Method* (Lincoln, Minn., and London).
Gribble, D. (1998), 'Narrator Interventions in Thucydides', *JHS* 118: 41–67.
Griffin, M. T. (1976), *Seneca: A Philosopher in Politics* (Oxford).
Grimm, G. (1977), *Rezeptionsgeschichte* (Munich).
Grote, J. (1851), *A Few Remarks upon a Pamphlet by Mr. Shilleto Entitled, Thucydides or Grote?* (Cambridge).
—— (1856), 'Old Studies and New', in *Cambridge Essays 1856*, (London) 74–114.
—— (1861), *A Few Words on Criticism* (Cambridge).
Gruen, E. S. (1984), *The Hellenistic World and the Coming of Rome 1–2* (Berkeley).
Gumbrecht, H. U. (1998), *In 1926* (Cambridge, Mass.).
Gummere, R. M. (1917), *Seneca: Ad Lucilium Epistulae Morales*, 3 vols. (London and New York).
Habinek, T. (1992), 'An Aristocracy of Virtue: Seneca on the Beginnings of Wisdom', in Dunn and Cole (eds.), 187–203.

HACHMANN, E. (1995), *Die Führung des Lesers in Senecas Epistulae Morales* (Munster).

HAHM, D. E. (1995), 'Polybius' Applied Political Theory', in A. Laks and M. Schofield (eds.), *Justice and Generosity: Studies in Hellenistic Social and Political Philosophy* (Cambridge), 4–47.

HALLETT, J. P. and VAN NORTWICK, T. (eds.) (1996), *Compromising Traditions: The Personal Voice in Classical Scholarship* (London).

HALPERIN, D. M. (1995), *Saint Foucault: Towards a Gay Hagiography* (New York).

—— WINKLER, J. J., and ZEITLIN, F. I. (eds.) (1990), *Before Sexuality* (Princeton).

HAMILTON, P. (1996), *Historicism* (London).

HANSON, V. D. and HEATH, J. (1998), *Who Killed Homer?* (New York).

HARARI, J. V. (ed.) (1979), *Textual Strategies: Perspectives in Post-Structuralist Criticism* (Ithaca, NY).

HARDIE, P. (1993), *The Epic Successors of Virgil* (Cambridge).

HARRISON, S. J. (1988), 'Vergil as a Poet of War', *Proceedings of the Virgil Society* 19: 48–68.

—— (1991), *Vergil: Aeneid 10* (Oxford).

—— (1992), 'The Arms of Capaneus: Statius *Thebaid* 4. 165–77', *CQ* NS 42: 247–52.

—— (1997), 'The Survival and Supremacy of Rome: The Unity of the Shield of Aeneas', *JRS* 87: 70–6.

—— (1998), 'The Sword-Belt of Pallas (*Aeneid* X.495–506): Symbolism and Ideology', in Stahl (ed.), 223–42.

—— (2000), *Apuleius: A Latin Sophist* (Oxford).

—— (ed.) (1990), *Oxford Readings in Vergil's 'Aeneid'* (Oxford).

—— (ed.) (1999), *Oxford Readings in the Roman Novel* (Oxford).

HARVIE, C. C. (1976), *The Lights of Liberalism: University Liberals and the Challenge of Democracy 1860–86* (London).

HAVELOCK, E. (1964), *Preface to Plato* (New Haven).

HAWTHORN, J. (1996), *Cunning Passages: New Historicism, Cultural Materialism and Marxism in the Contemporary Literary Debate* (London/New York).

HEATH, M. (1986), 'Thucydides 1. 23. 5–6', *LCM* 11: 104–5.

—— (1989) *Unity in Greek Poetics* (Oxford).

HEINZE, R. (1938), *Vom Geist des Römertums*, ed. E. Burck (Leipzig/Berlin).

HENDERSON, J(EFFREY) (ed.) (1980), *Aristophanes: Essays in Interpretation* (Cambridge).

HENDERSON, J(OHN) (1998a), 'Livy and the Invention of History', in Henderson (1998c), 301–19.

—— (1998b), 'Inventors of the past', review of Marincola (1997), *TLS*, 10 July, p. 26.

HENDERSON, J(OHN) (1998c), *Fighting for Rome* (Cambridge).

—— (1998d), *Juvenal's Mayor: The Professor who lived on 2d a day* (Cambridge).

—— (1998e), *Writing Down Rome* (Oxford).

—— (forthcoming), 'From Megalopolis to Cosmopolis: Polybius, or There and Back Again', in Goldhill (ed.).

HENDRICKSON, G. L. (1911), '*Satura*—the Genesis of a Literary Form?', *CPh* 6: 129–43.

HERSHKOWITZ, D. (1998), *Valerius Flaccus*' '*Argonautica*' (Oxford).

HEUBECK, A. (1980), '*Prophasis* und keine Ende (zu Thuk. I 23)', *Glotta* 58: 222–36.

—— and HOEKSTRA, A. (1989), *A Commentary on Homer's Odyssey II: Books ix–xvi* (Oxford).

HEXTER, R. J. and SELDEN, D. L. (eds.) (1992), *Innovations of Antiquity* (New York/London).

HINDS, S. E. (1992), '*Arma* in Ovid's *Fasti*', *Arethusa* 25: 81–149.

—— (1998), *Allusion and Intertext* (Cambridge).

HIRSCH, E. D., Jr. (1976), *The Aims of Interpretation* (Chicago).

HOPPER, E. (1971), *Readings in the Theory of Educational Systems* (London).

HORNBLOWER, S. (1991), *A Commentary on Thucydides: Volume I: Books I–III* (Oxford).

—— (1992), 'The Religious Dimension to the Peloponnesian War, or What Thucydides does not tell us', *HSCPh* 94: 169–97.

—— (1994a), 'Narratology and Narrative Techniques in Thucydides', in Hornblower (ed.), 131–66.

—— (1994b), *Thucydides*, 2nd edn. (London).

—— (ed.)(1994), *Greek Historiography* (Oxford).

—— (1996), *A Commentary on Thucydides: Volume II: Books IV–V.24* (Oxford).

—— and SPAWFORTH, A. (eds.) (1996), *The Oxford Classical Dictionary*, 3rd edn. (Oxford).

HOUSMAN, A. E. (1969), *The Confines of Criticism: The Cambridge Inaugural, 1911* (Cambridge).

HOW, W. W. and WELLS, J. (1928), *A Commentary on Herodotus*, 2nd edition (Oxford).

HUNTER, R. L. (1993), *The Argonautica of Apollonius: Literary Studies* (Cambridge).

—— (1997), '(B)ionic man: Callimachus' iambic programme', *PCPS* 43: 41–52.

—— (ed.) (1998), *Studies in Heliodorus* (Cambridge).

HUNTER, V. (1973), *Thucydides the Artful Reporter* (Toronto).

—— (1982), *Past and Process in Herodotus and Thucydides* (Princeton).

HUTCHINSON, G. O. (1985), *Aeschylus: Septem contra Thebas* (Oxford).

IGGERS, G. G. (1973), 'Historicism', in *Dictionary of the History of Ideas* (New York), II, 457–64.

IMMERWAHR, H. (1966), *Form and Thought in Herodotus* (Cleveland).

INGERSOLL, J. W. D. (1912), 'Roman Satire: Its Early Name?', *CPh* 7: 59–65.

IRMSCHER, J. (1979), 'Philologia perennis?' in: Irmscher (ed.), 39–44.

—— (ed.) (1979), *Antikerezeption, deutsche Klassik und sozialistische Gegenwart* (Berlin).

ISER, W. (1974), *The Implied Reader* (Baltimore).

—— (1978), *The Act of Reading* (London).

JACOBY, F. (1913), 'Herodot', in *Pauly–Wissowa, suppl. II*, cols. 205–520.

JAKOBSON, R. (1960), 'Closing Statement: Linguistics and Poetics', in T. A. Sebeok (ed.), *Style in Language* (New York), 350–77.

—— (1971), 'Two Aspects of Language and Two Types of Aphasic Disturbances', in R. Jakobson, *Selected Writings, Vol. 2* (The Hague/Paris), 239–59.

JAUMANN, H. (1995), *Critica: Untersuchungen zur Geschichte der Literaturkritik zwischen Quintilian und Thomasius*, Brill's Studies in Intellectual History, 62 (Leiden).

JAUSS, H. R. (1982), *Towards an Aesthetic of Reception* (Brighton).

JAY, A. (1996), *The Oxford Dictionary of Political Quotations* (Oxford).

JEFFERSON, A. and ROBEY, D. (1986), *Modern Literary Theory* 2nd edn. (London).

JENKINS, K. (1995), *On 'What is History?'* (London and New York).

JOCELYN, H. D. (1984), review of Grafton (1983), *LCM* 9: 55–61.

—— (1988), *Philology and Classical Education* (Liverpool).

—— (ed.)(1996), *Aspects of Nineteenth-Century British Classical Scholarship* (Liverpool).

—— and HURT, H. (eds.) (1993), *Tria lustra. Essays and Notes Presented to John Pinsent* (Liverpool).

JOHNSON, B. (ed.) (1982), *The Pedagogical Imperative: Teaching as a Literary Genre*, Yale French Studies, 63 (New Haven).

JOHNSON, G. (1994), *University Politics: F. M. Cornford's Cambridge and His Advice to the Young Academic Politician* (Cambridge).

JOHNSON, W. R. (1976), *Darkness Visible* (Berkeley).

JOLIFFE, J. W. (1956), 'Satyre: Satura: SATUROS. A Study in confusion', *Bibliothèque d'Humanisme et Renaissance*, 18: 84–95.

JOHNDORF, G. (1996), 'Marot's *Première Eglogue de Virgile*: Good, Bad, or Interesting?', in Ford and Jondorf (eds.), 115–132.

KAHANE, A. (1994), 'Callimachus, Apollonius, and the poetics of Mud', *TAPA* 124: 121–33.

KALLETT-MARX, R. M. (1995), *Hegemony to Empire: The Development of the Roman* Imperium *in the East from 148 to 62 B.C.* (Berkeley).

KÄPPEL, L. (1992) *Paian* (Berlin).

KASTER, R. A. (1997), 'Fruitful Disputes', *TAPA* 127: 345–7.

KATZ, E. and HALL, D. R. (1970), *Explicating French Texts: Poetry, Prose, Drama* (New York).

KEITH, A. M. (2000), *Engendering Rome: Women in Latin Epic* (Cambridge).

KENNEDY, D. F. (1989), review of Ovidian studies, *JRS* 79: 209–10.

—— (1993), *The Arts of Love* (Cambridge).

KENNER, H. (1976), 'The Pedagogue as Critic', in Young (ed.), 36–46.

KENNEY, E. J. (1974), *The Classical Text: Aspects of Editing in the Age of the Printed Book* (Berkeley, Los Angeles, and London).

KEYNES, J. M. (1973), *The General Theory of Employment, Interest and Money* [=Collected Works Vol. VII; orig.pub. 1936], (Cambridge).

KIERNAN, M. (ed.) (1985), *Sir Francis Bacon: The Essayes or Counsels Civill and Morall* (Oxford).

KING, K. C. (1980), 'The Force of Tradition: The Achilles Ode in Euripides' *Electra*', *TAPA* 110: 195–212.

KING, L. R. (1994), *The Beekeeper's Apprentice: On the Segregation of the Queen* (New York).

—— (1995), *A Monstrous Regiment of Women* (New York).

KLINGNER, F. (1943), *Römische Geisteswelt. Essays über Schrifttum und geistiges Leben im alten Rom* (Leipzig); 5th edn. 1979, ed. K. Büchner (Stuttgart).

—— (1956), *Catulls Peleus-Epos* (Munich).

KNEISSL, P. and LOSEMANN, V. (eds.) (1998), *Imperium Romanum. Studien zu Geschichte und Rezeption. Festschrift für K. Christ* (Stuttgart).

KNEPPE, A. and WIESEHÖFER, J. (1983), *Friedrich Münzer. Ein Althistoriker zwischen Kaiserreich und Nationalsozialismus* (Bonn).

KOHL, B. G. (1992), 'The Changing Concept of the *Studia Humanitatis* in the Early Renaissance', *Renaissance Studies*, 6: 185–92.

KÖNIGS, D. (1995), *Joseph Vogt: Ein Althistoriker in der Weimarer Republik und im Dritten Reich* (Basel/Frankfurt a.M.).

KOUMOULIDES, J. T. A. (ed.) (1987), *Greek Connections: Essays on Culture and Diplomacy* (Notre Dame, Ind.).

KRAUS, C. S. (1994), *Livy Ab urbe condita Book 6* (Cambridge).

KRAUSE, E., HUBER, L., and FISCHER, H. (eds.) (1991), *Hochschulalltag im 'Dritten Reich'. Die Hamburger Universität 1933–1954*. 2 vols. (Berlin/Hamburg).

KRAUSS, W. (1968), *Essays zur französischen Literatur* (Berlin und Weimar).

KRAYE, J. (ed.) (1996), *The Cambridge Companion to Renaissance Humanism* (Cambridge).

KRISTELLER, P. O. (1944–5), 'Humanism and Scholasticism in the Italian Renaissance', *Byzantion* 17: 365 ff.; repr. with updated notes in *Renaissance Thought* (New York, 1965), 110 ff.

KROLL, W. (1900), 'Studien über die Komposition der Aeneis', *NJb.* suppl. 22: 135–69.

—— (1903), 'Unsere Schätzung der römischen Dichtung', *NJb.* 6: 1–30.

—— (1905), 'Übersicht', *Bursians Jahresberichte*, suppl. 142.

—— (1924), *Studien zum Verständnis der römischen Literatur* (Leipzig).

KULLMANN, W. (1968), 'Vergangenheit und Zukunft in der Ilias', *Poetica* 2: 15–37.

KYTZLER, B. (1989), 'Bundesrepublik Deutschland. Latinistik', in *La filologia greca e latina nel secolo XX*, 2 (Pisa), 1043–63.

—— (ed.) (1973), *Ciceros literarische Leistung* (Darmstad).

LAIRD, A. (1993), 'Sounding Out Ekphrasis: Art and Text in Catullus 64', *JRS* 83: 50–62.

—— (1996), '*Ut figura poesis*: Writing Art and the Art of Writing in Augustan Poetry', in Elsner (ed.), 75–102.

LÄMMERT, E. (1955), *Bauformen des Erzählens* (Stuttgart).

LANSER, S. (1986), 'Toward a Feminist Narratology', *Style* 20: 341–63.

—— (1988), 'Shifting the Paradigm: Feminism and Narratology', *Style* 22: 52–60.

—— (1996), 'Queering Narratology', in K. Mezei, *Ambiguous Discourse: Feminist Narratology and British Women Writers* (Chapel Hill, NC, 1996), 250–61.

LATEINER, D. (1977), 'No Laughing Matter: A Literary Tactic in Herodotus', *TAPA* 107: 173–82.

—— (1982), 'A Note on the Perils of Good Fortune in Herodotus', *RhM* 125: 97–101.

—— (1989), *The Historical Method of Herodotus* (Toronto).

LAWALL, G. (1966), 'Apollonius' *Argonautica*: Jason as Anti-hero', *YCS* 19: 121–69.

LAWRENCE, D. H. (1936), *Phoenix: The Posthumous Papers of D. H. Lawrence*, ed. E. D. McDonald (London).

LE GOFF, J. (1992), *History and Memory* (New York).

LEACH, A. O. (1981–2), 'A Reply to Calder's Critics', *CW* 75: 362–3.

LEACH, E. (1970), *Lévi-Strauss* (London).

LEAVIS, F. R. (1952), *The Common Pursuit* (London).

—— (1962), *Two Cultures? The Significance of C. P. Snow* (London).

—— (ed.) (1968), *A Selection from Scrutiny*, 2 vols. (Cambridge).

LEE, D. E. and BECK, R. N. (1954), 'The Meaning of "Historicism"', *American Historical Review* 59: 568–79.

Lefkowitz, M. and Rogers, G. (eds.) (1996), *Black Athena Revisited* (Chapel Hill).

Leigh, M. (1997), *Lucan: Spectacle and Engagement* (Oxford).

Lemon, L. T. and Reis, M. J. (eds.) (1965), *Russian Formalist Criticism: Four Essays* (Lincoln, Nebr.).

Lesky, A. (1966), *A History of Greek Literature* (London).

Lévi-Strauss, C. (1963), *Structural Anthropology* (London).

Lewis, D. (1977), *Sparta and Persia* (Leiden).

Lloyd, G. E. R. (1979), *Magic, Reason and Experience* (Cambridge).

—— (1987), *The Revolutions of Wisdom* (Berkeley).

Lodge, D. (1988), *Modern Criticism and Theory* (London).

Lohse, G. (1991), *Klassische Philologie und Zeitgeschehen. Zur Geschichte eines Seminar an der Hamburger Universität in der Zeit des Nationalsozialismus*, in Krause *et al.* (eds.), ii. 775–826.

Loraux, N. (1986), 'Thucydide et la sedition dans les mots', *QS* 23: 95–134.

Losemann, V. (1977), *Nationalsozialismus und Antike. Studien zur Entwicklung des Faches Alte Geschichte 1933–1945* (Hamburg).

Luce, T. J. (1997), *The Greek Historians* (London).

Ludwig, W. (1986), 'Amtsenthebung und Emigration Klassischer Philologen', *Würzburger Jahrbücher für die Altertumswissenschaft* N.F. 12: 217–39.

McCanles, M. (1993), 'Historicism', in Preminger and Brogan (eds.), 529–33.

McGann, J. J. (1983), *The Romantic Ideology: A Critical Investigation* (Chicago).

McLaughlin, M. L. (1995), *Literary Imitation in the Italian Renaissance* (Oxford).

Macleod, C. W. (1983a), *Collected Essays* (Oxford).

—— (1983b), 'Rhetoric and History (Thucydides 6.16–18)', in Macleod (1983a), 68–87.

McManus, B. F. (1997), *Classics and Feminism: Gendering the Classics* (New York).

Malherbe, A. J. (1988), *Ancient Epistolary Theorists* (Atlanta).

Malinowski, B. (1929), *The Sexual Life of Savages in North-Western Melanesia* (London).

Malitz, J. (1998), 'Römertum im "Dritten Reich": Hans Oppermann', in Kneissl and Losemann (eds.), 65–82.

Malkin, I. and Rubinsohn, Z. W. (eds.) (1995), *Leaders and Masses in the Roman World: Studies in Honor of Zvi Yavetz* (Leyden).

Mandelker, A. (ed.) (1995), *Bakhtin in Context: Across the Disciplines* (Evanston, Ill.).

Mann, N. (1984), *Petrarch* (Oxford and New York).

—— and MUNK OLSEN, B. (eds.) (1997), *Medieval and Renaissance Scholarship* (Leiden).

MARCHAND, S. L. (1996), *Down From Olympus: Archaeology and Philhellenism in Germany 1750–1970* (Princeton).

MARINATOS, N. (1981), *Thucydides and Religion* (Königsheim).

MARINCOLA, J. (1997), *Authority and Tradition in Ancient Historiography* (Cambridge).

MARIOTTI, S. (1991), *Lezioni su Ennio* (Urbino: 1st edn. 1951).

MARTIN, R. (1993), 'Telemachus and the Last Hero-Song', *Colby Quarterly* 29: 222–40.

MARTIN, R. H. and WOODMAN, A. J. (1989), *Tacitus: Annals IV* (Cambridge).

MARTIN, W. (1986), *Recent Theories of Narrative* (Ithaca, NY).

MARTINDALE, C. (1993), *Redeeming the Text* (Cambridge).

MARTYN, J. R. C. (1972), 'Satis Saturae?', *Mnemosyne*, 4.25: 157–67.

MASO, S. (1980), 'Il problema dell'epicureismo nell'epistola 33 di Seneca', *AIV* 138: 573–89.

MATTHEWS, V. J. (1996), *Antimachus of Colophon: Text and Commentary* (Leiden).

MAURACH, G. (1970), *Der Bau von Senecas Epistulae Morales* (Heidelberg).

MAYENOWA, M. R. (1974), *Poetyka teoretyczna. Zagadnienia jêzyka* (Wrocław).

—— (ed.) (1971), *O spójnosci tekstu* (Wrocław).

MAYER, C.-A. (1951), 'Satyre as a Dramatic Genre', *Bibliothèque d'Humanisme et Renaissance*, 13: 327–33.

MAZZOLI, G. (1989), 'Le *Epistulae Morales ad Lucilium* di Seneca: valore letterario e filosofico', *ANRW* II 36.3: 1823–77.

MEINECKE, F. (1936), *Die Entstehung des Historismus* (Munich/Berlin).

—— (1972), *Historism: The Rise of a New Historical Outlook*, trans. J. E. Anderson with a foreword by Sir Isaiah Berlin (London).

MEISSNER, B. (1986), 'PRAGMATIKH ISTORIA: Polybios über den Zweck pragmatischer Geschichtsschreibung', *Saeculum*, 37: 313–51.

MENSCHING, E. (1992), *Nugae zur Philologie-Geschichte V. Eduard Norden zum 50. Todestag* (Berlin).

MERMIER, G. and BOILLY-WIDMER, Y. (1972), *Explication de Texte: Theorie et Pratique* (Glenview, Ill.).

MERQUIOR, J. G. (1985), *Foucault* (London).

MERRILL, E. T. (1910), 'On the Eight-Book Tradition of Pliny's *Letters* in Verona', *CPh* 5: 175–88.

MERTON, R. K. (1965), *On the Shoulders of Giants: A Shandean Postscript* (New York).

MIHAILESCU, C.-A. and HARMANEH, W. (1996), *Fiction Updated: Theories of Fictionality, Narratology and Poetics* (Toronto).

MILLAR, F. G. B. (1987), 'Polybius between Greece and Rome', in Koumoulides (ed.), 1–18.

MILLER, J. (1993), *The Passion of Michel Foucault* (London).

MILNES, R. M. (1857), 'The Dilettanti Society', *Edinburgh Review*, 105.

MINK, L. O. (1987), *Historical Understanding* (Ithaca and London).

MISCH, G. (1950), *A History of Autobiography in Antiquity*, vol. 2 (London).

MOLES, J. L. (1993a), 'Truth and Untruth in Herodotus and Thucydides', in Gill and Wiseman (eds.), 88–121.

—— (1993b), 'Thucydides', *JACT Review*, 10: 14–18.

—— (1993c), 'Livy's Preface', *PCPS* 39: 141–68.

—— (1995), review of Badian (1993), *JHS* 115: 213–15.

—— (1996), 'Herodotus Warns the Athenians', *PLLS*: 259–84.

—— (1999), 'ANATHEMA KAI KTEMA: The Inscriptional Inheritance', *HISTOS* 3.

MOMIGLIANO, A. (1974), *Polybius Between the English and the Turks* (Oxford).

—— (1977), 'Historicism Revisited', in *Essays in Ancient and Modern Historiography* (Oxford), 365–73.

MORGAN, J. R. (1993), 'Make-Believe and Make Believe: The Fictionality of the Greek Novel', in Gill and Wiseman (eds.), 175–229.

MORGAN, T. E. (1994), 'Plague or Poetry? Thucydides on the Epidemic at Athens', *TAPA* 124: 197–209.

MORRISON, J. V. (1992), *Homeric Misdirection: False Predictions in the Iliad* (Ann Arbor).

MOST, G. (1997), 'One Hundred Years of Fractiousness: Disciplining Polemics in Nineteenth-Century German Classical Scholarship', *TAPA* 127: 349–61.

MOTTO, A. L. (1985), *Seneca: Moral Epistles* (Chico, Calif.).

MURNAGHAN, S. (1986), 'Penelope's Agnoia: Knowledge, Power, and Gender in the Odyssey', *Helios*, NS 103–15.

MURRAY, G. G. A. (1915), 'German scholarship', *Quarterly Review* 223: 230–9.

MYNORS, R. A. B. (1972), *Vergilii Opera*, corrected second impression (Oxford).

—— (1990), *Virgil: Georgics* (Oxford).

NAGY, G. (1990), *Pindar's Homer* (Baltimore).

NIETZSCHE, F. W. (1872), *Die Geburt der Tragödie* (Leipzig).

—— (1997), 'On the Uses and Disadvantages of History for Life', in *Untimely Meditations*, trans. R. J. Hollingdale (Cambridge), 59–123.

NIGHTINGALE, A. W. (1995), *Genres in Dialogue: Plato and the Construct of Philosophy* (Cambridge).

NIMIS, S. (1984), 'Fussnoten: Das Fundament der Wissenschaft', *Arethusa*, 17: 105–33.

NISBET, G. (1997), review of Hallett and Van Nortwick (1997), *BMCR* 97.7.2.

NISBET, R. G. M. (1995), *Collected Papers on Latin Literature* (Oxford).

—— and HUBBARD, M. (1970), *A Commentary on Horace: Odes Book 1* (Oxford).

—— and —— (1978), *A Commentary on Horace: Odes Book II* (Oxford).

OKOPIEN-SLAWINSKA, A. (1985), *Semantyka wypowiedzi poetyckiej (Preliminaria)* (Worcław).

ONEGA, S. and GARCIA LANDA, J. A. (eds.) (1996), *Narratology* (London).

OOST, S. I. (1975), 'Thucydides and the Irrational: Sundry Passages', *CPh* 70: 186.

OSBORNE, R. G. and HORNBLOWER, S. (eds.) (1994), *Ritual, Finance, Politics: Athenian Democratic Accounts Presented to David Lewis* (Oxford), 53–68.

PÁLSSON, G. (1995), *The Textual Life of Savants: Ethnography, Iceland and the Linguistic Turn* (Chur).

PAGE, T. E. (1888), review of Orelli's Horace, *Classical Review* 2: 72–4.

PARRY, A. M. (1971), 'Introduction' in id. (ed.), *The Making of Homeric Verse: The Collected Papers of Milman Parry* (Oxford), pp. ix–lxii.

—— (1957/1981), *Logos* and *Ergon in Thucydides* (Cambridge, Mass.).

PARSONS, P. J. (1992), 'Poesia ellenistica: testi e contesti', *Aevum Antiquum* 5: 9–19.

PATON, W. R. (1922–7), *Polybius, The Histories, I–VI* (Cambridge, Mass.).

PEARSON, L. (1952), '*Prophasis* and *Aitia*', *TAPA* 83: 205–23.

—— (1972), '*Prophasis:* A Clarification', *TAPA* 103: 381–94.

PECERE, O. and REEVE, M. D. (eds.) (1995), *Formative Stages of Classical Traditions* (Spoleto).

PEETERS, K. (1998), 'Conceptions et critériologies post-genettiennes de la focalisation', online at *http://www.ufsia.ac.be/kpeeters/focalisation 1. html.*

PELLING, C. B. R. (2000), *Literary Texts and the Greek Historian* (London).

PERADOTTO, J. and SULLIVAN, J. P. (eds.) (1984), *Women in the Ancient World: The Arethusa Papers* (Albany).

PERKINS, D. (1992), *Is Literary History Possible?* (Baltimore and London).

PERUTELLI, A. (1979), *La narrazione commentata: studi sull'epillio latino* (Pisa).

PETERSMANN, H. (1977), *Petrons Urbane Prosa* (Vienna).

PFEIFFER, R. (1968), *A History of Classical Scholarship I* (Oxford).

PINKSTER, H. (1998), 'The Use of Narrative Tenses in Apuleius' *Amor and Psyche*', in Zimmerman *et al.* (eds.), 103–12.

PLETT, H. F. (ed.) (1991), *Intertextuality* (Berlin and New York).

POHLENZ, M. (1937), *Herodot, der erste Geschichtsschreiber des Abendlandes* (Leipzig).

POLLOCK, D. (1990), *Skywalking: The Life and Films of George Lucas* (Hollywood).

POPOVIC, A. (1978), 'Esteticka metakomunikacia', in F. Miko and A. Popovic (eds.), *Tvorba a recepcia* (Bratislava), 239–368.

POPPER, K. (1957), *The Poverty of Historicism* (London).

POTHECARY, S. (1995), 'Strabo, Polybius, and the Stade', *Phoenix* 49: 49–67.

PREMINGER, A. and BROGAN, T. V. F. (eds.) (1993), *The New Princeton Encyclopedia of Poetry and Poetics* (Princeton).

PRINCE, G. (1982), *Narratology: The Form and Functioning of Narrative* (Berlin).

—— (1987), *A Dictionary of Narratology* (Lincoln, Nebr.).

PROPP, V. (1958), *Morphology of the Folk Tale* (Bloomington, Ind.).

PUTNAM, M. C. J. (1998), *Virgil's Epic Designs* (New Haven).

QUINN, K. (1979), *Texts and Contexts: The Roman Writers and their Audience* (London, Boston, and Henley).

QUINT, D. (1993), *Epic and Empire* (Princeton).

RABINOWITZ, N. S. and RICHLIN, A. (eds.) (1993), *Feminist Theory and the Classics* (London).

RACE, W. H. (1992), 'How Greek Poems Begin', in Dunn and Cole (eds.), 13–38.

—— (ed.) (1997), *Pindar*, I: *Olympian Odes, Pythian Odes* (Cambridge, Mass.).

RANDOLPH, M. C. (1942), 'The Structural Design of Formal Verse Satire', *Philological Quarterly* 21: 368–84.

RAVENNA, G. (1974), 'L'ekphasis poetica di opere di arte in latino: temi e problemi', *Quad. Inst. Fil. Lat. Padova* 3: 1–52.

RAWLINGS, H. R. (1975), *A Semantic Study of Prophasis to 400 BC* (Wiesbaden).

—— (1981), *The Structure of Thucydides' History* (Princeton).

—— (1988), *Thucydides: History II* (Warminster).

RAWSON, E. (1989), 'Roman Tradition and the Greek World', in Astin *et al.* (eds.), 422–76.

REED, J. D. (1997), *Bion of Smyrna: The Fragments and the Adonis* (Cambridge).

REEVE, M. D. (1983), 'Statius: *Silvae*', in Reynolds (ed.), 397–9.

—— (1986), 'The Transmission of Livy 26–40', *RFil* 114: 129–72.

—— (1987), 'The Third Decade of Livy in Italy: The Spirensian Tradition', *RFil* 115: 405–40.

—— (1995), 'Conclusions', in Pecere and Reeve (eds.), 497–511.

REYNOLDS, L. D. (ed.) (1983), *Texts and Transmission* (Oxford).

—— and WILSON, N. G. (1991), *Scribes and Scholars: A Guide to the Transmission of Greek and Latin Literature*, 3rd edn. (Oxford).

RHODES, P. J. (1985), 'Thucydides on the Causes of the Peloponnesian War', *Hermes*, 115: 154–65.

RICHARDSON, J. S. (1979), 'Polybius' View of the Roman Empire', *PBSR* 47: 1–11.

—— (1990), 'Thucydides I. 23. 6 and the Debate about the Peloponnesian War', in Craik (ed.), 155–61.

RICHARDSON, S. (1990), *The Homeric Narrator* (Nashville).

RIMMON-KENAN, S. (1983), *Narrative Fiction: Contemporary Poetics* (London).

ROBERTS, D. H., DUNN, F. M., and FOWLER, D. (eds.) (1997), *Classical Closure* (Princeton).

ROMILLY, J. DE (1963), *Thucydides and Athenian Imperialism* (Oxford).

—— (1990), *La Construction de la vérité chez Thucydide* (Paris).

ROOD, T. (1998), *Thucydides: Narrative and Explanation* (Oxford).

ROSE, H. J. (1949), *A Handbook of Latin Literature* (London).

ROSE, P. (1992), *Sons of the Gods, Children of Earth: Ideology and Literary Form in Ancient Greece* (Ithaca, NY).

ROSSI, L. E. (1971), 'I generi letterari e le loro leggi scritte e non scritte nelle letterature classiche', *BICS* 18: 69–94.

RUDD, N. (ed.) (1972), *Essays on Classical Literature* (Cambridge).

RUSSELL, D. A. and WINTERBOTTOM, M. (1972), *Ancient Literary Criticism: The Principal Texts in New Translations* (Oxford).

RUSTEN, J. S. (1989), *Thucydides: The Peloponnesian War Book II* (Cambridge).

RUTHERFORD, I. (1996), 'Odes and Ends: Closure in Greek Lyric', in Roberts *et al.* (eds.), 43–61.

RUTHERFORD, R. B. (1992), *Homer: Odyssey Books XIX and XX* (Cambridge).

—— (1994), 'Learning from History: Categories and Case-Histories', in Osborne and Hornblower (eds.), 53–68.

RYAN, K. (1996), *New Historicism and Cultural Materialism: A Reader* (London).

STE. CROIX, G. E. M. DE (1972), *The Origins of the Peloponnesian War* (London).

SANDYS, J. E. (1903–8), *A History of Classical Scholarship*, 3 vols. (Cambridge).

SAUSSURE, F. DE (1916), *Cours de linguistique générale* (Paris).

SCHADEWALDT, W. (1938), *Iliasstudien* (Leipzig).

SCHAEFFER, J.-M. (1992), *Che cos'è un genere letterario* (Parma).

SCHEID, J. and SVENBRO, J. (1996), *The Craft of Zeus: Myths of Weaving and Fabric* (Cambridge).

SCHIESARO, A. (1998), 'Latin Literature and Greece', *Dialogos* 5: 144–9.

SCHMID, W. (1973), 'Cicerowertung und Cicerodeuting' in Kytzler (ed.), 33–68.

SCHMIDT, P. G. (1997), 'Pseudoantike Literatur als Philologisches Problem in Mittelalter und Renaissance', in Mann and Olsen (eds.).

SCHMIDT, P. L. (1985), 'Wilamowitz und die Geschichte der lateinischen Literatur', in Calder *et al.* (eds.), 358–99.

—— (1995), 'Zwischen Anpassungsdruck und Autonomiestreben: Die deutsche Latinistik vom Beginn bis in die 20er Jahre des 20. Jahrhunderts', in Flashar (ed.), 115–82.

SCHMITT, C. B. and SKINNER, Q. (eds.) (1988), *The Cambridge History of Renaissance Philosophy* (Cambridge).

SCHOECK, R. J. (1984), *Intertextuality and Renaissance Texts* (Bamberg).

—— (1991), ' "In loco intertexantur": Erasmus as Master of Intertextuality', in Plett (ed.), 181–91.

SCHUBERT, C. and BRODERSEN, K. (eds.) (1995), *Rom und der griechische Osten. Festschrift für Hatto H. Schmitt zum 65. Geburtstag* (Stuttgart).

SCOTT-KILVERT, I. (1979), *Polybius: The Rise of the Roman Empire* (Harmondsworth).

SEARBY, P. (1997), *History of the University of Cambridge*, vol. 3: *1750–1870* (Cambridge).

SEGAL, C. (1986), 'Foreword', in Conte (1986), 7–17.

SELDEN, D. (1994), 'Genre of Genre', in Tatum (ed.), 19–64.

SELDON, A. (ed.) (1988), *Contemporary History* (Oxford).

SEMIOTICA (1986), *Semiotica della novella latina: atti del Seminario interdisciplinare la novella Latina* (Rome).

SHACKLETON BAILEY, D. R. (1965), *Cicero's Letters to Atticus*, vol. 1 (Cambridge).

SHAPIRO, H. A. (1980), 'Jason's Cloak', *TAPA* 110: 263–86.

SHILLETO, R. (1851), *Thucydides or Grote?* (Cambridge).

SHIMRON, B. (1979–80), 'Polybius on Rome. A Reexamination of the Evidence', *SCI* 5: 94–117.

SHKLOVSKY, V. (1965), 'Art as Technique', in Lemon and Reis (eds.), 3–24.

SHOREY, P. (ed.) (1930), *Plato: The Republic* (Cambridge, Mass.).

SHRIMPTON, G. S. (1997), *History and Memory in Ancient Greece* (Montreal/London).

SHUCKBURGH, E. S. (1889), *The Histories of Polybius* (London).

SILK, M. S. (1971), *Interaction in Poetic Imagery* (Cambridge).

—— (1980), 'Aristophanes as a Lyric Poet', in Henderson (ed.), 99–151.

—— (1987), *Homer, The Iliad* (Cambridge).

—— (1995), 'Language, Poetry and Enactment', *Dialogos* 2: 109–32.

—— (1996), 'Tragic Language, the Greek Tragedians and Shakespeare', in Silk (ed.), 4.

—— (ed.) (1996), *Tragedy and the Tragic: Greek Theatre and Beyond* (Oxford).

—— and Stern, J. P. (1981), *Nietzsche on Tragedy* (Cambridge).

Silvermann, E. K. (1990), 'Clifford Geertz: Towards a More "Thick" Understanding', in Tilley (ed.), 121–59.

Skinner, M. B. (1997), 'Guidelines for Contributors', *TAPA* 127: 395.

Slater, N. (1989), *Reading Petronius* (Baltimore).

Slater, W. J. (1969), *Lexicon to Pindar* (Berlin).

Soffer, R. N. (1982), 'Why Do Disciplines Fail? The Strange Case of Sociology', *English Historical Review*. Oct. 1982.

Solmsen, F. (1982), 'Two Crucial Decisions in Herodotus', in *Kleine Schriften*, III, (Hildesheim—Zürich—New York), 78–109.

Sowerby, R. (1994), *The Classical Legacy in Renaissance Poetry* (London and New York).

Spurlin, W. J., and Fischer, M. (eds.) (1995), *The New Criticism and Contemporary Literary Theory: Connections and Continuities* (New York).

Stadter, P. A. (1993), 'The Form and Content of Thucydides' Pentecontaetia (1.89–117)', *GRBS* 34: 35–72.

Stahl, H.-P. (1966), *Thukydides: Die Stellung des Menschen im geschichtlichen Prozess* (Munich).

—— (ed.) (1998), *Vergil's Aeneid: Augustan Epic and Political Context* (London).

Stanford, W. B. (1967), *The Sound of Greek* (Berkeley).

—— (ed.) (1958–9), *Homer, Odyssey*, 2 vols., 2nd edn. (Bristol).

Stanley, K. (1965), 'Irony and Foreshadowing in *Aeneid* 1.462 ff', *AJP* 86: 267–77.

—— (1993), *The Shield of Homer: Narrative Structure in the Iliad* (Princeton).

Stein, H. (1883), *Herodotos, VII* (Berlin).

Stephenson, R. (1999), 'Records of Eclipses in Greek and Roman Historians and other Classical Authors', *HISTOS* 3.

Sternberg, M. (1978), *Expositional Modes and Temporal Ordering in Fiction* (Baltimore—London).

Stobart, J. C. (1911), *The Glory That Was Greece* (London).

—— (1912) *The Grandeur That Was Rome* (London).

Strasburger, H. (1956), 'Herodots Zeitrechnung', *Historia* 5: 129–61.

Strauss, B. S. (1997), 'The problem of Periodization: The Case of the Peloponnesian War', in Golden and Toohey (eds.), 165–75.

Stray, C. A. (1997a), '"Thucydides or Grote?" Classical Disputes and Disputed Classics in Nineteenth-Century Cambridge', *TAPA* 127: 363–71.

—— (1997b), Review, *JHS* 117: 229–31.

STRAY, C. A. (1998a), *Classics Transformed: Schools, Universities, and Society in England 1830–1960* (Oxford).

—— (1998b), 'Renegotiating Classics: The Politics of Curricular Reform in Late-Victorian Cambridge', *Echos du Monde Classique/Classical Views*, 42: NS 7.3: 1–22.

SUERBAUM, U. (1985), '*Intertextualität und Gattung*' in U. Broich-M. Pfister (ed.) *Intertextualität* (Tübingen), 59–77.

SULLIVAN, J. P. (ed.) (1962), *Critical Essays on Roman Literature: Elegy and Lyric* (London).

—— (ed.) (1963), *Critical Essays on Roman Literature*: *Satire* (London).

SUMMERS, W. C. (1910), *Select Letters of Seneca* (London).

SWAIN, S. (1993), 'Thucydides 1.22.1 and 3.82.4', *Mnemos* 46: 33–45.

—— (1994), 'Man and Medicine in Thucydides', *Arethusa* 27: 303–27.

SYNDIKUS, H. P. (1990), *Catull: eine Interpretation II* (Darmstadt).

TAPLIN, O. P. (1980), 'The Shield of Achilles in the *Iliad', G&R* 27: 1–21.

TARSKI, A. (1933), *Pojêcie prawdy w jêzykach nauk dedukcyjnych* (Warsaw).

TATUM, J. (1969), 'The Tales in Apuleius' *Metamorphoses', TAPA* 100: 487–527; rep. in Harrison (ed.) (1999), 157–94.

—— (ed.) (1994), *The Search For the Ancient Novel* (Baltimore—London).

THALMANN, W. G. (1998), *The Swineherd and the Bow: Representations of Class in the Odyssey* (Ithaca, NY).

THOMAS, B. (1991), *The New Historicism and Other Old-Fashioned Topics* (Princeton).

THOMAS, R. (1989), *Oral Tradition and Written Record in Classical Athens* (Cambridge).

—— (1997), 'Ethnography, Proof and Argument in Herodotus' *Histories', PCPS* 43: 128–48.

THOMPSON, W. E. (1985), 'Fragments of the Preserved Historians—especially Polybius', in *The Greek Historians: Literature and History. Papers Presented to A. E. Raubitschek* (Saratoga, Cal.), 119–39.

THOMSON, G. (1953), 'From Religion to Philosophy', *JHS* 73: 76–83.

—— (1960), 'Scientific Method in Textual Criticism: A Tribute to Walter Headlam (1866–1908)', *Eirene* 1: 51–60.

TILLEY, C. (ed.) (1990), *Reading Material Culture: Structuralism, Hermeneutics and Post-Structuralism* (Oxford).

TODOROV, T. (1977), *The Poetics of Prose* (Oxford).

—— (1990), *Genres in Discourse* (Cambridge).

—— (1993), *I generi del discorso* (Firenze).

TOMPKINS, J. (ed.) (1980), *Reader-Response Criticism* (Baltimore).

TOO, YUN LEE (1994), 'Educating Nero: A Reading of Seneca's Moral Epistles', in Elsner and Masters (eds.), 211–24.

TOOLAN, M. J. (1988), *Narrative: A Critical Linguistic Introduction* (London).

TUCKER, G. H. (1996), 'Clément Marot, Ferrara, and the Paradoxes of Exile', in Ford and Jondorf (eds.), 171–93.

TURYN, A. (ed.) (1952), *Pindari Carmina* (Oxford).

ULLMAN, B. L. (1913), '*Satura* and Satire', *CPh* 8: 172–94.

—— (1930), 'The Text of Petronius in the Sixteenth Century', *CPh* 25: 128–54.

—— (1955), *Studies in the Italian Renaissance* (Rome).

—— (1963), *The Humanism of Coluccio Salutati* (Padua).

—— and STADTER, P. A. (1972), *The Public Library of Renaissance Florence* (Padua).

VAN GRONINGEN, B. A. (1953), *In the Grip of the Past: Essay on an Aspect of Greek Thought* (Leiden).

VAN ROOY, C. A. (1966), *Studies in Classical Satire and Related Literary Theory*, 2nd edn. (Leiden).

VEESER, H. A. (ed.) (1989), *The New Historicism* (London).

VERDIN, H., SCHEPENS, G., and DE KEYSER, E. (eds.) (1990), *Purposes of History in Greek Historiography from the Fourth to the Second Century B.C.* (Louvain).

VERNANT, J.-P. (1991), *Mortals and Immortals* (Princeton).

—— and VIDAL-NAQUET, P. (1988), *Myth and Tragedy in Ancient Greece* (New York).

VICO, G. (1984), *The New Science of Giambattista Vico* (Cornell).

VIDAL-NAQUET, P. (1988), 'The Shields of the Heroes', in Vernant and Vidal-Naquet, 273–300.

VON FRITZ, H. (1967), *Die griechische Geschichtsschreibung* (Berlin).

WALBANK, F. W. (1946), *The Decline of the Roman Empire in the West* (Cambridge).

—— (1957–79), *A Historical Commentary on Polybius, I–III* (Oxford).

—— (1969), *The Awful Revolution* (Liverpool); revised version of Walbank (1946).

—— (1972), *Polybius* (Berkeley).

—— (1985), *Selected Papers* (Cambridge).

—— (1992) *Hypomnemata* (privately printed, Cambridge).

—— (1993) 'Polybius and the Past', in Jocelyn and Hurt (eds.), 15–23.

—— (1995a) ' "Treason" and Roman Domination: Two Case-studies, Polybius and Josephus', in Schubert and Brodersen (eds.), 273–85.

—— (1995b), 'Polybius' Perception of the One and the Many', in Malkin and Rubinsohn (eds.), 211–22.

—— (1998), 'A Greek Looks at Rome: Polybius VI Revisited', *SCI* 17: 45–59.

WALKER, A. D. (1993), '*Enargeia* and the Spectator in Greek Historiography', *TAPA* 123: 353–77.

WALSH, G. B. (1977), 'The First Stasimon of Euripides' *Electra*', *YCS* 25: 277–89.

WATERS, K. (1974), 'The Structure of Herodotos' Narrative', *Antichthon* 8: 1–10.

—— (1985), 'The Relationship of Material and Structure in the History of Herodotus', *Storia del Storiografica* 7: 123–37.

WATSON, P. (1985), 'Axelson Revisited: The Selection of Vocabulary in Latin Poetry', *CQ* NS 35: 430–48.

WEBB, R. H. (1912), 'On the Origin of Roman Satire', *CPh* 7: 177–89.

WEEDON, C. (1987), *Feminist Practice and Poststructuralist Theory* (Oxford, 1997).

WEGELER, C. (1996), '. . . *wir sagen ab der internationalen Gelehrtenrepublik'. Altertumswissenschaft und Nationalsozialismus. Das Göttinger Institut für Altertumskunde 1921–1962* (Vienna—Cologne—Weimar).

WEIDAUER, K. (1954), *Thukydides und die Hippokratischen Schriften* (Heidelberg).

WEINREICH, O. (1970) 'Nachwort', in *Heliodor. Die Abenteuer der schönen Charikleia* (Zurich).

WEINREICH, U. (1970), *Erkundungen zur Theorie der Semantik* (Tübingen).

WEINRICH, H. (1976), *Sprache in Texten* (Stuttgart).

WELLEK, R. (1955), *A History of Modern Criticism 1750–1950*, vol. 2: *The Romantic Age* (Cambridge).

WEST, D. (1995), 'Cast Out Theory: Horace *Odes* 1.4 and 4.7', Classical Association Presidential Address (Oxford).

WHEELER, A. L. (1912), '*Satura* as a Generic Term', *CPh* 7: 59–65.

WHITE, H. (1978), *Tropics of Discourse: Essays in Cultural Criticism* (Baltimore and London).

WHITMARSH, T. (1998), 'The Birth of a Prodigy: Heliodorus and the Genealogy of Hellenism', in Hunter (ed.), 93–124.

WIERZBICKA, A. (1971), 'Metatekst w tekscie', in Mayenowa (ed.), 105–121.

WILAMOWITZ-MOELLENDORF, U. (1982), *History of Classical Scholarship* (London).

WILLIAMS, G. W. (1968), *Tradition and Originality in Roman Poetry* (Oxford).

WILLIAMSON, G. (1951), *The Senecan Amble* (London).

WILSON NIGHTINGALE, A. (1995), *Genres in Dialogue* (Cambridge).

WILSON, J. (1982), 'The Customary Meanings of Words Were Changed—Or Were They? A Note on Thucydides 3.82.4', *CQ* 32: 18–20.

WILSON, M. (1987), 'Seneca's Epistles to Lucilius: A Revaluation', *Ramus*, 16: 102–21.

WILSON, N. G. (1992), *From Byzantium to Italy: Greek Studies in the Italian Renaissance* (London).

WIMSATT, W. K. and BEARDSLEY, M. C. (1954), *The Verbal Icon: Studies in the Meaning of Poetry* (Lexington, Ky.).

—— (1990), 'Penelope's Cunning and Homer's,' in *The Constraints of Desire: The Anthropology of Sex and Gender in Ancient Greece* (New York), 129–61.

—— WINKLER, J. (1985), Auctor & Actor: *a narratological reading of Apuleius'* Golden Ass (Berkeley/Los Angeles).

—— and ZEITLIN, F. (eds.) (1990), *Nothing To Do With Dionysos?* (Princeton).

WINSTANLEY, D. A. (1947), *Early Victorian Cambridge* (Cambridge).

—— (1950), *Later Victorian Cambridge* (Cambridge).

WISEMAN, T. P. (1979), *Clio's Cosmetics: Three Studies in Greco-Roman Literature* (Leicester).

—— (1988), 'Satyrs in Rome? The Background to Horace's *Ars Poetica*', *JRS* 78: 1–13.

—— (1993), 'Lying Historians: Seven Types of Mendacity', in Gill and Wiseman (eds.), 122–46.

—— (1997), 'Thucydides on *Logographoi*: A Modern Parallel?', *HISTOS* 1.

WOODMAN, A. J. (1988a), *Rhetoric in Classical Historiography* (London).

—— (1988b), 'Contemporary History in the Classical World', in Seldon (ed.), 149–64.

—— and WEST, D. A. (eds.) (1974), *Quality and Pleasure in Latin Poetry* (Cambridge).

WORTHINGTON, I. (1982), 'A Note on Thucydides 3. 82. 4', *LCM* 7: 124.

WORTON, M. and STILL, J. (eds.) (1990), *Intertextuality: Theories and Practices* (Manchester and New York).

WUCHER, A. (1956), *Theodor Mommsen: Geschichtsschreibung und Politik* (Göttingen).

YOUNG, D. (1987), 'Pindar and Horace against the Telchines (*Ol.* 7.53 & *Carm.* 4.4.33)', *AJP* 108: 152–71.

YOUNG, T. D. (ed.) (1976), *The New Criticism and After* (Charlottesville).

ZANKER, G. (1987), *Realism in Alexandrian Poetry* (London).

ZEITLIN, F. I. (1982), *Under the Sign of the Shield* (Rome).

ZIMMERMAN, M. *et al.* (eds.) (1998), *Aspects of Apuleius'* Golden Ass *II: Cupid and Psyche* (Groningen).

Index